The Tragedy of Political Science
Politics, Scholarship, and Democracy

DAVID M. RICCI

Yale University Press
New Haven and London

This publication was prepared under a grant from the
Woodrow Wilson International Center for Scholars,
Washington, D.C. The statements and views expressed
herein are those of the author and are not necessarily
those of the Wilson Center.

Designed by James J. Johnson
and set in Electra and Janson types by Huron Valley Graphics.
Printed in the United States of America by
Vail-Ballou Press, Binghamton, New York.

*The paper in this book meets the guidelines for
permanence and durability of the Committee on
Production Guidelines for Book Longevity of the Council
on Library Resources.*

Library of Congress Cataloging in Publication Data

Ricci, David M.
   The tragedy of political science.

   Includes index.
   1. Political science.   I. Title.
JA71.R48   1984   320   84–3510
ISBN 0–300–03088–6

10   9   8   7   6   5   4   3   2   1

For my mother and father,
who deserve this book very much;

for Iry, Ronit, and Anat,
who have been my support for so long;

and for Tali,
who came last, but not least.

Contents

Preface

This book originated in my perception of two important trends that have characterized the development of modern political science. The first emerged in the history of political thought. For the most part, the ideas which form the basis of that history are found in writings of men like Plato, Aristotle, Augustine, Aquinas, Bodin, Locke, Burke, and Marx, whose works are considered to be part of the corpus of great books that come down to us as a legacy of Western civilization. For centuries, those books served in the academic world as the touchstone of teaching about politics, but they were not themselves mainly the product of an academic environment. Some of their authors taught for a living, but most were busy with practical affairs, and their tradition of discourse therefore owed more to experience in the realms of culture and society than to enthusiasm for a narrow and scholarly view of public life.

Who, then, are the great thinkers of today? To ask this question is to become aware of the first trend that marks the development of modern political science, because, according to most political scientists, the line of first-rate thinkers in the Western tradition came to an end around the close of the nineteenth century. Thus on the subject of, say, liberalism, not since John Stuart Mill, roughly speaking, has a really impressive political thinker appeared. Now oddly enough, just at about the time that men like John Stuart Mill were presumably becoming so scarce, universities were unquestionably growing into the enormous centers of learning that they are today. Here was a second trend relevant to political science, because, as the universities expanded and provided academic appointments for political scholars, they stressed the importance of a scientific approach to natural and social affairs, in fields ranging from biology and physics to anthropology, sociology, and political science.

The longer I thought about the declining number of great thinkers and the growing prominence of universities, the more I was convinced that these two trends must be significantly related. What happened, or so it seemed to me, was that people teaching politics in the ever-expanding universities managed to replace the old tradition of political thought with their own work. This they did by expounding the virtues of a scholarly way of analyzing politics, whereupon, by comparison, any more traditional sort of speculation about public affairs appeared to be either less incisive or plainly mistaken. As the years passed, great quantities of that scholarly work accumulated, while more and more prestige accrued to the universities in return for the scientific knowledge which their faculty members, in various fields, produced and placed at the service of society. Eventually, the new expertise of academicians as a class became so highly regarded that, for political scientists at least, it seemed reasonable to honor the older tradition of political ideas more for its historical stature than for any recent representatives. Ergo the present situation, where most college courses on politics are designed to stress not an aggregate wisdom of the ages but the contemporary conclusions of political science professors regarding what, on the basis of scholarly research, appears to them true of the political world.

The peculiar consequence of all this is that, beginning quite recently, large numbers of American citizens have come to learn about public life from a particular aggregation of academic specialists rather than, as in the past, from a tradition based upon the works of great men in many walks of life. Yet we know very little about those specialists and about how shared vocational circumstances may affect the quality of their teachings. What if, for example, the conditions of work in universities direct the findings of political research in some specific directions and not in others? And what if, as a result, political scientists, as a group, tend to endorse certain views of the polity as opposed to others? In short, what is the nature of political science as a learned discipline, and what is the impact of that character on the form and content of political education in America today?

Such broad questions may indicate the need for an inquiry larger than any one investigator can handle comprehensively, because thousands of political scientists have taught and written in America since universities emerged a century ago, and no one can possibly read, or otherwise acquaint himself with, all they have said. I will concede this point even before my critics make it. I will also add that, having attempted the job, I probably know better than anyone else just how painfully limited one researcher's talents are in relation to the enormous quantity of materials that might be surveyed. Nevertheless, operating under the assumption that if nothing were ventured, nothing would be gained, I decided that a basic overview of the discipline's development, and of representative works which its members published in several eras, could lead at least to some enlightenment on the subject of political studies. And that is what I set out to achieve.

In its final form, one written aspect of *The Tragedy of Political Science* deserves explanation. With no male chauvinism intended, the book refers more frequently to men than to women. Part of this imbalance I caused by avoiding stylistic awkwardness while dealing with matters entailing gender, especially in the singular. Most of the disparity, however, stems from my concern for human beings taken collectively. Men and women all belong to the species of man, as in Charles Darwin's *Descent of Man* and Jacob Bronowski's *Ascent of Man*, and no other term but that one, and its derivatives, can yet evoke so powerfully the qualities of grandeur and achievement that lie within our grasp as members of the human race. In the text, I sometimes speak of individuals, persons, and people, in order to preclude being written off as an incorrigible troglodyte. But I have not yielded to modern usage entirely, because replacing the older terms with newer expressions on every occasion means losing some of the historical and emotional connotations still conveyed by the former. And some of those connotations I wished to retain because this is, after all, a book about tragedy, which encourages readers to recall and reaffirm the ideals of a great civilization where those are embodied, as the term *tragedy* itself, in an age-old tradition of humanistic discourse. I therefore ask the same readers for forbearance and hope that they will tolerate what may be rated, nowadays, an eccentric ratio of masculine to feminine references.

Acknowledgments

Some of the early research for this book was conducted while I spent a sabbatical leave at the University of Pennsylvania during the academic year of 1976–77. I am grateful to the Penn-Israel Exchange Program for financial support received during that year. Drafting of the manuscript took place mainly from September 1981 to September 1982, when I was a Fellow at the Woodrow Wilson International Center for Scholars in Washington, D.C. Members of the staff there provided library facilities and administrative services that made possible the completion of the writing within its appointed time. Moreover, conversation with other Fellows, and attendance at the Center's many seminars and colloquia, provided intellectual stimulation throughout the year and contributed many ideas that found a place in my writing.

For their critical reading of the manuscript, I am grateful to my father, Thomas A. Ricci, to Marian Neal Ash of Yale University Press, and to Robert E. Brown. James C. Scott and Richard J. Bernstein were very helpful for uncovering some unexplained assumptions in my work, and these I strove to explicate fully before going to press. For tracking down many detailed citations, I owe a special note of thanks to J. David O'Donnell, my research assistant in Washington.

For whatever merit this book enjoys, all those who helped me are entitled to share the credit. The errors I accept as mine alone.

Introduction

1

Political Science as a Profession

The Tragedy of Political Science tells a story of American political science as an academic discipline. As the book's subtitle indicates, this story has three focal points: "politics," or the subject of political science inquiry; "scholarship," or the way in which inquiry is conducted by the discipline; and "democracy," or the entity that political studies in America presumably serve. Moreover, as the book's title suggests, this is a story of how "tragedy," in the literary sense of that term, emerges from an interplay of the same three factors. As the story unfolds, all of these matters will be explained at length.

This book differs from most other writings on political science in that they focus on what might be called "input," whereas my work shall be more concerned with "output." Thus standard accounts of the discipline of political studies highlight what practitioners are expected to bring to the discipline's in-box, in terms of the sort of research that political scientists should do. This is the meaning of book after book taken up mainly with discussion of how to formulate a plausible hypothesis about political affairs, how to test it for validity, and how to link one's research conclusion to some generalization that will predict regularities of political behavior.[1] The same writings pay much less attention, however, to what emerges from political science's out-box, after works by individual political scholars have been received, considered, and approved or disapproved by their colleagues. Yet practitioners tend to expound notions they believe their colleagues will accept, and they are reluctant to suggest ideas they assume will be less attractive, for one reason or another, to the discipline as a

1. See the many books with titles like *Conducting Political Research, Handbook of Political Science Methods, The Conduct of Political Inquiry, The Craft of Political Research, A Primer of Political Analysis, Introductory Problems in Political Research*, and so forth.

whole. As a result, the end-product of knowledge generated by political science, and passed down over the years, is shaped by institutional pressures that strongly affect both the kinds of assertions which are advanced within the profession and the sort of ideas which are accorded the status of certified truth there. It follows that a comprehensive understanding of political studies must take into account some aspects of their collective existence that standard works on the subject have disregarded until now.

It is the larger view, then, regarding political science's long-run agenda, so to speak, that I shall emphasize in this book. Practically speaking, there are sound reasons for this emphasis, for even when scholarly input resulting from individual research efforts and findings is important, it should not be permitted to overshadow a learned discipline's collective output of knowledge and consensual teachings. The latter, after all, constitutes the service rendered by political scientists to society at large, whereas the former consists mainly of ideas that crop up from time to time and satisfy largely a passing curiosity of men and women within the community of political scholars. My inclination is therefore to concentrate on the discipline's overall product and to ask how it is that work conducted within political science relates to the discipline's social role; that is, how political scientists, as one group of professionals among many, are discharging their duties, or failing in their obligations, to the human community within which they live. Here is where the tragedy appears.

Organizations, Expertise, and Higher Education

One may begin to appreciate the need for an inquiry centering upon political scientists' product by considering broadly the structure of society today, within which the study of politics proceeds. Around the turn of the twentieth century, scholars started to realize that bureaucracies are a crucial element, if not the sine qua non, of modern life. It seemed almost a truism that many human activities in an increasingly complicated world must be handled by large-scale organizations—from General Motors to the German General Staff—whose work is performed in very special, if not always satisfactory, ways. Recent events confirm this reality but diminish its relative importance, for bureaucracies have been joined by a second crucial feature of contemporary living. This is the extent to which organizations—including government agencies, churches, labor unions, universities, chambers of commerce, armies, medical associations, learned disciplines, and more—are increasingly staffed by men and women of quite singular character, whose distinctive training and outlook make them somewhat similar from organization to organization. As one result, a certain type of individual, with exceptional propensities and proclivities, counts nowadays for just as much as the panoply of collective entities.

Understanding the nature of this modern person is difficult, because so many kinds of organizations exist today, each serving society in its own way. As a result, we have no single name for their workers but speak variously of "bureaucrats," "functionaries," "officialdom," "the meritocracy," "experts," "professionals," "the scientific estate," "the new class," or whatnot.[2] Likewise, because the people in question are numerous, dispersed, and active in so many realms of human endeavor, their typical and shared qualities are difficult to measure precisely. Nevertheless, distinctive attitudes and comportment are continually on display, for even while people of this nature work according to technical imperatives associated with their immediate institutions, they simultaneously manifest preferences and aspirations brought to their jobs from elsewhere. A doctor, for example, may work for a municipal hospital, but she remains a doctor. Similarly, an economist can be employed by the Department of Agriculture, but at heart he is still an economist. Or, a manager will strive to make the firm he serves more profitable, but his efforts to that end will be guided by an outlook acquired at the Harvard Business School.

Such cases indicate that a measure of expertise—of notable competence at dealing with things or processes or people—is the hallmark of that special quality which an "organization man," or woman, exercises in the workplace. Yet, in realms where expertise is common, it is also powerful, and here is a matter that warrants careful consideration, because the exercise of power may be socially beneficial or it may not. Once upon a time, most Americans believed that they knew how to bring up their children. Today, on the other hand, many people are convinced that, in this realm as in others, they must first consult the opinions of an expert such as Dr. Spock. This example is probably so commonplace as to excite little reflection. But when multiplied over and over again, the influence of experts has enormous impact on life in virtually all of its modern dimensions. They have the decisive word, or at least a great deal to say, with regard to ascertaining what people should eat, what sort of housing they should inhabit, how their children should be educated, how the country should be defended, what Washington should do about waste and pollution, how many unemployed should remain out of work, what level of interest and inflation are nationally tolerable, and so forth.

Under the circumstances, it is not surprising that apprehension has arisen

2. Many of the new workers, and the occupational environment which requires their presence and molds their character, are described by Peter F. Drucker, *The Age of Discontinuity: Guidelines to Our Changing Society* (New York: Knopf, 1969), esp. pp. 263–310; David T. Bazelon, *Power in America: The Politics of the New Class* (New York: New American Library, 1971), esp. pp. 307–32; Daniel Bell, *The Coming of Post-Industrial Society: A Venture in Social Forecasting* (New York: Basic Books, 1973), esp. pp. 167–265; and Alvin W. Gouldner, *The Future of Intellectuals and the Rise of the New Class* (New York: Seabury, 1979).

concerning the growing power of expertise over so many aspects of life today, from the trivial to the vital.[3] If ordinary citizens must turn to experts for advice on the manufacture, deployment, and use of nuclear weapons, how can we be sure that their knowledge is tempered by prudence and moderation? Given that chemists and physicists seem uniquely qualified to fathom the country's energy situation, how will we know whether or not their research into exotic fuels will serve to sustain a good society in the long run? If parents want to raise their children in a traditional way, no matter in which tradition, will they be able to stand up to a social environment shaped by the progressive views of family experts ranging from pediatricians to child psychiatrists to social workers to juvenile court officials to schoolteachers?[4] And so it goes, on and on.

It is but a short step from recognizing the importance of expertise to asking where most of the experts come from. The answer is obvious: they matriculate in the nation's system of higher education, dominated by great universities. In these schools the people who staff America's large organizations are tutored, and there they acquire habits of mind that accompany them throughout vocational life. In fact, universities transmit a great deal more than specific and precise skills. True, those who train as engineers, lawyers, accountants, and physicians will emerge from the academy with particular learning as to the nature of their work, who their clients are, how they are to be served, and what kinds of words and concepts will suffice for discussing vocational matters. But even those who pursue general studies, such as liberal arts, take from the university a distinctive view of the world and of social relationships, an outlook that tends to be skeptical, secular, and scientific. Later, general students obtain tangible skills at the office, in occupational slots for which no university program of studies corresponds exactly. But higher education has already fitted them with the attitudes that infuse the world of expertise, and only an immediate skill is lacking. In the cases of both the liberal arts major and the occupational specialist, therefore, university education instills certain sensitivities and inclinations in young men and women who go on to become tomorrow's organization people, working in associations, corporations, professions, disciplines, bureaus, institutes, and more.

The Discipline of Political Studies

By identifying organizations as frameworks for the employment of expertise, and by tracing the source of experts back to their higher education, we are led to

3. See Jethro K. Lieberman, *The Tyranny of the Experts: How Professionals Are Closing the Open Society* (New York: Walker and Company, 1970); and Daniel Guttman and Barry Willner, *The Shadow Government: The Government's Multibillion-dollar Giveaway of Its Decision-making Powers to Private Management Consultants, 'Experts,' and Think Tanks* (New York: Pantheon, 1976).

4. See Christopher Lasch, *Haven in a Heartless World: The Family Besieged* (New York: Basic Books, 1977).

recognize political science as one component in the system of special training that underlies the outlook and behavior of experts in various jobs today. Some academic disciplines deal with precise and marketable knowledge, such as that which enables them to train physicists. Political science belongs to another group of learned disciplines, embracing most of the humanities and social sciences, which impart a more general understanding of their subject to students among whom only a few will work at a job based solely on the acquired knowledge. Immediate vocational payoffs aside, such disciplines are responsible for investigating immense realms of social phenomena, for translating the findings of their research into coherent teachings, and for conveying to all who would listen, be they students or the public, a sense of what constitutes reasonable behavior toward their fellow men.

Among the general disciplines, political science is charged with surveying the province of public affairs and institutions, with the resultant knowledge transmitted to citizens in such a way as to encourage civility, tolerance, moderation, patriotism, an appreciation of rights and of obligations, and, not the least, a willingness to support wise governmental policy. To learn of such matters is not to acquire one of the marketable skills imparted by disciplines such as biology or chemistry. After all, political scientists are not in the business of training students who intend to seek gainful employment as politicians, although some of them may. But formal knowledge of politics, like the residue of many other general studies, does make up part of the mental furniture of many who go on to staff the nation's great organizations. Political science thus serves to shape part of the overall outlook of such people, and it thereby becomes an educational enterprise of no small importance.

The Old Learning and the New

The beginning of wisdom concerning this enterprise of political studies is to note that a century ago there were very few college courses on current political affairs, although many students did study some political history, in one form or another, including the classics. This explains why, during the 1880s and 1890s, American universities awarded only three or four doctorates each year in the subject of political science, while around 1900 the total number of full-time teachers of politics in America seems to have been somewhere between fifty and one hundred.[5] These figures indicate that most citizens at the turn of the century still learned about public affairs from authorities outside the university, from people other than political scholars. However, as college enrollment expanded, students increasingly chose to study the subject formally, and a growing number of teachers were needed to instruct them. By the late 1940s, as many as 115

5. Albert Somit and Joseph Tanenhaus, *The Development of American Political Science: From Burgess to Behavioralism* (Boston: Allyn and Bacon, 1967), pp. 23, 58.

doctorates in political science were awarded every year,[6] and membership in the American Political Science Association, which numbered only 214 in 1904,[7] rose to more than 4,000.[8] In the early 1970s, new doctorates mounted to an average of more than 700 annually,[9] while membership in the Association reached around 17,000, embracing 6,000 graduate students and some 8,400 teachers.[10] By this time, it would be no exaggeration to say that a very substantial portion of the total college population, destined to become experts and enter the nation's organizations, was receiving some instruction, if only a course or two, in political science.

In later chapters we shall see how, over the past century, political scientists disengaged themselves from scholars working in related fields such as history, economics, and sociology—how they founded graduate programs, established departments, developed new courses, and certified a very special sort of research as the discipline's overriding goal, with a number of intended and unintended consequences. In the process, the rise of political science was accompanied by a new locus of concern that superseded the traditional pedagogical perspectives appropriate to a few students and their even fewer teachers of a century ago. Thus in mid–nineteenth-century America the study of politics, apart from the slavery question, was largely a reflection of cultural consensus. In the traditional school-ing, colleges charged teachers with conveying to their students various conven-tional truths about the nature of man and the proper form of government. As educators and responsible men, most teachers believed in these truths, but then again, so did people in all walks of life. In the typical college, time was set aside for debate and discussion while instruction took place. Still, classroom work concentrated mainly on Western civilization's great books and on a few second-ary texts that celebrated the virtues of Anglo-American constitutionalism.

Then two things happened simultaneously. For one thing, as time passed, scientific ideas, such as Darwin's theory of evolution, strongly challenged the old orthodoxies about man and society. With this, the theories and principles offered by inherited political works no longer seemed patently true or acceptable. For another, political science students and teachers came more and more to focus their energies upon writings that the teachers produced and that their students were required to read. By an imperative of academic life known as the rule of

6. Ibid., p. 158.
7. "Report of the Secretary," *Proceedings of the American Political Science Association*, vol. 1 (1904), p. 28.
8. Thomas E. Mann, "Political Science Faculty and Student Data," *PS* (Summer 1976), p. 283.
9. Walfred H. Peterson, "Doctoral Output in Political Science—Tables for 1970–72," *PS* (Fall 1972), p. 427.
10. "Report of the Executive Director," *PS* (Summer 1972), p. 323.

"publish or perish," the number of these new writings quickly grew to exceed by far the number of old and established favorites. But, because so many former political notions were no longer compellingly persuasive, they were incorporated less and less frequently into the new writings, which tended to speak for the teachers themselves rather than to reflect broader opinions widely espoused.

The importance of the new learning as compared to the old can hardly be overstated. A rough approximation of how far the scales tipped may be gained by considering the case of America's fifth president. James Madison studied the premodern curriculum and went on to write substantial portions of the Constitution and the Federalist Papers. Yet when he attended the College of New Jersey, which eventually grew into Princeton University, its library contained a collection of no more than 1,300 books, covering all collegiate subjects.[11] And when he took the senior course dealing with politics, his syllabus contained fewer than 50 items, mostly well-known works and classics.[12] By contrast, in 1962 a committee of the American Political Science Association estimated that a well-stocked undergraduate library on political science alone should contain at least 2,500 volumes, largely of the new variety;[13] and by 1976 the number of journals publishing articles of interest to political scientists had risen to more than 60,[14] even as the output of newly published political books clamoring for attention approached 400 per month.[15] These figures do not indicate that works by unquestionable authorities such as Aristotle, Locke, Jefferson, Marx, Mill, Lenin, and Keynes have disappeared from university studies. But they have been massively supplemented by constantly updated professorial views of ever-changing political facts and by books that Professors Jones, Smith, and Brown write in order to explain to us what Aristotle, Locke, Marx, and the rest, *really* meant.

The Organization of Political Studies

This thumbnail sketch adds an enormously important truth to what I have already pointed out about political science. The discipline is an intellectual enterprise playing a noteworthy role in the general system of higher education, by which young Americans acquire the skills and outlooks that fit some of them, at least, for working in the nation's great organizations. Within this reality we

11. Dennis F. Thompson, "The Education of a Founding Father: The Reading List for John Witherspoon's Course in Political Theory, as Taken by James Madison," *Political Theory* (November 1976), p. 523.

12. Ibid., pp. 525–28.

13. Committee on Standards of Instruction of the American Political Science Association, "Political Science as a Discipline," *American Political Science Review* (June 1962), p. 419.

14. Michael W. Giles and Gerald C. Wright, Jr., "Political Scientists' Evaluations of Sixty-three Journals," *PS* (Summer 1975), pp. 254–56.

15. See the estimates in Nelson W. Polsby, "Report of the Managing Editor," *PS* (Fall 1971), p. 541.

now have another, which is that political scientists have generated a very large body of literature intended mainly for students and teachers and only marginally including items that were universally considered important to political learning and practice in the past. In this sense, what flows from political science is a new and significant contribution to political thought, a compendium of ideas—introducing the new and reinterpreting the old—which the discipline offers to society as the most reliable and authoritative knowledge presently available on public affairs.

Most significantly, this body of expert thought—politics according to political scientists—is produced by men and women working together, in a community of scholars, where one man's writing is another man's reading, and where standards of excellence are generated by the peers of one's particular realm. To recognize the existence of this community is to recall some of the matters touched upon earlier, namely the importance and power of organizations and the special mentality of people who work within them. Paradoxically, what obtains here is a situation where the exponents of expertise, which will be used within large organizations, themselves constitute an organization of sorts. In this sense, teachers of political science serve not only as individual pedagogues but stand collectively somewhere between society at large and their students, jointly investigating the way in which citizens deal with public affairs and together expounding the results of their investigations.

Now if political scientists dispense expertise that their literature reveals as having been devised mainly by themselves, and if their acts of intellectual creativity take place within a community of scholars, we are entitled to cast upon such works a gaze no less critical than that warranted by other manifestations of expertise in modern society. If these are our experts in this particular realm, are their opinions balanced and prudent? If they do their work in an organized way, are they not susceptible to occupational pressures that can affect the very substance of their teachings, that is, the political thought which they transmit from one generation to the next? Once questions of this sort are posed, it seems logical to assume that when political scholars work together, the facts they discover and the knowledge they transmit will almost inevitably, given the orthodoxies encouraged by organized endeavor, constitute a very special and perhaps dangerously incomplete version of the real world they are responsible for studying. But this is to anticipate our story.

Terms of Analysis

To comprehend political science as a collective endeavor, one must use terms appropriate to the quest. Many practitioners tell their students that political inquiry is mainly a matter of constructing plausible hypotheses about political behavior carefully, and then testing the same propositions ingeniously. Although the textbooks that convey such teachings do not explicitly avow it, their main effect is to signify that what counts professionally is how individual researchers do their research and draw the appropriate conclusions. Yet if we are to explore the nature of political science in the round, we must develop an approach more concerned with how the work of individuals is related to that of their reputable colleagues, to the point where a scholarly community grows enthusiastic about certain investigations and cool to others, receptive to some findings and hostile to alternatives. In brief, we must think in terms that embrace phenomena such as the origins of vocational motivation, the mechanics of collective endeavor, and the parameters of orthodox ambitions.

Bureaucracy

One such term, the progenitor to many of the rest, is bureaucracy. When Max Weber, the great German sociologist, spoke of bureaucracies, he was intrigued by the way they organize work. He therefore made much of their ability to standardize tasks, to apportion the overall job to many different people, and to institute an impersonal chain of command more effective than small-scale administration based on prebureaucratic systems such as family authority. Later students of bureaucracy, seeking to describe its complicated structure of penalties and rewards, costs and benefits, would say that such matters entail specialization, hierarchy, status, authority, oligarchy, co-optation, rationality, and efficiency.

For our purposes, two aspects of bureaucratic behavior seem particularly important. The first concerns power. Weber himself was impressed by the ability of bureaucrats to amass power, and he attributed this capacity to their penchant for accumulating knowledge.[16] By creating so many regulations that ordinary citizens can hardly cope with them all, or by developing a jargon virtually incomprehensible to the layman, bureaucrats are able to create a situation wherein only they understand the job their organization is doing, a milieu wherein outsiders must defer to officials in order to receive from them either valuable information or effective policy. As a second point, scholars following Weber's lead have often noticed that even while bureaucrats tend to create and conserve knowledge, the substance of that knowledge is not necessarily useful to society. That is, although bureaucracies are presumably designed to fulfill the nation's needs for goods and services, a bureaucrat is likely to favor his organization's immediate ends instead, where so long as the work contributes to the survival and prosperity of the institution, it is deemed satisfactory by his

---

16. See Hans H. Gerth and C. Wright Mills, eds., *From Max Weber: Essays in Sociology* (New York: Oxford, 1946), chapter 7, "Bureaucracy," pp. 196–244, but esp. 233–35.

colleagues.[17] If either, or both, of these two bureaucratic tendencies—to self-serving power or to social irrelevance—were to infect an academic discipline, we would be justified in suspecting the quality and validity of that discipline's teachings.

Manifest versus Latent Functions

Viewed as an entity, the members of an organization presumably supply the nation with some product or service, such as defense, new automobiles, frozen food, legal advice, or health care. One can therefore say that each organization serves a "function" with regard to a society's conditions of existence. It is important to note, however, that there exist functions other than those stated in a government agency's enabling act, or in a private company's advertising, high-minded though these may be. In order to deal with variety in this area, we should be alert to the distinction between "manifest" and "latent" functions.[18] The former are consequences intended and recognized by members of the organization and the surrounding society, whereas the latter are not so consciously intended or recognized by anyone. Political machines are a classic example of the difference between these two different kinds of function.[19] Formally, party organizations exist in order to unite people who agree to certain political principles, and to win elections so as to shape public policy in accordance with a platform animated by those principles. At the same time, though, such organizations are busy helping various interest groups, mediating between them and government officials, and providing constituents with patronage appointments and other economic favors. As a result, many members of the machine remain faithful to it in return for services entirely unrelated to whatever principled stand the machine announces as its ostensible function. The political party is an example indicating that learned disciplines, too, may serve many latent functions—such as providing job security for practitioners—which remain unstated beside the customarily avowed purpose of providing knowledge for the ultimate benefit of mankind.

Functional versus Substantive Rationality

Long ago, Karl Mannheim described the classic tension that may exist between various functions served by a single bureaucracy, or an organization by any other name. Mannheim noted that collective entities seek to behave rationally, when they break work down into manageable tasks and try to administer the execution

---

17. On the tendency of bureaucracy to serve its own goals, see Ralph P. Hummel, *The Bureaucratic Experience* (New York: St. Martin's, 1977), pp. 56–91.

18. Robert K. Merton, *On Theoretical Sociology* (New York: The Free Press, 1967), pp. 73–138.

19. Ibid., pp. 125–36.

of those tasks impersonally. But rationality comes in two varieties, he concluded, and while organizations are quite capable of one of these, they are almost always incompetent at the other. By "functional rationality" Mannheim meant a series of actions organized so as to achieve a preordained goal.[20] Once the goal is known, some actions will be more effective with regard to its attainment, and therefore more rational, even while other actions do little to promote that end, and therefore are less rational. As an example of functional rationality, Mannheim wrote of a soldier effectively carrying out orders, and he noted that military service often entails behavior aimed at efficiently achieving ends laid down in advance. In modern life, the quantity of functional rationality may increase as the number of organizations grows and as the people within them gain more and more ability to solve problems defined by their superiors. However, substantive rationality is another matter entirely, and it may decrease apace with the growth of organizations.

By substantive rationality, Mannheim meant thought and action that reflect an intelligent grasp of events constituting a given situation, including insight into their implications and selection of the most appropriate course of response.[21] Now clearly, this second sort of rationality does not aim at serving ends already laid down but at considering whether established objectives are adequate and, if not, what must replace them in our affections and behavior. To use the military example once more, if a soldier must carry out orders as effectively as possible, his chief of staff must decide which orders to give, in light of a situation that demands intelligent calculation of the national interest. Students of this problem are aware, however, that people who work within organizations are adept mainly at manipulating means to attain short-term ends, which is how they prosper at work and advance in their careers. The result is that even the boss of a large-scale enterprise, having normally risen from a subordinate position, will be poorly equipped to elevate his sights above the day-to-day objectives of organizational life—sheer survival for both the worker and the institution—and decide what larger ends the group should promote beyond those it has traditionally pursued. In short, organization men are not rewarded for stepping outside their immediate context and considering the imperatives of substantive rationality. It is a point worth keeping in mind with regard to academic disciplines, where a scholar's day-to-day work of research, publication, and teaching of received truth may dull both his appetite and his ability for considering larger questions that do not fit easily within the vocation's usual terms of reference.

20. Karl Mannheim, *Man and Society in an Age of Reconstruction* (New York: Harcourt, Brace, and World, 1940), pp. 51–60, but esp. 53.
21. Ibid.

Functionaries and Roles

The term *bureaucracy* has the disadvantage of connoting a certain structure of operations—such as that in the Pentagon—entailing considerable hierarchy of command and physical proximity among workers. But since many organizations, such as the Democratic party and the American Medical Association, actually rank low on a scale of such characteristics, it is sometimes helpful to think of large-scale enterprise in terms of special behavior rather than distinctive structure. Thus a "functionary" is a person who, in realms as far apart as farming, medicine, law, public administration, and industry, shapes his occupational personality so as to behave rationally and contribute to overall efficiency.[22] It does not matter much where he works, and he may move occasionally from one organization to another. What is crucial, instead, is the functionary's tendency to internalize at any moment the standards of the organization that he serves, seeking at every turn to help it operate in society as smoothly and effectively as possible. Most important, functionaries are so dedicated to their employer's ends as to act out, in the office at least, a "role" that they play to advance those ends. The distinguishing feature of such roles is their reference point within the organization itself.[23] For example, Jones becomes an assistant vice-president in charge of marketing for Universal Widgets, whereupon her talents are applied to selling as many widgets as that organization decides is proper for a person playing the role signified by her title. Eventually, Jones will embrace the duties of her vice-presidential role so thoroughly as to be unable to imagine that alternative standards might guide her and the company's other employees. She will sincerely contend that modern society cannot live well without a steady and reliable source of widgets, and she will be incapable of balancing the nation's need for them against human requirements for, say, low-cost housing. Here the tension between functional and substantive rationality becomes apparent.

Professions, Markets, and Scientific Communities

If organization men may be regarded less as members of particular institutions than as bearers of the special mentality which marks a functionary, what should we expect of people known as members of a "profession"? On the surface, at least, traditional professional people such as doctors, lawyers, dentists, accountants, clergymen, and professors, do not seem to resemble standard organization men. For one thing, they are likely to be independently employed and therefore not beholden to a hierarchy of superiors. In this respect, the *structure* of bureaucracy does not normally constitute an important factor in professional lives. In addition, they are trained to work according to an enlightened ethic that makes

---

22. William F. Howton, *Functionaries* (Chicago: Quadrangle, 1969), passim.
23. Ibid., pp. 22–23f.

the interests of their client more important than any end of the profession. On this count, the institutional *loyalty* of functionaries is presumably a sentiment which professionals would disdain.

Nonetheless, some aspects of professional life place practitioners squarely within a collective framework.[24] For example, regardless of where they work, inside or outside of a bureaucratic entity, members of a particular profession are generally products of the same education and speak a common vocational language. In addition, as a result of this shared training they tend to read the same vocational journals—from *Science* to the *New England Journal of Medicine* to the *Harvard Law Review*—and therefore continue to participate in an ongoing collegiality of knowledge. Furthermore, professionals tend to have a very strong sense of who is a member of their guild and who is not, of whom to defer to with regard to vocational standards and whom to ignore. And finally, people of the same profession are bound together by a feeling that they are destined to play a very special and beneficial role in society. Having once acquired this feeling, they rarely leave their profession and join another. In all of these senses, professionals belong to a very real community of their own, which is surely a collective entity, although far-flung and less tangible than organizations of an obviously bureaucratic character.[25]

Significantly, the collective dimensions of professional life vary from profession to profession. Engineers, for example, are most often employed within organizations whose goals are so clearly defined as to minimize the influence exercised by professional impulses. Professors, on the other hand, are most likely to enjoy academic freedom and to work in ways beholden to little more than guidelines set within their disciplines. One useful way of considering the range of professions in this regard is to remember that there are, roughly speaking, two arenas of human interaction within which professions come to operate; that is, organizations and markets.[26] In organizations per se, such as in the State Department, some few people are authorized to set the goals for all, toward which ends transactions are mainly internal and largely controlled from above. These conditions sustain a true hierarchy, whereby workers are kept in line with common objectives by means of direct reward and punishment. There exists, however, a second form of occupational context for professions, and it is the market situa-

24. For a useful collection of articles on the nature of professions, see Howard M. Vollmer and Donald L. Mills, eds., *Professionalization* (Englewood Cliffs, N.J.: Prentice-Hall, 1966). For an analysis of professions that is particularly appropriate to the learned disciplines, see William J. Goode, "Community Within a Community: The Professions," *American Sociological Review* (April 1957), pp. 194–200.

25. Goode, "Community," p. 194.

26. On organizations and markets, see James G. March and Herbert A. Simon, *Organizations* (New York: Wiley, 1958), p. 4, and passim.

tion. Markets come into being when the creator of a product or service must offer the fruit of his efforts to people outside of the immediate workplace, where, as a consequence, he cannot avoid thinking in terms of the price a potential customer is willing to pay.

The market model provides important clues as to what kind of collective sanctions are important to professionals. Thus many professional people will be associated with a specific workplace—such as a government agency or private hospital—but they will try to work in ways that earn the respect and recognition of their colleagues elsewhere. A lawyer, for example, may work directly with a large firm and for its clients, but he will take care to do the job in such a way as to maintain the esteem of other lawyers, implementing their ethical standards and doing nothing that would detract from the public's regard for his profession as a whole. In this sense, there is a market dimension to most professions, where the practitioner seeks status and prestige by offering his work for the approval of professional peers, it being clearly understood that willingness to keep a proper profile in their eyes will eventually be translated into vocational rewards.[27]

It is possible to place the various professions along a spectrum, from those whose collective standards are least influential in shaping vocational behavior, to those whose community is supremely powerful in this regard. On such a spectrum, the learned disciplines would be among those most conscious of, and responsive to, collective standards. Because their members work in the nation's universities, they do yield to some hierarchical imperatives of traditional administration, such as the timing of classes and the filing of unending registration and grade forms. But most professors regard such matters as more of an annoyance than the guarantee of vocational success. In consequence, they spend much of their time pursuing professional status by doing research and by publishing the results in order to be judged by their scholarly peers nationwide.

At the least bureaucratic end of the spectrum, each learned discipline forms a "scientific community."[28] Its members work together concurrently rather than in physical proximity, to discover new truths and to advance vocationally by demonstrating competence to other members of the same community, wherever located. All of this activity proceeds in a very marketlike manner, joining one university to another. But the market is inhabited by "buyers" and "sellers" of knowledge who display many of the habits—such as orderliness, secular skepticism, short-range rationality, attention to properly marshaled data, etc.—of bureaucratically inclined functionaries. Scientific communities therefore display a

27. On the process of gaining professional recognition by offering one's research results to the scientific community, see Norman W. Storer, *The Social System of Science* (New York: Holt, Rinehart and Winston, 1966), pp. 20–26.

28. Warren O. Hagstrom, *The Scientific Community* (New York: Basic Books, 1965).

paradoxical mixture of open-ended and close-minded processes and people, for which students of human affairs have yet to construct a simple and serviceable sociological model. We shall see how such a community came into being for political scientists, and how it has affected their work.

The Sociology of Knowledge
Regardless of where they work, most people will entertain views closely reflecting the social circumstances that surround them, circumstances of family, or work-place, and of political community. On this score, we may say that functionally rational thinking and behavior reflects "the sociology of knowledge," the fact that our place in society causes us to believe certain things, and even convinces us that those things are objectively true.[29] This tendency toward self-deception is a problem highlighted by Marxists, who contend that economic class membership is a sociological force which determines our world views and leads us to believe that those views are eternal verities rather than fleeting reflections of "false class consciousness." This same tendency, at the organizational as well as the class level, might cause a president of General Motors to say sincerely that what is good for General Motors is also good for America.

For our purposes, it is noteworthy that Mannheim tried to overcome the sociology of knowledge by trying to find some people free of sociological influence and therefore able to develop objectively true knowledge, of the sort necessary for achieving substantive rationality. Arguing directly against Marx, Mannheim claimed that intellectuals are capable of detaching themselves from class ties and purging themselves of class bias.[30] Presumably, they can form a very special community, which will speculate upon public questions, investigate social problems, criticize each other's work, and from time to time draw conclusions as to how men should confront the world in a truly rational way. As time passed, Mannheim's position easily shaded over into the notion that scientific communities, as collections of intellectuals dedicated to special investigatory techniques and stringent testing of research results, can somehow overcome the bias of sociological rootedness and produce a constant stream of reliable knowledge concerning just about anything that society needs to know. As we shall see, the political science discipline has consistently aspired to be such a scientific community, seeking knowledge that is not merely the functionally rational stuff of organized life but the objectively true data that facilitates substantive reasoning.

29. On the sociology of knowledge, see Peter L. Berger and Thomas Luckmann, *The Social Construction of Reality: A Treatise in the Sociology of Knowledge* (Garden City, N.Y.: Doubleday Anchor, 1967), esp. pp. 1–19.

30. Karl Mannheim, *Ideology and Utopia: An Introduction to the Sociology of Knowledge* (New York: Harcourt, Brace, 1936), pp. 136–46.

Intramural Discontent

Bureaucracy, manifest and latent functions, functional and substantive rationality, functionaries and roles, professions, markets, scientific communities, the sociology of knowledge—these are the sort of terms that point us in the right direction for understanding the nature of learned disciplines. Suggestive as they are, such terms do not indicate that political science in particular requires investigation. After all, to conceive of political scientists as working in a scholarly community does not automatically imply that their occupational environment imposes functional rationality so powerfully as to produce a view of politics that is ultimately distorted and incomplete. But there are very clear signs that some members of the discipline are themselves unhappy with its condition, and their unease bespeaks the need for our inquiry.

Collective Dissatisfaction
A study of more than four thousand students and scholars in eighteen academic and professional disciplines, published in 1960, showed that graduate faculty members and recent recipients of the doctorate in political science shared the feeling that conditions in their discipline were unsatisfactory. Of all eighteen fields, including physics, mathematics, psychology, sociology, history, English, engineering, and education, the political science respondents together were least likely to answer "yes" when asked if they believed the present state of their discipline was "very satisfactory."[31] A later survey, of hundreds of thousands of students and faculty members in many academic fields across the country in 1969, found that political science students and other social science majors were generally "more dissatisfied and critical than their counterparts in the natural sciences and the applied fields."[32] As for faculty, "nearly half the political science professors at major colleges and institutions in the United States hold the opinion that graduate education in their subject is not doing a good job training students."[33] And finally, the latest survey, made in 1976, revealed that, from 1963 to 1976, political scientists grew increasingly unhappy with their profession, to the point where only 24 percent said they would choose the same profession if given a chance to start over again.[34]

31. Bernard Berelson, *Graduate Education in the United States* (New York: McGraw-Hill, 1960), p. 212.

32. Seymour M. Lipset and Everett C. Ladd, "Portrait of a Discipline: The American Political Science Community, Part I," *Teaching Political Science* (October 1975), p. 30.

33. Ibid., p. 36.

34. Walter B. Roettger, "The Discipline: What's Right, What's Wrong, and Who Cares?" paper presented at the 1978 Annual Meeting of the American Political Science Association, New York City, 1978, p. 30.

Individual Protest

Statistics such as these reflect an undercurrent of suspicion that something is wrong, somewhere, with the professional study of politics. For more precise indications of what is in fact the trouble, we may turn to statements made by practitioners who, from time to time, have charged the discipline with a very wide range of faults. For example:

> The current interests and role of the [discipline's] professional journals is best illustrated, perhaps, by recounting a discussion that took place recently among a group of political scientists. Those present agreed that the most interesting and suggestive articles on the American and world scenes were appearing in the following journals: *Commentary, The New Leader, Dissent, The New Statesman & Nation, The Economist, Partisan Review, Monthly Review, Encounter, Bulletin of the Atomic Scientists,* and *The Nation.* . . . No one mentioned the names of any of the professional journals in political science.[35] (Arnold Rogow, 1957)

> Generally speaking, one may wonder whether the new political science has brought to light anything of political importance which intelligent political practioners with a deep knowledge of history, nay, intelligent and educated journalists, to say nothing of the old political science at its best, did not know at least as well beforehand.[36] (Leo Strauss, 1962)

> What must be abandoned is the hope that political analysis can be either objective or scientific. . . . There may be cooperation among political scientists in the sense that they share and criticize each other's research. However, this communication does not produce an agreed upon body of knowledge. . . . At this time, it is hard to point to any 'findings' that have been accepted by the scholarly community. As matters now stand, there are cliques, coteries, and lone wolves talking past one another or to themselves.[37] (Andrew Hacker, 1967)

> Political disorder does not favor political scientists; it deranges their theories and cracks their time-honored assumptions. But the shortcomings of political science during . . . [the 1960s] are not to be found in the poor

35. Arnold A. Rogow, "Comment on Smith and Apter: or, Whatever Happened to the Great Issues?" *American Political Science Review* (September 1957), p. 770.

36. Leo Strauss, "An Epilogue," in Herbert J. Storing, ed., *Essays on the Scientific Study of Politics* (New York: Holt, Rinehart and Winston, 1962), p. 312.

37. Andrew Hacker, "The Utility of Quantitative Methods in Political Science," in James C. Charlesworth, ed., *Contemporary Political Analysis* (New York: Free Press, 1967), p. 147.

advice political scientists gave to authorities. . . . The somber fact of the matter was that, on most of the fundamental questions underlying disorder, the discipline of political science simply did not have anything to say one way or the other.[38] (Theodore Lowi, 1972)

. . . students and citizens in general have an instinctive awareness of what politics is, but political science does not have any view of what it is, or at least not one that in any way corresponds to or refines that untutored awareness. . . . Now the awareness of which I speak is that politics has to do with justice and the realization of the good life. . . . The citizen has . . . certainly been frustrated by political science from which he had a right to expect instruction and clarification about the ends of politics and the means available for fulfilling them.[39] (Allan Bloom, 1977)

The Tragedy of Political Science

There are common denominators to complaints of this kind, such as the feeling that political science does not conclusively point the way to a good society, or that its teachings do not come together and reinforce each other so as to present any particular lesson that all should heed. Moreover, the critics share a sense of urgency, provoked by the conviction that university students, who will staff America's great institutions and organizations, really need an understanding of politics beyond that which political science in its present form is able to impart. In the course of this book, I shall analyze various reasons why political science gives rise to such complaints, how it is that the discipline's members work together in good conscience while continuing, with regard to key questions, to produce strikingly unsatisfactory results. For the moment, let us note that they are trapped in a situation with tragic overtones, where professional efforts in accord with the scholarly community's highest standards seem unable to generate a product capable of providing the nation with all the political knowledge it needs.

Tragedy as a Literary Concept

The term *tragedy* sheds light on political science's condition only if we are aware that, in serious literature, the same term is reserved for conveying complex

38. Theodore J. Lowi, "The Politics of Higher Education: Political Science as a Case Study," in George J. Graham and George W. Carey, eds., *The Post-Behavioral Era: Perspectives on Political Science* (New York: McKay, 1972), p. 11.

39. Allan Bloom, "Political Science and the Undergraduate," in Vernon Van Dyke, ed., *Teaching Political Science: The Professor and the Polity* (Atlantic Highlands, N.J.: Humanities Press, 1977), p. 118.

connotations which reach far beyond those associated with its common use as a synonym for everyday words such as *calamity*, *catastrophe*, and *disaster*. In fact, the latter refer to situations where pain and suffering are mainly inexplicable, as when a plane crashes and kills its passengers, or when a dam bursts and the consequent flood destroys both life and property downstream.[40] Tragedy, on the other hand, is written by authors who seek to make the trials of life intelligible and instructive, in which case it is a categorical error for us to ask, after hearing the word *tragedy* in conversation or in a news broadcast, "Who died?" instead of "In which theater?"[41]

As for theaters, Aristotle tried hard to define exactly what took place when Greek tragedies—such as *Agamemnon*, by Aeschylus, or *Oedipus the King*, by Sophocles—were performed on the stage. To this end he described tragedy as a play imitating serious action, and as involving people of high social rank or character, whose misfortunes are brought about not by evil acts but by mistakes in judgment.[42] Since Aristotle's time, many works of great emotional power—such as *King Lear*, by Shakespeare, and *The Master Builder*, by Ibsen—have been added to the world's repertoire of tragic drama. The result is somewhat paradoxical. Literary scholars today largely agree on which plays belong to the realm of tragedy, for something elemental in those works, no matter how diverse they are by historical epoch and native culture, decisively identifies their genre. The same scholars differ considerably, however, as to which specific features of the same plays, so varying in characterization and plot, are truly tragic and therefore qualify them for that title.[43]

Exact definitions aside, we may take our cue on the subject from the self-evident case of Achilles, who had to decide whether to stay at Troy and die heroically in the siege or to quit the war and sail home to a comfortable but undistinguished life instead. Achilles himself, in Homer's *Iliad*,[44] recounts the choice as a painful dilemma, which we can at once recognize as tragic even without characterizing its parameters precisely: "My mother Thetis the goddess of silver feet tells me / I carry two sorts of destiny toward the day of my death. Either, / if I stay here and fight beside the city of the Trojans, / my return home is gone, but my glory shall be everlasting; / but if I return home to the beloved

40. Henry Alonzo Myers, *Tragedy: A View of Life* (Ithaca, N.Y.: Cornell University Press, 1956), pp. 153–54.

41. David Lenson, *Achilles' Choice: Examples of Modern Tragedy* (Princeton, N.J.: Princeton University Press, 1975), p. 4.

42. See the text from his *Poetics* in S. H. Butcher, *Aristotle's Theory of Poetry and Fine Art*, 4th ed. (New York: Dover, 1951), pp. 23, 25, 45–47.

43. Herbert J. Muller, *The Spirit of Tragedy* (New York: Knopf, 1956), p. 10.

44. The *Iliad of Homer*, trans. Richard Lattimore (Chicago: University of Chicago Press, 1951), p. 209.

land of my fathers, / the excellence of my glory is gone, but there will be a long life / left to me, and my end in death will not come to me quickly."

Achilles' choice suggests that there is an important sense in which tragedy flows from the clash of opposing ends and values, where men see alternative paths of action which seem desirable but which also exact a terrible price from those who choose one to the exclusion of any other. Hegel was the first modern writer to emphasize this aspect of tragic situations,[45] and he took *Antigone*, by Sophocles,[46] as the classic example. In that play, King Creon upholds law and order in Thebes by refusing to bury the dead rebel Polyneices. Antigone, the sister of Polyneices, then insists that justice according to the gods requires that she bury her brother. She does so, and later dies according to Creon's command. In short order, her despairing betrothed, Creon's son Haemon, takes his own life and is followed closely in suicide by his grieving mother, Eurydice. As A. C. Bradley pointed out, what actually occurs in such a tragedy "is not so much the war of good with evil as the war of good with good."[47] In other words, tragedy is an affair of men and women choosing between ideals such as civic duty and family obligation, which are severally dear to them, when no one alternative is patently superior to the rest, and where failure to compromise, if compromise is possible at all, leads to downfall and destruction.

In modern drama, similar clashes of opposing goods are the basic themes in *Billy Budd*, by Herman Melville,[48] in *Saint Joan*, by George Bernard Shaw,[49] and in *The Crucible*, by Arthur Miller.[50] On board a British man-of-war, the good sailor Billy Budd inadvertently kills Claggart, an evil petty officer. Subsequently Captain Vere, guided by naval law instead of his sense of equity, is compelled to execute Billy in the interest of military order rather than civilian justice. In *Saint Joan*, according to Shaw's version of the historical events, Joan calls successfully upon French soldiers to fight against the English for the sake of God and France. Then she is abandoned by her King and various religious officials, who leave the Maid to burn at the stake because they fear that her ideas on nationalism and individual conscience will destroy the great and useful institutions of feudalism and the Church. In *The Crucible*, Miller writes of the

45. Georg Wilhelm Friedrich Hegel, *Aesthetics: Lectures on Fine Art*, trans. T. M. Knox (Oxford: Oxford University Press, 1975), vol. 2, pp. 1196, 1212–13.

46. See the text in L. R. Lind, ed., *Ten Greek Plays in Contemporary Translations* (Boston: Houghton Mifflin, 1957), pp. 83–109.

47. *Oxford Lectures on Poetry* (London: Macmillan and Company, 1909), pp. 71–72. See also Lionel Abel, "Is There a Tragic Sense of Life?" in Abel, ed., *Moderns on Tragedy* (New York: Fawcett, 1967), p. 183.

48. See Louis O. Coxe and Robert Chapman, *Billy Budd* (London: Heinemann, 1966).

49. (Baltimore: Penguin, 1951).

50. (New York: Bantam, 1959).

Salem, Massachusetts, witch trials, wherein John Procter is falsely accused of traffic with the devil and sentenced to death. Later, Procter refuses to confess the deed and save his life, because lying under oath would be a sin and earn him the everlasting fires of Hell.

Politics, Scholarship, and Democracy
In a very broad sense, then, literary tragedy entails the confrontation of at least two good ends, where a dialectic of choice and responsibility may be forced upon a single character, such as Achilles or Hamlet,[51] or where the conflict of good with good is revealed in a collision between the agents of opposing ends, as in *Antigone*. Either way, there is no reason for supposing that tragedy of this sort can be acted out only on the stage and not in our own lives. Moreover, once we begin to think of tragedy as taking place in the real world, we can easily see that its protagonists may be large groups of people rather than just a few actors in the theater.[52] There are, for example, tragic conflicts between nations, where two claim the same territory and neither is able to moderate its respective aspirations.[53]

    Political science is a collective protagonist, of course, and its tragic predicament grows out of the fact that, like Achilles torn by indecision, or like Creon and Antigone simultaneously pursuing cross-purposes, the discipline is committed to two ends which, from time to time, turn out to be incompatible. For one thing, practitioners are on the whole devoted to pursuing the study of public life in scientific fashion. This does not mean that every political scholar accepts the need for scientific political inquiry, for no discipline is so monolithic as to impose absolute conformity on each of its members. Nor does it mean that those who enthusiastically share this commitment agree on exactly what science is and what it is not, since science is too massive yet diffuse a phenomenon to be defined in only one way. Still, as we shall see, the mainstream of political science does portray its work as a scientific form of social analysis. And this conception of what is proper to academic research has very deep and powerful roots, for it reflects an interest of all the learned disciplines in maintaining the university's reputation for discovering and communicating precise and reliable knowledge to modern society. Given this larger context of university life, within which deference and prestige flow especially to those professors whose accomplishments buttress the social status of all who work in higher education, it is

    51. Thus Hamlet's famous soliloquy, "To be, or not to be, that is the question," in William Shakespeare, *Hamlet*, act 3, sc. 1, lines 56–88.
    52. Oscar Mandel, *A Definition of Tragedy* (New York: New York University Press, 1961), p. 107.
    53. Sidney Hook, "Pragmatism and the Tragic Sense of Life," in Robert W. Corrigan, ed., *Tragedy: Vision and Form* (San Francisco: Chandler, 1965), p. 67.

unlikely that mainstream political scholars will turn their backs on science and develop an interest in some other road to knowledge, such as revelation.

As a scholarly community in America unlike that, for instance, in the Soviet Union, political scientists share a second commitment, which is their devotion to democratic politics. Some call for a thorough overhaul of existing political institutions and practices, while others recommend enthusiastic support for the status quo. But, except for a few avowed Marxists and a monarchist or two, most practitioners hope to produce, within the guidelines of a scientific style, research findings and scholarly teachings which will help to sustain a good society as defined by the nation at large, that is, a democratic society.

It is between these two commitments of the discipline—acceptance of scientific techniques and attachment to democratic ideals—that trouble begins. Political scholars aspire to study politics in a scientific way, which is logical for their community. But such studies do not always shed positive light on the very object of their inquiries. For one thing, scientific research continually denies central tenets of democratic ideology, such as the rationality of ordinary citizens.[54] This is the case, for example, when voting studies repeatedly reveal that most Americans are only vaguely informed about who the candidates are and where they stand on important public issues. For another, the same research is conducted via techniques that cannot fully grasp or assess some of democracy's most vital features, including patriotism or respect for one's fellow citizens. According to the scientific canon, discussion of such intangible matters must be reserved for men of the cloth, the sword, or the scepter.

As individuals, political scientists are often aware of the possible tension between their commitments to science and to democracy. Yet they collectively persist—and here is where the pressures of an organizational framework are crucial—in doing their scholarly work in ways that perpetuate the tension, for they are unable to develop other professionally acceptable guidelines to modern teaching and research. Accordingly, in the chapters to come, we should think of political science as an enterprise constantly moving in a circle among three poles of concern. To begin with, there is the intrinsic importance of politics, which practitioners seek to study because an understanding of public life is presumably desirable wherever men live together. Second, there are the imperatives of schol-

---

54. Some political scientists are convinced that a free society can get along with few rational citizens. The tenet of rationality nevertheless remains in force as far as many Americans are concerned. See Lester C. Thurow, *The Zero-Sum Society: Distribution and the Possibilities for Economic Change* (New York: Penguin, 1981), p. 16: "To be workable, a democracy assumes that public decisions are made in a framework where there is a substantial majority of concerned but disinterested citizens who will prevent policies from being shaped by those with direct economic self-interests. Decisions in the interests of the general welfare are supposed to be produced by those concerned but disinterested citizens."

arship, which demand that politics be studied scientifically, in accord with certain standards of precision and reliability. And finally, there is the objective of a democratic society, of political scientists' shared determination to help maintain the behavior and institutions characteristic of a free people. Circular movement occurs, figuratively, when scholars select at the first pole of politics some event or phenomenon susceptible to research, move to the second in order to study it properly, and then discover that they have arrived at their destination with findings and teachings that do not really foster democracy. Unhappy there, the discipline returns to politics, the point of departure, in hopes of doing new research that will produce a more satisfactory result.

The subtitle of this book, *Politics, Scholarship, and Democracy,* is designed to help readers keep in mind a cycle that has been traveled more than once in this century. At the same time, the book's title, *The Tragedy of Political Science,* should draw attention to the fundamental significance of this professional orbit. As a tragic protagonist, the discipline's collective shortcoming is located in a stubborn insistence on studying politics scientifically, even though inquiry in that mode cannot insure the health of a democratic society. In Aristotle's terms, we would expect the errors of this way to lead to downfall or destruction. Fortunately, however, American democracy is still going strong. Moreover, it would be unfair to blame the discipline of political science, among all possible factors, if the national regime were to collapse. Still, signs of persistent civic disillusionment and public disorder have appeared in recent generations, with ominous implications that political scientists have noted repeatedly. It follows that something is tragically amiss in a discipline which knows of these things yet continues working in ways that do little to serve the object it sincerely reveres.[55]

55. For a comprehensive critique of political science for doing too little to improve the quality of American political life, see Donald W. Hanson, "The Education of Citizens: Reflections on the State of Political Science," *Polity* (Summer 1979), pp. 457–77.

The Early Years

2

The Locus of Higher Education

Political scientists do their work of teaching and research in the world of higher education. The signal achievements of this learned discipline come essentially from practitioners in those great universities that play a key role in the complex of institutions, including universities, research institutes, libraries, and so forth, all devoted to acquiring and disseminating knowledge in America. It is therefore appropriate to begin an inquiry into the shape of modern political studies by seeking an appreciation of the nature of those universities. All academic political scientists, each in his or her own way, understand perfectly well that they must formulate and expound ideas according to standards laid down in their school for the success of all scholars who labor there, whichever their discipline. This much is so obvious as to constitute no more than a truism. Yet it is also true, and odd, that although historians know a great deal about how the nation's colleges and universities began and grew, the same scholars have only recently begun to explore the larger significance of academe within a modern, urbanized, industrialized, bureaucratized, and professionalized American society. Thus attention is just now coming to bear on the fact that so many academic disciplines, including political science, emerged formally about a century ago, in a unique university setting, which was founded at that time, and which continues even today to shape both the form and the content of scholarly work. Since it is in that workplace that political science remains, mediating between the political world and those who seek knowledge of it, we must know something of where the discipline stands.

The Rise of Universities

Universities are indeed strange places. According to Clark Kerr, former chancellor of the University of California, the large and pace-setting educational centers of modern America may properly be called "multiversities."[1] Each is composed of many academic departments and institutes, with greatly diversified scholars and research centers, where the sum of the parts adds up to a nominal whole joined by no organizational principle or rationale other than administrative convenience. Each multiversity presumably produces and transmits knowledge to society, but it does so only haphazardly, and indirectly, through the virtually uncoordinated efforts of its semiautonomous professors, departments, institutes, colleges, and faculties. The modern university president, who is formally responsible for giving coherent direction to all this activity, is less a leader of the whole institution than a competent middleman smoothing out a balance of power among parents, students, university neighbors, football enthusiasts, media, and other interested parties.[2] Subject only to budgetary limitations, a multiversity's component parts proliferate on the spur of the moment with Parkinsonian frenzy, and a typical school may eventually offer more than three thousand courses,[3] including fifty to one hundred in political science alone. How did all this come to be, and what does it signify for the discipline of political studies?

Old-Time Colleges

In America before the Civil War, there were no universities in the modern sense. Even those that bore the name were, in reality, mostly small and sectarian colleges with no more than six to eight teachers and perhaps fifty to a hundred students.[4] By 1860, about two hundred of these schools dotted the countryside. Most of them resembled the earliest American colleges such as Harvard, Princeton, Columbia, William and Mary, and Dartmouth, all founded in order to assure an adequate supply of piety and denominational ministers.[5] Most importantly, each college reflected the comprehensive world view of its founders, a matter on which they were in agreement and in deference to which they worked to mold their students. A sense of shared purposes thus emerged very clearly when one chronicler described the first days of Oberlin College, established in 1833: "The school was to be surrounded by a Christian community, united in the faith of the gospel and in self-denying efforts to establish and build up the school."[6]

1. Clark Kerr, *The Uses of the University* (New York: Harper and Row, 1966), esp. pp. 1–45.

2. On the various publics served by universities, see ibid., pp. 29–41, and Jacques Barzun, *The American University* (New York: Harper and Row, 1970), p. 165.

3. Kerr, *University*, p. 14.

4. Richard Hofstadter, "The Revolution in Higher Education," in Arthur M. Schlesinger, Jr. and Morton White, eds., *Paths of American Thought* (Boston: Houghton Mifflin, 1963), p. 271.

5. Harvard was founded by Congregationalists, Princeton by Presbyterians, Columbia by Episcopalians, William and Mary by Anglicans, and Dartmouth by Congregationalists.

6. James Harris Fairchild, *Oberlin, Its Origins, Progress, and Results* (Oberlin: R. Butler, 1871), p. 3, quoted in Wilson Smith, "Apologia pro Alma Mater: The College as Community in

The contrast between these antebellum colleges and today's multiversities could not have been greater. Where the various college presidents and boards of trustees believed that they knew what was worth knowing and imparting to the young, they maintained firm control over a standard course of instruction. Usually this was rooted in the classical curriculum, emphasizing the study of Greek, Latin, some mathematics, a little history, moral philosophy, and a few other subjects. Such knowledge was regarded as the "improving" kind rather than an ever-expanding quantity of information and speculation that we have grown accustomed to in the modern world;[7] and colleges therefore regarded students mainly as vessels to be filled up with an appropriate measure of the stuff. Moreover, it was generally accepted that whatever specific facts the student needed could be transmitted in such a way as to train his mind rather mechanically—via repetitive drills in grammar, rhetoric, mathematics, the dead languages, and more—instead of stimulating his personality to develop unpredictably in line with individual talents.[8]

In all of this, not surprisingly, there was little room for independent thought, and classroom discipline was valued more highly than vigorous discussion. Moreover, most teachers had neither the time nor the means to acquire a depth of learning much greater than that of their students. In fact, because the system called for assimilating only limited stocks of knowledge, teachers were expected to deal with a number of subjects, assuming that the extent of wisdom in each was manageable. It was not unusual, therefore, for a single person, humanistically inclined, to be charged with instruction in rhetoric and criticism, English composition, logic, grammar, moral philosophy, natural theology, composition, forensic discussions, natural and political law, and metaphysics.[9] Or, a professor more interested in the natural sciences might be called upon to

Ante-Bellum America," in Stanley Elkins and Eric McKitrick, eds., *The Hofstadter Aegis: A Memorial* (New York: Knopf, 1974), p. 131.

7. "Improving knowledge" is the term used by Edward Shils, "The Order of Learning in the United States: The Ascendency of the University," in Alexandra Oleson and John Voss, eds., *The Organization of Knowledge in Modern America, 1860–1920* (Baltimore: Johns Hopkins University Press, 1979), p. 28.

8. The classical curriculum's objectives were summed up at Yale in 1828 by a faculty committee whose report was published in "Original Papers in relation to a Course of Liberal Education," *The American Journal of Science and Arts*, 15 (1829), pp. 297–351. See esp. p. 300: "The two great points to be gained in intellectual culture, are the discipline and the furniture of the mind; expanding its powers, and storing it with knowledge."

9. These were the courses assigned to the professor of moral philosophy at the University of Pennsylvania in 1826, according to Anna Haddow, *Political Science in American Colleges and Universities, 1636–1900*, ed. and introd. William Anderson (New York: Appleton-Century Crofts, 1939), p. 44.

teach mechanics, ballistics, hydrostatics, climatology, meteorology, electricity, optics, and astronomy.[10]

Were a college teacher to dabble in so many fields today, he would surely be considered professionally incompetent, jack-of-all-trades and master of none. But this only shows how much expectations in higher education have changed since the college era. Today, universities demand depth of learning in both faculty and students, whereas more than a century ago, beyond expounding certain important truths in each field, educators strove primarily to create excellent character. How would the graduate behave in later years? That was the central question. Indeed, because virtue and comportment were vital goals of the college, the school assigned grades not just for unadorned intellectual achievement but on the basis of scholarship and conduct combined, with students penalized for unexcused absences, missing church services, misconduct at recitations, and the like. In 1642, President Henry Dunster of Harvard wrote that a degree would be granted only when, after fulfilling his residence requirements, the student "has maintained a blameless life and has sedulously observed all public exercises."[11] This was the college ideal, and not until 1870 did Harvard resolve that "the scales of scholarship and conduct should hereafter be kept distinct."[12]

The Beginnings of Change

The most powerful statement of old-time educational philosophy came at mid-century when, ironically, the college ideal was about to be challenged and eventually overshadowed by the rise of America's great universities. According to John Cardinal Newman,[13] students deserved a "liberal education." By this he meant they should study in a school where teachers, with generous respect for each other and for their respective fields of knowledge, strive to achieve a balanced view of the various realms of wisdom and an inspiring sense of how all parts relate to the whole, which is God's plan for man and the world. In such a school, said Newman, a student "profits by an intellectual tradition . . . which guides him in his choice of subjects, and duly interprets for him those which he chooses. He apprehends the great outlines of knowledge, the principles on which

10. These were some of the courses taught by James Renwick at Columbia in the 1820s. They are mentioned in Richard Hofstadter and Walter Metzger, *The Development of Academic Freedom in the United States* (New York: Columbia University Press, 1955), pp. 283–84.

11. Quoted in Louis F. Snow, *The College Curriculum in the United States* (New York: Columbia University Press, 1907), p. 26.

12. The resolution is quoted in Mary Lovett Smallwood, *An Historical Study of Examinations and Grading Systems in Early American Universities* (Cambridge: Harvard University Press, 1955), p. 74.

13. John Cardinal Henry Newman, *The Idea of a University* (orig., 1852; Oxford: Clarendon, 1976).

it rests, the scale of its parts, its lights and its shades, its great points and its little. . . . A habit of mind is formed which lasts through life, of which the attributes are freedom, equitableness, calmness, moderation, and wisdom."[14] Newman called his ideal school a university, whereas today we would call it a college, and in order to preserve its intellectual coherence he specifically warned that professors must teach current wisdom rather than produce new knowledge.[15] The intellectual ferment of research and discovery Newman left for independent bodies such as national academies and learned societies. His school would permit only occasional and carefully monitored curricular reforms designed to teach, with no damage to the old, worthy new items of knowledge created outside of its gates.

But such a vision was losing its power to persuade in the New World even as Newman wrote in the Old, for after the Civil War, one American school after another transformed itself into that larger entity known as the modern university, while entirely new universities were founded where not even a college had existed before. And the hallmark of all this rebuilding and creating was precisely the quest for, and the dissemination of, new knowledge in a host of areas, some of them outgrowths of the classical curriculum and others unrelated to it. Thus one factor in the rise of universities was enactment of the Morrill Act of 1862, which provided public land endowments in each American state to subsidize "at least one college where the leading subject shall be, without excluding other scientific and classical studies . . . to teach such branches of learning as are related to agriculture and the mechanic arts . . . in order to promote the liberal and practical education of the industrial classes in the several pursuits and professions in life."[16] Together with the second Morrill Act of 1890, here was the financial wherewithal for the famous land-grant colleges, which in most cases eventually turned into large state universities such as Michigan, Wisconsin, and California, and where over the decades subject after subject was added to the old curriculum so that a rapidly industrializing and urbanizing nation could provide training in the practical arts necessary to its commercial success.

Philanthropic capital also went into college reform, thereby demonstrating that building universities appealed to men of private means as well as to ordinary citizens acting through government. What clearly obtained was a widespread belief that the new form of higher education was somehow central to the nation's continued power and prosperity, and that all should therefore willingly support it, each in his own way and with his particular resources. Ezra Cornell, rich

14. Ibid., pp. 95–96.
15. Ibid., p. 8.
16. Excerpts from the Morrill Act of 1862 appear in Richard Hofstadter and Wilson Smith, eds., *American Higher Education: A Documentary History* (Chicago: University of Chicago Press, 1961), vol. 2, pp. 568–69.

from Western Union stock, gave $500,000 for the establishment of a school, and when this was combined with the Morrill Act endowment for the state of New York, Cornell University began classes in 1869 under the leadership of President Andrew D. White.[17] Johns Hopkins, a Baltimore business magnate, left $3.5 million to a university incorporated in his name, and the Johns Hopkins University opened its doors in 1876, headed by President Daniel Coit Gilman.[18] With a little encouragement from his Baptist friends, John D. Rockefeller agreed to contribute some of his oil profits to the University of Chicago, which in 1892 was rebuilt by President William Harper on the basis of an earlier charter and received $30 million of Rockefeller largesse.[19] Leland Stanford, who made his fortune in rails, founded Stanford University in 1885 and gave it $20 million.[20] And so it went, in an outburst of philanthropy unprecedented in the nation's history. Between 1878 and 1908, private donors gave $140 million to all branches of higher education.[21]

The Academic Culture

Where colleges did not hold pure learning to be their overriding objective, no "academic culture" could exist before the Civil War.[22] Practitioners moved in and out of college teaching as an adjunct to other vocations, salaries were too low to attract outstanding talent, libraries existed for supplying required texts rather than for creative reading and original research, teachers were hired for their orthodox opinions instead of a notable depth of knowledge, and the school took little interest in individual students except insofar as each was expected to conform to the same demands made of every other student. Those who laid down rules governing both the shape and substance of instruction held, in their respective schools, that fixed and proper guidelines contributed mightily to America's welfare, by molding some students for inspiring leadership and by preparing others to follow and maintain the general moral tenor of society. But the whole enterprise was driven by notions brought to the college from beyond its bounds

17. On the founding of Cornell, see Walter P. Rogers, *Andrew D. White and the Modern University* (Ithaca: Cornell University Press, 1942).

18. On the founding of Johns Hopkins University, see John C. French, *A History of the University Founded by Johns Hopkins* (Baltimore: Johns Hopkins University Press, 1946).

19. On the founding of the University of Chicago, see Thomas Wakefield Goodspeed, *A History of the University of Chicago, Founded by John D. Rockefeller* (Chicago: University of Chicago Press, 1916).

20. On the founding of Stanford University, see Orrin Leslie Elliott, *Stanford University: The First Twenty-Five Years* (Stanford: Stanford University Press, 1937).

21. Hofstadter, "The Revolution in Higher Education," p. 275.

22. On the "academic culture," see Burton J. Bledstein, *The Culture of Professionalism: The Middle Class and the Development of Higher Education in America* (New York: Norton, 1976), pp. 269–86. See also Hofstadter, "The Revolution," p. 283.

rather than by standards created and maintained within its walls; and in this sense a modern social scientist would say that such colleges were no more than a dependent variable in American life. They undoubtedly did an educational job that some people wanted done, but the schools themselves did not act independently either in defining the job or in deciding how to do it.

Then came the university era, when the input of public and private support produced a most unexpected output, which was the academic culture whose absence before the Civil War was so striking compared to its commanding presence in today's world of education. One necessary step was to weaken the hold exercised over course work by classical studies. Intentionally or unintentionally, this was accomplished by introducing new schools and subjects laterally into the universities. As a result, faculty members were no longer confined as previously to a few standard fields of knowledge, and undergraduates were released from the uniform requirement of studying what all their classmates had to learn. A second step came when graduate programs were added vertically to the growing variety of substantive fields available in the universities, with advanced studies starting from scratch in the 1860s and graduate enrollment rising to almost ten thousand students in 1910.[23] Graduate work embraced some entirely new subjects—such as sociology and psychology—but its main effect was to deepen old knowledge so extensively as to challenge the balance and coherence of the classical curriculum, which had been rooted in a limited quantity of facts and theories to be expounded and assimilated.

As a new curriculum emerged via the widening and deepening of an old range of studies, and as universities were founded and colleges upgraded, a great number of teaching positions became available. In response, intensively trained graduate students tended to stay in the universities after receiving their advanced degrees, creating networks of personal and vocational contacts that reached across the new institutions and the land with a consciousness of shared enterprise, confusing as their efforts might be when compared with the eternal verities of classical learning. From 1876 to 1886, for example, Johns Hopkins awarded sixty-nine doctorates, with fifty-six of the recipients appointed to teach at more than thirty colleges and universities.[24] By 1926, the same school could count more than one thousand of its graduates as faculty members throughout the country.[25] These figures reflect a situation that characterizes higher education today, where, in contrast to the era of small colleges, there are several hundred

23. *Historical Statistics of the United States: Colonial Times to 1970* (Washington, D.C.: Bureau of the Census, 1975), vol. 1, p. 383.

24. W. Carson Ryan, *Studies in Early Graduate Education: The Johns Hopkins, Clark University, The University of Chicago* (New York: Carnegie Foundation, 1939), p. 32.

25. Frederick Rudolph, *The American College and University: A History* (New York: Knopf, 1965), p. 336.

large universities—not equally prestigious or productive, of course—where hundreds of thousands of men and women teach locally but communicate professionally with peers in similar universities nationwide. With all of these scholars, in theory at least, pressing forward on the frontiers of knowledge, there is a distinct feeling that universities collectively, unlike their college forebears, generate their own product and their own standards. By the turn of the century there could be no doubt that higher education had moved far from its original status and come closer than ever before to achieving the rank of independent variable in American life.

The Commitment to Science

Thus far, the university picture is in broad outline. We must dig deeper, however, to uncover the factors that fostered the academic culture—within which political science would take its place—and imparted to it a character that still exists today. In fact, no academic culture could have developed and survived without there occurring a fundamental shift in expectations concerning institutions of higher education and the teachers they employed. Thus universities actually became a more independent force in America than the old colleges because they grew into the leading producers and custodians of scientific knowledge, a new fund of wisdom that was generated mainly in the universities rather than outside, and which was both constantly growing and commonly judged indispensable to the nation's continued well-being.

An academic culture based on science: that is what modern universities are really about. Before the Civil War, science was often considered a practical affair rather than an enterprise of basic research aimed at discovering new principles and regularities.[26] Indeed, some college trustees insisted that research should be discouraged because professors might waste time on irrelevant intellectual fancies and neglect to drill their students in the limited but necessary requirements of classical knowledge.[27] In addition, however, and more importantly, there had long been a widespread belief that natural events can be explained only by reference to some divine plan.[28] So long as science was thus seen as a handmaiden to theology, there seemed no reason to transform her into a queenly presence in her own right.

As the century wore on, college attitudes toward science changed dramatically, although not suddenly. This was especially so after the publication of Charles Darwin's *Origin of Species* in 1859, from which the scientific enterprise acquired enormous prestige. It was inevitable that some part of society would be

26. Hofstadter and Metzger, *The Development of Academic Freedom*, pp. 286–87.
27. Ibid., p. 286.
28. Ibid., p. 288.

charged with searching out such knowledge, and it was the universities, collectively, which accepted the commission. In this sequence of events, Darwin's ideas of natural selection and evolution so thoroughly captivated leading scientists and publicists as eventually to undermine the very logic of classical education. Most colleges were dominated by clerical views, woven deeply into the standard learning and enforced by trustees determined to mold students into decent and steadfast Christians. But Darwin's theory strongly suggested that Christian theology depended upon faulty geology and biology, and that God's plan amounted, at best, to no more than an open-ended struggle for survival in a cosmos indifferent to man's fate. To those who agreed with Darwin, the theological underpinnings of classical truth seemed no more than a matter of habitual and fruitless citation of authorities lacking in demonstrable knowledge. The more stubbornly clerical educators clung to the old universe of values and discourse, the more they provoked the new men of science to look upon them as anachronistic obstacles to the attainment of an accurate understanding of the world. As one historian described the move at Johns Hopkins away from traditional standards, "the old-time college had all the truth it needed in revealed religion and in the humanistic tradition." By contrast, "the new university in Baltimore substituted a search for scientific truth."[29]

And so, rather than confine themselves to what Newman had envisioned and recommended, the new universities sought to become the champions of new wisdom, institutions of science where knowledge would be acquired and added to the existing classical compendium. When President Gilman of the Johns Hopkins University described his school, its true functions were "the acquisition, conservation, refinement, and distribution of knowledge."[30] Or, as President William Folwell of the University of Minnesota claimed, "we have discovered what is that informing spirit which is to give life to the limbs and elements of the University; which can fuse, connect, and compact them into a harmonious organization. It is science."[31] Not only university presidents, as interested parties, hitched their schools to the rising scientific star. The country as a whole also anticipated the general benefits of such science and expected the academy to facilitate their appearance. Thus Senator George F. Hoar, speaking at the opening of Clark University in 1889, predicted "great advantage to the country, both in wealth and power, and in the comfort and moral improvement of the people, by the application of science to the useful arts."[32]

29. Rudolph, *The American College and University*, p. 274.

30. Daniel Coit Gilman, *The Benefits which Society Derives from Universities, an Address* (Baltimore: Johns Hopkins University Press, 1885), p. 16.

31. See his "Inaugural," in William Watts Folwell, *University Addresses* (Minneapolis: H. W. Wilson, 1909), p. 18.

32. Quoted in Ryan, *Graduate Education*, p. 70.

Some transformations in the college regime, made inevitable by the commitment to science, were foreseen as early as 1850, by Francis Wayland in his *Report to the Corporation of Brown University*.[33] President Wayland conceded that the classical curriculum had taught several subjects well. But he argued that new skills, linked to vast new realms of knowledge, would be necessary for life in an increasingly complex and sophisticated society. Yet if the new knowledge was so important as to warrant introducing it in the old curriculum, which Wayland believed, then either the old wisdom would have to coexist with new courses in the college program, or the program of studies would have to be lengthened beyond the traditional three or four years.[34] Both steps were eventually taken, as new courses were offered to undergraduates and as graduate programs added to the overall time of studies. Either way, classical wisdom was severely derogated, by intent or by neglect. Its relative importance within the general framework of cumulative wisdom, including the new, simply had to shrink; and concomitantly the creators of the new wisdom, indebted less to their forebears and more to their own efforts and creativity, began exercising greater and greater power over the content and goals of higher education. The declining influence of traditional educators and their once-controlling pedagogical conception showed up unmistakably in a steadily declining number of clerical trustees for colleges and universities throughout the land. In fifteen private institutions from 1860 to 1930, clergymen constituted 39 percent of the trustees in 1860, no more than 23 percent in 1900, and only 7 percent in 1930.[35] In other words, to the extent that scientific knowledge overwhelmed the world view of classical education, there was less demand for clergymen to oversee the training of America's young adults. Trustees could be chosen more as they are today, for an ability to help universities provide the material conditions and intellectual climate that enable independent scholars to do the scientific research and teaching considered essential in modern society.

Science versus Theology

The quest for science gave universities a new role in American life, and this quest provided a rallying point around which an academic culture could grow out of a shared sense of vocational purpose. What kind of science did they have in mind, these spokesmen of the new mood? The main object was to distinguish very clearly the new science from the old theology, and thereby to lay out a road

33. Francis Wayland, *Report to the Corporation of Brown University, On Changes in the System of Collegiate Education, Read March 28, 1850* (Providence, R.I.: G. H. Whitney, 1850).

34. See the discussion of Wayland's report in Richard J. Storr, *The Beginnings of Graduate Education in America* (Chicago: University of Chicago Press, 1953), p. 60f.

35. Earl McGrath, "The Control of Higher Education in America," *Educational Record* (April 1936), pp. 259–79.

to valuable knowledge that only certain people were equipped by training and outlook to travel. Gradually, there came into being the idea that science, which occasionally dazzles by its discoveries—as with Darwin's conclusion that there is an evolutionary process of natural selection—is actually a matter of methods rather than results.[36] That is, if the right methods are used, one may expect useful consequences, which are simply a welcome by-product of the methods, with the methods themselves remaining the essence of science. Textbooks of the time did not offer very detailed descriptions of the scientific method, as modern textbooks do, but there were frequent exhortations to collect important facts—in whatever realm of knowledge—and then subject them to open-minded discussion and verification.

The idea that science is really a matter of methods must be seen for what it was historically, a bold claim by certain thinkers and investigators—from physicists to historians—that they, having learned the right methods of research and analysis, were capable of providing uniquely useful advice to society, whereas certain other people, untrained in the necessary techniques, were incapable of making the same contribution to human welfare. The idea that Darwin's real accomplishment lay in his careful analysis of the species, even more than in his theoretical conclusion, was therefore a very large step toward certifying a new class of experts, men of refined knowledge who would henceforth play a vital role in American life. Here, in terms of science, was the actual basis for an academic culture, for the feeling that scholars, acting in concert with their colleagues, were engaged in a communal endeavor deserving recognition and respect for its original and valuable contributions to American society.

To strengthen their claims, the new men of science did not hesitate to compare their work with that of theologians, the old paragons of educational virtue and presumably the ultimate sources of authority for much of the truth embodied in classical studies. As President Andrew White of Cornell wrote,[37] when Galileo argued that Jupiter was surrounded by moons he proved the contention scientifically with empirical evidence, the view through a telescope. In reply, his clerical opponents insisted that "the Bible showed . . . that there could be only seven planets; that this was proved by the seven golden candlesticks of the Apocalypse, by the seven-branched candlestick of the Tabernacle, and by the seven churches of Asia." Accordingly, if Galileo continued to see moons circling Jupiter, they could only be an illusion created by the Devil to test his Christian faith. Less dramatically, but equally emphatically, President David

36. On the shift from science as results to science as methods, a philosophical stance which may be called "scientific naturalism," see Edward A. Purcell, Jr., *The Crisis of Democratic Theory: Scientific Naturalism and the Problem of Value* (Lexington: University Press of Kentucky, 1973), pp. 3–12.

37. Andrew D. White, *The Warfare of Science* (New York: Appleton, 1876), pp. 35–36.

Starr Jordan of Stanford University made White's point more succinctly: "The clerical mind is irrevocably committed to untestable assumptions."[38] Or, as Professor Alexander Winchell complained along the same lines, when he was discharged from Vanderbilt University for teaching evolution, opposition to Darwin's theory was actually "ecclesiastical proscription for an opinion which must be settled by scientific evidence."[39]

The New Organization

The commitment to science, defined as an enterprise continually expanding the scope of knowledge available to mankind, was not merely a matter of pedagogical rhetoric and vocational principle. Of necessity, that commitment also brought on far-ranging organizational changes in higher education, to the point of creating an unprecedented pattern of studies, along with a new administrative apparatus designed for overseeing it. As is so often the case in revolutionary breaks with the past, there was no master plan by which colleges were transformed into universities. Nonetheless, school after school, from coast to coast, managed to acquire roughly the same structure during the decades of great change from the end of the Civil War to World War I. Substantive instruction varied from place to place, of course, as one school stressed the humanities and another the sciences, or business, or engineering, or whatever. But the modern university's form, in virtually a Platonic sense of Forms, emerged quite clearly and consistently in those years, almost as if an underlying logic guided those who fashioned specific changes for the special circumstances of their respective schools.[40]

Curricular Reform
The logic of this educational metamorphosis began to unfold when American scholars moved to emulate their German brethren.[41] Nineteenth-century German universities were widely admired in America for encouraging scientific research and for maintaining *Lehrfreiheit*, or faculty freedom to teach whatever professors deemed interesting and important, and *Lernfreiheit*, or student liberty

38. Written in 1891; quoted in Hofstadter and Metzger, *Academic Freedom*, p. 348.
39. From a letter by Winchell to the *Nashville* (Tennessee) *Daily American*, June 16, 1878, reprinted in Hofstadter and Smith, *American Higher Education*, 2, p. 8.
40. Laurence R. Veysey, *The Emergence of the American University* (Chicago: University of Chicago Press, 1965), pp. 267–68, argues that the absence of a master plan for reform at the beginning of the university era compels the historian "to reason backward from the evidence of how the academic system functioned toward the causes for its appearance."
41. Hofstadter and Metzger, *Academic Freedom*, chapter 8, "The German Influence," pp. 367–412; and John S. Brubacher and Willis Rudy, *Higher Education in Transition, An American History: 1636–1956* (New York: Harper and Brothers, 1958), chapter 9, "The Influence of the German University," pp. 171–95.

to attend whichever courses they judged intriguing and worthwhile.[42] After 1865, a generation of American scholars—from biologists to geologists to historians to psychologists—returned from Germany, where they had gone to study because graduate education was almost nonexistent in America. In their enthusiasm for scientific work, these academicians, with only a few exceptions, wound up devising and installing an elective program of studies as America's response to the German example.

The switch to elective courses received an imprimatur of respectability in 1869, when President Eliot announced his intention to remake Harvard's curriculum according to the new principle.[43] On the one hand, Eliot attacked the classical notion that a student's mind can be trained only by proper exposure to the right subjects. To the contrary, he argued, a student can acquire mental competence by strict attention to any important and challenging field of study. On that basis, the university would do well to permit each young person to study what he wishes, more or less, and thereby foster special talents even while molding general intellect. On the other hand, Eliot held that traditional studies confined teachers unnecessarily and wastefully. The elective system would put a stop to that, by encouraging faculty members to study intensively what interested them, in order occasionally to prepare materials for entirely new courses in their favorite fields. As a result, teachers would be free to make scientific discoveries rather than spend the bulk of their time drilling students in the classical catechism year in and year out.

In effect, Eliot proposed that higher education become an analogue of the scientific method, where if the process is carefully and conscientiously maintained, desirable results will be assured, for both students and teachers. That the new system found quick favor was surely a sign of the times. In 1872, Harvard abolished subject requirements for seniors; in 1879, junior requirements were eliminated; in 1884, sophomore requirements went the same way; by 1897, even freshmen had only to study a foreign language.[44] And Harvard was not alone, for a study of ninety-seven undergraduate programs in 1901 showed that fifty-six schools had abolished half or more of all their subject requirements.[45]

While the elective system envisioned a pair of active parties to the new learning, the two still had to be brought into contact fruitfully. This came about when traditional recitations were gradually replaced by lectures and seminars.

42. Ibid., pp. 171–72.
43. His "Inaugural Address," in Charles William Eliot, *Educational Reform: Essays and Addresses* (New York: Century, 1898), pp. 1–38, gives a summary of Eliot's early opinion of electives.
44. Rudolf, *The American College and University*, p. 294.
45. Ibid., pp. 302–03. The original study is in E. D. Phillips, "The Elective System in American Education," *Pedagogical Seminary* (June 1901), pp. 206–30.

Eventually, lectures would govern the undergraduate program, and would enable scholars to convey their new ideas and discoveries to students in an interesting and challenging way. In the process, knowledge was constantly reexamined and augmented rather than remaining confined to standard textbooks and assigned in bits and pieces for memorization and exposition, a process that had bored both students and teachers in the old-time colleges. Seminars, which became the hallmark of graduate education, were patterned after those in Germany, to facilitate widespread reading and discussion of the latest research findings in various fields. Here, professors and their advanced students worked out exciting partnerships between masters and disciples in the common pursuit of new knowledge.

As the college ideal yielded to electives, lectures, and seminars, many of the new-style courses were gathered together into graduate schools, a rubric of learning that overshadowed the college entirely and was destined to become the very sign and symbol of modern universities. The German model was not strictly copied, since in Germany higher degrees were still awarded only in the traditional medieval faculties of law, medicine, theology, and philosophy, whereas in America advanced study also took place in newly established schools such as those for agriculture, engineering, and business. Still, American reformers grasped the European idea that graduate studies were necessary as the capstone of an educational structure designed to widen and deepen human knowledge. Yale awarded its first Ph.D. in 1861, while Harvard reorganized itself to create a graduate school in 1871, with Michigan, Columbia, Wisconsin, and other institutions closely following suit. In 1876, the Johns Hopkins University opened its doors, in a signal act of creation that marked a point of reform from which there would be no return. In plain terms, the Baltimore school committed itself wholeheartedly to graduate education, and to that enterprise's characteristic pursuit of knowledge in the new fashion. As President Gilman reported, "In selecting a staff of teachers, the Trustees have determined to consider especially the devotion of the candidate to some particular line of study and the certainty of his eminence in that speciality; the power to pursue independent and original investigations, and to inspire the young with enthusiasm for study and research."[46] Conspicuous by its absence was even a parenthetical aside to the importance of developing moral character and proper behavior, which would have accorded well with classical goals.

Departments and Markets

The logic of change not only pervaded course innovations but also imbued the question of how the new courses might be administered. Gone were the days of

46. Daniel Coit Gilman, *The Launching of a University* (New York: Dodd, Mead, and Co., 1906), p. 43.

important schools with only a president, a few tutors, and several scores of students. As America's undergraduate population grew from 54,300 in 1870 to 597,900 in 1920,[47] with graduate studies proliferating apace, something had to be done to tie together the hundreds of new courses at every university with the thousands of students and teachers. The administrative solution to this problem, cutting across undergraduate and graduate programs alike, was a flexible system of academic departments. Even though textbooks in every discipline today explain how, by the nature of things, there is a reasonable division of academic labor among the various disciplines, with an appropriate portion assigned to each one, reformers in the late nineteenth century did not act according to a controlling blueprint for constructing the new house of knowledge, with so many rooms here and so many tenants there. Instead, departments were added as scholars learned more and more about their respective interests, multiplied the number of lectures and seminars they wanted to offer on related subjects, and attracted students who thought the new courses interesting and worthwhile. For administrative convenience, it seemed appropriate to group together men of like interests, whose courses would then constitute distinctive programs of study.[48]

Together with this administrative rearrangement, old subjects were deepened and broadened, and new departments were created from within old fields or in the gaps between them. Sometimes the process was gradual, as we shall see in the case of political science. However, it could also be sudden, as in 1893 when the University of Chicago divided its Department of Biology into five new departments—Zoology, Botany, Anatomy, Neurology, and Physiology.[49] By about 1900, the tendency to create new departments lost much of its force. The academic world had largely been divided up among those disciplines we recognize today, and the existing range of departments was so firmly established that there would be little further fragmentation of the world of learning.[50]

The new departments needed staff, and on this score the process of departmentalization was nourished by a growing national job market for teachers in all fields. Here was a remarkable but insufficiently appreciated phenomenon in American higher education. European countries after the American Civil War, and especially Germany, were not committed to the support of many schools or a large number of students and faculty members.[51] European scholars in any single

47. *Historical Statistics*, 1, p. 383.

48. On the relationship between departmentalization and administrative convenience, see Veysey, *Emergence of the American University*, pp. 320–24.

49. Goodspeed, *History of the University of Chicago*, p. 322.

50. Veysey, *Emergence of the American University*, pp. 321–22.

51. On the differences between German and American universities with regard to market conditions, see Joseph Ben-David, *The Scientist's Role in Society* (Englewood Cliffs, N.J.: Prentice-Hall, 1971), pp. 117–60.

country were therefore likely to enjoy only limited employment opportunities, with working conditions fairly standardized by authorities who administered mainly state-run educational systems. In America, by contrast, there were hundreds of colleges and universities run by churches, citizen groups, philanthropic societies, and all levels of government. Everywhere, energetic school presidents were eager to bid against each other in order to hire professors who would raise their institution's standards and reputation. As a result, in schools large and small, aspiring teachers kept their eye on the main chance, which was sometimes far from where they were working at the moment. Alert and ambitious citizens of the new academic culture were aware, for example, that in 1893 President Harper raided Clark University, in Worcester, Massachusetts, to take away some of that school's best faculty members, at handsome increases in salary, in order to staff his newly founded University of Chicago.[52] Or the historians, to take another case, would hear rumors about Frederick Jackson Turner, their colleague whose thesis on the relation of the frontier to democracy made him a rising academic star, whereupon he parlayed his fame into higher income and better research facilities at the University of Wisconsin, whose president was afraid of losing Turner to a tempting offer from Harvard.[53]

But how does one measure the value of a candidate in the national job market? That was the question both potential employers and employees had to answer, the former to know the quality of available staff and the latter to make themselves maximally attractive to outstanding buyers. Here the market's two sides were well served by the fact that science required dissemination as well as discovery of new knowledge. When research findings were expounded, in published form, the job market gained a handy yardstick for estimating each scholar's worth in comparison to that of his colleagues in the shared pursuit of scientific progress.

Because commercial publishers could not be relied upon to find scientific publishing profitable and therefore worth doing—how many potential buyers are there, after all, for esoteric books on topics ranging from Jurassic sedimentation to the grammar of *Beowulf*?—a substantial part of the dissemination network had to be created by the universities themselves, in the form of facilities for bringing out scholarly books and journals. This was done with such thoroughness, and has since become so commonplace a part of university science, that few people today realize how suddenly and comprehensively this feature of academic life came into being in the late nineteenth century. University presses were established at Johns Hopkins, Chicago, Columbia, and the University of California

52. On Harper's raid, see Goodspeed, *History of the University of Chicago*, pp. 211–12.

53. Merle Curti and Vernon Carstensen, *The University of Wisconsin: A History, 1848–1925* (Madison: University of Wisconsin Press, 1949), pp. 615–17.

in the 1890s, while those of Harvard, Yale, and Princeton appeared soon after the turn of the century.[54] Around and beside them, a variety of scholarly journals were created, sometimes sponsored by the universities and sometimes by learned societies. For instance, the *American Journal of Mathematics* (1878), the *American Chemical Journal* (1879), the *American Journal of Philology* (1879), the *American Journal of Psychology* (1887), the *American Geologist* (1888), the *American Historical Review* (1891), the *Journal of Political Economy* (1892), and the *American Journal of Sociology* (1894) constitute only a small sample of the important journals founded before World War I.[55]

Once so many publishing outlets were available, it seemed reasonable to conclude that any scholar who managed to get into print thereby demonstrated his worth as a contributor to new knowledge. Accordingly, the supply and demand sides of the academic marketplace came together in mutual interest. Professors were intent on publishing and attaining "scholarly visibility," and university administrators were constantly on the lookout to see who was visible and therefore worth hiring or promoting. It was at this historical and logical point that the rule of publish or perish became so important a part of academic life. The first signs of publishing potential revealed themselves when a young scholar earned his doctorate, which required writing up a substantial piece of research that usually appeared, sooner or later, in book or article form. In the college era, many teachers never acquired a Ph.D. At Harvard in 1884, for example, only 19 out of 189 faculty members had the doctorate; at Michigan in the same year, only 6 out of 88 had it.[56] But the times changed rapidly, and by 1900 the Ph.D. was virtually mandatory for a permanent post at any prominent school. Thus Arthur T. Hadley, the president of Yale, announced in 1901 that promotion for young scholars would henceforth depend on "productive work" that leads to a "national reputation."[57] There can be no doubt here as to the existence of the national market, and its standards for visibility. As one college dean remarked in the same era, the school's best teacher would not be promoted when his appointment came up for renewal. Why not? Because "he hasn't done anything!"[58] that is, published enough.

54. On the founding of university presses, see Rudolf, *The American College and University*, p. 407.

55. For a sampling of the early journals, see James McKeen Cattell, *Scientific Societies and Associations*, no. 17, *Monographs on Education in the United States*, ed. Nicholas Murray Butler (Albany: J. B. Lyon, 1900), vol. 2, pp. 17–20.

56. Rudolph, *The American College and University*, p. 395.

57. Quoted in Veysey, *Emergence of the American University*, pp. 176–77.

58. Quoted in Claude Charleton Bowman, *The College Professor in America: An Analysis of Articles Published in the General Magazines, 1890–1938* (Philadelphia: University of Pennsylvania Press, 1938), p. 122.

Larger Trends

Little by little, an academic culture, commitment to science, electives, lectures, seminars, graduate programs, departments, a national job market, publications, and scholarly visibility took shape between the Civil War and World War I. When historians today seek to place such developments in the widest context, some significant trends begin to emerge. Recent interpretations of the period in question place great emphasis on two broad phenomena existing in America at that time. These were the growing influence of middle-class values and forms of behavior, and a concerted move toward professionalization in many occupations. In truth, the two trends were so intertwined and dependent upon each other that only for analytical purposes can they be separated.

The Rise of the Middle Class

Robert Wiebe has described the changing social environment which, in late nineteenth- and early twentieth-century America, encouraged people to adopt middle-class values and behavior.[59] In his analysis, the old and antebellum society that emphasized deference and stable social ranks broke down as industry and urban areas grew tremendously after the Civil War, thereby severely reducing in importance the small and intimate villages, towns, and cities that Wiebe called "island communities."[60] In the search for a new social order, innovations in communication and transportation—all part of the growing impact of science, of course—drew people out of their territorial isolation, where neighbors knew each other and accepted traditional values as necessary to maintain collective life in the established pattern. Henceforth, men were thrust into contact with regional, nationwide, or even global networks of trade and information where no one knew who should set guidelines or what those should be. Under the circumstances, familiar skills and modes of behavior were no longer sufficient to command either success or prestige, and new skills and knowledge were sought, eagerly or not, by those who aspired to take a place in the new order—a truly national society—that was emerging.[61]

In Burton Bledstein's extension of Wiebe's thesis, the middle-class dimension of searching for a new order was defined as an American's state of mind rather than his relation to the means of production as might be said of a European in the Old World's more stratified societies.[62] For Bledstein, the ascendant idea in post–Civil War America was a notion that old-time standards of honesty and civility, although commendable, were no longer sufficient to qualify a man

---

59. Robert H. Wiebe, *The Search for Order, 1877–1920* (New York: Hill and Wang, 1967).
60. Ibid., pp. 4, 44–77.
61. Ibid., pp. 111–63.
62. On the middle class as a state of mind, see Bledstein, *The Culture of Professionalism*, p. 6.

for social deference and financial success in the rapidly growing and constantly changing communities of the new regime. Instead, professional skills and competence, earned through long study and training, were necessary for an aspiring person to attain, regardless of his original station in life, an enviable new place.[63] In this sense, middle-class men for Bledstein were those united in their disdain for permanent class privilege and their determination to choose "vocation, rank, and order" on the basis of new attitudes and work habits.[64] Here was the common ground upon which people from various traditional niches in the old society could stand together and build the new.

Professionalization
Now, when Wiebe and Bledstein spoke of the search for order, it is clear that they had in mind (1) a groping toward new patterns of social life, and (2) a quest for knowledge concerning the structure of nature and society, with the underlying assumption being that people engaged in the latter quest, and working through scientific specialization, could lay claim to special competence with regard to the question of how social life ought more properly to be arranged. But "specialization," although accurate, is a term that fails to connote all the important qualities of social change that beset America in this era.[65] For that purpose, "professionalization" is more serviceable.

Before the Civil War, there were three great professions: divinity, law, and medicine. People with other skills, such as farmers, merchants, and manufacturers, were respected for having vocations but not professions. After the war, practitioners of many occupations sought to acquire professional status, which conferred a special reputation, deserved or not, of serving the public with both technical competence and moral integrity.[66] As Bledstein pointed out, this was the time when many of the modern professional rituals and trappings of office were first created, including an abundance of academic degrees, licenses, publications, associations, jargon, special instruments, uniforms, and more, "in the medical doctor's office, the home, the school, the seminar room, the athletic arena, the fraternity house, the settlement house, and the charity ward."[67] This was also the era in which many occupations became organized, with the found-

63. Ibid., pp. 172–73.
64. Ibid., p. 18.
65. For an excellent essay that does use the term "specialization" to analyze many aspects of the era during which universities rose to prominence, see John Higham, "The Matrix of Specialization," in Oleson and Voss, *The Organization of Knowledge*, pp. 3–18.
66. Thomas L. Haskell, *The Emergence of Professional Social Science: The American Social Science Association and the Nineteenth-Century Crisis of Authority* (Urbana, Ill.: University of Illinois Press, 1977), pp. 65–85.
67. Bledstein, *The Culture of Professionalism*, p. 95.

ing of the American Federation of Labor, the National Association of Manufacturers, the Grange, the Farm Bureau Federation, the Chamber of Commerce,
and others. Some of these were broadly oriented toward business and trade
interests rather than public service; and it is therefore clear that not all the new
organizations, so necessary for supporting a new order and its occupational—
rather than geographical—communities, were strictly professional in character.
But pervading it all was what Bledstein called the "culture of professionalism,"
the idea that at key points in the new order there was room for experts of unique
skill and perspective whose access to a "special understanding of a segment of the
universe"[68] constituted a scarce and necessary resource to be placed at society's
service in a very distinctive way. In every area of public and private life, the shape
of modern society would be determined more and more by professional
knowledge and skills, or at least by intensively trained people who claimed
professional rank. Into the family via social workers, psychiatrists, doctors, and
teachers; into the workplace via scientific management and engineering; into the
realm of public ceremony via urban planners, architects, funeral directors, and
public relations specialists; and into government via economists, sociologists,
defense analysts, and more: at every turn the nation would be increasingly
beholden to the new experts at manipulating people, things, and the conditions
of modern life.

It is no exaggeration to say that universities became the linchpin of the
entire complex of professions in the new order. The facts are beyond dispute.
The spectacular growth of the student population came mainly from the ranks of
those who sought entrance to the middle class or those who, already inside,
strove to remain.[69] Accordingly, higher education became the nation's instrument for molding, or socializing, young people in accordance with the needs of
modern life, until they turned into the sort of men and women whom business
and the newly professionalized occupations sought out, and whereby they became adept at playing those roles that had to be filled if the great institutions of
industry, trade, professions, government, and urban life were to be maintained
in a style to which America quickly became accustomed.

The universities thus became a key element in what Bledstein called "the
vertical vision."[70] The old-time colleges had provided "moral apprenticeship for
the children of the gentry,"[71] instilling in them the manners admired in classical
education and in the small communities then constituting traditional America.
But this "horizontal vision," as Bledstein called it, lost authority for many when

68. Ibid., p. 90.
69. On the middle-class character of most enrollees, see Christopher Jencks and David Riesman, *The Academic Revolution* (Garden City, N.Y.: Doubleday Anchor, 1969), pp. 61–154.
70. Bledstein, *The Culture of Professionalism*, pp. 105–28.
71. Ibid., p. 209.

the small community lost its commanding role in American life, when people were forced by new circumstances to look outward and upward to regional, national, and even global communities for guidelines to security, knowledge, and success. In the vertical vision, higher education gave everyone a chance to change along with the times. In this sense, universities became a sheer necessity for modern America sometime between 1850 and 1900,[72] providing a way station in life where the old ways could be discarded and the new acquired. In the process, with enormous and unforeseen consequences for the future, the world of academe gained great and unexpected power over the form and content of higher education. As Dorothy Ross observed, "the middle class public turned from the moral advice of the clergy to the expert advice of the university social scientists, from the old elite's conception of society as hierarchically ordered by virtue to the new elite's conception of society as a meritocracy, hierarchically ordered by competence."[73]

Authority for the Learned Disciplines
What was it that clothed the university's professors with authority, if not the long established theological certainties that had given legitimacy to the clergy and their classical curriculum? For Thomas Haskell, all learned disciplines, including the social sciences, gained authority from a widespread belief that the new order had to deal with what Haskell called "interdependence."[74] In science, the watchword was evolution, which, while indicating that changes are always taking place, at the same time taught that all things are constantly linked to everything else. Darwin had written of the species, but examples of linkage in everyday life were commonplace as society became more complex, such as when a country doctor, only a general practitioner, could be upstaged by a specialist trained at Massachusetts General Hospital. Understandably, it became clear to many people that the old maxims of common sense simply could not explain everything that needed explaining. Instead, interdependence drained the immediate world of its one-time meaning and forced men to look for hidden or remote causes of previously familiar phenomena.[75] In Haskell's terms, professionalism, or the rise of experts in every realm of knowledge, was therefore not simply a drive to power by people who lacked standing, but a social necessity created by the need to replace old patterns of authority with new guides to action and virtue.[76] The demand was for a new breed of men who, apparently able to at least

72. Ibid., p. 127.
73. Dorothy Ross, "The Development of the Social Sciences," in Oleson and Voss, *The Organization of Knowledge*, p. 121.
74. Haskell, *The Emergence of Professional Social Science*, pp. 15–16, 18–23, 28–30.
75. Ibid., pp. 40–44f.
76. Ibid., pp. 65f.

partly pierce the veil of uncertainty that shrouded interdependence, would be available for consultation at critical moments in the lives of individuals or society as a whole. Authority flowed, therefore, to the professions. But it was the learned disciplines, based mainly in the universities and ostensibly at the very forefront of scientific research into the mysteries of interdependence, which acted as mentor to all the other professions by virtue of the university's many training programs for middle-class positions. As a result, professors became perhaps the most authoritative of all the new professionals.[77]

Within the learned disciplines, authority was gradually parceled out by a process of diffusion that permitted each academic speciality to partake of the leadership and legitimacy that had devolved on higher learning as a whole. We have already seen how departments were created when science so deepened the fund of knowledge that narrow areas of concern became the rule. The sum total of these departments, nationwide, constituted the various academic disciplines, more or less as they exist today, where peer groups of scholars, each taking a specific realm of knowledge for its own, decided what constituted reliable and valuable truth there. In order to facilitate the dissemination of research findings and stimulate fruitful communication among its members, each discipline organized nationally, publishing scholarly journals and holding frequent conventions and symposia where scholarly papers were read and matters of common professional interest discussed. In this regard, the developing academic culture was buttressed by specific professional structures which, one after another, came into being to give shape to the new disciplines: the American Historical Association (1884), the American Economic Association (1885), the American Statistical Association (1888), the American Mathematical Society (1888), the Geological Society of America (1888), the American Anthropological Society (1902), the American Sociological Society (1905), and more.[78]

It is important to note that, because specialized knowledge accumulated very rapidly in the new situation, it soon became clear that only one's immediate colleagues, rather than scholars in other disciplines, were qualified to judge whether one's work was done well or poorly. A historian, for example, being unacquainted with the relevant body of research findings, was simply unable to say whether or not some economist's latest published paper constituted a valuable contribution to economic knowledge. This meant that for the purposes of each academic subject under study, every discipline became an exclusive "com-

---

77. Wiebe, *The Search for Order*, p. 121: "By 1900 they [the universities] had an unquestioned power to legitimize, for no new profession felt complete—or scientific—without its distinct academic curriculum; they provided centers for philosophizing and propagandizing; and they inculcated apprentices with the proper values and goals."

78. For a listing of some of the major scientific societies established at this time, see Cattell, *Scientific Societies*, pp. 11–16.

munity of the competent,"[79] with professorial ranks carefully assigned on the basis of recognized scholarly contribution.[80] As such, the various communities saw their authority accepted by the public, which sent its children to learn at the universities with experts who would provide suitable certification for studious achievement. After all, who could be more competent than the community of the competent?

From ASSA to AAUP

The life story of the American Social Science Association (ASSA) tells an instructive tale illustrating many of the general trends spelled out above.[81] The ASSA was founded in 1865 by traditional men of affairs and by college-educated scholars who confronted the complexities of interdependence in search of new knowledge that would permit reasonable solutions for the nation's growing social problems, especially those arising from poverty, crime, labor unrest, and business cycles produced by urbanization and industrialization. In the broadest sense, these reformers sought knowledge that would generate authoritative advice about how society might ease its growing pains, in light of the fact that old knowledge seemed inadequate to the job.

The key to the ASSA's failure as an organization lay in the fact that a new view of science, personified by members of the new academic disciplines, would eventually regard the notion of a comprehensive social science organization as a contradiction in terms. One by one, the American Historical Association in 1884, the American Economic Association in 1885, the American Anthropological Association in 1902, and others, broke away from the ASSA when new and specialized research led teachers further and further into their respective disciplines and away from former colleagues in other disciplines. Indeed, rather than respond to the ASSA's continued calls for common efforts and understanding, they saw a growing need to establish those professional networks which would guarantee each discipline exclusive authority over a specific domain of knowledge. In plain terms, their insistence on going their own way was a flat denial of the ASSA's hope that authority in the new order would be shared as it had in the old, by a single class or group of people.

Two events associated with the growing power of universities and professionalism showed how impossible it was to maintain, in the new order, a traditional form of shared authority. In the late 1870s, President Gilman of Johns Hopkins

79. Haskell, *The Emergence of Professional Social Science*, pp. 66f.

80. On the appearance of standardized ranks and levels of professional achievement in the learned disciplines, see Veysey, *The Emergence of the American University*, pp. 317–20.

81. For two complementary versions of the story, see Haskell, *The Emergence of Professional Social Science*, and Mary O. Furner, *Advocacy and Objectivity: A Crisis in the Professionalization of American Social Science, 1865–1905* (Lexington: University Press of Kentucky, 1975).

rejected an ASSA proposal to merge the Association somehow with the new university. In Gilman's view, the objectives of the ASSA simply did not equate with those of the university, for the school was much less interested than the association in various forms of agitation designed to influence public opinion and policy directly. And so the various disciplines at Johns Hopkins and other universities continued to develop and specialize, eventually to split knowledge asunder irrevocably.[82] Then, six years after the ASSA finally collapsed, the American Association of University Professors (AAUP) was established in 1915.[83] Theoretically, it was an opportunity to bring the disciplines back together, as they had been in embryonic form in the ASSA much earlier. But the AAUP stood for no particular content in scholarly work whatsoever and came into existence only to protect academic freedom. Here, the argument was made that the AAUP served an interest of the university community as a whole, protecting the right of its members to discover the truth scientifically and to speak it fearlessly.[84] At the same time, the AAUP's indifference to intellectual substance revealed that each discipline refused to countenance any wide-ranging organization of professors that might interfere with affairs better controlled by separate communities of the competent.

A Change of Constitution

In *The Academic Revolution* (1969), Christopher Jencks and David Riesman described many of the major features of educational reform that accompanied the triumph of the universities over the college ideal. Extending their analysis into recent years, they concluded that the single most important effect of all the reforms together was "the rise to power of the academic profession."[85] With this phrase, Jencks and Riesman highlighted the fact that various pedagogical and structural innovations had changed the very constitution, in an Aristotelian sense, of Amer-

---

82. Haskell, *Emergence*, pp. 144–67.

83. A "General Declaration of Principles," adopted by the AAUP in 1915, is reprinted in Hofstadter and Smith, *American Higher Education*, 2, pp. 860–78. An account of how and why the AAUP was founded, appears in Hofstadter and Metzger, *The Development of Academic Freedom*, pp. 468–80.

84. See the "Report of the Committee on Academic Freedom and Tenure" of the AAUP, in Hofstadter and Smith, *American Higher Education*, p. 872: "It is . . . inadmissible that the power of determining when departures from the requirements of the scientific spirit and method have occurred, should be vested in bodies not composed of members of the academic profession. Such bodies necessarily lack full competency to judge of these requirements; their intervention can never be exempt from suspicion that it is dictated by other motives than zeal for the integrity of science; and it is, in any case, unsuitable to the dignity of a great profession that the initial responsibility for the maintenance of its professional standards should not be in the hands of its own members."

85. Jencks and Riesman, *The Academic Revolution*, p. xvi.

ica's institutions of higher education. The typical school was now a university rather than a college. But the ideal college based on a classical curriculum had been run by people who themselves gave the tone to their school and who knew what they wanted taught. Their school was thus constituted vertically. Its governors, either a board of trustees or the president acting on their behalf, chose to employ certain teachers because as employees they agreed to do the work defined by their employer. This was the sort of hierarchical arrangement we now associate with bureaucracy, where instructions descend from the top to the bottom of an organizational ladder. In such a situation, where leaders have a firm conception of the task at hand, followers will comply with dictated guidelines. And the colleges did know what their task was, for, as the *Report of the Faculty of Yale* declared in 1829, "there are certain common subjects of knowledge, about which all men ought to be informed, who are best educated."[86]

The enthusiasm for scientific research changed all of that. University administrators could hardly claim to know what was worth knowing, because knowledge expanded so rapidly that no one could acquaint himself with more than a sizable fraction of the sum total. Consequently, men at the top no longer seemed competent to say what sort of educated man should be produced by their school. Instead, the elective principle implied just the opposite, that so long as science could produce such vast quantities of useful knowledge, "educated men need not know the same things."[87]

It followed that administrators lacked a rationale for imposing hierarchical command over universities. Power was therefore assumed by the various learned disciplines, for they alone were deemed competent to judge the true worth of scholars laboring in their respective fields. Over time, entire faculties came to be composed of men and women selected by their departmental colleagues rather than by the school's nonacademic staff. Of course, formal decisions with regard to rank and salary were made somewhere in the university's administrative structure, and decisions as to how many positions there should be in various departments—as matters of intellectual and financial balance—were fought out in administrative forums. But the new-style faculty in truth recruited themselves, on the basis of unchallengeable expertise, with administrators in effect ratifying decisions made in the university's departments and institutes.[88] As Jencks and Riesman pointed out, science created a situation where scholars, rather than university presidents or trustees, "decide what a student ought to know, how he should be taught it, and who can teach it to him."[89] In this sense, if we measure the degree of professionalization by a group's claim of the right to regulate itself,

86. "Original Papers," p. 325.
87. Rudolph, *The American College and University*, p. 305.
88. Barzun, *The American University*, p. 42.
89. Jencks and Riesman, *The Academic Revolution*, p. 510.

because of unique experience and expertise, it may be said that the learned disciplines achieved the very highest rank of professionalism among all groups claiming that status in America in the late nineteenth and early twentieth centuries.[90]

Here is one explanation for the nature of Kerr's multiversity. The move from a college to a university ideal by no means eliminated the vertical imperatives of academic bureaucracy. If it had, we would know less today of IBM cards, course regulations, and the endless paperwork of academic life. But the existence of nationwide disciplines did introduce a companion principle of horizontal reference to higher education. This was the world of hundreds of academic departments scattered across the land, where scientific progress took place in different places and at different times, and where outstanding practitioners were located physically at one school while at the same time integrated professionally with colleagues elsewhere. While the market rather than the bureaucratic principle held sway, it was not clear that a professor had colleagues in his own university at all, except those, for the most part in his department, who might take a personal interest in his work. Here is the multiversity with its congeries of departments, institutes, faculties, and programs of study, where administrators have all they can do just to hold the disparate parts together and pay for them all, and where each discipline pursues scientific knowledge in its own way, recognizing no common authority in the school capable of providing a set of goals that all can pursue together rather than remain apart.

The Temple of Science

The new situation can be portrayed graphically, which will help keep it in mind for future reference. In Western society, starting with the Greeks, and continuing into Christian culture and the curriculum developed around classical and Christian values down through the nineteenth century, science entailed various fields of knowledge, or "episteme," and did not correspond exactly to what we mean by science today.[91] In the *Nichomachean Ethics*, for example, Aristotle wrote of a great many theoretical, practical, and productive kinds of knowledge, including geometry, astronomy, physics, biology, rhetoric, music, poetry, logic, and more.[92] In a sense, all of these were separate sciences, or realms of knowledge. Yet in the minds of learned men and women for more than two thousand years in the West, it was as though the diversified sciences comprised one great Temple of Science, with specific fields constituting columns while a

90. Ibid., p. 238.

91. On the differences between the classical and the modern view of science, see the preface to G. E. R. Lloyd, *Early Greek Science: Thales to Aristotle* (London: Chatto and Windus, 1970).

92. On Aristotle's typology of the sciences, see *The Nichomachean Ethics of Aristotle*, trans. and introd. Sir David Ross (London: Oxford University Press, 1954), pp. 140–47.

realm of wisdom served as the pediment and roof somehow linking the columns together. That is, in classical thought there reigned a notion that some basic body of wisdom, science, or reliable ideas by any other name, provided a means for holding together an edifice of knowledge, whose columns separately provided a great deal of useful information but which could not, by themselves, tell us how human communities should be built and run.

The new vision of science looked quite different. Thus for Daniel Coit Gilman, as one Johns Hopkins professor recalled in later years, scholarship should not rest upon mere erudition but must offer each scholar "the unique experience of having contributed some tiny brick, however small, to the Temple of Science, the construction of which is the sublimest achievement of man."[93] In Gilman's praise for narrowly focused but effective scientific research, one can discern the confidence of an age, based on the fact that scientific discoveries and technological developments were then making enormous contributions to human well-being in fields ranging from health and agriculture to communications and transportation. But what was missing from the university reforms was sufficient thought to the fact that the Temple of Science needed a realm of synthesizing wisdom, of concern for the general design and welfare, and that someone would therefore have to take responsibility for the roof of knowledge. There was some recognition of the danger that students taking many scattered electives and specialized courses might remain educationally impoverished, unable to appreciate the great bodies of wisdom and good taste that had accumulated in Western history down through the centuries. Special programs of general education were devised in places like Columbia, Harvard, and Chicago to counter the intellectual fragmentation that accompanied the rise of universities.[94] But these programs, even though imitated in some other schools, never found a firm rationale, not in the philosophical sense of proving the importance of humanities in an age of science, and not in the vocational sense of explaining how humanistic training would outfit a student for work in those occupations and professions that became characteristic of modern America.[95]

Here, then, was a painful paradox that accompanied the deepening of knowledge in every field, with specialization gaining so much ground as to leave

93. From G. Stanley Hall, *Life and Confessions of a Psychologist* (New York: D. Appleton, 1923), pp. 248–49; quoted in Hofstadter and Smith, *American Higher Education*, 2, p. 650.

94. See Daniel Bell, *The Reforming of General Education: The Columbia College Experience in its National Setting* (New York: Columbia University Press, 1966); *General Education in a Free Society; a Report of the Harvard Committee* (Cambridge: Harvard University Press, 1945); and *The Idea and Practice of General Education: An Account of the College of the University of Chicago* (Chicago: University of Chicago Press, 1950).

95. See Robert M. Hutchins, *The Higher Learning in America* (New Haven: Yale University Press, 1936), and Harry D. Gideonese, *The Higher Learning in a Democracy: A Reply to President Hutchins' Critique of the American University* (New York: Farrar and Rinehart, 1937).

no one qualified to say what each field meant in relation to the whole, or even to a few others. Most of the new disciplines could safely shrug off responsibility for the lack of an all-embracing vision. After all, they were expected to tend to their own realms of learning and inquiry. But in the case of political science, to which we now turn, it was not easy to delegate to someone else the responsibility for formulating, or at least persuasively expounding, society's ultimate goals. And the discipline's obligations in this matter were especially troublesome when its members tried to deal with urgent problems of democratic theory and practice.

3

The Contradictions of a Political Discipline

The study of politics enjoys an honorable history that stretches, by conventional reckoning, all the way back to ancient Greece.[1] But as a learned discipline, and not merely an adjunct of other scholarly concerns, political science was born together with America's modern universities and grew apace with their tendency to foster specialization in the world of knowledge. In this saga, even while the discipline developed structural characteristics similar to those of other learned disciplines in order to establish itself within the university environment, political scientists inherited substantive obligations that clashed with their professional hopes and expectations. Within this dialectic, setting structure against substance, lay the seeds of a tragedy for political science. They remained dormant and hardly noticed as the discipline grew out of the college milieu and into the university setting, but they burst forth with annoying vigor and caused considerable soul-searching when most of the nation, including political scientists, sought to defend democracy before World War II.

The Development of Political Science

Political science per se did not appear in the classical curriculum. In the college era, the titles of "disputations" and "commencement theses"—roughly equivalent to today's term papers and senior essays—indicate that political topics were studied intensively. Thus a survey of such works up to 1825 revealed many with titles like: "Are the people the sole judges of their rights and liberties?" "Is party

1. William Anderson, *Man's Quest for Political Knowledge: The Study and Teaching of Politics in Ancient Times* (Minneapolis: University of Minnesota Press, 1964).

spirit beneficial?" "Ought the poor to be supported by law?"[2] However, issues of this sort were not discussed in courses specifically labeled as political science and offered in departments of that name. For example, in 1841 the University of Pennsylvania listed two courses in "The Law of Nations" and "Political Law." Both were taught in the Department of Rhetoric and English Literature, presumably because the chief source of texts for such subjects were classical works broadly accepted as models of rhetoric and literature.[3]

In general, the colleges raised political questions in comprehensive senior-year courses under the name of "moral philosophy" or "moral science."[4] In most instances, these courses were offered to advanced students by the college president, a man of extraordinary scholarly breadth when measured by today's disciplinary standards. It was not unusual for the senior course to include logic, rhetoric, philosophy, natural law, the law of nations, politics, and political economy. Accordingly, the typical college president would enjoy an imposing academic title, such as "Professor of Moral and Mental Philosophy, Political Economy, and Polite Literature," and would be responsible for teaching subjects ranging from constitutional law to evidences of Christianity.[5] He was, in fact, a personification of the classical notion that some sort of a roof must be provided for the Temple of Science, that an overarching synthesis of wisdom must combine various realms of learning—the Temple's columns—into a comprehensive point of view. As one teacher of the subject observed, moral philosophy "is related to the whole business of active life. The languages, and even mathematical and natural knowledge, are but hand maids to this superior knowledge."[6]

In the course of presenting the requisite synthesis, standard textbooks on moral philosophy dealt with "theoretical ethics," or maxims concerning virtue, conscience, and religion, and then applied these to "practical ethics," which encompassed the requirements of love of God and duties to man, the last touching upon slavery, property rights, slander, truth and contracts, civil rights, the forms of government, the proper structure of society, and more.[7] Most impor-

---

2. Anna Haddow, *Political Science in American Colleges and Universities, 1636–1900*, ed. and introd. William Anderson (New York: Appleton-Century Crofts, 1939), pp. 31–40, 101–10.

3. Ibid., p. 125.

4. On moral science and philosophy, see Donald H. Meyer, *The Instructed Conscience: The Shaping of the American National Ethic* (Philadelphia: University of Pennsylvania Press, 1974).

5. This was the title, and these were some of the course assignments, of Andrew Wylie, president at Indiana University in the 1830s. See Oliver Peter Field, *Political Science at Indiana University, 1829–1951* (Bloomington: Bureau of Government Research, Indiana University, 1952), p. 5.

6. John Witherspoon, *Lectures on Moral Philosophy and Eloquence*, 3rd ed. (Philadelphia: William W. Woodward, 1810), p. 141.

7. The division between theoretical and practical ethics may be seen in Francis Wayland, *The Elements of Moral Science*, 2nd ed. (orig., 1835; Boston: Gould and Lincoln, 1872).

tantly, senior courses based on moral philosophy addressed political questions within a framework of concern that combined attention to facts with consideration for values, that touched upon matters of God and of civil society, of virtue and of necessity, of business and benevolence, of the formal bonds of citizenship and the intimate ties of familial love. In the amalgam of facts and values, a unifying theme was always reference to the twin standards of right and obligation. As John Witherspoon wrote, "Right and obligation are correlative terms. Whatever others have a right or title to claim from me, that is my duty, or what I am obliged to do to them."[8] Although much of moral philosophy could be explained in terms of a well-reasoned contract theory of government and society, without reference to divine will, there could be no gainsaying that, in the last analysis, human happiness consists, as Francis Wayland held, "in the gratification of our desires within the limits assigned to them by our Creator. . . . And hence the greatest happiness of which man is, in his present state, capable, is to be attained by conforming his whole conduct to the laws of virtue, that is, to the will of God."[9]

Courses in moral philosophy eventually disappeared from college catalogues when increasing devotion to Darwinism made their religious fundament seem out of place at the university. Thus when scholars began to believe that the universe is characterized by perpetual flux and is indifferent to human existence, many of them concluded that no invariant moral standards could be discovered by research into, as it were, the nature of things: commandments to be revealed and expounded in church, yes; imperatives to be discovered and taught at the university, no. At the same time, the expansion of scientific knowledge after 1865 encouraged academic disciplines—including political science—to extract from the moribund senior course specific concerns capable of being fashioned into separate scholarly fields. In the time of transition, teachers did not necessarily break sharply with the past. Thus Francis Lieber, the first American to hold a professorship of political science, faithfully mirrored in his own teachings the condition of political studies as they began to emerge from the field of moral philosophy and to form the substance of a new discipline. From 1857 to 1865, Lieber served at Columbia University as Professor of History and Political Science. His very title thereby indicated that political science was first regarded as inseparable from other concerns, in this case history. At the same time, Lieber always believed that political right entails moral obligation, and that the science of government must seek to implement political ethics.[10] Here, Lieber resembled those moral philosophers who refused to separate the secular aspects of politics

8. *Lectures*, p. 57.
9. *Elements*, p. 103.
10. Haddow, *Political Science*, pp. 141–42.

from the theological side of all things. In this sense political science was, at its inception, still linked to philosophy.

Departments and Programs of Study

We have seen how universities came into existence after the Civil War, and how their commitment to scientific research was accompanied by the introduction of elective courses. These controlling features of modern academic life encouraged scholars to specialize and made the establishment of disciplinary departments inevitable. Along this road, political science proceeded in step with other disciplines, even though neither an overall marching order nor a common destination were fixed in advance. Thus where the elective system was introduced, political studies seemed a natural area for expansion. Accordingly, when Cornell University set up its six original instructional divisions in 1868, one of them was called the Department of History, Social, and Political Science.[11] Soon afterward, in 1876, Johns Hopkins unveiled America's most advanced graduate programs, offering a combination of historical and political studies, which attracted Woodrow Wilson to study there and become the early discipline's most famous recipient of a political science doctorate. And in 1880, at Columbia University, John Burgess established the School of Political Science, a graduate institute whose founding has been described as the event that marked the birth of political science "as a learned discipline."[12]

The Columbia program,[13] together with graduate studies at Johns Hopkins, set an example for other universities interested in developing courses and degrees in political studies. At Columbia, undergraduate students could take their fourth year in the School of Political Science, and after a total of three years in that school, plus the completion of a doctoral dissertation, would receive their Ph.D. award. The curriculum was full of comparative history, popular in many schools until around 1900. This entailed an endeavor to understand how various political habits, rights, procedures, and institutions developed in the United States as compared to European countries or their antecedents. Attention focused mainly on the "State" as a whole and on the American states and local governments as parts of the federal system.

At Columbia and elsewhere, political science as a separate learned discipline did not emerge distinctly at the very start. Although it dwelt in what was called the School of Political Science, only gradually was a line drawn between political studies and the other subjects that were taught there, which included

11. Ibid., p. 190.

12. Albert Somit and Joseph Tanenhaus, *The Development of American Political Science: From Burgess to Behavioralism* (Boston: Allyn and Bacon, 1967), p. 21.

13. See John W. Burgess, "The Study of the Political Sciences at Columbia College," *International Review*, 12 (1882), pp. 346–57.

courses in what today would be called history, economics, sociology, anthropology, and modern languages. But what really became important in those programs, as in the universities at large, was the commitment to original scientific research, to the idea that, as Burgess said, "there was a great deal of truth still to be found."[14] Where this notion took hold, teachers would tend to delve deeply into those subjects that interested them most. As a result, bodies of specialized knowledge were generated within the faculty of loosely grouped scholars at places like Columbia, and it was inevitable that around those funds of knowledge specific bands of men—scholars and students—would gather, having more and more in common with one another and less and less to share with other people in the same school. At Columbia, then, and at other universities where political studies began in conjunction with various scholarly concerns, the field of political science little by little detached itself from related realms of knowledge. By the early 1890s, its School of Political Science had three internal administrative groupings, for "Economics and Social Science," for "History and Political Philosophy," and for "Public Law and Comparative Jurisprudence."[15] The latter gradually became a department concerned solely with political science. At Harvard in 1890, a "Faculty of Arts and Science" was created, with one of its twelve divisions devoted to "History and Political Science." In 1895 this division contained two departments, of "History and Roman Law" and "Political Economy." By 1910, these two had been transformed into "History and Government" and "Political Economy," with "Government" achieving the status of independent department in 1911.[16]

And so it went, with departments of political science, under titles as varied as "Public Law and Jurisprudence," or "Government," or "Politics," gaining recognition as independent academic units while the old moral philosophy languished and had its parts distributed to separate disciplines. Political science acquired departmental status at the University of California in 1903, at the University of Illinois in 1904, at the University of Wisconsin in 1904, at the University of Michigan in 1911, at the University of Minnesota in 1915, and at Stanford University in 1919, among others. As of 1914, 40 out of 531 colleges and universities surveyed by the American Political Science Association supported independent departments of political science, while approximately 200 offered political science courses in departments embracing also history, econom-

14. John W. Burgess, *Reminiscences of an American Scholar* (New York: Columbia University Press, 1934), p. 148.
15. Ralph Gordon Hoxie, et al., *A History of the Faculty of Political Science, Columbia University* (New York: Columbia University Press, 1955), pp. 60–61.
16. Kimball E. Elkins, "Instruction and Degrees in Political Science at Harvard," in Arthur Maas, ed., *Philosophiae Doctores in Scientia Politica* (Cambridge: Harvard University Press, 1967), p. 10.

ics, ethics, sociology, or philosophy.[17] This steady trend toward specialization continued over the years, and in 1960 the Association reported 466 independent departments, as opposed to 320 still linked to social science or humanistic disciplines.[18]

The substantive interests of political scholars came to light, and the distinctive shape of their modern discipline began to emerge, when courses given in political science became more and more sharply focused. Thus in 1872–73 Harvard's catalogue contained offerings in a category called "Political Science," but the courses in fact dealt with political economy, Roman law, and the American Constitution[19]—hardly the sort of concentrated attention to modern political affairs reflected in the course titles of a typical political science program today. By 1899–1900, this disciplinary vagueness had all but disappeared, and Harvard courses in "Government" carried titles that strongly resembled mature political science offerings, such as "Constitutional Government," "Leading Principles of Constitutional Law," "Elements of International Law," "Federal Government: History and Administration," "Constitutional Law in the United States," and "International Law as Administered by the Courts."[20] At the University of Wisconsin in the same year, the discipline's courses were similarly specific but covered even more political territory, from "Party Government" and "Elements of Political Science," to "Municipal Government in Europe and the United States," "International Law," "State and Federal Administration," "Constitutional Law," and "History of Political Thought and Philosophy of the State."[21]

This growing curricular variety, at many different schools, was sufficiently confusing to provoke the Association into studying the matter in some detail, and in 1915, an APSA committee decided that fifteen basic course areas comprised "the scope of Political Science."[22] The official list could easily be taken to describe most of the program of studies in any large university department of political science today. One may conclude, therefore, that within half a century political science grew out of moral philosophy into substantially what it is now, give or take some subjects of latter-day concern such as politics in the Third World and theories of nuclear strategy.

17. *The Teaching of Government* (New York: Macmillan, 1916), p. 1. This volume consists of the "Report to the American Political Science Association by the Committee on Instruction."

18. "Political Science as a Discipline. A Statement by the Committee on Standards of Instruction of the American Political Science Association," *American Political Science Review* (June 1962), p. 418.

19. Elkins, "Instruction and Degrees," p. 9.

20. Haddow, *Political Science*, p. 1.

21. Ibid., p. 212.

22. "Report of the Committee of Seven on Instruction in Colleges and Universities," *American Political Science Review* (May 1915), pp. 356–57.

Organizing the Discipline

As departments of political science appeared in many different schools, their members shared the conviction of university scholars in all regions of the country that finally, in the age of science, professors could make original contributions to human welfare and not merely transmit cultural artifacts from one generation to the next in a program of studies laid down by traditionally minded college administrators. This new belief, as the basis of an "academic culture," led to such heightened self-awareness among scholars that, in order to assure scientific progress, they created the system of peer-group endeavor and review, which engendered nationwide disciplines linked to a coast-to-coast job market. It was only natural that political scientists would follow suit and bind together their far-flung departments into a well-organized discipline like the others.

The first signs of extra-local organization appeared with the establishment of publishing outlets, as necessary instruments for the dissemination of scientific discoveries and for the achievement of scholarly visibility. In 1883 Johns Hopkins founded *The Johns Hopkins Studies in Historical and Political Science*, and in 1886 Columbia set up the *Political Science Quarterly*. In 1890 the University of Pennsylvania added the *Annals of the American Academy of Political and Social Science*, and in 1891 Columbia began to publish its *Studies in History, Economics, and Public Law*. While there was an early inclination to insure that each journal afforded scholarly visibility to men at the school responsible for its actual publication, it is also true that, as time passed, more than local dissertations and articles gained entry. By 1904, for example, almost half of the articles appearing in the *Political Science Quarterly* were authored by scholars from outside of Columbia, proof that, to a considerable extent, the journals were already functioning as clearinghouses for research done by members of the discipline throughout the country.[23]

At the start of the century there were from fifty to one hundred full-time teachers of political science in America,[24] and some of them began to think of establishing an organization that would cater specifically to their scholarly needs. This entity came into being in 1903, when the American Political Science Association (APSA) was founded.[25] It was a creative act constituting one of the final denials of the prediscicplinary approach to science that had characterized the American Social Science Association since 1865. In the case of political scholars, the immediate cause for separatism was a desire to detach themselves from the field of history, which already operated within a national framework main-

---

23. Somit and Tanenhaus, *The Development of American Political Science*, p. 45.

24. Ibid., p. 258.

25. On the founding of the Association, see "The Organization of the American Political Science Association," *Proceedings of the American Political Science Association*, vol. 1 (1904), pp. 5–15.

tained by the American Historical Association since 1884. The first annual meeting of the APSA was held in New Orleans in December of 1904. Two hundred and fourteen memberships were taken out in that first year, and the Association grew steadily, if not always rapidly, so that by 1913, there were about fifteen hundred members, in 1946 about four thousand, in 1960 more than seven thousand, and in 1976 over fourteen thousand.[26]

The APSA immediately started publishing the proceedings of its annual meeting,[27] and in 1906 it added the first issues of the *American Political Science Review* (APSR), a quarterly journal that served as an official house organ. Both the *APSR*, and the APSA's conventions and committee activities, contributed enormously to a sense of shared endeavor for the new discipline's members. Publication in the former or delivering a paper to, or being elected an officer in, the latter clearly indicated who was capable of doing highly regarded research and therefore entitled to such esteem among his peers as to appear certified by the "community of the competent" that presumably existed in every learned discipline. The national organization also contributed, in less visible ways, to fostering those social and personal ties, of vocation or friendship, that permit any learned discipline to function effectively in an academic world spread across hundreds of colleges and universities throughout the land. By the 1890s, a network of such ties was firmly in place, and graduate faculty members were becoming adept at finding jobs for their political science doctors within the ever-expanding university system.[28] The APSA did much to maintain that network, continually discussing and examining its members' scholarly accomplishments—or lack thereof—and negotiating job offers either at annual meetings or via contacts created there among beginners, established scholars, and interested universities.

To the extent that the new discipline was a member of the rising professions in the post–Civil War era, its formal organization predictably operated in such a way as immediately to gather in many political scientists and gradually to exclude most other people. After all, professionals are respected because the public assumes that they are "competent" and that their organizations avoid conferring membership on anyone who is "incompetent." Physicians, to take a very clear case, are charged with performing surgery and refuse membership in the American Medical Association to barbers, who once did most medical operations in America. As for a learned discipline, if it were to foresake exclusivity, its mem-

26. Membership figures appear from time to time in the *American Political Science Review* or the journal *PS*. See also the table in Heinz Eulau and James G. March, eds., *Political Science* (Englewood Cliffs, N.J.: Prentice-Hall, 1969), p. 68.

27. Publication of the *Proceedings* ended with vol. 10 in 1912.

28. See Hoxie, *History of the Faculty*, pp. 55–56, on the successful placement of Columbia graduates in this era.

bers would be hard pressed to maintain a reputation for knowing something that other people—such as journalists—do not.

The APSA's constitution declared that "Any person may become a member of this Association" upon payment of annual dues.[29] Formally, at least, the intention was to make membership available to anyone especially interested in the subject of politics. Still, the Association's own figures reveal that, whereas in 1912 only 20 percent of the members were "professors and teachers," by 1932 these educators already constituted a majority of the noninstitutional membership, that is, individual members as distinguished from subscribing libraries and research institutes.[30] And by the 1970s, more than 75 percent of the APSA members were academicians.[31] What happened was obviously a consequence of intensified specialization, to the point where the Association's meetings and the *APSR* became less interesting and intelligible to nonacademic generalists, to people interested in politics but not necessarily in scholarly studies of that subject.

In retrospect, the hallmarks of increasing specialization are obvious. For example, at the APSA's first annual meeting, 14 scholarly papers were presented consecutively, each read to the entire attending membership.[32] Under the circumstances, it is safe to assume that the audience took some interest in all of the matters then discussed. However, the Association's successive convention programs gradually became much more dense, so that in 1940 more than 190 papers were read at the annual meeting.[33] By 1970 there were 156 "panels" devoted to various political topics, with most panels allocated enough time for reading two or three papers.[34] With all of this activity compressed into a convention span of no more than four days, it was necessary for fifteen or twenty panels to meet simultaneously, although in separate quarters. Such overlap became a normal course of events, not even worth remarking, because practitioners knew very well that multiplying the number of topics went hand in hand with focusing on such narrow subject matters as to make each respective work interesting to only a small fraction of the Association's total members. Yet the effect of this same process, of fewer and fewer people hearing more and more about less and

29. See the "Constitution of the American Political Science Association," *Proceedings of the American Political Science Association*, vol. 1, pp. 16–17.

30. Somit and Tanenhaus, *The Development of American Political Science*, pp. 55, 92.

31. Thomas E. Mann, "Report on a Survey of the Membership of the American Political Science Association," *PS* (Fall 1974), p. 382.

32. See the "Programme," in *Proceedings of the American Political Science Association*, vol. 1, pp. 25–26.

33. Frederick A. Ogg, "News and Notes," *American Political Science Review (February 1941)*, pp. 116–32.

34. See "The Daily Program," *PS* (Spring 1970), pp. 139–87.

less, could be none other than exclusionary, as most nonacademicians were even less interested than their scholarly colleagues in the sort of work being displayed and discussed.

Footnoting practices in the *APSR* offer additional evidence of ever-increasing specialization within the discipline. Articles in 1906 averaged ten footnotes apiece, demonstrating that an intelligent statement of political opinion at that time could be made with only a few citations to specialized literature. By 1977, articles in the *APSR* had an average of forty-five footnotes, with many of them conveying multiple citations so that, in effect, a latter-day essay was embellished by far more than four times the sources of a typical 1906 article. The result was that nonacademicians, with neither the time nor the inclination to read so deeply in specialized literature, were implicitly branded as incompetent to engage in such scholarly work. It is not surprising, then, that as the years passed fewer and fewer nonacademicians bothered to join the APSA, and it is a mark of their insignificance to the organization that only one of the Association's presidents since 1945, Ralph Bunche, held a nonacademic post at the time of his election.[35]

Professional Characteristics

In the light of our understanding of the world of higher education generally, we know that learned disciplines fit into a larger trend, whereby in the search for a new social order toward the end of the nineteenth century, America conferred professional status on the university's constituent parts in return for scholars making scientific discoveries and placing them at the service of society. With respect to political scientists, this collective professional standing seemed justifiable for two reasons, which had to do with the how, and the why, of their disciplinary efforts—that is, how they would approach their subject more effectively than ever before, and why society stood to benefit from their endeavors. The case seemed plausible on both counts.

The first point of the discipline's professional character stressed the value of being scientific at work. Historians of the discipline agree that, by the turn of the century, many political scientists were strongly committed to doing science rather than anything else.[36] In this respect, political scientists shared in the widespread faith—a sort of "scientism"—that universities must rely on science rather than on revelation to inform their teachings on natural or social phenomena. Of course, by today's standards this early notion of science was not very

35. The small number of nonacademicians serving as officers of the APSA is noted by Allen Schick, "Political Science Isn't as Political Science Does," *PS* (Summer 1976), p. 277.

36. See Dwight Waldo, "Political Science: Tradition, Discipline, Profession, Science, Enterprise," in Fred I. Greenstein and Nelson S. Polsby, eds., *The Handbook of Political Science* (Reading, Mass.: Addison-Wesley, 1975), vol. 1, p. 28.

sophisticated. It therefore entailed very little in the way of statistics, survey research, formal modeling, game theory, and so forth, but relied mainly on strenuous efforts to collect the facts and to consider them without prejudice. Nonetheless, the commitment to making political studies more scientific than ever before was really quite strong, and it could hardly have been otherwise, in an age marked by the growth of universities dedicated to that same principle in all disciplines. Thus where political science was concerned, James Bryce, the APSA's fourth president, called upon his colleagues to "stick close to the facts." Above all, he said, researchers should avoid losing themselves in "abstractions," meaning that the time had come to abandon the traditional search for wisdom on matters such as "sovereignty," "law," or the "state," via "efforts of thought" and "the methods of metaphysics." In the era of science, or so it seemed to Bryce, more empirical research was needed, to see "what forms the state has taken and which have proved best, what powers governments have enjoyed and how those powers have worked." Bryce did not advocate a complete disregard for "philo-sophical generalizations" about politics, but he did strongly insist that political inquiry needed a new approach to its subject, and that such generalizations would be justifiable only after the thoroughgoing examination of facts which political science could provide.[37]

The second point of professional character claimed by the discipline went hand in hand with scientism, and suggested that there was some intrinsic social usefulness to whatever facts political scientists might collect in the new manner. Here, the idea was that a continual amassing of reliable political knowledge would serve to enlighten America's people with regard to the rudiments of good government and politics.[38] On the matter of promoting good citizenship—for rulers and the ruled, leaders and plain citizens—there was surely some measure of continuity between the old moral philosophy and the young political science, even if the discipline depended less on ethical exhortation and more on scientific information. Thus old-time senior courses had been designed to elevate the moral standards and behavior of their students in future public life, and the new School of Political Science at Columbia carried this intention forward by con-sciously imitating the Ecole Libre des Sciences Politiques in Paris, an early institute for training senior civil servants.[39] At Cornell, Andrew White had both lawmakers and citizens in mind when he addressed the subject of "Education in

37. See Bryce's "The Relations of Political Science to History and to Practice," *American Political Science Review* (February 1909), p. 4.

38. See the frequent references to this point, in terms of citizenship training, in Somit and Tanenhaus, *The Development of American Political Science*, passim. See also Bernard Crick, *The New Science of Politics: Its Origins and Conditions* (Berkeley: University of California Press, 1959), pp. 19–36, 73–74.

39. Hoxie, *History of the Faculty*, pp. 11–12.

Political Science" and observed that "The demand of this nation for men trained in History, Political and Social Science, and General Jurisprudence, can hardly be overstated."[40]

No sooner had the APSA opened for professional business than its attention was drawn to the dismal state of political knowledge among young Americans. From a survey of students in ten universities, William Schaper concluded that most of them knew very little about national elections, the officers of county governments, the Supreme Court, procedures for amending the Constitution, and so forth.[41] In such a state of affairs, political science had a crucial role to play in higher education, even if the introduction of political science courses there might make it necessary to eliminate some traditional subjects of study. With political ignorance widespread, it was surely less important that "the future American citizen" would be able "to translate the language of the ancient Romans and talk learnedly of Ephors, Areopagus, Praetors and Consuls than that he should know how our candidates are nominated, how our citizens are governed, how our senators are elected, how our juries are drawn and how our national and State courts are constituted."[42] And these political matters are just what, presumably, political scientists wanted to teach, on the basis of their special ability to study politics scientifically and discover the facts required for living together well.

In 1915, the discipline moved far to make its commitment to citizenship training official. In a report by the Association's "Committee on Instruction in Political Science in Colleges and Universities," entitled *The Teaching of Government*, departments of political science were charged with three tasks. The first was to train people for citizenship; the second was to prepare students for professions such as the law; and the third was to educate experts who would work for government.[43] Apart from the business of providing preprofessional studies for potential lawyers and such, the major tasks amounted to citizenship training, broadly conceived, for the people at large or for their servants in office. And since this service to society struck most political scientists as their natural and appropriate academic lot, by 1930 the central importance of teaching citizenship came out even more clearly. In that year, the "Report of the Committee on Policy" of the APSA declared that "The activities of political scientists fall into three main

40. Andrew D. White, *Education in Political Science, an Address Delivered on the Third Anniversary of the Johns Hopkins University, Feb. 22, 1879* (Baltimore: John T. Murphey and Co., 1879), p. 3.

41. William A. Schaper, "What Do Students Know About American Government, Before Taking College Courses in Political Science?" *Proceedings of the American Political Science Association*, vol. 2 (1905), pp. 207–28.

42. "Report of the Committee of 5," ibid., vol. 5 (1908), p. 234.

43. *The Teaching of Government*, p. 187.

divisions: (1) research, (2) publication, and (3) instruction, including training for citizenship and for the public service. These three activities are inextricably bound together."[44] In fact, they may all be reduced to one, which is citizenship training in the widest sense, because publication can take place only after research is done, and because the purpose of research is to produce knowledge that facilitates the right sort of instruction in civics. The immediate university course might cover state and local government, and the research at hand might concern theories of international relations, but the fundamental objective, in all cases, would be to help people conduct their public affairs more smoothly and efficiently, whether as private citizens or public servants, so that all would prosper to the extent humanly possible.

The Disciplinary Dilemma

Just as parts of the university system developed logically, rather than according to an overall plan, so too there was something eminently appropriate to both sides of political science's professional character. For one thing, it was natural for the discipline to aspire to study politics scientifically. That course permitted political scholars to join other students of society in claiming a share of the new authority that, in Thomas Haskell's terms, centered on the universities as a replacement for old-time professions and classical virtues. In addition, it seemed equally fitting that scholars devoted to political studies—as distinct from biology, or physics, or literature, or history, or whatever—should seek professional recognition for helping people maintain, and improve, the very community in which they all lived. If not the promotion of good citizenship, what conceivable service could a political discipline render, except for tendering advice to wealthy clients? But if political scientists had concentrated on the latter, their discipline would have forfeited the special regard granted to those who serve the public rather than private interests.

Unfortunately, even though the commitment to science and the devotion to good citizenship each made sense intrinsically, so to speak, there was another sense in which they did not fit together comfortably at all, a case similar to that in chemistry where two substances, safe when separate, produce an unpleasant reaction when thrown together. In this regard, the two principles underlying political science have long suffered a certain confusion of means to ends, which persists even until today. Thus if the discipline is wedded to the scientific technique (a point shared by other university disciplines), and if it seeks to use that technique in the pursuit of even a commonly accepted goal (as other disciplines

44. "Report of the Committee on Policy," *American Political Science Review* (February 1930), p. 3.

pursue unexceptional objectives), there may be something special about the end purpose of political science which turns out to be incompatible with its means (highly regarded as those may be in principle). In most fields, scientific research produced discoveries that were patently useful in the solution of physical and social problems. This is why, apart from an occasional incident such as the malfunction at the Three Mile Island nuclear reactor in 1979, society admires science and technology. In political studies, by contrast, it was never entirely clear that a science of politics would produce the sort of teachings required for good citizenship and better government. Let us begin to consider how, in America at least, this was so.

The Liberal Context

The fundamental dilemma of political science sprang from the fact that, although the discipline was born in a university environment of science, it dwelt in a national context of liberalism. This meant that, even while the new political scholars worked according to the university's standards and requirements for professional repute, the goals of their work were always linked, in complex ways, to the hopes and fears of an entire country. These in effect presented the discipline with standards of good citizenship and effective government that would somehow have to be maintained and reinforced by scholarly work. But there was the rub. The discipline was not really asked, directly or otherwise, to follow the dictates of science wherever they might lead, to dissect political reality as dispassionately as other disciplines were called upon to analyze things in their realms of respective concern. Instead, because America was so overwhelmingly devoted to the principles and practices of democratic liberalism, the end for political science was virtually laid down in advance, and any discoveries the discipline might make would either engender support for that end or—and here was the danger— detract from existing support by revealing the existence of bad citizenship and encouraging more of the same.

According to writers such as Louis Hartz, "the liberal tradition" is America's political orthodoxy, and most Americans have long been liberal in the sense of being uniformly devoted to a set of middle-class ideals and practices.[45] In other countries, those ideals are constantly challenged by nonliberal notions—ranging from socialism to fascism to Islamic "republicanism"—espoused by various social classes or political movements. Inside America, of course, there have always been differences of emphasis with regard to specific policies and with respect to degrees of enthusiasm for any particular part of the liberal canon. This explains

45. Louis Hartz, *The Liberal Tradition in America* (New York: Harcourt, Brace and World, 1955), passim, esp. pp. 3–32. In support of Hartz's thesis, see Donald J. Devine, *The Political Culture of the United States: The Influence of Member Values on Regime Maintenance* (Boston: Little, Brown, 1972), passim, esp. pp. 51–58.

why the nation has had Federalists, Republicans, Whigs, Democrats, independent voters, and more. Still, there are many political matters which receive enormously widespread public support in America, and their nonpartisan character testifies to the existence of strong and persistent attachments to a shared core of political ideals. Thus one political scientist has held that the elements of democratic ideology in America include "consent, accountability, limited or constitutional government, representation, majority rule, minority rights, the principle of political opposition, freedom of thought, speech, press and assembly, equality of opportunity, religious toleration, equality before the law, the rights of juridical defense, and individual self-determination over a broad range of personal affairs."[46] These concepts were present, or implied, when a philosopher suggested that "Liberalism is a political theory linked these days with such democratic machinery as checks and balances in government, an uncontrolled press, responsible opposition parties, and a population which does not live in fear of arbitrary arrest by the government. A liberal state is one where most actions of the government are taken with the consent of at least a majority of the population. A liberal political philosophy is a description of this kind of state, combined with the attempt to work out the general principles which can best rationalize it."[47]

More specifically, what were "the general principles" that could "best rationalize" a liberal state and how did political scientists deal with them? For there can be no doubt that most political scholars in America have, in fact, worked within the liberal tradition since as early as 1825, when the Board of Visitors insisted that several basic liberal documents—including John Locke's *Second Treatise of Government*, the Declaration of Independence, the Constitution, and Washington's "Farewell Address"—be used as texts at the University of Virginia.[48] And in 1928, William B. Munro, as twenty-second president of the APSA, observed that "the science and art of government still rest upon . . . the postulate that all able-bodied citizens are of equal weight, volume and value, endowed with inalienable rights, vested with the attribution of an indivisible sovereignty."[49] As late as 1976, Dwight Waldo reviewed the accomplishments of the discipline and noted an "American experience" which is "written deeply into American political science," and which embraces features such as "a written Constitution . . . , a bill of rights, a territorial

46. Herbert McClosky, "Consensus and Ideology in American Politics," *American Political Science Review* (June 1964), p. 363.

47. Kenneth R. Minogue, *The Liberal Mind* (New York: Vintage, 1968), p. 1.

48. On the consensus concerning political teachings before the Civil War, and on the situation at the University of Virginia then, see Crick, *The New Science of Politics*, pp. 14–15ff, and Haddow, *Political Science*, pp. 127–33.

49. "Physics and Politics: An Old Analogy Revised," *American Political Science Review* (February 1928), p. 3.

division of powers, and a functional separation of powers, . . . the development of an enduring two-party system and a luxuriant group life with political associations . . . and a deep and pervasive sense that the American experience is or will become the *human* experience."[50]

Because the liberal tradition is as large and complex as America's very political culture, sprawling over the centuries and across the better part of a continent, students of the subject will always disagree among themselves about which of liberalism's features have been the most important and representative.[51] It seems fair to say that four postulates underlay the political side of this tradition, while a fifth, about the efficacy of science, encouraged Americans to regard liberalism as "a special kind of hope" for the outcome people may expect when society functions properly, or liberally.[52]

The first liberal postulate was fundamentally moral and clearly articulated in Jefferson's phrase, from the Declaration of Independence, that "all men are endowed by their Creator with certain unalienable rights." This means that human beings, without regard to the particular circumstances of whatever polity in which they happen to live, are entitled to certain rights and the treatment from their fellow men implied by those rights—all simply because they are equal in the sight of God. The theology of this liberal postulate has never been a matter of complete consensus in America, where diverse groups have espoused different churchly faiths throughout the generations. We may best regard it, therefore, as an axiom of simple decency that, in a society where God was assumed to have granted all men certain natural rights, it was considered morally reprehensible for some men to deprive others of those rights. Slavery, of course, was the great test case and exception to this rule, plunging the nation into a civil war precisely because it violated the first liberal postulate.

The second, third, and fourth liberal postulates combined to explain how a democratic polity may be constructed and maintained. That is, granted that citizens are entitled to some unalienable rights, what happens next? At this point, a second liberal postulate came into play, which was a presumption of human rationality. Americans have long held that ordinary people, in their capacity as citizens, are capable of thinking through their situation and achieving a firm understanding of what their own interest requires them to do. When the Declaration of Independence, for example, stated that "We hold these truths to be self-evident," it was another way of saying that men have a capacity for clear

50. Waldo, "Political Science," p. 20.
51. For a survey of nineteenth and twentieth century American liberalism, see Harry K. Girvetz, *The Evolution of Liberalism* (New York: Macmillan, 1963). For a wider view, including Europe and starting with the seventeenth century, see Roberto Manageira Unger, *Knowledge and Politics* (New York: Free Press, 1975).
52. On liberalism as a special kind of hope, see Minogue, *The Liberal Mind*, p. 2.

and consistent thinking, by which they can recognize the features of political reality and act accordingly. This ability to reason did not imply, as its corollary, that citizens will always behave reasonably. Indeed, against the near certainty that they often will not, the Founding Fathers expressly provided that government be constructed with a great many built-in safeguards against tyranny. But the basic idea was plain, that a typical citizen either has the ability to reason now or can acquire it by proper education and training. Ideally, no one need make political decisions for someone else as if that person were incompetent. That every man will enjoy political rights, then, may be considered a necessary provision of the means which he needs in order to advance the interests he comes to ascertain rationally.

A third liberal postulate concerned the activity of political groups, which may be expected to form since individuals are unlikely to gain their political objectives without banding together with others of like mind to amass power for the pursuit of joint objectives. In the liberal tradition, it was an article of faith that, once church and state were separated, most political groups would behave rationally, with shared knowledge of their common interests. This did not mean that they necessarily would behave reasonably, and therefore James Madison, in the *Federalist*, observed that factions of citizens must have their interests checked and balanced by those of other factions, so that a compromise constituting the public interest can emerge in the end.[53] Still, Americans have long assumed that factional activity is legitimate, and that the constitutional rights of free speech and assembly will provide opportunities for people to work together politically rather than merely raise their voices individually. The nation therefore accepted the growth and influence of political parties—the vehicles of group interest par excellence—on the grounds that they legitimately express the will of collections of people advancing their interests as part of the rational "consent of the governed" called for by various liberal manifestos.[54]

With individuals and groups encouraged to act and given the means to do so, a fourth liberal postulate was required, this one concerning responsible government. In the final analysis, liberalism meant believing that, in a large and pluralistic society, with a bewildering array of individual and collective interests struggling for expression, people can come together and manage their public affairs democratically, with government responsive to the people's will. Here, we may consider the many democratic devices that Americans either created for themselves or borrowed from other times and places, including separation of powers, federalism, frequent elections, various civil rights, political parties, the

53. "Essay No, 10," in *The Federalist*, ed. Jacob E. Cooke (Middletown, Conn.: Wesleyan University Press, 1961), pp. 56–65.

54. See Richard Hofstadter, *The Idea of a Party System: The Rise of Legitimate Opposition in the United States, 1780–1840* (Berkeley: University of California Press, 1970), esp. pp. 212–71.

referendum, initiative, recall, and so forth. Underlying them all is a pervasive conviction that structures and procedures of government can be established in such a way as to assure that, even where the power to rule comes into being, it can be hedged in and limited so as to compel leaders and officials to serve the public rather than merely personal gain. In the words of Abraham Lincoln, it was worth fighting the Civil War so that "government of the people, by the people, and for the people, shall not perish from the earth."[55] Yet to believe the sacrifice justified, one had first to believe in liberalism's fourth postulate, that responsible government is truly possible.

These four postulates of liberalism constituted a package of precepts describing what liberal polities should look like more or less. There was, however, an additional point of liberal faith, concerning science, which came into being independently of the others and which did not belong to them alone. Perhaps a belief in the efficacy of science is now a universal reality, with people of many different cultures and political principles hoping that science will somehow improve their lives. At any rate, the proponents of liberalism have long expected that continual additions to scientific knowledge will constitute positive contributions to the general welfare. On this score, we may anticipate occasional major breakthroughs, such as those in biology, chemistry, and physics, which have generated great scientific inventions and the miracles of technology. Yet just as important are small but steady increments of scientific information in all realms of knowledge, leading to a fuller understanding for every man of the physical and social world around him. The liberal faith in science may therefore be interpreted as an extension of the second liberal postulate, the assumption of a human capacity for reasoning. The more scientific knowledge that becomes available to men, the more they will be able to comprehend their circumstances accurately and act with due regard for desirable outcomes. In this sense, in a liberal society of constantly clashing political interests, science is the midwife of social progress and enlightenment, a beneficial factor capable of improving the content of political life. While not directly related to the mechanisms of liberal politics, then, an ever-growing fund of scientific knowledge can be their welcome companion nonetheless.

Values and Facts in a Science of Politics

Liberalism's five postulates constituted a national context—a set of American expectations—within which the discipline of political science had to operate, while its members worked according to research standards laid down by the university for all disciplines in order to assure professional authority and prestige

---

55. "The Gettysburg Address," in *The Collected Works of Abraham Lincoln*, ed. Roy P. Basler (New Brunswick, N.J.: Rutgers University Press, 1953), vol. 7, p. 23.

for their accomplishments. The trouble was that, given the very distinctive nature of politics in general and of democratic politics in particular, political scientists might do their professional work so well as to treat its subject matter unsatisfactorily. In this regard, two danger areas were quickly spotted, and others would appear in the course of time.

One difficulty had to do with values, or how men ought to behave. The first liberal postulate held that society was bound to treat all people equally, that everyone should enjoy certain rights while also fulfilling concomitant obligations. It was a universal American belief in each person's intrinsic worth. Unfortunately for political scholars who sought to practice science in order to advance in the university world, it was never clear what they could say authoritatively about that belief—was it justified or not?—for such an idea belongs to the realms of spiritual and ethical knowledge.

The quandary for political science on this score may best be understood in terms of our image of a Grecian Temple of Science. For moral philosophers, the Temple's roof had incorporated an element of values, showing how knowledge of men, of society, and of nature—the Temple's individual columns—came together to provide an obligatory blueprint for the good life and good society. Yet this intangible dimension of political knowledge and affairs did not fit easily into the proper scope of professional inquiry on such a subject. Woodrow Wilson, speaking as the eighth president of the APSA, told his colleagues that nothing in human life is "properly foreign to the student of politics." By this he meant that he did not know "how some students of politics get along without literature . . . or without art, or any of the means by which men have sought to picture to themselves what their days mean or to represent to themselves the voices that are forever in their ears as they go their doubtful journey." Political scientists who stick too closely to "the facts," he said, will "miss the deepest facts of all, the spiritual experiences, the visions of the mind, the aspirations of the spirit that are the pulse of life."[56]

However, Wilson's admonitions stemmed from a perspective acquired before the discipline took modern shape, and they did little to alter his colleagues' collective course. The exhortation was elegant, but it lacked a prescription for truly professional conduct. The dilemma therefore remained: could political scientists *as scientists* discover a way to make authoritative statements concerning what men ought to want and ought to do? Apparently not, because the APSA's constitution declared that its members would not collectively "assume a partisan position upon any question of practical politics."[57] But, alternatively, could a

56. The citations above are from Wilson's "The Law and the Facts," *American Political Science Review* (February 1911), p. 2.

57. See the "Constitution of the American Political Science Association," in *Proceedings*, vol. 1, p. 16.

science devoted to maintaining liberalism be true to its mission while ruling out expressions of professional opinion with regard to what should be done in situations that trouble the citizens of a democratic polity? Moral philosophers had treated public affairs from the standpoint of what is right, and what that standard commands us to do. Was neutrality on such matters a satisfactory discharge of professional responsibilities?

The second danger area for political scientists did not relate to the moral learning that practitioners had difficulty in expounding but to the scientific knowledge which, in their enthusiasm for the new vocational style, they would surely produce. Here, the danger had to do with liberalism's second, third, and fourth postulates—the progressive assumptions of rationality—and with how well they might stand up to sustained research into the actual politics of a democratic country. Jesse Macy, eleventh president of the APSA, held that to foreswear telling a lie and to seek the truth were ancient biblical injunctions, wherefore "The modern scientific spirit is simply the Christian spirit realized in a limited field of experience." From this conjunction of science and Christianity it followed, for Macy, that scientific truth could be the basis of modern democracy, which he described as a society serving those qualities, known to science, "which are essential to human well being."[58]

Henry Jones Ford, fifteenth president of the APSA, was impelled in 1920 to point out a paradox inherent in this faith. Political radicals in the postwar era, he said, and among them many young Americans, were convinced that democracy cannot bring liberty and justice to all. At the same time, works by the most respected students of politics, including Tocqueville from 1835, Bryce from 1888, and Ostrogorski from 1902, had taught, and were still teaching, that democracy was not as fair as had been supposed, and that to some extent it dealt very badly with the poor. From all of this, Ford inferred a disturbing question: "What is the matter with political science if it may serve to undermine institutions of government? Has it no settled criteria of political value, no methods of analysis by which it can accurately discern the causes of bad government and prescribe the means of cure?"[59] What Ford highlighted, in other words, was the fact that scientific investigations, carefully carried out with intent to improve society, might instead so contradict popular expectations as to undermine faith in democracy and therefore weaken the very regime that political scientists in good conscience sought to support. Here was a possibility which, in the 1920s and 1930s, became more and more of a reality.

58. "The Scientific Spirit in Politics," *American Political Science Review* (February 1917), pp. 6–7.

59. "Present Tendencies in American Politics," *American Political Science Review* (February 1920), pp. 3–5.

The Theory and Practice of Democracy

The first generation of political scientists worked from 1880 to 1900, mainly after the fashion of comparative history, and succeeded in firmly establishing the early programs of political studies, such as these were. The second generation pressed forward from 1900 to 1920, setting up the APSA, consolidating collegial departments, and working out a sense of collective identity quite distinct from that of all other disciplines, such as history, economics, and sociology. In the third generation, from 1920 to 1940, the emphasis on science finally came of age, with aspiration turning more and more to practice, as older political scientists gave way to younger men better trained in the techniques of modern research.[60] In America at large, this was an age of disillusionment, of realization that World War I signaled a loosing of forces, both domestic and international, that would make human progress less than automatic and more an objective to be obtained only by extraordinary efforts, if at all. For those interested in politics, it seemed time for taking stock, for seeing where the nation presently stood, where things were going well and where they were not. This they felt after decades of political invention and reform that produced the referendum, the initiative, the recall, nonpartisan elections, city managers, direct election of Senators, suffrage for women, and considerable substantive legislation.

Many political scientists, such as Charles Merriam, were active in reform circles prior to 1920.[61] Their commitment to the liberal tradition thereafter persisted, but it was tempered by skepticism concerning the outcome of that tradition in practice. The mood was summed up, in retrospect, by Bernard Crick when he observed that political scholars, together with many other Progressive intellectuals, "had worked hard to return politics to the people, and the people had returned Harding."[62] Under the circumstances, there seemed good reason for academics to involve themselves less directly in politics than before the war, and to discharge their civic responsibilities instead by emphasizing scholarly research within the university. By studying political phenomena closely, they said, scientific knowledge would emerge and contribute to improving the quality of public life in America. This renewed dedication to scientific inquiry found formal expression in the APSA's sponsorship of three National Conferences on the Science of Politics, in 1923, 1924, and 1925. It also appeared in the Associa-

60. On the three early generations of political scientists, see Richard Jensen, "History and the Political Scientist," in Seymour Martin Lipset, ed., *Politics and the Social Sciences* (New York: Oxford University Press, 1969), pp. 1–13.

61. On Merriam, see Barry D. Karl, *Charles E. Merriam and the Study of Politics* (Chicago: University of Chicago Press, 1974).

62. *The New Science of Politics*, p. 134.

tion's strong support for the creation of a Social Science Research Council in 1923, with the Association entering as one of several founding disciplines.

The 1920s and 1930s came to be marked, then, by a steady flow of empirical research and descriptive studies, designed to enlighten first political scientists, and then their students and the public, as to the condition of American politics and the way in which all citizens might maintain and improve the nation's democracy. There is no need to review all of this material here, some of it entirely original in character and some of it incorporating broad ideas from earlier decades. The fact is that many of these writings were repetitive, and many of the rest focused upon contemporary issues of such limited concern as to enjoy only antiquarian value today. A brief survey of some salient points in the literature, however, will suffice to show that, as the years passed, political scientists found themselves confronting the contradictions between scientific form and professional substance; that is, the danger that practitioners might, in a scientifically acceptable way, produce a research product whose effect would be to undermine the very object which the discipline was professionally committed to support, namely, the democratic polity. In uneasy awareness of what their prewar writings had already revealed, and with growing concern for the mounting evidence displayed in their postwar research, political scientists were eventually forced to admit that liberalism's second, third, and fourth postulates—matters of common expectation concerning human and institutional behavior in politics— were strongly challenged by the facts.

The Postulate of Rational Men

Liberalism's "most fundamental assumption," as Edward S. Corwin put it in 1929, was the notion "that man is primarily a rational creature, and that his acts are governed by rational considerations." Indeed, upon this assumption rests "the doctrine that the people should rule."[63] Yet the political behavior of real people, when closely analyzed, did not seem rational enough to fit the bill.

On this point, the findings of psychology could not be overlooked. Sigmund Freud had long claimed that human personality is a complicated alloy of id, ego, and superego, with the id and the ego driven by elemental forces of instinct only weakly constrained by reason and the superego's injunctions of conscience.[64] Political scientists did not always endorse Freudian categories of analysis, but they did more and more conclude that if human beings were largely irrational, politics could not be far behind. Thus Graham Wallas observed that "representative democracy is generally accepted as the best form of government; but those

63. "The Democratic Dogma and the Future of Political Science," *American Political Science Review* (August 1929), pp. 570–71.

64. For a summary of Freud's basic position, see his *The Ego and the Id* (orig., 1923; London: L. and Virginia Woolf at the Hogarth Press and the Institute of Psycho-Analysis, 1927).

who have had most experience of its actual working are often disappointed and apprehensive."[65] For Wallas, the assumption of rationality in politics amounted to what he called the "intellectualist fallacy," which held "that all motives result from the idea of some preconceived end."[66] To the contrary, he argued, the "empirical art of politics consists largely in the creation of opinion by the deliberate exploitation of subconscious non-rational inference."[67] Using the art of advertisement to illustrate his point, Wallas held that both the commercial and the political worlds of persuasion rely on deliberate manipulation of "entities"—like "country" or "party" or "justice" or "right"—which constitute our images of the world but which are in fact complicated mixtures of fact, instincts, and emotions that do not permit orderly and accurate thinking.[68]

Walter Lippmann built upon Wallas's work when he contended that "the deepest error of our political thinking" is "to talk of politics without reference to human beings."[69] A realistic view of men in public life, according to Lippmann, must take account of the fact that they do not behave rationally. As he put it, no "genuine politician treats his constituents as reasoning animals. This is as true of the high politics of Isaiah as it is of the ward boss. . . . The successful politician—good or bad—deals with the dynamics—with the will, the hopes, the needs and the visions of men."[70] For Lippmann, close attention to the historical masters of political thought, rather than unquestioning reliance on democratic dogma, would reveal men's true and nonrational nature. Thus the "rare value of Machiavelli" was his "lack of self-deception," for he in effect described how men take what they want and justify their desires only afterwards, rather than before the event.[71] As Lippmann said, "We find reasons for what we want to do." It follows that "man when he is most creative is not a rational, but a willful animal."[72]

Irrational men, those who respond to manipulation of their instincts and emotions, willful men: what did such people in politics imply for the liberal notion of informed public opinion, which was supposed to instruct government and to hold it in check? A. Lawrence Lowell, in his major work on public opinion, began by noting that "the elder breed of political and economic philosophers erred in regarding man as a purely rational being."[73] Rather, he said,

65. *Human Nature in Politics* (London: Archibald Constable, 1908), p. ix.

66. Ibid., pp. 23–25.

67. Ibid., p. xi.

68. Ibid., pp. 59–97.

69. *A Preface to Politics* (New York: Mitchell Kennerley, 1914), p. 32.

70. Ibid., p. 217.

71. Ibid., p. 212.

72. Ibid., p. 213.

73. *Public Opinion and Popular Government* (New York: Longmans, Green, and Co., 1913), p. 16.

men act in accordance with their traditions and a Weltanschauung, which together mix up opinion, knowledge, beliefs, and so forth,[74] even though the consequent ideas in our heads may be "inconsistent with actual facts or wholly foreign to the real benefits received."[75] One result, according to Lowell, is that their nature causes citizens to be so ill-informed on most political issues that after an election it is difficult, from the returns, to know which interests they thought to advance; or, as he made the point, "it is often impossible to ascertain on which of the issues involved the people have rendered their verdict."[76] But if the people do not express a clear sense of their interests, for whatever reason, how can representative government be possible, in the traditional sense? This was precisely the question raised by Merriam and Harold Gosnell in their classic work on nonvoting, when they studied the reasons why more than 50 percent of the potential electorate in Chicago's municipal elections of 1923 either did not register to vote or, once registered, did not cast their ballot on election day. Confronted by the fact that 44 percent of the nonvoters gave "general indifference or some form of inertia" as their reason for ignoring election day,[77] Merriam and Gosnell concluded that every effort must be made to bring more voters to the polls, else the country would be ruled, in effect undemocratically, by the minority who voted regularly but only in order to advance interests narrower than those of the citizenry as a whole.[78]

In all, the literature on voters and rationality revealed two problems: the first was irrational action spurred by observable impulse, and the second was a failure to act due to patent indifference. To both of these manifestations of behavior as revealed in research, the most comforting reaction was to claim that with enough additional research the situation might improve. And thus, while conceding that psychological evidence shows human behavior to flow from an amalgam of reason and passion, Merriam argued that intelligence is rooted partly in genetic abilities and partly in environmental influences. We need not be entirely pessimistic, according to him, concerning future political behavior, for scientists may eventually improve intelligence through genetic selection or via the right sort of education, in sufficient quantities.[79]

This response to revelations of political irrationality was not entirely satisfactory because, apart from its reliance on genetic solutions that have still not

74. Ibid., p. 19.

75. Ibid., p. 18.

76. Ibid., p. 25.

77. Charles E. Merriam and Harold F. Gosnell, *Non-Voting: Causes and Methods of Control* (Chicago: University of Chicago Press, 1924), p. 158.

78. Ibid., pp. 232–49.

79. "The Significance of Psychology for the Study of Politics," *American Political Science Review* (August 1924), pp. 476–77ff.

materialized, the plea for more education, though natural to educators, too easily slid over into a prescription for offering citizens constant help in order to fulfill their democratic responsibilities—in which case, how much democracy is left? The dilemma was highlighted in Harold Lasswell's work. "The findings of personality research show that the individual is a poor judge of his own interest," said Lasswell,[80] and he proceeded to study not just voters but also political leaders as irrational individuals. From Lasswell's psychoanalytic viewpoint, it was logical to conclude that the quality of public life will improve when political activists are guided and advised by social science professionals, presumably those trained in psychology.[81] It seemed the scientific thing to say, but there was no clear link between this sort of process and that of democracy itself, a matter of free interplay between opinions expressed by men and women from all regions and walks of life. In fact, Lasswell was both explicit and scientific concerning open discussion of public affairs: he opposed it, charging that such discussion endangered society by expressing interests in such a way as to expose personal problems—irrational fixations and compulsions—and thereby complicate political confrontations unnecessarily.[82] Oddly enough, in his recommendations for overcoming irrationality in the political process, Lasswell came very close to advocating the same sort of techniques for manipulating public opinion that he, among others, had condemned when they were used by propagandists in World War I. After the war, Lasswell deplored the way in which governments on both sides had created consensus by controlling the minds of their peoples, when truth and reason were casualties of a public relations effort unrestrained by "the canons of critical veracity."[83] But concerning the cause of peace he was quick to suggest that, in a world of irrational men, stable order must rely on a "universal body of symbols and practices sustaining an elite which propagates itself by peaceful methods and wields a monopoly of coercion which it is rarely necessary to apply to the uttermost."[84] At that point, science had come a long way from democracy, no matter how admirable the intent.

The Unreason of Groups

What science said about irrational men bore directly upon the role of groups within a democratic society since, after all, such groups are but composites of individuals. In contrast to what liberals had long expected from groups in the way

80. *Psychopathology and Politics* (orig., 1930; Chicago: University of Chicago Press, 1977), p. 183.

81. The guidance would facilitate what Lasswell called "preventive politics." See ibid., pp. 173–203.

82. Ibid., 191–97.

83. *Propaganda Technique in the World War* (New York: Knopf, 1972), p. 206.

84. *World Politics and Personal Insecurity* (New York: McGraw-Hill, 1935), p. 181.

of concerted but rational action, observers were struck by the fact that group activity could be as irrational as that of individuals. For example, there was the opinion of Gustave Le Bon, a Frenchman, that collective behavior is ruled by "the law of the mental unity of crowds."[85] By this, Le Bon meant that a very special kind of entity is created when people congregate, an entity that is not simply the sum of the individual personalities forming the group but something that acquires a personality of its own, easily swayed into irrational action by passion, impulse, or the bombast of a demogogic leader. Robert Michels was another European student of collective unreason who was widely read by American social scientists, and he, arguing from the data of research into political parties, held that there is an "iron law of oligarchy" that works in all organizations.[86] As Michels explained this law, administrative necessity and unequally distributed political talents assure that when men come together to advance their interests, the assemblage will invariably fall under the control of leaders who may, and often do, act against the joint interests of the group's members in order to protect narrower interests instead, that is, their own.

Intrigued by such theoretical "laws," students of American politics turned their attention to political groups of various kinds and discovered many manifestations of group irrationality or, at the least, failure to serve clearly defined collective interests. Parties, for example, were persistently disappointing.[87] Thus Frank Kent, who described most voters as knowing little of public affairs, wrote of people and party machines who play "the great game of politics." Unfortunately for democracy, machines and their boss leaders played the game for money, rather than on behalf of the public welfare.[88] They could do this—selling offices and legislative favors—precisely because voters, instead of thinking for themselves, responded to political slogans rather than facts, thereby leaving the party in control of a small elite, as Michels had predicted. Arthur N. Holcombe was more charitable to parties, and to the role that principle, rather than hucksterism, presumably played in their behavior. Looking beyond the realm of bosses, who operated mainly at state and local levels, he examined the two

85. See his *The Crowd: A Study of the Popular Mind* (orig., 1895; New York: Macmillan, 1938), pp. 25–38.

86. On this law, see Michels *Political Parties: A Sociological Study of the Oligarchical Tendencies of Modern Democracy* (orig., 1915; New York: Dover, 1959), pp. 377–92. In "Some Reflections on the Sociological Character of Political Parties," *American Political Science Review* (November 1927), pp. 753–72, Michels summarized his overall view of oligarchical tendencies in political organizations.

87. See Charles E. Merriam, *The American Party System*, rev. ed. (New York: Macmillan, 1929), p. 456, for the standard charges against parties in this era.

88. *The Great Game of Politics: An Effort to Present the Elementary Human Facts About Politics, Politicians, and Political Machines, Candidates and Their Ways, for the Benefit of the Average Citizen* (Garden City, N.Y.: Doubleday, Page, and Co., 1924), p. 79.

national parties and concluded that they represented America's great sectional interests, where citizens banded together, more or less, because the long-term possession of those interests and the habits created by shared political activity forged an enduring collective entity.[89] However, even Holcombe was disturbed by the inability of major parties to formulate clear positions with regard to "important issues of the day."[90] This he attributed to the fact that each such party embraced so many constituent groups as to fear offending any of them by taking a clear stand on matters in dispute. The raising of new issues Holcombe therefore left to third parties, smaller and more homogeneous than the main two.[91] However, his reliance on third parties was a tacit admission that, where they do not exist or do not exercise significant influence, the normal course of two-party events can fail to produce rational policy with regard to a great many important public affairs.

Beyond parties, a particular set of groups caused special difficulty for political scientists intent on reconciling liberal theory with democratic reality, and these were the groups advancing special interests, perhaps benign but certainly not as broad as the public interest itself, whatever that might be. Thus Kent observed that party leaders were not able to formulate issues out of rational consideration and then discuss them with the voters, but instead were forced to consider an agenda of needs created by powerful special interest groups whose desires had to be placated in order to assure reelection. As Kent said, those who run for office "are subjected to a persistent and unrelenting pressure from groups and elements in their communities, which makes intelligent and independent conduct in office . . . tremendously difficult."[92] Just how powerful and effective these forces could be, both inside and outside of party circles, was revealed by Peter H. Odegard when he wrote of the most successful of them all, the Anti-Saloon League, which was organized in the 1870s and agitated for several decades until it persuaded enough national and state politicians to accept the 18th Amendment and Prohibition.[93] And just how many of these powerful groups there were, at the national level alone, was described by E. Pendleton Herring, in a study of more than one hundred lobbying organizations with offices in Washington, D.C.[94] Herring made it clear that such groups, with their offices, public relations experts, contacts with the mass media, experienced witnesses

89. *The Political Parties of Today: A Study in Republican and Democratic Politics* (New York: Harper and Brothers, 1924), p. 349.

90. Ibid., p. 352.

91. Ibid., pp. 342–44.

92. *The Great Game*, p. 263.

93. *Pressure Politics: The Story of the Anti-Saloon League* (New York: Columbia University Press, 1928).

94. *Group Representation Before Congress* (Baltimore: Johns Hopkins University Press, 1929).

before congressional committees, and well-heeled masters of Washington entertaining, were in the nation's political life to stay. Exactly where they fit into the
liberal notion of democracy, in an era when mass irrationality and voter indifference were widely recognized, was not so clear.

A final body of political analysis concerning groups centered on the concept
of "publics," which were less organized than parties and formal interest groups,
but which nevertheless played an important role in democratic theory. Walter
Lippmann, who did influential work along these lines, started from the fact that
people tend to think in terms of "stereotypes"[95]—such as the "wily Oriental," the
"Georgian redneck," and the "pedantic professor." These building blocks of
inference convey a simplified picture of our social surroundings, because men
cannot acquire and assimilate all the facts available on public matters. But
because by their very nature stereotypes are incomplete, "democracy in its original form never seriously faced the problem which arises because the pictures
inside people's heads do not automatically correspond with the world outside."[96]
What happens, in fact, is that when matters of collective import are considered
by the polity, various "publics" will arise, some already organized and long
interested, others temporary and only lately concerned. Among these publics,
opinions will be expressed and, via political pressures and electoral decisions,
leaders will eventually be induced to take one action or another. For Lippmann,
the problem was that, given their habit of thinking in stereotypes, most people
who belong to publics will not really know what the facts of an issue are. Must we
then leave the fate of a democratic society in the hands of these ignorant publics,
assuming that the right to vote and act politically cannot be withdrawn because it
is an inviolable part of American life? All Lippmann could conclude was that
publics should not seek to make government behave according to preconceived
plans but should instead vote and thereby express a judgment as to policies and
decisions proposed by various small and more knowledgeable groups—elites,
really—who have enough of a grasp on the facts to propose some course of
action but too much of a stake in the outcome that they might safely be left
unrestrained by the larger body of citizens.[97] In other words, Lippmann held that
America's common men could not chart the nation's path by themselves but
should leave the job of conceiving and initiating policy to some other force. It
was a realistic theory, firmly rooted in the latest research, but far from the
expectations of a liberal tradition.

95. Lippmann dealt with the term "stereotype" and its meaning in his *Public Opinion* (New
York: Harcourt, Brace, 1922), passim.
96. Ibid., pp. 30–31.
97. *The Phantom Public* (New York: Harcourt, Brace, 1925), pp. 54–62.

Responsive Government

The fourth liberal postulate had to do with democratic government, and with the conviction that even where political power must, of social necessity, be exercised by the nation's leaders, they could, by employing various devices, be held responsible to public opinion and the people's interests. Political science as a discipline thus strongly supported the existing institutions and practices of liberalism. With only an occasional intimation that some individual political scientist might favor an avowedly nondemocratic reform,[98] most practitioners continued to write books and journal articles praising constitutional rights, frequent elections, federalism, competitive parties, and so forth. However, as the evidence on individual and group irrationality mounted, many members of the discipline felt constrained to advocate an approach to American politics designed to compensate for some of democracy's perceived shortcomings, and here they virtually admitted the impossibility of democracy's functioning according to the liberal vision. Specifically, it became commonplace among political scholars to recommend setting aside a certain realm of public activity and, in the name of efficiency, maintaining it beyond the range of day-to-day democratic control.

Woodrow Wilson, in the classic statement of this position, wrote as early as 1887 that political thinkers had spent two thousand years addressing the problem of who should make basic decisions for society. Democrats, of course, had decided in favor of the people. The time had come, Wilson argued, to think more about how the same decisions might be executed well, for it was actually "getting to be harder to *run* a constitution than to frame one."[99] In his opinion, to run the country efficiently and to carry out decisions effectively, there must come into being a realm of "administration," charged solely with overseeing the everyday business of government and operating beyond the proper sphere of politics. As he put it, "Administrative questions are not political questions. Although politics sets the tasks of administration, it should not be suffered to manipulate its offices." To make the new concept even clearer, Wilson suggested that "Politics is . . . the special province of the statesman, administration of the technical official."[100] In Wilson's scheme of things, it is right that electorates and the elected will exercise ultimate control over America's administrative officials, but not every day and not with direct impact on every conceivable administrative function. Formal democracy aside, his intention was to expound the notion that some specially trained people are necessary for government to operate smoothly,

98. For example, see Walter J. Shepard, "Democracy in Transition," *American Political Science Review* (February 1935), pp. 18–19.

99. "The Study of Administration," *Political Science Quarterly* (June 1887), reprinted in *Political Science Quarterly* (December 1941), pp. 481–506. The quotation is from p. 484.

100. Ibid., p. 494.

although to the extent that these people and their work come to embody and reflect expertise and specialization, actual democracy is surely attenuated.

Frank Goodnow foreshadowed this eventuality in his book *Politics and Administration*, which incorporated Wilson's terminology into its very title. Goodnow argued that there are two "distinct functions of government," among which "Politics has to do with policies or expression of the state will" and "Administration has to do with the execution of those policies."[101] It followed that much administration could be detached from politics because "it [administration] embraces fields of semi-scientific, *quasi*-judicial and *quasi*-business or commercial activity," that is, work having to do with the proper running of public transportation, the efficient operation of public sewers, the impartial assignment of contracts for public works, the scientific application of public health standards, and the like.[102] Following Wilson's lead, Goodnow encouraged the public to play a democratic role by electing many officials and by expressing its will via referenda and initiatives. But he, too, defined administration as an activity requiring people of special training and competence, almost as if they would substitute for the rationality that seemed lacking in democratic practice. As Goodnow put it, government needed "a force of agents" that would be "free from the influence of politics because of the fact that their mission is the exercise of foresight and discretion, the pursuit of truth, the gathering of information, the maintenance of a strictly impartial attitude toward the individuals with whom they have dealings."[103]

The idea of a realm of administration standing next to that of politics now seems a natural outgrowth of those general trends described by Mary Furner[104] and Thomas Haskell,[105] whereby developing professions in the late nineteenth century created specialized knowledge and offered it to society in exchange for status and authority. In the specific case of political science, as we have seen, the discipline committed itself to promoting good citizenship, broadly conceived, and that mission entailed training young people for ordinary political participation and/or government service. What evolved was a program of studies serving two ends, not always entirely compatible with each other. Political science professors taught courses to instruct students in the principles of good citizenship, that is, to believe in democracy's great institutions and to fulfill their expected role in public life. However, the same professors, or their departmental colleagues, also taught courses in which students learned the principles of ad-

101. *Politics and Administration: A Study in Government* (New York: Macmillan, 1900), p. 18.

102. Ibid., p. 85.

103. Ibid.

104. See n. 81, above.

105. See n. 66, above.

ministration, or how to run government agencies expertly. As Dwight Waldo has shown, right up to World War II this two-track notion reigned almost unchallenged in the discipline.[106] It eventually collapsed not because the contradiction between democracy and expertise became intolerable, but when political scientists realized that real-life administration was as political as politics can be.

When political scientists recommended expertise and administrative skill as an antidote to some of democracy's ills, their specific suggestions reflected the discipline's persistent and deepening commitment to science itself, which we have already noted as a postwar phenomenon. The reports of the three National Conferences on the Science of Politics, held from 1923 to 1925, were full of exhortations to produce scientific knowledge that would help to improve the quality of political life in America. As Merriam wrote, "unless a higher degree of science can be brought into the operations of government, civilization is in the very gravest peril from the caprice of ignorance and passion."[107] Or, "The whole scheme of governmental activity requires a body of scientific political principles for even reasonable efficiency and success. It is the function of political science to provide this science of politics."[108] And, "The need of today is for developing the power-controlling sciences until they equal the efficiency of the power-creating disciplines [active in World War I], to the end that mankind can become the conscious arbiter of its own destiny. We must evolve a system of social control by which reason rather than passion will be the dominating power."[109]

The general idea, which political scholars shared with other social scientists of the age, was that what Lippmann called "organized intelligence,"[110] wielded by experts, would help Americans stop "muddling through" and finally "apply scientific methods to the management of society as we have been learning to apply them in the natural world."[111] In the vocabulary of political science, familiar since Plato used the same concepts under other names, the goal was to let knowledge, rather than mere opinion, rule the realm of public affairs.[112] Many advocates of the new approach seem not to have realized how seriously

106. *The Administrative State* (New York: Ronald Press, 1948) passim, esp. pp. 12–21, 159–66.

107. "Progress Report of the Committee on Political Research," *American Political Science Review* (May 1923), p. 295.

108. "Reports of the National Conference on the Science of Politics," ibid. (February 1924), p. 119.

109. "Reports of the Second National Conference on the Science of Politics," ibid. (February 1925), p. 110.

110. See Lippmann, *Public Opinion*, part 8, "Organized Intelligence," pp. 369–418.

111. James T. Shotwell, *Intelligence and Politics* (New York: Century, 1921), p. 26.

112. The preference for knowledge rather than opinion was highlighted in Benjamin F. Wright, "The Tendency Away from Political Democracy in the United States," *Southwest Social Science Quarterly* (June 1926), pp. 28–29.

their clamor for scientific expertise denied the validity of liberalism's second, third, and fourth postulates. And if their enthusiasm for knowledge over opinion implicitly raised the question of who, in the modern era, might serve as latter-day Platonic philosopher kings—or who Lasswell's "political psychiatrists" might be—they did not see fit to discuss this question at great length. But it was being asked and answered, with stunning effect, in the world at large, and with consequences that American political science could hardly ignore.

The Challenge of Authoritarianism

In 1933, William F. Willoughby, twenty-seventh APSA president, addressed his colleagues and spoke of the weaknesses of democracy, of "the tendency of the voters . . . to demand or approve the reckless occurrence of debt and extravagance in the expenditure of public funds; . . . of blocs in our legislative bodies to put special or class interests above those of the general welfare. To these may be added the difficulty encountered in making popular government a reality . . . in the sense of preventing real political powers from becoming vested in self-seeking, and often corrupt, political rings."[113] Willoughby touched upon, albeit unintentionally, the failure of liberal democracy in exactly those three areas—of individual citizenship, political groups, and responsible government—where it was not supposed to fail, according to America's most fundamental expectations. His remarks indicated, then, that by the early 1930s the discipline as a whole had reached a point where its scientific findings could not be discounted as separate curiosities but constituted, instead, a coherent body of testimony to the notion that something in democracy either needed radical repair or—always a possibility when old faiths are challenged—a new and reassuring explanation.

The Political Scene
The liberal faith certainly was challenged, and severely so, throughout the 1920s and 1930s. Authoritarian governments seemed everywhere on the march, and Americans were unprepared to confront them, either in theory or in practice. Extraordinary historical events followed one another with trip-hammer rapidity. From 1917 to 1920, the Communists took over Russia; in 1922, Mussolini seized control of Italy; in 1925, 1929, and 1934, dictatorships were established in Portugal, Yugoslavia, Austria, and Bulgaria; in 1931, the Japanese invaded Manchuria; in 1932, the Nazis captured a plurality of seats in the Reichstag; in 1933, they won a majority and suspended parliamentary rule; in 1935, the Italians conquered Ethiopia; in 1936, Hitler dispatched troops to the Rhineland; in the

113. "A Program for Research in Political Science," *American Political Science Review* (February 1933), pp. 3–4.

same year the Berlin-Rome Axis was announced, with Japan joining in shortly afterward; from 1935 to 1938, the Moscow Trials were held, where old-time Bolsheviks confessed to crimes that everyone knew they did not commit; in 1939, Franco won the Spanish Civil War and imposed fascism on Spain; also in 1939, the Molotov-Ribbentrop nonaggression pact revealed collusion between Stalin and Hitler; within weeks, Europe hurtled into World War II.

The existence of modern authoritarianism embarrassed American liberals in two ways. On the one hand, it impressed upon them the fact that democracy had failed almost entirely to take hold in Europe after World War I. This was especially disturbing where it had been established in Eastern Europe after Woodrow Wilson's calls to make the world safe for democracy and self-determination, although the plague of repression was not confined there. By the mid-1930s, authoritarian regimes held sway in Italy, Germany, Turkey, Austria, Bulgaria, Greece, Portugal, Hungary, Poland, Romania, Yugoslavia, Latvia, Lithuania, Russia, and Japan. All this led many Americans to conclude that democracy was not a viable form of government except under special circumstances, or with a development period measured in generations if not centuries. More significantly, this political reality, when considered soberly, suggested that men are not naturally created with a capacity, or even a desire, for self-rule. In consequence, Americans increasingly wondered whether, contrary to their liberal faith, the nation's institutions might be artificial rather than the model of a natural order for mankind.

On the other hand, not only authoritarian circumstances but also their attendant ideologies, such as Marxism and National Socialism, argued directly against the notion that America's democratic institutions and procedures were appropriate for modern man. The fundamental rationale for dictatorship, on both the Left and the Right, was that people are not rational, that they are swayed by their emotions, that individuals have no right to congregate in groups such as independent churches or free labor unions in order to express their private interests but must subordinate those as against the nation's destiny, that parliamentary representation with multiple parties can only lead to confusion and a perversion of the national will, and that countries must therefore be ruled undemocratically either by a single and exclusive party or by a dominant and charismatic leader. In fact, the whole point of authoritarian ideology, as Karl Loewenstein explained, was to claim that people lack sufficient reason to rule themselves temperately with laws and constitutions, wherefore they must be led, on the basis of intoxicating sentiment, by some agent—either party or dictator—who will address them with emotional propaganda and primitive symbols in order to create consent that is apparently spontaneous but actually imposed.[114]

---

114. "Militant Democracy and Fundamental Rights," *American Political Science Review* (June 1937), p. 418.

As the 1930s wore on, events in the real world made authoritarian theory more plausible than ever before. For one thing, there was the Great Depression, which turned financial securities into worthless paper and proud workers into forgotten men. Everywhere, democratic governments stood accused of sheer inability either to confront the complex conditions of modern life or to handle them intelligently. But if such governments were incompetent, was stronger leadership required? Ideologists of the authoritarian camp never tired of proclaiming that it was. In addition, however, to their constant verbal assault on democracy, there was the military-political threat of dictatorship itself. The fascists in particular—from Italy to Germany to Japan—seemed bent on military conquest, and democratic governments in Britain and France, striving to meet the challenge, appeared at best confused and at worst appeasing. The result was a feeling that, whatever its rank in the realm of virtue, a democratically organized polity might be less able than authoritarian states to cope successfully with international affairs. This foreboding, of course, merely complemented the suspicion that, in domestic affairs as well, democratic leadership led to inefficiency.

The Problem of Values

If the second, third, and fourth postulates of liberalism seemed less and less tenable owing to scientific research findings and pressing events in the political world itself, there remained a logical fall-back position for those who nonetheless wished to support free institutions and practices. Regardless of the perceived facts, liberalism still enjoyed a moral basis, summed up in the first postulate, which declared that all men are created equal in some fundamental sense, wherefore they deserve equal rights and respectful consideration from their fellows. In light of this postulate, spokesmen for democracy could say that authoritarian states per se are an affront to common decency. No matter what research might reveal about man's political competence in the short run, then, there was something inherently wrong with basing political rule on force and terror, backed up by truncheons and concentration camps.

Unfortunately, the general trend toward elevating science at the expense of other forms of social analysis made professional elaboration of the equality postulate unpersuasive, if not impossible. To begin with, in the light of scientific discoveries, it became clearer and clearer that the notion of men being intrinsically equal was chiefly persuasive when coming from a revelation that God creates them that way. Yet the Darwinian revolution had assigned the role of science to academicians and conferred authority on their work only to the extent that it did not resemble theology. As a result, people in the university's regular academic departments—including all of the social sciences—were not professionally qualified to lend support to what might have been the strongest possible arguments in favor of the liberal tradition. In the matter of God's will, their work was irrelevant.

At the same time, academicians might have expounded some secular arguments for moral equality, but these lacked persuasive force as a consequence of uncertainty within the tradition of scientific reasoning itself.[115] There was a time when, even apart from humanity's faith in a divine Presence, the nature of things seemed to demonstrate the soundness of a belief in inherent equality. But the very structure of reasoning that had once led to such a conclusion, say in the eighteenth century, no longer seemed reliable. For example, Immanual Kant had argued deductively, from certain axiomatic statements, that we are logically obliged to conclude that men must treat each other as ends in themselves, rather than as means to someone else's ends.[116] On the basis of this conclusion, which he called "the categorical imperative," equal rights and democratic government were required. But Kant's tool of logical deduction, used also by Jeremy Bentham to justify democracy,[117] was severely battered by the science of mathematics in the nineteenth century. Euclidean geometry, the classic example of powerful and effective deduction from obvious axioms to inescapable conclusions, fell by the wayside as various forms of non-Euclidean geometries came to the fore, based on impeccable logic but leading to apparently absurd conclusions. In 1915, Albert Einstein published his general theory of relativity, in which he argued that one particular set of non-Euclidean equations, seemingly in violation of common sense, was actually true for the real world.[118] In 1919, Arthur Eddington, making careful measures of starlight during an eclipse of the sun, confirmed the prediction of Einstein's theory, that light would bend under the force of gravity as it passed the sun on its journey to Earth from the stars.[119]

Einstein's work eventually contributed a great deal to scientific and technological progress, but for philosophy his theory had retrogressive implications. The trouble lay in his notion of relativity—of all things being relative to all others rather than having absolute character in time and in space. Relativity in this sense seemed to destroy forever the rationale for saying that there is a natural,

115. The next three paragraphs in the text were guided by the analysis set forth in Edward A. Purcell, Jr., *The Crisis of Democratic Theory: Scientific Naturalism and the Problem of Value* (Lexington: University Press of Kentucky, 1973), pp. 47–73.

116. *Foundations of the Metaphysics of Morals*, trans. Lewis W. Beck (Indianapolis: Bobbs-Merrill, 1959).

117. A *Fragment on Government and an Introduction to the Principles of Morals and Legislation*, ed. and introd. by Wilfrid Harrison (Oxford: Basil Blackwell, 1960).

118. *Relativity; the Special and the General Theory, a Popular Exposition*, trans. by Robert W. Lawson (London: Methuen, 1920).

119. Sir Joseph Thompson, "The Deflection of Light by Gravitation and the Einstein Theory of Relativity," *Scientific Monthly* (January 1920), pp. 79–85.

fixed order of things, within which men have a certain and equal status. It did not help, in the 1920s and 1930s, that the science of anthropology seemed bent on discovering a wide-ranging world of social relativity right here and now. John Witherspoon, in the heyday of moral philosophy, had held that "the principles of duty and obligation must be drawn from the nature of man. That is to say, if we can discover how his Maker formed him, . . . that certainly is what he ought to be."[120] But in the 1920s and 1930s, anthropologists like Bronislaw Malinowski, Margaret Mead, and Ruth Benedict[121] were doing research on tribes in faraway places and writing to say that, as opposed to man's having any fixed nature at all, it was his society that had constant needs to be served, in a variety of ways. The anthropologists advanced a new theory of society, in which certain collective *functions*, such as reproducing the species or providing food and shelter, could be carried out by a variety of *structures*, or social institutions and practices. Within the terms of this theory, study after study showed that various primitive tribes managed to live successfully from generation to generation while evincing forms of behavior never predicted by Freud, who expected to find the Oedipus complex in all men, reflecting their basic human nature. But if every society has its own culture, which de facto serves important collective needs, who can say which set of institutions and practices—such as equal civil rights and constitutional rule—should be labeled the best for mankind? In fact, moral relativism with regard to another people's practices seemed to most anthropologists the scientific stance to adopt, even though we may be sure that they did not have concentration camps in mind when they formulated their scientific research conclusions.

Scientific Naturalism and Value Relativism

Edward Purcell has described the general crisis of democratic theory in the 1920s and 1930s as flowing from scholarly dedication to "scientific naturalism," whose devotees were convinced that "No *a priori* truths existed, and metaphysics was merely a cover for human ignorance and superstition. Only concrete, scientific investigations could yield true knowledge, and that knowledge was empirical, particular, and experimentally verifiable."[122] Arnold Brecht, who studied the effect of this conviction on political science in particular, used another name for the same phenomenon, which he called "scientific value relativism."[123] In

---

120. *Lectures*, p. 8.

121. Bronislaw Malinowski, *Sex and Repression in Savage Society* (New York: Harcourt, Brace, 1927); Margaret Mead, *Coming of Age in Samoa* (New York: W. Morrow, 1928); Ruth Benedict, *Patterns of Culture* (Boston: Houghton, Mifflin, 1934).

122. Purcell, *The Crisis of Democratic Theory*, p. 3.

123. *Political Theory: The Foundations of Twentieth-Century Political Thought* (Princeton: Princeton University Press, 1959), passim, but esp. pp. 117–35.

Brecht's opinion, scholars of this persuasion set such store in scientific methods and research techniques that they saw no way of dealing with values adequately and therefore left them as the province of people devoted to nonscientific modes of social analysis. In Brecht's version of the story, we can recognize the advent of scientific value relativism, in America at least, as a feature of the triumph of universities over the college ideal, marked by the emergence of new academic disciplines as professions within the world of higher education. His powerful account especially provides, however, an addendum to the standard version, that is, a description of the sense of shock which reverberated throughout the world of political studies when the long-run effects of the new outlook finally became apparent.

For several decades before and after 1900, many Europeans and Americans aspired to uphold civilized values such as the dignity of man and freedom of conscience. Although colonial policies were harsh, it was a time when savants and common men alike believed, in the words of one chronicler, that there should be "independent judges, equality before the law, no slaves, no torture, no cruel punishment," and that "science, art, and press must go uncensored."[124] Given the era's general confidence in a single set of self-evident answers, this consensus set many moral questions aside as hardly worth pursuing. But the truth is that scientific value relativism had left a "scientific void," a realm of social speculation and concern—temporarily unproblematical—which could not be filled by science if the established consensus were to wane and people were to demand new and authoritative expositions of basic morality.[125] And then the crisis did come, when Marxists, fascists, and National Socialists began to argue, and to act, as if there should be no regard for the values embraced in the onetime consensus. For the authoritarians, civil rights could be violated with impunity, free speech was a luxury that society could not afford, competitive political parties were a threat to national survival, and all who disagreed with the party line must be crudely suppressed. Yet when liberal, democratic scholars were confronted by these notions, they found, in Brecht's terms, that "science was unable to define Western civilization by reference to fundamental principle,"[126] for the scientific method "does not enable us to state, in absolute terms, whether the purpose pursued by us or by others is good or bad, right or wrong, just or unjust, nor which of several conflicting purposes is more valuable than the other. It only enables us to answer those questions in relative terms."[127]

In a way, it was the triumph of professional creed over liberal context, where

124. Ibid., pp. 6–7.
125. Ibid., p. 7.
126. Ibid., p. 8.
127. Ibid., p. 124.

the entire corpus of scientific knowledge seemed unable to provide a course for society to follow, and where in 1939 Robert S. Lynd called into question the scientific enterprise itself in the very title of his book, *Knowledge for What?* [128] Nevertheless, many political scientists seemed unable to refrain from persisting in their commitment to the scientific approach, almost as if its shortcomings were irrelevant to their professional objectives. For example, William Munroe argued in 1928 that his colleagues' "immediate goal . . . should be to release political science from the old metaphysical and juristic concepts upon which it has traditionally been based."[129] We should, he said, "discard our allegiance to the absolute, for nothing would seem to be more truly self-evident than the proposition that all civic rights and duties, all forms and methods of government, are relative to one another, as well as to time and place and circumstance."[130] Did he really think that, for Americans, loyalty to the Constitution was relative, a matter of fleeting taste? George E. G. Catlin expounded the case for science very plainly when he suggested that "The business of the scientist is to study those methods which a man must adopt to attain this or that end *if* he happen to choose it."[131] Was he really ready to let political scientists choose to inquire into the most efficient ways to overthrow America's government, and then publish the results? George Sabine, who specialized in the history of political thought, carried this line of detachment to its natural conclusion when he held that "there is no logical reason why a social philosopher should not postulate any value he chooses, provided only that he avows what he is doing and does not pretend to prove what he is merely taking for granted."[132] Was Sabine really convinced that civilization can endure if its philosophers advocate whatsoever "values" they may fancy, as if "right" and "wrong" are entirely meaningless terms?

Triumph and Tragedy

Consider for a moment how far political science had come by the late 1930s, and what it had done in order to get there. Seeking to work scientifically, so as to acquire a share in the authority generated by the new professions, political scientists organized, did their research, published the results, and generally did what universities expected them to do. It was a triumph of successful adaptation to new circumstances in the world of higher education. This is not to say that

128. *Knowledge for What? The Place of Social Science in American Culture* (Princeton: Princeton University Press, 1939).

129. "Physics and Politics," p. 10.

130. Ibid., p. 8.

131. "Appendix: Commentary," in Stuart A. Rice, ed., *Methods in Social Science* (Chicago: University of Chicago Press, 1931), p. 93.

132. "What Is a Political Theory?" *Journal of Politics* (February 1939), p. 13.

every political scholar worked in the approved scientific fashion, but the trend was clear.

All along, as the discipline's members in effect strove to fulfill liberalism's fifth postulate, on the efficacy of science, they knew that the substance of their work was to bolster democratic goals widely endorsed by America's citizens. Yet, as the commitment to science translated itself into research practice, its results made liberalism's postulates with regard to expected political behavior seem less and less true. At that point only the first liberal tenet, on moral equality, could be considered beyond empirical disproof. Yet as to that precept, even though nothing compellingly persuasive could be said against the moral equality of men, neither could the same proposition be professionally expounded in conclusive fashion. In short, faced with a crisis in the real world, political science had little constructive to say because there was little interface between the enterprise of scientific scholarship and the realm of old-fashioned virtue. And here was the tragic condition—a matter, in literary terms, of pursuing one good end so single-mindedly as to lose out on another.

We shall explore the relationship between political science and tragedy more fully in chapter 9. For now, let us note that the conjunction of triumph and tragedy contained a historical irony. The difficulty was not, after all, due to any idiosyncracy of individual political scholars, since most of them were whole-heartedly committed to American democracy. In fact, the difficulty flowed from success, for, throughout the universities, teachers of all sorts were together con-summating their collective victory over the college system of administrative control for curriculum and teaching, whereupon political scholars, along with the rest, finally gained the right to profess what they thought should be professed. Almost immediately, however, political scientists discovered that they did not know where they should stand collectively with regard to some of the most important questions being addressed to their field.

Of course there were many political scientists who responded energetically to the multiple crises of American democracy in the 1930s, to the economic failures at home and the strategic confusions abroad. But what cannot be denied is that, for all their enthusiasm and genuine commitment to liberal values and devices, they were not professionally persuasive in support of democracy in its hour of need. For example, Charles Beard called upon American educators to instruct young people in the ideals and practice of democracy. He admitted, however, that "Our democracy rests upon the assumption that all human beings have a moral worth in themselves and cannot be used for ends alien to human-ity. This is an assumption and cannot be proved."[133] Carl Friedrich conceded

133. "Democracy and Education in the United States," *Social Research* (September 1937), p. 394.

that academic freedom, when "vindicated in terms of neutral truth" in an age of ideological confrontation, can only be farcical. But he could offer, in place of such truth, only "faith in the development of the free personality as the ultimate ideal of humanity."[134] For Charles Merriam, there were four principal "assumptions" of democracy, including "the essential dignity of man" and the "perfectability of mankind."[135] It is clear from his exposition of the subject that he supported every sort of common decency and deplored its absence. But he never explained whether his "assumptions" referred to fact or to aspiration, and what compelling reasons there might be to adopt those assumptions if they were, after all, only aspirations. John Lewis was equally ingenious at sidestepping the inconvenient findings of scientific research. In his argument supporting democracy, he advocated equality of suffrage, of opportunity, of citizens before the law, and so forth, on the ground that people's right to the means of controlling their own destiny flows from "the postulate of the ethical value of individual personality. . . . This postulate is perhaps simply an article of faith, but it is the one article of faith thoroughly basic to democratic theory."[136]

In their enthusiasm for the home team, political scientists who supported a free society during the 1930s may have been effective cheerleaders. As professionals, however, in an age so thoroughly committed to science, they advocated the right objectives in terms that carried very little weight. Some members of the discipline recognized the problem and feared that insufficient attention to values would somehow undermine both American patriotism and commitment to democracy. They therefore urged their colleagues to remember that political science must always retain a "normative" character, that it must teach values as well as the facts of political life.[137] Arguments of this sort had some emotional appeal, but the Cassandras were not noticeably effective in changing the discipline's professional course. Their more forward-looking associates preferred to await a new theory of democracy that could assimilate the results of scientific political research while continuing to find strength in science itself rather than in traditional morals. Fortunately, that theory was not far off.

134. "Education and Propaganda," *The Atlantic Monthly* (June 1937), pp. 693, 701.

135. "The Assumptions of Democracy," *Political Science Quarterly* (September 1938), p. 329.

136. "The Elements of Democracy," *American Political Science Review* (June 1940), p. 468.

137. One persistent critic of the trend toward a scientific political science was William Y. Elliot. See his *The Pragmatic Revolt in Politics* (New York: Macmillan, 1928), and "The Pragmatic Revolt in Politics: Twenty Years in Retrospect," *Review of Politics* (January 1940), pp. 1–11.

The Mid-Century
Liberal Matrix

4

The New View of Science and Politics

It was a difficult situation that confronted political science just before World War II. Some facts of public life contradicted democracy in theory and practice, and many political scientists recognized the danger. The same scholars also agreed, however, that while such facts provoked disillusion and disarray in the democratic camp, no one there could persuasively argue them out of existence. The academic mind just would not take seriously world views which, as a matter of principle, ignored solid research findings. This hostility to premodern inference was summed up neatly by the philosopher T. V. Smith in 1926, when he proclaimed that "Increased knowledge will prove more fruitful than any resort to holy names."[1]

The Mid-Century Liberal Matrix

Under the circumstances, it was logical for political scientists in their collective role to create or adopt a new theory of democracy—one that would praise existing liberal practices and institutions and, at the same time, find new reasons for accepting their sometimes disappointing outcome in the real world. Most importantly, the requisite new view could not afford to renounce the practice of science in social research, since no other form of inquiry in the twentieth century seemed capable of analyzing society's ills in terms that could reach beyond special pleading. Likewise, however, insofar as science would surely continue to produce potentially disheartening research findings, the new theory would have to explain why, no matter how uninspiring the political scene might appear momentarily, it actually constituted a situation of some value, wherein

1. *The Democratic Way of Life* (Chicago: University of Chicago Press, 1926), p. 35.

any necessary reform could be undertaken without recourse to authoritarian devices that would destroy democracy itself.

As it happened, just before the war there was one comprehensive view of American society which appeared suitable—for remaining loyal to science and, simultaneously, for assimilating the results of its exercise. Some political scientists did adopt parts of this view, which we shall call Deweyism, after its leading exponent, John Dewey. Then, after the war, a second theory appeared, similar to Deweyism in many respects, but even more serviceable to social scientists. A substantial majority of all political scientists eventually endorsed this second view, which may be called Popperism, after its foremost advocate, Karl Popper. While neither Dewey nor Popper was a political scientist, what they had to say reflected a new and tough-minded version of liberalism, one that worked its way deep into the discipline of political studies.

It is unfortunate that American social scientists are not more like their European counterparts, who have a fondness for comprehensive theories in the grand style of Karl Marx and Max Weber. Had such an attitude prevailed in the New World in the late 1930s and early 1940s, someone might have produced a seminal work embracing every element of the new outlook and capable of attracting disciples who would henceforth cite it repeatedly as a fount of integrating wisdom. But American intellectual history rarely works that way, in the tradition of "great books" and commentary upon them.[2] As a result, although the writings of Dewey and Popper are instructive concerning the way in which various parts of a new liberal position made sense together, they were in no way exemplars of a phenomenon that can be defined and described with precision. What they represent, therefore, may best be characterized as a new "matrix" of liberal discourse concerning science, knowledge, politics, democracy, and related subjects.

That is to say, around the time of World War II, there came into being a universe of discussion and debate, based on arguments and ideas, concepts and terms, which constituted the catch-all frame of reference within which most American scholars, including political scientists, investigated and spelled out the meaning of American society after the war. A matrix of discourse in this sense did not reflect unanimity but only the sentiments of people likely to make similar, though not necessarily identical, assumptions and understand contemporary events in similar, yet not always identical, ways. As a frame of reference, this matrix did not impose answers to every conceivable political question; nor, in fact, did it propose solutions to all immediate issues on the nation's agenda. On the first count, its component elements were not sufficiently authoritative to

---

2. For example, in Edward S. Corwin, "The Democratic Dogma and the Future of Political Science," *American Political Science Review* (August 1929), pp. 569–692, a distinguished political scientist wrote about the most fundamental assumptions of democratic doctrine without citing any sources as the origin of those assumptions.

impose an inflexible orthodoxy, and therefore some scholars working within its bounds endorsed one set of specific ideas even while others rested upon a different set instead. On the second score, precisely because the matrix could not enforce conformity, men who embraced only part of its elements found that, even while concurring on fundamental notions, they could disagree with other men as to how particular social problems should be approached and resolved.

What the matrix offered, then, was a configuration of considerations to be used in social analysis, sometimes explicitly and sometimes implicitly, and always selectively rather than with indiscriminate enthusiasm. In this sense, regardless of the different ways in which various scholars drew upon it, the matrix served as an intellectual mold within which certain ideas were patently valid and commendable, while others seemed misleading and therefore dangerous, where some social institutions were judged useful and worth supporting, while others appeared harmful and deserved condemnation. Once accepted, this was the universe of discourse that would enable political scientists to overcome the contradictions of their discipline and reconcile, for a scholarly generation, the twin professional impulses toward science and liberalism. It was also this matrix that came under attack in the 1960s and consequently lost its ability to make the findings of political research easily compatible with faith in democracy.

Deweyism

Some of the matrix's basic notions were foreshadowed in the teaching of John Dewey, who served as professor of philosophy at the University of Chicago from 1894 to 1904, and then at Columbia University from 1904 to 1929, after which he remained active as professor emeritus and founding member of the New School for Social Research. Charles Frankel, with perhaps some exaggeration, claimed that Dewey was "generally regarded as the most influential philosopher in American history."[3] Surely he was the dean of his colleagues during the 1920s and 1930s. His ideas were well known in the academic world, on the basis of publishing a new book every few years, plus numerous articles in popular and scholarly journals.

As a young man in the late nineteenth century, Dewey struggled to throw off the immutable verities of theology and Kantian ethics, preferring instead an evolutionary notion of truth such as that found in Hegelian dialectics. As time went on, however, he also found Hegelianism unsatisfactory and transferred his allegiance to the sort of ideas advocated by American philosophers like Charles Sanders Peirce and William James, who favored a continual and open-ended

---

3. "Dewey, John," in David L. Sills, ed., *The International Encyclopedia of the Social Sciences*, vol. 4 (New York: Crowell, Collier and Macmillan, 1968), p. 155.

program of inquiry and constant revision of social beliefs. Against the background of this intellectual odyssey, Dewey's thought is usually described by commentators as some form of "pragmatism," or "instrumentalism," or even "radical empiricism."[4] Such terms invite dispute, for they evoke unsettled technical considerations still capable of generating discord among philosophers. Rather than use them, therefore, we may employ "Deweyism" as a more neutral label for the major ideas that Dewey espoused and advanced. By keeping those ideas in mind, and especially their overall shape and thrust when taken together, one may grasp the contours of the emerging liberal matrix.

The Nature of Science

Dewey wrote a great deal on many subjects. Analytically speaking, however, he started from the premise that scientists in classical times had understood the world to be fixed and bounded.[5] It followed that the goal of philosophy was to discover nature's character once and for all, after which men would live accordingly. In this world view, men first assumed that eternal truths exist and then proceded to find them. Dewey himself stressed the importance of such apparent truths in the great pagan and Christian notions of man's essential character and the role he should play in God's universe. To all such theories of a static universe, natural or moral, Dewey assigned the name of "absolutism."[6] In his own career, he began by opposing absolutist philosophies as they presented themselves in theology. In this regard, he was typical of many professors in the same era, when late nineteenth-century universities were moving away from the college ideal based on religious certainty.

In Dewey's terms, the old-time philosophers had used their capacity for reason to seek out the Ideal, which was then called the Real, as in Plato's dialogues, and which became the standard by which mankind's behavior should be measured.[7] As an alternative, Dewey recommended what he called "experimentalism," which was an entirely different form of science, based less on contemplation and more on a process of seeking experience via experiments.[8] In

4. See the essays on Dewey in Paul A. Schilpp, ed., *The Philosophy of John Dewey*, 2nd ed. (New York: Tudor, 1951). See also Morton G. White, *The Origin of Dewey's Instrumentalism* (New York: Columbia University Press, 1943), and Horace Thayer, *The Logic of Pragmatism: An Examination of John Dewey's Philosophy* (New York: Humanities, 1951).

5. John Dewey, *Reconstruction in Philosophy* (orig., 1920; Boston: Beacon, 1948), pp. 53–76.

6. Ibid., p. 97.

7. Ibid., chapter 5, "Changing Conceptions of the Ideal and the Real," pp. 103–31.

8. David W. Marcell, *Progress and Pragmatism: James, Dewey, Beard, and the American Idea of Progress* (Westport, Conn.: Greenwood, 1974), chapter 5, "John Dewey: The Experimentalist Criterion," pp. 196–257, esp, pp. 232–46. For a good short description of the experimentalist, as opposed to the absolutist pursuit of knowledge, see John Dewey, *The Public and Its Problems: An Essay in Political Inquiry* (New York: Henry Holt and Co., 1927), pp. 202–03.

this program of inquiry, reason is not abandoned but supplemented by data which we can gather by using our senses in a special and systematic way. As Dewey put it, if a man wants to know something today, "the last thing he does is merely to contemplate. He does not look in however earnest and prolonged a way upon the object expecting that thereby he will detect its fixed and character- istic form. . . . He proceeds to *do* something," and this act of doing is the experimental process.[9]

By experiments, Dewey meant activity whereby a scientist pushes, pulls, prods, weighs, measures, and otherwise works on his or her environment. Sci- ence of this kind implies a thorough denial of the fundamental premise of old-time philosophies, for the very work of science causes the modern scientist to change the world, to alter its components and their relation to one another, or, as Dewey put it, to engage in a "process of transforming the existent situation."[10] Of course, a world that is capable of being altered cannot justify absolutist assumptions concerning its eternal and invariable nature, and for Dewey the consequences of the new science were clear. Instead of serving to reveal an order to which men must conform, science in the modern era works continually to shape that order in ways most congenial to human needs, whatever those may be at the moment.

In consequence of defining science as an approach to knowledge different from the traditional mode, Dewey was able to insist that its distinguishing feature lies not in any particular truths it discovers but rather in the manner of doing research itself. That is, absolutist science might point to a set of ideas— such as Newton's laws of motion—and hold that they represent *the* findings of science, whereupon people must agree to act as if they will always hold true. For Dewey, such a claim was literally nonsensical. According to his under- standing of the matter, insofar as true science combines reason and experience, its experiential component must constantly change, as scientists succeed in performing additional experiments and adding to their stock of knowledge. But if that is the case, our definition of science cannot validly refer to its accom- plishments but must focus on its special mode of inquiry. As Dewey made the point, "when methods are employed which deal competently with problems that present themselves, the physician, engineer, artist, craftsman, lay claim to scientific knowing."[11]

As a distinctive method, science mixes pure cogitation with "directed observations"[12] and produces a unique sort of knowledge. The result is what

9. *Reconstruction*, pp. 112–13.

10. Ibid., p. 177.

11. John Dewey, *The Quest for Certainty: A Study of the Relation of Knowledge and Action* (New York: Minton, Balch, 1929), p. 199.

12. Ibid., p. 200.

Dewey called "organized intelligence."[13] That is to say, when men work together at what we call science, the methods they employ individually are reinforced by their interaction collectively, and the ever-increasing joint capacity to understand the world adds up to organized intelligence. It is, without doubt, an intelligence that can be counted upon to exceed in power or balance that of the ordinary individual. It is also by its nature a constantly progressive force, in the sense that, as the scientific enterprise unfolds over time, it will present each human generation with a more advanced starting point of knowledge than that enjoyed by the previous generation.

The Shape of Democracy

In human affairs, the analogue of science was democracy, which Dewey recommended as the scientific method writ large. This view of democracy held true both for the state's institutions and for the character of its citizens. On the one hand, Dewey suggested that the meaning of democracy lies in its essence as "a mode of government, a specified practice in selecting officials and regulating their conduct as officials."[14] In these terms, democratic institutions resemble the scientific method, where science is a way in which inquiry is conducted rather than the particular result of any inquiry. On the other hand, if democracy is an open-ended system for considering political matters, it follows that citizens of that state should comport themselves as scientists do at work, so that their democracy will operate as effectively as the scientific community. Dewey made precisely this point when he argued that scientists have developed a certain "morale," which entails skepticism, doubts, a willingness to consider new ideas, going to where the evidence points rather than where preconceptions lead, and so forth.[15] Given the effectiveness of those attributes when scientists seek to fathom the natural world, Dewey was convinced that a free society should cultivate the same sort of morale among its citizens, in order most probably to arrive at reliable political knowlege and act upon it. In his words, "The crisis in democracy demands the substitution of the intelligence that is exemplified in scientific procedure for the kind of intelligence that is now accepted" in public affairs.[16]

Just as in scientific communities diverse and conflicting hypotheses are analyzed and judged valid or not, Dewey argued that a democratic state is necessary for accommodating the ideas of different groups and social classes. In this sense, making political rights available to all can bring various interests to

13. John Dewey, *Liberalism and Social Action* (orig., 1935; Capricorn, 1963), p. 51, and passim.

14. *The Public*, p. 82.

15. John Dewey, *Freedom and Culture* (New York: Putnam's Sons, 1939), p. 145.

16. *Liberalism*, pp. 72–73.

light so that matters can be resolved in favor of "more inclusive interests than are represented by [any of them] . . . separately."[17] The crucial predicate underlying this reasoning was its rejection of the absolutist notion that some interests invariably deserve promotion, even at the expense of others. In Dewey's terms we have no scientific way of deciding in advance that some interests are superior to others, and therefore what we must confront is a modern situation of constant change and social evolution, where "new forces"—social and economic, rural and urban, racial and religious, rich and poor—appear on the political stage and require adjustment and compromise. Since the powerful and continuing dynamism of modern society, driven by a permanent revolution in science and technology, will inevitably bring such new forces into being, Dewey pointed out that "It is not that liberalism creates the need, but that the necessity for adjustment defines the office of liberalism."[18]

Here in the overall constellation of his ideas Dewey introduced a strong plea for maintaining America's democratic institutions and practices, from constitutionalism to frequent elections. These devices correspond to a scientific community's means for productively exchanging ideas. As Dewey said, "The strongest point to be made in behalf of even such rudimentary political forms as democracy has already attained, popular voting, majority rule and so on, is that to some extent they involve a consultation and discussion which uncover social needs and troubles."[19] Or, in another formulation of the same idea, it is only "by extending the application of democratic methods, methods of consultation, persuasion, negotiation, communication,[and] co-operative intelligence" that we can guarantee the sort of social results which an understanding of natural science leads us to expect.[20]

Operative Conclusions

At least two operative conclusions, for policy and for ideology, could be inferred from what Dewey had to say about science and democracy. For one thing, his arguments led straight to condemning authoritarian rule. Marxism, fascism, and National Socialism all adhered rigidly to the premise of a single and fixed truth, to be discovered either by a party or a leader and then accepted without question by the mass of citizens. In Dewey's terms, these were absolutist world views,[21] congruent with the classical idea that where truths are unitary, there must come into being a ruling elite—of priests or philosopher kings—to interpret and apply the eternal verities. The trouble with such regimes, in the present as well as in

17. Ibid., p. 79.
18. Ibid., p. 49.
19. *The Public*, p. 208.
20. *Freedom*, p. 175.
21. Ibid., pp. 93–94.

the past, is that by laying down unalterable guidelines for social action, they freeze the condition of human intelligence at whatever level it may have attained by the time absolutist rule begins. For Dewey, then, regimes of this sort must be denounced if only because they fail to permit science to function as organized intelligence, which alone is capable of providing men with increasingly accurate and useful information about the natural and social world in which they live.

A second conclusion for Dewey, the correlative to condemning authoritarian government because it holds knowledge and men back, was to praise liberal government for doing precisely the opposite, for permitting and encouraging men to make discoveries and improve their lot. Here Dewey's understanding of science and society provided solid grounds for championing the commitment to individual rights and equality—"individualism"—which scientific research results had apparently challenged. Like Lippmann, Dewey conceded that the "omnicompetent" individual of traditional liberal thought was nowhere to be found.[22] But the failure to discover such individuals did not discourage him, for he argued that faith in their existence—a tenet of "the old liberalism"—merely reflected an early view of democracy, progressive for its day, which could be discarded in the light of more recent scientific knowledge.[23] In effect, Dewey said that the accumulating stock of scientific knowledge will foster a citizenry far more competent than those of today. That is, as the scientific enterprise builds on the achievements of the past, the separate capacities of individual men will be enhanced by the information brought to light via the organized intelligence of science.[24] In the reign of this "new individualism," as Dewey called it, science and a democratic society can work hand in hand to assure that each future generation of citizens will be more mature and rational than its predecessor. Accordingly, rather than look to nondemocratic reforms to compensate for the obvious irrationality of some citizens today, the more promising option is to strengthen and expand the realm of democratic procedure instead, so that society can weigh and disseminate most effectively whatever new knowledge science may produce. As Dewey summed up this very positive approach to the discouraging situation that political research had revealed concerning the nature of people in public life, "the cure for the ailments of democracy is more democracy."[25]

Underlying both conclusions—opposition to authoritarianism and enthusiasm for democracy—was an important shift in the fundamentals of political argument from matters of principle to effective results. Here was the technically pragmatic element in Dewey's work. It came in recognition of a persistent reality

22. *The Public*, p. 158.
23. Ibid., p. 145.
24. John Dewey, *Individualism Old and New* (New York: Minton, Balch, 1930), chapter 8, "Individuality in Our Day," pp. 146–71.
25. *The Public*, p. 146.

in human affairs, that absolutist theorists are sometimes capable of offering extraordinarily persuasive arguments in favor of their antidemocratic views. As Dostoevsky demonstrated in his tale of the Grand Inquisitor, men do not live by bread alone but also by faith in powerful symbols of good and evil, salvation and damnation.[26] In order to combat the sheer style of arguments which deal with such matters, and which may convince but err at the same time, Dewey urged that absolutist principles be tested by their consequences rather than by their logical, rhetorical, aesthetic, or emotional elegance. And he made this point very directly, "It is both astonishing and depressing that so much of the energy of mankind has gone into fighting for . . . the truth of creeds, religious, moral and political, as distinct from what has gone into efforts to try creeds by putting them to the test of acting upon them."[27] In short, Dewey wanted to know not what authoritarians may promise but what they are likely to deliver. It was a point whose importance would grow as Americans became acquainted with the excesses of dictatorial regimes, first from afar, and then at first hand when Allied ground forces entered Europe during World War II.

The New Look in Political Science

Absolutism, experimentalism, science as method, organized intelligence, democracy as method, scientific morale, the new individualism, the test of effective results: what Deweyism offered to social scientists was a comprehensive set of interlocking ideas that could be used to appraise the nation's political situation and still maintain liberal confidence. Not every scholar who accepted the general thrust of these ideas endorsed each of them, or, with regard to any particular one, employed Dewey's vocabulary faithfully. But in the prewar era, some students of democracy did begin to speak as if various concepts, similar or identical to those espoused by Dewey, could be applied fruitfully to the nation's ills. In our terms, they were putting together the early parts of a new matrix of liberal discourse. No single work by Dewey, or by anyone else, itemized all the points in that matrix and explained how they related to each other. What transpired instead was a collective groping toward common ideas, during which, in typical American fashion, scholars acknowledged no central theory as their source of ultimate coherence but proceeded to cultivate shared opinion in a proximate and practical way instead.

Some advantages the new matrix unquestionably did enjoy. Most political scientists before World War II clung to the old terms of discourse when discuss-

26. Fyodor Dostoevsky, *"Notes From the Underground" and "The Grand Inquisitor"* (New York: Dutton, 1960), pp. 119–41.
27. *The Quest for Certainty*, p. 277.

ing the condition of American society. They had difficulty, therefore, producing persuasive democratic commentary within the traditional frame of reference, the five basic liberal postulates. For the few practitioners who went over to Dewey's sort of ideas, however, it was as if social analysis had turned a corner and permitted them to approach their subject from an entirely new, and unexpectedly fruitful, angle. To such scholars, Deweyism proposed a way of dealing with democracy that would skirt the pitfalls awaiting those who argued for or against democratic morals as the key to a strong and confident liberalism. Before the war, men who recoiled from the findings of science and urged exposition of democratic morals were open to the charge that ethical principles cannot be confirmed scientifically. How could righteous teachers be sure of competing successfully against ideologues who place antidemocratic versions of morality before the American people? Alternatively, those who were not wedded to morals, but to science instead, found themselves vulnerable when sincere patriotism and good citizenship were debated. On such occasions, the moralists charged that democratic citizens who lack passionate commitment to decent standards of behavior will easily fall into despair when authoritarians begin to harp upon the momentary difficulties of democracy in action.

As a third approach to the entire subject, Deweyism suggested considering the world of politics, rather than principles, and concentrating on very practical considerations concerning the capacity of liberal or authoritarian regimes, rather than theorists, to deal with that world. In the process, it might be possible to portray democracy as an imperfect but necessary mechanism, in words so plain that recourse to the tricky ground of ethical analysis and explication could be avoided entirely. Charles Beard summed up the situation in 1937, in terms that fit well within the new matrix of discourse. "A monarchy or a despotism," he said, "is like a beautifully rigged ship [in terms of absolutist theory and ideology] . . . when she hits a rock in a storm she turns over and they [the leader and his followers] all go to the bottom with her. Democracy is like an old scow; your feet are always wet, there is always disorder aboard, but you can't sink her."[28]

And so it was that the test of effective results began to appear in political science works, concentrating attention not on traditional liberal expectations— concerning the second, the third, and the fourth liberal postulates on individuals, groups, and responsible government—but on the function of liberal institutions and practices, such as they really were, in the modern world. As early as 1930, Francis G. Wilson argued that "A pragmatic interpretation and the scientific method must be used in investigating modern democracy."[29] His own contribu-

28. "Democracy and Education in the United States," *Social Research* (September 1937), p. 392.
29. "The Pragmatic Electorate," *American Political Science Review* (February 1930), p. 32.

tion was to analyze the significance of nonvoting, which seemed so dangerous from the traditional point of view. In Wilson's opinion, "ultimate participation is more important than constant participation," and by this he meant that "the vote is in reality a check on those who govern," which need not be exercised at every opportunity but only when citizens feel that their interests are not served by government policy.[30] Scholars such as Merriam and Gosnell had contended that everyone must vote, in order that the best people will contribute to electoral mandates and restrain party machines. In contrast, Wilson pointed out that there really was no evidence that "the more capable" were, in fact, the nonvoters. It followed that there was no good reason for assuming that higher rates of voting would qualitatively improve any mandate.[31] Besides, as he saw it the real objective of voting is to balance interests rather than voters, wherefore electoral abstention may satisfactorily be explained by the fact that many men whose interests are prospering will not bother to cast a ballot.[32] In short, Wilson made the argument that a major source of liberal discontent, the low rate of voter turnout, does not necessarily violate the primary function of a democratic polity, which is to represent society's great interests. It was an argument which closely paralleled Dewey's on the need to "adjust" political forces. If Wilson was correct, there was no need to consider nondemocratic remedies for the country's ills, for they would detract from civilized behavior without contributing toward the goal of representing the interests of all.

By 1937, Walter Lippmann was advocating an even more explicitly Deweyian view of the political system. The straight, unvarnished truth about political expression is that many citizens do it poorly, that they are largely uninformed about important issues and usually unable to articulate their views impressively. The result is a democratic regime that sometimes appears foolish for letting such people speak freely, in ways that influence the shaping of public policy. No matter, concluded Lippmann, what really counts is the opportunity to speak, and not what people say. In his terms, "civilized men must cherish liberty—as a means of promoting the discovery of truth," where "out of all the speaking and listening, the give and take of opinions, the truth should be arrived at."[33] Of course, the democratic system "may not produce the truth, or the whole truth, all the time, or often, or in some cases ever. But if the truth can be found, there is no other system which will normally and habitually find so much truth."[34] In effect, Lippmann did exactly what Dewey recommended. He posited an overall goal for democracy and then showed how, regardless of day-to-day events that

30. Ibid., p. 18.
31. Ibid., pp. 26–27.
32. Ibid., pp. 32–33.
33. "The Indispensable Opposition," *Atlantic Monthly* (August 1939), pp. 187–88.
34. Ibid., p. 187.

may seem unsatisfactory in the short run, there is an overriding utility to maintaining the very liberal institutions which Americans already enjoyed. Errors there will always be. In Lippmann's view, however, this did not mean that democratic rights, as a system, encourage mistakes, but only that occasional detours are inevitable on the road to truth.

The political scientist who employed the new liberal matrix most consistently before World War II was E. Pendleton Herring, later to serve as forty-eighth president of the APSA. In *The Politics of Democracy* (1940), Herring began by saying that he would attempt "to evaluate the political process as a method for reconciling change with stability."[35] That is, he reiterated Dewey's dictum that democracy must be defined as a method rather than any substantive, and perhaps momentarily disappointing, result. In Herring's opinion, the key to that method, which must accommodate change without sacrificing political stability, is a system of competitive parties. Here he was quite explicit. Where some commentators had criticized American parties for insufficient devotion to principle and for lack of clear-cut policy positions, Herring instead viewed the major parties as welcome forums within which many voices could be raised and interest groups heard, as arenas for working out the compromises required in a time of transition that Dewey had noted and that Herring was determined to control.[36] As he put it, "The accomplishment of party government lies in its demonstrated ability for reducing warring interests and conflicting classes to co-operative terms."[37] In this process, "A distinctive party stand inevitably incurs the danger of internal and factional dispute," whose bitterness and strife would make compromise in the long run more difficult to attain.[38]

In sum, Herring did exactly what the emerging liberal matrix and political science's professional situation called for. He accepted the facts as revealed by research and then placed upon them a democratic interpretation more optimistic than that permitted by traditional liberal expectations. For example, in his scheme of things, American parties were praiseworthy for their disarray and confusion, the very qualities which had so disappointed earlier observers. He therefore suggested that the rise to power of a principled third party, which Holcombe had viewed somewhat sympathetically, would be a sign of "serious rigidities in our political system. It would . . . indicate . . . that our party leaders had failed in their task of harmonizing and adjusting the economic and social forces of their communities."[39] As for stability, Herring hailed the party

35. *The Politics of Democracy: American Parties in Action* (orig., 1940; New York: Norton, 1965), p. viii.

36. Ibid., chapter 7, "Standards for Judging the American Party System," pp. 100–16.

37. Ibid., p. 132.

38. Ibid., p. 232.

39. Ibid., p. 179.

system in its contemporary form for helping "to preserve existing social institutions by blurring sharp issues and ignoring others."[40] Once again, the failure to live up to exacting standards became a matter for celebration rather than cause for despair. In Herring's view, not only should citizens and leaders both be excused from devotion to principles, but the same political actors deserve praise for their abstinence. As he said of citizens, "The concept which seems most suited to a society of conflicting aims is tolerance. . . . Tolerance of belief or disbelief is basic not only to science but also to the full use of intelligence in the direction of human affairs."[41] Here was the Deweyian conjunction of scientific "morale" and good citizenship. So much for public adherence to fixed ethics. With respect to leaders, in Herring's view the function of democratic politicians "is to stand for relativity in the struggle of absolute values and thus to promote continuity and cohesion in social relations."[42] It followed, in this Deweyite scheme of things, that "The strength of Charles F. Murphey, boss of Tammany, lay in his moderation."[43] In the older liberal world, with its emphasis on rationality and responsive government, Murphey's "moderation" would have been labeled "corruption," since the boss's indifference to principles sustained a willingness to sell favors to the highest bidder.

In the final analysis, Herring's position paralleled Dewey's even unto the notion that absolutist formulations are powerfully misleading, wherefore they cannot be fought with philosophical arguments but must, instead, be put to the test of effective results. Thus in his words, "The liberal can never know the comfort that comes to the true believer who bases his faith on an identification of the public interest with particular classes or institutions and then projects this picture into the future."[44] Admittedly, absolutist theory and rhetoric speak directly to the human soul, and to its hunger for certainty and peace of mind. "This is the easy road," said Herring, but its real-world price should not be overlooked, and it is that such comfort "leads to dogmatism and ends in that bitterest conflict—the battle between true believers."[45] Democracy, by contrast, is not "a perfect system for adjusting rival interests or ideas." But "its words and its forms permit a higher degree of flexibility and experimentation in the adjustment of human affairs than man has yet achieved through any other means."[46]

40. Ibid., p. 131.
41. Ibid., p. 433.
42. Ibid., p. 136.
43. Ibid., p. 137.
44. Ibid., p. 429.
45. Ibid.
46. Ibid., p. 25.

Wartime Lessons

Some parts of the mid-century liberal matrix were worked out before the war; others appeared only afterward. Of the latter, several emerged from lessons taught by the war itself, serving as the test par excellence of effective results. As wars go, the nation had waged this one efficiently and successfully, and this was proof for most Americans that their way of life was inherently sound. An enormous military machine had been created and deployed to every corner of the earth, it had prevailed in battles of unprecedented size and scope, industry had produced a remarkable quantity and quality of military supplies for the nation and its allies, and farmers had managed to feed their countrymen better than during the Depression, even while providing food for friendly states of the Atlantic Alliance. Moreover, the greatest of accomplishments had come in just those realms of production and regimentation where dictatorial governments were presumably at an advantage over bickering democrats. Yet America had achieved her wartime goals without resorting to authoritarian means. The nation's democratic institutions—Congress, the Presidency, the courts, elections, free speech, and the rest—had all worked smoothly, with only an exceptional denial of civil rights such as when Japanese-Americans were interned on the West Coast.

The commendable performance of democracy under stress highlighted, in unmistakable fashion, the fact that totalitarian governments had behaved badly. They had, at the very least, precipitated the terrible war itself, and so, if for no other reason, most Americans concluded that the political principles which justify elevating dictators to power must be fundamentally flawed. In this respect, Europe's condition after the reign of Hitler was de facto proof of the virtues of democracy, of civil rights, competitive parties, frequent elections, peaceful change of governments, and more. Samuel Lubell, for example, summed up his impression of the war-torn continent with these words: "Some poet ought to write an Ode to a Stable [democratic] Government. It really is a thing of beauty and a joy forever."[47] Americans who had looked upon Auschwitz refused to be sidetracked by philosophical niceties, anthropological discoveries, scientific demonstrations, or the like. Some things were right, and others were wrong. And that was that.

The war revived American optimism concerning the nation's institutions and character, and this optimism became part of scholarly consciousness during the Cold War, to the point where it may be viewed as an unstated presumption underlying most conventional writings about American politics until about 1965. To be thus hopeful was an overall element of form in the liberal matrix rather than a specific point of technical argument or theory. In this shape, it

47. *The Future of American Politics*, (New York: Harper, 1952), p. 245.

made various postwar descriptions of American democracy persuasive simply because, even though the facts—embodied in research findings—had not changed, the larger context within which academic research and writing proceeded was more receptive to the status quo than during the 1930s. Earlier, the practical Deweyian perspective, comparing democracy to authoritarianism on the basis of concrete results, seemed only one among various possible ways of analyzing American society. Later, the same approach was regarded as virtually stating the obvious.

And so Frank Tannenbaum made the case for democracy in a political science article that seemed eminently sound in 1945, whereas five or ten years earlier it would have been severely challenged. As he put it, in phrases which carried overtones of the Deweyian perspective in every line of text, "the end of government is not victory [of inflexible principles] but compromise. . . . With us democracy is a method [as with Dewey]. . . . With us the majority is right, but only temporarily [as scientific truth is subject to change]. . . . The American way is by compromise in little bits, by persuasion, by much talk and little bitterness [as in scientific communities]. . . ."[48] Moreover, "what the people want is what they need. . . . [for] no one knows better than the people themselves what they need at the moment [as opposed to absolutist theories and authoritarian leaders or parties]. . . . In the long run, wisdom is tested by experience [that is, by effective results rather than philosophical subtleties]."[49]

In technical terms, the pervasive optimism that burst forth after World War II found expression in an argument of "ethical relativism," which held that authoritarian theory and practice combine to impose error on entire societies, while in a democratic state errors can be recognized and policies revised accordingly.[50] This was a point that entered the new liberal matrix and would be expounded again and again, in various forms, during the Cold War. It was clearly expressed, for example, when Hans Kelsen wrote in 1946 of the conflict between absolutism and relativism in philosophy and politics.[51] It is in the nature of man that he cannot know the truth perfectly, said Kelsen, but this does not mean that all men are aware of their own limitation. In fact, majorities of like mind may occasionally decide that they have somehow grasped the whole truth,

---

48. "On Certain Characteristics of American Democracy," *Political Science Quarterly* (September 1945), p. 350.

49. Ibid., pp. 345–46.

50. On the shift to an assessment of democracy rooted in "ethical relativism," see Edward A. Purcell, Jr., *The Crisis of Democratic Theory: Scientific Naturalism and the Problem of Value* (Lexington: University Press of Kentucky, 1973), chapter 11, "Toward a Relativist Theory of Democracy," pp. 197–217.

51. "Absolutism and Relativism in Philosophy and Politics," *American Political Science Review* (October 1948), pp. 906–14.

now and forever. The lesson to be learned from their vanity is that we must espouse and maintain democracy for its ability to preserve minority views, recognizing that a minority may at times be right and should have the means to try to become a majority, with power to remake public policy in line with a more correct version of the truth. Kelsen came down on the side of "relativism" because he concluded that all men's beliefs are, at best, correct only relative to their circumstances. Since circumstances continually change, however, and since science encourages us to analyze even old circumstances in new ways, we must admit that our beliefs are fallible and subject to revision. In Kelsen's words, "It may be that the opinion of the minority, and not the opinion of the majority, is correct. Solely because of this possibility, which only philosophical relativism can admit—that what is right today may be wrong tomorrow—the minority must have a chance to express freely their opinion and must have full opportunity of becoming the majority."[52]

Popperism

In sum, the mid-century liberal matrix emerged around World War II as a pattern of discourse which assumed that authoritarian political theories could be written off as absolutist. They were incapable of assimilating new truths, whereas democratic society should be lauded for maintaining institutions which promote social flexibility and facilitate the transfer of devotion from outworn standards to those that keep abreast of the times. Still, even if American social scientists after the war were ready to entertain an outlook which assumed the usefulness and validity of political compromise, adjustment, experimentalism, discussion and debate, and experience rather than preconception, this did not mean that they would do so in terms of Dewey's particular theory of knowledge and its origins. In fact, Dewey's work was important because it showed how American scholars could create important elements of the new matrix and how those elements could make sense together. But his portrait of science was not sharply drawn, and it thereby testified to a common shortcoming of American notions of science in the 1920s and 1930s. As Bernard Crick remarked, Charles Merriam and his associates spoke a great deal about the subject of science, and were even enthusiastic in its cause, but they said very little about what, exactly, it was.[53] They did agree that science was an open-ended system which, by its nature, invalidated

---

52. Ibid., p. 914. See also similar ideas expressed by Herman Finer, "Towards a Democratic Theory," *ibid.* (April, 1945), pp. 249–68.

53. *The New Science of Politics: Its Origins and Conditions* (Berkeley: University of California Press, 1959), pp. 138–39, 144–45. See also p. 214: "I have not suppressed Merriam and Lasswell's writings on the philosophy of science; they simply do not exist."

the presumptions of authoritarian ethics and regimes. Yet their "philosophy of science"—to use a modern term—which had to justify this conclusion, consisted mainly of generalities, and did not even glitter.

It was as if Deweyism had set the stage, where the play in its rough outlines was predictable, and where it remained only to bring in new furniture to replace some of the old and thereby adopt the sets to America's new mood and situation after World War II. And so, as more and more American scholars swung into line to employ the new liberal matrix after 1945, they cast about for an impressive vocabulary that would impart to their research even more power to persuade than that which success in war had already assured. It was a classic case of working within the liberal tradition, where the end was established by national consensus and the right techniques had to be devised for getting there. As it turned out, the shortcomings of a native American conceptual scheme here would be overcome by paying less attention to men such as Dewey and more to European scholars,[54] the most congenial of whom, for the liberal persuasion, was Karl Popper.

Popper provided the requisite new philosophy of science, in terms much more specific than those used by Dewey. His most authoritative statement of this philosophy, linking it directly to democratic politics, appeared in *The Open Society and Its Enemies* (1945).[55] In the next decade, this was the stance that informed many polemics of the Cold War, as liberal scholars and other American writers spoke up in a confrontation with their nonliberal counterparts, mostly abroad. We may call this stance Popperism, using the general title as a way of avoiding philosophical terminology that might describe the new notions more precisely but also more contentiously. Of course, Popper was not the author of all the ideas he so successfully integrated in his work, and later advocates of the new outlook did not acquire their convictions from his work alone. Our concern is not for intellectual pedigree, however, but for the content and meaning of political thought. In this, Popper was uniquely instructive and his name can serve well as a shorthand expression for important aspects of the new view.[56] In microcosm, his writings showed how various liberal arguments

54. Robert Dahl has noted the importance of an influx of European scholars and European concepts into American political science in the 1940s. See his "The Behavioral Approach in Political Science: Epitaph for a Monument to a Successful Protest," *American Political Science Review* (December 1961), p. 764.

55. 4th ed. (orig., 1945; New York: Harper and Row, 1963), 2 vols.

56. For the reception accorded Popper's work, see Alfred Cobban, "The Open Society: A Reconsideration," *Political Science Quarterly* (March 1954), pp. 119: "Professor Karl R. Popper's book, *The Open Society and Its Enemies*, attained almost the standing of a classic with its first appearance."

finally fell into place side by side, that is, how liberalism's major logical and practical problems were related to one another and linked to a well-rounded theoretical perspective which "solved" them, at least for a generation in American political science. No less important, it was Popper's philosophy of science which, at the end of that generation, was severely challenged by Thomas Kuhn, in *The Structure of Scientific Revolutions* (1962),[57] with the result that political science eventually lapsed back into its former despond.

Four Basic Tenets

A native of Austria who fled from Nazism and took up a teaching post in philosophy at the London School of Economics,[58] Popper has written that as far back as in 1919 he began to consider the question: "Is there a criterion for the scientific character or status of a theory?"[59] In those days, opinions on the subject varied greatly. For example, Nazis argued that "Jewish" science was somehow less reliable than its "Aryan" counterpart, and Marxists were convinced that the output of "bourgeois" investigations was false as compared to knowledge produced by "proletarian" dialectics. Then too, there were the "scientific" assertions by psychologists of the Freudian and the Adlerian persuasions, whose conclusions about human nature seemed occasionally useful but always resistant to firm proofs.[60] Quarreling over the definition of science was no mere verbal exercise. Rather, the mantle of science was eagerly contested for the prestige it automatically conferred on any claim to true knowledge. Popper sought, therefore, a way to resolve, with finality, opposing claims as to which ideas are scientific, sound, reliable—whatever adjectives be used—or, in the realm of social thought with its enormous consequences, what is true and what is false. And so he urged that four criteria be recognized as the hallmarks of truly scientific work: testability, falsification, tentativity, and the importance of methods over results.

All statements of science, said Popper, are scientific to the extent that it is possible to associate them with unambiguous evidence, such as when Eddington checked Einstein's theory of relativity by measuring the curvature of starlight around the sun during a solar eclipse. That is, a belief is entitled to be called scientific if it is expressed in terms that can clearly be proved or disproved, as distinguished from moral or religious statements couched in terms of values that cannot be conclusively supported or contradicted. This was the notion of test-

---

57. 2nd ed. (orig., 1962; Chicago: University of Chicago Press, 1972).

58. For an intellectual biography, see Bryan Magee, *Karl Popper* (New York: Viking, 1973). For descriptive and critical essays on Popper's work, see Paul A. Schlipp, ed., *The Philosophy of Karl R. Popper*, 2 vols. (LaSalle, Ill.: Open Court, 1974), pp. 185–957.

59. See the title essay in Karl Popper, *Conjectures and Refutations* (London: Routledge and Kegan Paul, 1963), p. 33.

60. Ibid., pp. 34–35.

ability, the idea that scientists must shape their work so that any conclusion they draw can be tested by their colleagues.[61]

It is sometimes very difficult to prove what we believe about humanity, society, or nature, Popper continued. This is because the world is so full of small events that "inference to theories [large truths] from singular statements which are 'verified by experience' . . . is logically inadmissible. Theories are, therefore, *never* empirically verifiable."[62] In the language of formal logic, the point is that induction, which is the test procedure for proving large generalizations to the extent that they accord with small particulars, can never be absolutely convincing. After all, it is not possible for scientists to observe all small events relevant to a particular generalization. At some future date, a hitherto undiscovered fact may contradict and disprove a large generalization. Thus since Newton's time all apples have fallen, but one may someday rise instead.

If scientists cannot conclusively prove their claims, they can sometimes find the fact that disproves, and disproof can itself be the source of knowledge. Popper argued, therefore, that scientists have a duty to state their beliefs about the world in such a way that critics can bring to bear against those beliefs at least the weight of any evidence human beings are capable of gathering. This is what he called the principle of falsification. It is "not the verifiability but the falsifiability of a system" that permits people to call certain work science.[63] Thus whoever claims that the Devil causes earthquakes makes an unscientific assertion, because no one can collect enough concrete evidence about Satan to show conclusively that he does *not* shake the world.

The state of knowledge advances when scientists demonstrate that a great many beliefs are actually false. What remains is a body of claims that are apparently but not necessarily true, because they are not, and cannot be, supported by absolute proof. As Popper stated this notion of tentativity—his third criterion for science—the evidence tending to support any scientific truth is inherently "inconclusive" and "therefore liable to revision at any time."[64] Unlike a moralist or a theologian, the scientist is a man whose mind must forever remain receptive to new propositions or revisions of received wisdom. He cannot be certain that a new idea will be absolutely true, but it may seem, on the basis of available evidence, more tentatively true than previous knowledge.

Popper's ideas about testability, falsification, and tentativity merged to support a fourth notion, which was that method is more important than results in science. He illustrated the point by asking, hypothetically, how one should

61. *The Logic of Scientific Discovery*, rev. ed. (orig., 1934; New York: Harper and Row, 1965), p. 40.

62. Ibid. See also *Open Society*, 2, p. 220.

63. *Logic*, pp. 40, 78–92, and *Open Society*, 2, pp. 13f.

64. *Open Society*, 2, p. 221.

characterize two identical books, the first written by a clairvoyant and the second by a scientist working strictly according to Popper's version of the scientific method.[65] Being identical, the two books contain the same facts and conclusions, but this does not warrant calling the clairvoyant's knowledge scientific. What makes his counterpart's propositions scientific, and hence worthy of special consideration and confidence, is the way in which they are arrived at, via testing, striving to falsify, and a willingness to consider alternative proposals.

In short, science is a matter of methods and not results. Indeed, a scientist's work may produce very few of the latter. But if he faithfully employs the proper methods, his findings will be maximally reliable. And reliability, for Popper, was an exceedingly worthwhile objective. Only when it is achieved can we disregard the labels that some people affix disdainfully to hypotheses they wish to discredit, such as when the Nazis dismissed Einstein's theory of relativity for being no more than a piece of "Jewish" science. In work that is truly scientific, the quality of its conclusions can rise above any personal idiosyncracies occasioned by a scientist's social origins.

The Scientific Community
These several points underlay Popper's basic thesis as to the nature of scientific work performed by individuals. He further concluded that the scientific community, or the collectivity of individuals working in a scientific way, can play a very special role in mankind's search for reliable knowledge. In this Freudian era, one can hardly deny that all members of society are shaped by their social origins, and so there can be no certainty that these background forces will not distort even those ideas which are seriously called scientific. How, then, can a reliable body of beliefs be built upon the collective work of men who are separately imperfect? This problem has been called "the sociology of knowledge," on the grounds that the sociological characteristics of every scientist presumably influence his choice of beliefs so strongly that, in principle at least, he must always wonder if what he concludes from his studies is in fact so.

Popper conceded that every member of the scientific community is biased, each in his or her own way. But by virtue of employing the scientific method, their propositions can be tested by all of their colleagues. From this interplay of individual research efforts emerge reliable propositions which, at least temporarily, are capable of withstanding very stringent challenges. In these circumstances, when a scientific proposition is finally accepted by members of the community, the origin and predilections of its author are reduced to insignificance by their collective approval.[66]

65. Ibid., p. 218.
66. On the scientific community, see ibid., pp. 221–23.

But what if some shared bias might lead the entire scientific community to believe some things that are untrue, as, for example, when nineteenth-century biologists were sure that human races are inherently unequal? Popper was alert to this problem. In his terms, it reflected the fact that inductive reasoning is so weak as to deny absolute validity even to those propositions that are accepted and endorsed by the scientific community as a whole. This means that all scientific knowledge, at the level of the community as well as at the level of the individual scientist, is tentative and subject to later revision or rejection. Thus the theory of relativity is widely endorsed today, but tomorrow it may be superseded.

The Open Society

There was a special corollary to this scientific reality. Scientists study either the physical world or society, and then, on the basis of their research findings, make recommendations for action to improve the human condition. In either case, Popper said, their recommendations must be offered in a spirit of experimentation and only partial commitment. Any policy based upon the current state of scientific knowledge can be no more trustworthy than that knowledge itself. Accordingly, science permits people to try any course of action, see if it works to satisfaction, and continue to pursue it for as long as it fulfills its promise. Beyond this kind of policy experimentalism, science can offer no certainty of success. And thus, if Popper understood the nature of science correctly, it implies a permanent caveat against absolute confidence in any one social policy, against irrevocable commitment to any one plan for organizing society.

Starting with this idea that science stands in permanent opposition to fixed social commitments, Popper wrote of the closed and, more important, the open society.[67] In his analysis of history, closed societies have appeared in many eras, including our own. Always, they are linked to some sort of political ideology that recognizes the existence of only one legitimate objective for society, be it called Truth, Justice, the interest of the Working Class, the needs of a General Will, the reign of a Master Race, or some other end. Invariably, such limited and immutable objectives have led people in closed societies to ask: "Who shall rule the state?"[68] Unfortunately, the answer to this question then necessarily appears as a function of the exclusive objective itself, so that the end is seen as requiring unswerving support for a ruling group which possesses unique competence in respect of realizing the community's special aim. The result may be allegiance to Plato's philosopher kings, or to their modern authoritarian counterparts in fascist, communist, or extreme nationalist parties.

67. On closed and open societies, see ibid., 1, pp. 169–201.
68. Ibid., p. 120.

Popper labeled the political thinking of closed societies utopian,[69] because it presumes both that men can discover absolute and correct goals rationally and that they can construct an all-powerful government which will shape a perfect society according to such preconceived ends. But in fact science, as Popper understood it, is standing proof of man's inability to acquire more than tentative knowledge about the world and its people. If, given the nature of scientific knowledge, the human capacity for certainty about anything is so limited, it follows that no closed society is ever justified. Some men will always be convinced that their social beliefs are absolutely true, now and forever, yet the inherent fallibility of scientific knowledge makes it impossible for them to prove that such beliefs are indeed true. And therefore, in Popper's opinion, there can be no compelling reason why one group rather than another should continue to rule any state in pursuit of one set of ends rather than another.

The link here between the nature of science and the ideals of politics was inescapable. Like Dewey, Popper argued that a good society must resemble the archetypical scientific community, for it too must be a collection of people fully capable of dealing with new ideas, in this case political ideas. As he put it, because men cannot agree on ends, closed societies must give way to open societies. In the latter, citizens will continually discuss ultimate ends but, since lasting consensus is impossible, governments will endorse only selected programs aimed at achieving some ends on a tentative basis. Of course, as politics proceed in an open society, various interested groups will propose alternative policies, and any government of the moment that chooses to administer one such program will necessarily represent less than the hopes and aspirations of all its subjects. Under the circumstances, with part of the citizenry always disagreeing with whatever end a particular government is committed to pursue, a new and fundamental political question must be asked: "How can we organize political institutions so that bad or incompetent rulers can be prevented from doing so much damage?"[70] That is, how can people be free to replace one government with another, when the existing rulers and their programs become unacceptable to a significant number of citizens?

Merely to ask this question is to concede that utopia is unattainable, and so Popper posited what he called "institutional democracy" as a necessary condition of open societies.[71] What is needed, lest a majority of voters some day agree to install a totalitarian government that will ignore the needs of a minority of their neighbors, is a procedural system that can exist and survive apart from the ever-changing and sometimes tyrannical mood of the people themselves. Popper

69. Ibid., p. 158.
70. Ibid., p. 121.
71. Ibid., p. 126.

did not describe his concept of institutional democracy in detail, but he recommended an arrangement of democratic institutions capable of absorbing policy changes while keeping an electoral door perpetually open to new opinions, new programs, new ends, and new governments. Such was the good society based on uncertainty, the larger instance of a scientific community, so to speak.

The Efficacy of Popperism

Testability, falsification, tentativity, open and closed societies, utopian thinking, and institutional democracy were all terms that confirmed the basic thrust of Deweyism while sharpening its focus and multiplying its connotations. Popperism thereby did much to accommodate the new liberal matrix to the needs of postwar political science. This was especially so with regard to the way in which the restated matrix dealt with vexing questions concerning the nature of science and the efficiency of scientific research, both of which had created tension between the discipline of political studies and the liberal context within which it operated.

The Reconciliation with Traditional Liberalism

In terms of the five traditional liberal postulates, Popperism of course favored the fifth, which spoke of the need for scientific research, but it also strongly supported the second, third, and fourth, on democratic practices, while neatly sidestepping the first, on moral equality. Logically speaking, the point of departure was a scientific understanding of the world, which sees complete rationality in human affairs as impossible, for men can attain only an imperfect and partial grasp of the truth, whatever that may be. Some will be more rational and others less; about this matter, science can only lead us to believe that, given the progress of science itself, people may be lifted to higher levels of rationality, although not to perfection per se. Accordingly, indications of human irrationality—as seen in voters, interest groups, parties, elected officials, judges, bureaucrats, policies, programs, or whatever—will occasionally show up in scientific research into politics. These are to be expected. They do not, however, justify despair but rather should encourage us to work hard at making the political system ever more open and democratic so that the diffusion of information and knowledge will have a salutary effect on existing irrationality and reduce its incidence in the future.

Here is a shift of perspective, whereby reason is said to be an outcome of the political system rather than an input in distressingly short supply. On these grounds, Popper followed Dewey and declared that existing democratic institutions were basically sound, the American holding that the cure for democracy's ills was more democracy, and the European contending that institutional democracy can keep an open society sufficiently flexible to cope with its problems as they arise. The usefulness of this stance to students of American society should not be underestimated. Instead of holding on uncomfortably to research findings that placed them constantly at odds with existing patterns of liberal practice, social scientists could start from the presumption that liberalism's most obvious structures—elections, parties, federalism, civil rights, and so forth—are necessary parts of the great mechanism by which a free people conduct their affairs intelligently. From this presumption it did not follow that passivity was in order, for democracy's necessary parts would occasionally require reform or redesign, or supplement by new parts aimed at making the mechanism more effective. But simply to take for granted the worthiness of America's existing political system was to reduce enormously science's ability to create perpetual tension between scholarly discoveries and the devotion of an entire society to its liberal past, present, and future. Here, then, was an important outcome of the new outlook on science, clothed with Popper's philosophy and terminology. It said, in effect, that even where an apparently unsatisfactory situation is discovered by the discipline's preferred mode of inquiry, one may conclude that America's perceived ills are only a temporary annoyance and that the country's political devices, suitably reformed, can be made to produce more desirable results.

Even as Popperism moved positively to support liberal institutions, it just as significantly enabled social scientists to avoid entanglement with liberalism's first postulate, on moral equality. We have seen how the problem of continuing to justify liberalism morally arose only when science had thoroughly undermined confidence in the efficacy of democratic practices from a practical point of view. That is, existing practices did not seem to work as once expected. Yet most of the learned disciplines had opted for scientific reasoning, and their practitioners knew of no way to speak professionally to the matter of morals. Then came the new liberal matrix, which led social scientists to conclude that the Popperian view of democratic practices was correct, and that those practices deserve praise and support for their usefulness according to the new understanding of how men acquire and employ knowledge. With this there was no need to rely upon liberalism's first postulate and to defend democracy in terms of philosophical arguments which, by their very nature, seemed unpersuasive and inconclusive to those of a scientific cast of mind. It was not, therefore, that the new liberal matrix dealt satisfactorily with the first liberal postulate. Rather, it downplayed the old maxims and made possible postwar debate on the nature of American society in terms that permitted participants to avoid dealing with moral questions at all. According to Popper, scholars remained free to be inspired by considerations of moral decency, and no doubt many of them were.[72] In the world of Popperism,

---

72. Popper never said that moral affairs are unimportant. What he said was that science can ascertain nothing about the truth or falsity of moral notions. See his *Conjectures and Refutations*, pp. 39–40.

however, they did not have to explain their conscience but could rely on other arguments in support of democracy instead.

A Role for Social Scientists

All these ties between the new outlook and the old make sense only in the context of both Dewey and Popper arguing that scientific truth is tentative, meaning that men have to live with institutions that permit new ideas to be tested, rejected, and/or confirmed. But if scientific knowledge is uncertain, and surely to be revised at some later date, why accept the advice of social scientists at all, based as it is on no more than today's research results? At this point, Popper provided even more clearly than Dewey a fruitful conception of the nature of scientific communities, including those formed by social scientists. Within those communities, devotion to the scientific method was supremely important, for it assured that research results would be maximally reliable even if only tentative. As Popper defined the task of people working in such communities, "The only course open to the social sciences is . . . [to] tackle the practical problems of our time with . . . the methods of trial and error, of inventing hypotheses which can be practically tested, and of submitting them to piecemeal tests. *A social technology is needed whose results can be tested by piecemeal social engineering.*"[73]

If the road to progress entails piecemeal social engineering rather than seductive certainty, we are enjoined to take the advice of social scientists not because their word is unimpeachable but because their findings are the best available. To foster widespread adoption of this view, the first step for interested scholars was to champion the scientific method so that everyone would understand it was a scheme for producing tentative knowledge rather than permanent peace of mind. The next step was to use that method in professional work so as to make modest proposals for reforming small parts of society one at a time—here a welfare service, there a wildlife program, here a state legislature, and there a military procurement budget. Together, such reforms would constitute piecemeal social engineering as opposed to a dangerous utopian program for reforming all parts of society totally and simultaneously. All citizens, naturally, would have the right to recommend reforms, and to that end institutional democracy would guarantee a hearing to all suggestions. But were the scientific method clearly understood and widely appreciated, from step one, the views of social scientists would be deemed especially valuable for flowing from investigations based on that method and being checked by public tests within the community of scientists. For social scientists, here was the road to prestige and professional success.

73. *Open Society*, 2, p. 223. For further comments on the need for piecemeal social engineering, see ibid., pp. 134, 158–59, 161–63, and Karl Popper, *The Poverty of Historicism* (orig., 1957; New York: Harper and Row, 1961), pp. 58–71.

There was even the added attraction that Popper's view justified critical research conclusions, which were likely to flow from scholarly investigations into a society that was, after all, far from perfect. With the analogy between science and democracy adding strength to the notion that America's political system really was an open society, more or less, a social scientist could extol various virtues of the existing political framework even while his work demonstrated the need for making that framework more efficient. In principle, it could be argued that the body politic was basically sound, and this overriding truth, both constant and reassuring, could be advanced again and again, in teaching, together with the idea that there would always be small discoveries waiting to be made—with the results published, of course—and small reforms suggested. Political scientists eventually worked out a very thorough understanding of the institutions of American politics and how these together constituted an open society in need of only minor and occasional changes. This, almost inevitably, became their new teaching.

The Challenge of Marxism

If Popperism suggested how social research might be conducted and justified within a liberal society, it also indicated how that society might be defended against threats from without. By 1945, Americans knew very well that fascism was bankrupt, practically and ideologically. That particular authoritarian belief system might still be unchallengeable in the realm of anthropological relativity, as a matter of strict logic and inference. But it no longer attracted the attention of serious people, except insofar as they were willing to investigate its perversions and publish their findings so that it would never again tempt the civilized world. Against the backdrop of World War II, most Americans were convinced that long into the future there would be no meaningful challenge to liberalism from the right. And so even today, fascism receives very little space, and even less sympathy, in standard political science textbooks that describe modern political ideologies.

There remained, however, the extremely serious problem of Marxism. As an ideology rather than a political movement, Marxism was much more sophisticated and attractive than the bombast of a Mussolini or the rantings of a Hitler. In fact, Marxism offered a well-balanced and highly plausible set of political ideas—the dialectic, the theory of surplus value, the inevitability of class conflict, an explanation of imperialism, a strategy for revolution, and more—where the proletarian dictatorship that *ought to be* is continually shown as inevitable by the class war that *is*, as discovered endlessly by Marxian inquiry.

All of these notions directly challenged both liberal ideas and democratic practices. To be sure, much evidence suggested that Marxist thinking, such as in the phrase "the dictatorship of the proletariat," fosters authoritarian government, as in Russia. And so there was considerable liberal willingness to conclude that Marxism, even as pure ideology, failed the test of effective results as surely as did fascism. Still, some held that Marxism does not necessarily require dictatorial rule, for did not Engels, and later Lenin, both say that the state will eventually "wither away"?[74] For such disciples, Marxism, detached from the reputation of its real-world offspring, was a powerful intellectual tool enjoying intrinsic value as an aid to political analysis and understanding. Thus the postwar generation of American scholars needed a conclusive answer, beyond what were to them the war's obvious lessons, as to why the Marxian viewpoint was wrong and invalid. They needed it to guarantee political confidence at home and, as the Cold War developed, they needed it to argue persuasively the American case abroad.

The basic difficulty with combating Marxism arose from the fact that its disciples presented their ideas as true on the basis of scientific reasoning, with the science, of course, a Marxian sort based on dialectical materialism.[75] Then Popperism arrived and, reaffirming Dewey's rejection of absolutist ideologies but expressing the disclaimer in fashionable terminology, attacked Marxian claims by redefining the very nature of science itself. Popper said that Marxists cannot "scientifically" interpret history so as to establish conclusively that there exists some ultimate goal which can only be achieved by special representatives of the working class. No matter how many specific examples of historical events and trends Marxists can cite as proof for their convictions, the citations reflect only a process of inductive reasoning which cannot, in principle, establish the infallibility of their doctrine. In fact, the inherent worth of Marxist ends is just as impossible to prove as are the value of diverse ends sought by other social groups. It is thus only dogmatic moralists, unfettered by the rule of true science, who can insist that among all known social programs, Marxism is historically determined to be absolutely necessary. The international community of scholars has not even tentatively accepted a Marxian definition of the proletariate's needs, and it is not likely to do so and thereby disparage the needs of other classes. Marxism's claim to the mantle of science, with all the legitimacy that a successful claim would imply, was thus put to rest.[76]

74. Frederick Engels, *Socialism, Utopian and Scientific* (New York: International Publishers, 1935), pp. 69–75; and V. I. Lenin, *State and Revolution* (New York: International Publishers, 1932), pp. 15–20.

75. For example, see Howard Selsam, *What Is Philosophy? A Marxist Introduction* (New York: International Publishers, 1938), p. 16: "Dialectical Materialism is not only a world outlook and a way of life. It is a philosophy of science too. . . . It is . . . the generalization of the principles science employs, the picture of our world science gives us, the study of the techniques and methods that science uses, and the theory of their function in the whole sphere of human life."

76. For a Marxian reply to Popper, see Stanley Ryerson, *The Open Society: Paradox and Challenge* (New York: International Publishers, 1965).

The End of Ideology Movement

With an infusion of Popperism, the new liberal matrix was ready for adoption shortly after the war ended. The question is, to what extent did this Popperism actually triumph over earlier liberal conceptions, which had aimed at many of the same ends but suffered so much dissatisfaction en route? Were the new way of analyzing American society to become the general liberal view, political scientists could take their collective cue from what would then be a conventional wisdom and work according to that wisdom within a supportive and rewarding intellectual climate. And so, for our story to continue smoothly, it was necessary that a large-scale shift to Popperism take place. It did, conveniently, in what came to be called "the end of ideology" movement.

The overall mood was optimistic. From the late 1940s and well into the 1960s, many leading scholars and literary figures in the United States agreed that Western society had progressed beyond any need for ideologies capable of providing sweeping remedies for whatever political ills remained. In the opinion of men such as Seymour Martin Lipset, Daniel Bell, Edward Shils, Arthur Schlesinger, Jr., George Kennan, and many other influential writers, there were two parts to the argument that ideologies were, or ought to be, considered properly defunct. At times it was said that most political parties in the West paid only lip service to ideology anyway, while they went about the business of finding practical and technical solutions to immediate social issues. And sometimes it was claimed that there remained so few social issues that only practical, rather than ideological, solutions had to be found. When Shils made the first point, he was convinced that the great countries of the West had "increasingly considered their major domestic policies without regard for the standard distinctions of 'left' or 'right,' of socialism and laizzez-faire, but in a matter-of-fact way which recognized no general principles and treated each emerging situation on its own merits.[77] And as Lipset made the second point, "the fundamental political problems of the industrial revolution have been solved: the workers have achieved industrial and political citizenship; the conservatives have accepted the welfare state."[78] Under the circumstances, "social revolution in the West ends domestic politics for those intellectuals who must have ideologies or utopias to motivate them to political action."[79]

There were, to be sure, some scholars and intellectuals who never did accept either the empirical claim or the moral judgment that ideologies were, as

---

77. Edward Shils, "The End of Ideology?" *Encounter* (November 1955), p. 54.

78. Seymour Martin Lipset, *Political Man: The Social Bases of Politics* (Garden City, N.Y.: Doubleday, 1960), chapter 13, "The End of Ideology?" p. 406.

79. Ibid.

Bell put it, "exhausted."[80] Like the first group, these men also published scholarly and popular articles on the theme of ideology, and thus there arose a small but intense debate about the need for, or the absence of, ideology.[81] The question of exactly who "won" the debate may be left to the cognoscenti, but it is perfectly clear that the anti-ideologists represented the dominant American mood after World War II. In the popular view, the nation had endured a bitter depression and a costly war against radical ideologies and regimes, and yet had survived while preserving prosperity at home and achieving peace abroad. Many people were apprehensive lest the military power of Russia and/or China, wielded in the course of the Cold War, might endanger the American way of life. But it was widely held that the Cold War was largely a military affair, and that the fundamental decency and social efficiency of American politics had been conclusively proved between 1930 and 1950. A *Partisan Review* symposium in 1952, entitled "Our Country and Our Culture," evoked mainly praise from its distinguished contributors, with remarks such as:

> The American artist and intellectual no longer feels "disinherited" as Henry James, or "astray" as Ezra Pound did in 1913.[82] (Editorial Statement)

> As for the Jamesian version of Europe as the "rich, deep, dark Old World," its appeal has been markedly reduced by a series of social upheavals, revolutions, and two world wars.[83] (Philip Rahv)

> Next to Himmler, even Babbit began to look good.[84] (Arthur Schlesinger, Jr.)

> The Second World War completed the course of spiritual reinstatement. In the briefest span it showed that the promises of the "New Orders," whether based on myth [fascism] or Marx, were fraudulent; that European folly, treachery, and disregard for human rights refuted the claim of superior "civilization."[85] (Jacques Barzun)

80. Daniel Bell, *The End of Ideology: On the Exhaustion of Political Ideas in the Fifties* (New York: The Free Press, 1960), p. 402.

81. For collections of essays in the debate, pro and con, see Chaim L. Waxman, ed., *The End of Ideology Debate* (New York: Simon and Schuster, 1969); and Mostafa Rejai, ed., *Decline of Ideology?* (Chicago: Aldine-Atherton, 1971).

82. Newton Arvin, James Burnham, et al., "Our Country and Our Culture: A Symposium," *Partisan Review* (May–June 1952), p. 283.

83. Ibid., p. 305.

84. Louise Bogan, Richard Chase, et al., "Our Country and Our Culture III," *ibid.* (September–October 1952), p. 591.

85. William Barrett, Jacques Barzun, et al., "Our Country and Our Culture II," ibid. (July–August 1952), p. 426.

Confidence ran so strongly that at the Milan Conference on ideology, in 1955, where many anti-ideologues presented papers extolling anti-ideological politics, one American participant described the proceedings as taking place in an "atmosphere of a post-victory ball."[86]

The Concept of Totalitarianism

In their optimism, the anti-ideologues did not respond to their critics separately and directly but used the term *totalitarianism* to lump fascism and communism together as perverted forms of political thought rather than two substantively different critiques of liberal society.[87] On this score, liberalism's advocates did not have to rely on Popper alone but could refer to several distinguished treatises on authoritarian government that appeared after the war. In 1951, Hannah Arendt's *The Origins of Totalitarianism* was published, written by a refugee from Nazi Germany.[88] Arendt showed how European intellectual history had prepared the moral groundwork, or morass, upon which fanatics had built a system of government that she called totalitarianism and which she portrayed as more tyrannical than even traditional dictatorships. In 1956, in *Totalitarianism, Dictatorship, and Autocracy*, Carl J. Friedrich and Zbigniew K. Brzezinski offered an empirical description of totalitarianism, defining it as a regime more oppressive and dangerous than mere dictatorship.[89] Using Nazi Germany and Soviet Russia as their examples, Friedrich and Brzezinski demonstrated that totalitarianism was characterized by an official set of beliefs or ideology, a single mass-party, a terroristic secret police, a monopoly of government control over mass communications, exclusive power over the instruments of armed force, and a centrally administered economy. In this view of totalitarianism, it matters not at all where one starts in substantive criticism of liberalism, from the political right or the left. The practical consequences are invariably the same, and always deplorable.

It was the test of effective results, with a fresh label and more evidence than ever before. From the new analysis there flowed an obvious and powerful Popperian imperative: Stay away from ideology, for it leads only to political disaster. Assuming that America had avoided such a disaster in the past, how fitting it would be to show that the nation's historic good fortune was somehow linked to a habit of eschewing ideological political thought. In 1953, Daniel J. Boorstin argued precisely this conclusion in *The Genius of American Politics*.[90] Boorstin

86. Shils, "The End of Ideology?," p. 54.
87. On the origins of the term "totalitarianism," see Les Adler and Thomas Paterson, "Red Fascism: The Merger of Nazi Germany and Soviet Russia in the American Image of Totalitarianism, 1930's–1950's" *American Historical Review* (April 1970), pp. 1046–64.
88. (orig., 1951; New York: Meridian, 1958).
89. (Cambridge, Mass: Harvard, 1956), pp. 3–11.
90. (Chicago: University of Chicago Press, 1953).

observed that long ago Americans had established their political institutions on the basis of some very simple ideas about what is natural and fair for free men and free women. With the years, some reforms had been effected, but always as a prudent extension of the original vision rather than as a necessary change dictated by some grand ideological plan. For this Boorstin praised his countrymen, saying that "while many nations have filled their sanctuaries with ideological idols, we have had the courage to refuse to do so."[91] By simply behaving decently, and by demonstrating an open-minded willingness to try out new ideas when they seem worthwhile, Americans "have traditionally held out to the world, not our doctrine, but our example."[92]

Agreement on Fundamentals

If the condemnation of ideology was essentially Popperian, so was the confident recital of what should be done. The anti-ideologists wrote separately; there was no conscious agreement among them to constitute a single school of thought; they often explored the politics and ideologies of different countries; and their works therefore differed on many points of detail. Nevertheless, what they all said, albeit in various forums and contexts, added up to a prescription for Popperian science and society. It is a point not much stressed by intellectual histories of the era, but of some importance for our story.

Daniel Bell, for example, announced the exhaustion of ideology with satisfaction. The fault with utopian thought, he argued, was not that people discussed high ideals, but that such discussion often took place in simplistic and dangerous ideological terms. Debate itself must continue, he said, since there will always be those who need a lofty vision of social affairs to help them fuse "passion with intelligence" in the continual effort to improve society. Bell argued that the new vision must be empirical, however, and by empirical he meant that a workable approach to the problems of society must specify exactly what is to be done, how it is to be done, what the benefits will be, and who will pay the costs.[93]

The key Popperian element here was Bell's idea that a vision of future policies must rest upon empirical realities. In the very concept "empirical" there resides an implicit understanding that the quality of testability will distinguish any empirical plan from some older, ideological scheme. This means that if utopian thinking is justified at all, it must indicate, without dangerous uncertainty, just what will result from the implementation of one or another proposal for improving society. In other words, it is the Popperian quality of testability that makes possible an intelligent choice among divergent proposals for social change

91. Ibid., p. 170.
92. Ibid., p. 186.
93. Bell, *End of Ideology*, p. 405.

where results can be assessed and therefore approved in advance. And it is exactly this prescience that will enable mankind to avoid the excesses in human behavior that ideologies, uncritically espoused and unswervingly pursued, have often produced in the past.

Like Bell, Edward Shils did not wish totally to deny people the satisfaction of pursuing utopian goals, and he even believed that adherence to traditional liberal ideals makes the public at large more prone to support excellent democratic institutions. Shils too, however, deprecated the ideological cast of most utopian thinking, and he insisted that the case for freedom and democracy had to reargued without reference to ideological generalities. He did not specify what this revised liberal thinking would look like in the end, but he did say that it must proceed to the point where all errors are revealed and only "the permanently valid element(s) in our historical ideals" will be "salvaged."[94] Here, again, the whole conception was Popperian, for Shils's emphasis on finding the "permanently valid" elements of democratic idealism implied a series of falsification tests that would strip away misconceptions and ignorance in order to reveal a core of democratic beliefs that are both useful and true. For Popper, the inherent limitation of falsification tests was that whatever knowledge survives rigorous testing can only be tentatively true. Significantly, the anti-ideologists agreed with him. Thus Raymond Aron set the tone for the entire anti-ideological school by calling for the abolition of ideological fanaticism and "the advent of the skeptics" who will "doubt all the models and utopias."[95]

Like Popper, the anti-ideologists criticized ideologies of the right and the left even while, again like Popper, their concern after World War II was mainly with Marxism. As opposed to that school of thought, they followed Popper in his solution to the sociology-of-knowledge problem. Marxists were adamant about possible biases, and they often claimed that their opponents' political beliefs could only be false owing to an origin in middle-class prejudices and preconceptions. Thus to Marx it was obvious that capitalists figuratively carry their hearts about in their purses. In turn, the anti-ideological school charged that Marxism was no more immune to the sociology of knowledge than any other set of beliefs. The overall solution to this ideological quibbling, they said, was to lay aside traditional justifications for liberalism and start opposing Marxism with a reliable political vision based upon scientific knowledge about society. As Bell made the point, and as Popper equally stressed, natural science is itself a standing negation of the Marxist theory that there is a necessary "social determination of [all] ideas."[96] To oppose Marxism successfully, therefore, required a scientific kind of

94. Shils, "End of Ideology?" p. 57.
95. Raymond Aron, *The Opium of the Intellectuals* (Garden City, N.Y.: Doubleday, 1957), "Conclusion: The End of the Ideological Age?," p. 324.
96. Bell, *End of Ideology*, p. 397.

thinking in the social field that would avoid ideological error. And this, in the last analysis, was what men like Bell, Shils, and Aron recommended, via empiricism, falsification, and tentatively espoused truths.

The society that Bell, Shils, Aron, and the other anti-ideologues sought to preserve or to fashion resembled nothing so much as Popper's vision of an open society. There was to be no "large-scale social planning," because the ideological thinking necessary to sustain such planning had to be discouraged and curtailed.[97] Instead, research was to be based upon extensive scientific thinking, which would lead to many suggestions for small and tentative changes in public policy. Over the years, such changes as were attempted might come to constitute a significant reform or they might not, depending upon whether or not they passed the empirical test of effective results. As Lipset described the whole affair, a democratic society was needed where citizens could decide unexciting but nonetheless important small issues such as the price of milk or a marginal raise in wages for metalworkers.[98] Such a society might not measure up to an ideologue's dream of the perfect world, but it would, in keeping with Lipset's less demanding and Popperian criteria, be "the good society itself in operation."[99] It would facilitate some change, at least in the direction of better living conditions, and it would avoid the political rigidities, and therefore frustrations, that can cause tyrannical power to fall into the hands of only a few citizens. So long as "the give-and-take of a free society's internal struggles" are preserved, said Lipset,[100] the possibility of social progress is assured, and the danger of paralysis or regression is avoided. The goal, in Popperian terms, was institutional democracy. What more could be expected by reasonable, skeptical, and scientific people, as opposed to dogmatic and dangerous ideologues?

Popperism and Political Science

The rise of Popperism was an enormously important event for the discipline of political studies, even though most young political scientists today are probably unaware of exactly what happened to their profession four decades ago. At long last, democracy seemed to hold together scientifically and liberally. Employing at every turn the test of effective results, the Popperian scholar had at hand a powerful range of analytical concepts such as testability, falsification, tentativity, the scientific community, the sociology of knowledge, institutional democracy, piecemeal social engineering, and totalitarianism. Moreover, widespread accep-

97. This point is made by Henry David Aiken, "The Revolt Against Ideology," *Commentary* (April 1964), p. 32.
98. Lipset, *Political Man*, p. 406.
99. Ibid., p. 403.
100. Ibid.

tance of the new outlook as part of the Cold War meant that is was not merely available but also acceptable. And thus it became professionally advisable for academicians to adopt Popperism and use it in their work, for by doing so they could step easily and respectably into the mainstream of postwar American hopes and expectations. This is just what many political scientists did, on the basis of an approach to political analysis that they called "behavioralism."

5

The Behavioral Persuasion

In 1950, the American Political Science Association numbered 5,126 members.[1] At the same time, 2,659,021 students were enrolled in American colleges and universities,[2] with 7,173 of them completing degrees in political science.[3] Together, both the discipline and the world of higher education overall would grow, until by 1970 more than 13,500 had joined the Association[4] while student population nationwide stood at 7,136,075,[5] with 27,901 of the enrolled receiving degrees in political science.[6] Here, finally, was the setting for a full flowering of the professional trends born long before, as hundreds, and then thousands of new political scientists found teaching positions, attended conventions, kept up with the literature, obtained research grants, trained graduate disciples, executed research projects, submitted article manuscripts for publication, put books into print, and held themselves available to move to better jobs with higher pay or rank. It was a time for becoming thoroughly engrossed in the profession and enthusiastically true to its standards.

Two scholarly propensities characterized much of the discipline's work in the period from roughly 1945 to approximately 1970. First, zeal for a scientific mode of research persisted but found expression in innovative ideas unfamiliar to prewar political science. On this important point, the standard historical accounts are

1. Heinz Eulau and James G. March (eds.), *Political Science* (Englewood Cliffs, N.J.: Prentice-Hall, 1969), p. 68.
2. W. Vance Grant, ed., *Digest of Education Statistics* (Washington, D.C.: National Center for Education Statistics, 1982), p. 105.
3. Ibid., p. 129.
4. "Report of the Executive Director," *PS* (Summer 1978), p. 386.
5. Grant, *Digest*, p. 105.
6. Ibid., p. 129.

unintentionally misleading. Earlier practitioners had collected much factual information concerning political institutions, and from that data base they had drawn interesting conclusions. According to the commonly understood meaning of science in their time, many political scholars from 1920 to 1940 had already engaged in scientific endeavors. But the younger generation who came to power in professional circles after World War II claimed that previous works of political inquiry had together assembled only a large quantity of data with no significantly revealing qualities, that is, a sterile "hyperfactualism," as one critic charged.[7] They therefore called upon their colleagues to practice science in a new style. To some of the Young Turks, it was as if the discipline had yet to enter the age of science. In reality, however, it was a typical case of practitioners in a learned discipline honing both professional skills and vocational reputation while riding the shifting tides of twentieth-century academic life, where terms and techniques keep changing along with intellectual fashion. In this sense, it was only natural that the very commitment to science would undergo redefinition from time to time.

Second, the revised conception of science found strong justification in the mid-century liberal matrix of discourse. To remain loyal to science was to endorse the long-term depreciation of revelation and tradition, a phenomenon which had fostered the universities in nineteenth-century America and which helped to maintain their special place in society afterward. But beyond that, political scientists after World War II worked within a climate of conventional opinion embracing highly satisfactory arguments to the effect that, when properly done, scientific research and teaching can make valuable contributions to public welfare. Thus the strictures on how political scholars should practice a new sort of science, as opposed to unimaginatively persisting with the old business of data collecting, fit comfortably within a wider view assigning social utility to the whole enterprise.

Defining Behavioralism

What were the major characteristics of political science during an era when the profession seemed to move not only with the historical tide but also in a direction that could fairly be said to lead to the nation's greater good? We may begin with the renewed dedication to scientific research, which ordinarily justifies calling these years the age of "behavioralism." Robert A. Dahl,[*8] a leading postwar

7. David Easton, *The Political System: An Inquiry into the State of Political Science*, 2nd ed. (New York: Knopf, 1971), pp. 66–78.

8. Since analysis of behavioralism can be based only on some of the many available sources, and may therefore be vulnerable to charges of inappropriate selectivity, I have placed an asterisk beside the name of every former president of the APSA cited in this chapter, but only where that name first appears, to indicate that my views of the subject are at least based upon the works of important and representative figures in the political science discipline.

practitioner whose opinion should be accorded great weight, observed that "the behavioral approach" captured and pervaded the discipline by 1962.[9] It was never quite clear, however, what kind of science behavioralists wished to pursue, or how thoroughly the same scholars were wedded to each of its tenets. In fact, members of the discipline spoke vaguely about where political scientists should stand in relation to the formal models of science then available. And thus the discipline's writings sometimes equated the behavioral approach with no more than "the" scientific method, as when Evron M. Kirkpatrick, the Executive Director of the American Political Science Association, said that behavioralism assumed that "the concepts and theory of the social sciences can and ought to be made identical with those of the natural sciences."[10] Or, definition was sometimes sidestepped entirely, as when Arthur S. Goldberg asserted that "the exact nature of the system [of scientific thought] is a matter of some controversy, and it is felt that a discussion of these controversies . . . could prove more confusing than beneficial."[11] Even when behavioralists were inclined to be specific, they did not concur as to which scientific principles were at stake. David Easton* listed eight assumptions and objectives of behavioralism when he sought to explicate "the current meaning" of the subject.[12] Later, Albert Somit and Joseph Tanenhaus asked political scientists what they thought behavioralism was and then agreed with Easton that the answers reflected eight "key behavioral articles of faith."[13] But Easton's eight items and those of Somit and Tanenhaus were not identical. Alternatively, Kirkpatrick offered four points that he found indispensable to researchers engaged in "the behavioral revolution."[14] Avery Leiserson* also offered four points, as did A. James Gregor.[15] Yet theirs did not match each other, nor those of Kirkpatrick. If we take these scholars to be either behavioral-

9. "The Behavioral Approach in Political Science: Epitaph for a Monument to a Successful Protest," *American Political Science Review* (December 1961), p. 770.

10. "The Impact of the Behavioral Approach on Traditional Political Science," in Howard Ball and Thomas Lauth, eds., *Changing Perspectives in Contemporary Political Analysis* (Englewood Cliffs, N.J.: Prentice-Hall, 1971), p. 79.

11. "Political Science as Science," in ibid., p. 47.

12. "The Current Meaning of 'Behavioralism' in Political Science," in James Charlesworth, ed., *The Limits of Behavioralism in Political Science* (Philadelphia: The American Academy of Political and Social Sciences, 1962), pp. 7–8.

13. *The Development of Political Science: From Burgess to Behavioralism* (Boston: Allyn and Bacon, 1967), pp. 177–79.

14. "The Impact of the Behavioral Approach," pp. 73–76. He later offered a list of eight "salient characteristics" of the "political behavior" movement, in Evron M. Kirkpatrick, "From Past to Present," in Donald M. Freeman, ed., *Foundations of Political Science: Research, Methods, and Scope* (New York: Macmillan, 1977), pp. 23–24.

15. Leiserson, "The Behavioral Approach," in Robert Connery, ed., *Teaching Political Science* (Durham: Duke University Press, 1965), pp. 61–62; Gregor, *An Introduction to Metapolitics* (New York: Free Press, 1971), pp. 19–20.

ists or neutral observers, the avowed critics were no more consistent.[16] It is not surprising, then, that Bernard Susser despaired of achieving a theoretical description and in 1974 concluded that behavioralism, for practical intents and purposes, was "nothing more than the application of precise scientific methods to the study of politics"[17]—whatever those methods might be.

If behavioralism had any definite character, it does not appear in the contradictory accounts of points of fact and theory involved in the postwar switch to a new form of science. Yet there was a certain behavioral understanding of how to proceed professionally in support of a free society, and it can be seen by reconstructing what happened in the discipline of political science after World War II. In that analysis, it becomes clear that behavioralism strongly resembled Popperism in many respects. The congruence between the two goes far to explain why the behavioral approach was originally attractive for combining science with socially useful research, and why its usefulness was consequently challenged, when the mid-century liberal matrix became less persuasive and Popperism as an overall scheme for social inquiry began to fall from grace during the late 1960s.

Basic Behavioral Tenets on Science

Early and leading behavioralists, such as Gabriel A. Almond,* David Easton, and David B. Truman,* very strongly but only generally committed themselves to scientific inquiry in the late 1940s and early 1950s. Later they and their disciples gradually worked out and recorded the details of that commitment, as they sought in the 1950s and 1960s to instruct and persuade others to accept their point of view. Seen thus as an organic whole, slowly unfolding, the behavioral approach to political analysis was predicated upon what we may call an "initial dichotomy" between science and nonscience.

The Initial Dichotomy

What joined behavioralists from the start was a presumption that a kind of inquiry exists which deserves the name and reputation of science, whereas other intellectual efforts fall short of this goal and should only be called unscientific. In the very simplest terms, the key to this dichotomy was the distinction between

16. For example, see the account of behavioralism in Marvin Surkin, "Sense and Non-Sense in Politics," in Marvin Surkin and Alan Wolfe, eds., *An End to Political Science* (New York: Basic Books, 1970), pp. 13–33; and the critique of modern political science expounded by John S. Gunnell in his *Philosophy, Science, and Political Inquiry* (Morristown, N.J.: General Learning Press, 1975). Both of these authors use categories of analysis not directly compatible with any of the lists of behavioral characteristics offered by the sources cited in notes 12–15, above.

17. "The Behavioral Ideology: A Review and a Retrospect," *Political Studies* (September 1974), p. 272.

the realm of what is and the realm of what ought to be. Science deals with what is, and nonscience—which might be theology, ethical theory, ideology, or something else—takes as its province those things that ought to be.

We can now recognize this initial dichotomy as vital to Popperism, since Popper too aimed at resolving contradictory claims with respect to what is scientific and what is not. Both the behavioralists and Popper saw nothing inherently wrong with nonscientific beliefs, for no one can be certain these are devoid of truth. Indeed, the realm of nonscience, so to speak, being the realm of what ought to be, is unquestionably important, and people wish to know how they should live with regard to the issues addressed by nonscientific study and the resolutions proposed by its practitioners. Behavioralists, however, in the hope of avoiding controversy over intangible matters, took as their proper concern the realm of investigations into concrete actuality, which they chose to call science. And so Harold Lasswell* and Abraham Kaplan held that "the basic concepts and hypotheses of political science" should contain "no elaborations of political doctrine, or what the state and society *ought* to be."[18] Or, as David B. Truman concluded for behavioralism specifically, "inquiry into how men *ought* to act is not a concern of research in political behavior."[19]

Testability

How, exactly, does science differ from any other way of seeking knowledge of the real world? Popper held that the hallmark of science properly so-called is a very special sort of research method, and behavioralists followed him in affirming the principles that were fundamental to his point of view. Thus, like Popper, leading behavioralists held that "testability" is a crucial requirement of scientific propositions. "In the language of science," wrote Heinz Eulau,* "definitions must be operational. No matter how concrete or abstract conceptually, they must be relevant empirically."[20] Or, in Somit and Tanenhaus's description of behavioral research, "inquiry should proceed from carefully developed theoretical formulations which yield . . . 'operationalizable' hypotheses, that is, hypotheses which can be tested against empirical data."[21]

This proposition was repeatedly restated by behavioralists. Indeed, it was fundamental to the point where Easton argued that the vital difference between most pre–World War II political scientists and behavioralists lay precisely in the latter's insistence on testability.[22] Ideally, adherents of the new approach would

18. *Power and Society: A Framework for Political Inquiry* (London: Lowe and Brydone, 1952), p. xi.

19. "The Implications of Political Behavior Research," *Items* (December 1951), pp. 37–38.

20. *The Behavioral Persuasion in Politics* (New York: Random House, 1963), p. 6.

21. *The Development of Political Science*, p. 178.

22. "The Current Meaning of 'Behavioralism,' " p. 15.

frame political statements in such a way that their propositions could be denied or confirmed, and thereby add to the general stock of political knowledge. Nevertheless, writings based on nonscientific approaches to political analysis continued to crop up in the discipline's professional literature from time to time, and provided frequent examples of the sort of formulations which, to behavioralists, seemed impossible to check and assimilate into a fund of reliable learning. For example, there would be no way of grappling scientifically with the assertion, by Thomas I. Cook and Malcolm Moos in 1952, that "a genuine foreign policy necessitates absence of hypocrisy."[23] How can one test empirically for the absence, or presence, of hypocrisy? And who can confirm, or deny, that a foreign policy is genuine?

Falsifiability

Logically, of course, anyone who asserts that science is an enterprise based upon testable propositions must come to grips with the problem of what constitutes correct and useful techniques of testing. Again in agreement with Popper, behavioralists recognized that the difficulties of reasoning by induction make absolute verification impossible. They therefore accepted the process of disproving as an integral part of science properly understood. As Goldberg said, "the heart" of the scientific enterprise consists first of an imaginative hypothesis and then "verification (more properly, falsification)."[24] Reiterating the same point, Lawrence Mayer held that "A scientific statement consists of a statement . . . that implies or specifies a precise category of conceivable observations that would be logically incompatible with it."[25]

Popper had observed that falsification tests can at least remove a great many mistaken beliefs from the accepted stock of political knowledge. Eulau made the same point when he claimed that "the methods of science do not so much function to create knowledge as to reduce ignorance."[26] Karl W. Deutsch* agreed when he recommended that political scientists pursue what he called "implication analysis."[27] For example, Plato's theory of human nature implies that a certain proportion of children will be born gifted. The present population may be studied in order to test this implication and, if it turns out to be false, Plato's theory is either entirely invalid or in need of modification. In Deutsch's

23. "Foreign Policy: The Realism of Idealism," *American Political Science Review* (June 1952), p. 352.

24. "Political Science as a Science," p. 47.

25. *Comparative Political Inquiry* (Homewood, Ill.: Dorsey, 1972), p. 46.

26. "Comment on Professor Deutsch's Paper," in James Charlesworth, ed., *A Design for Political Science: Scope, Objectives, and Methods* (Philadelphia: The American Academy of Political and Social Science, 1966), p. 182.

27. "Recent Trends in Research Methods," in ibid., p. 169.

opinion, political scientists would do well to use this kind of analysis to shed a realistic light on all basic political beliefs.

Tentativity

The function of falsification procedures is negative rather than positive, inasmuch as such tests serve to deny rather than to confirm our beliefs. This reality led Popper to accept "tentativity" as a corollary to the tenet of falsifiability. Behavioralists took the same step, for, as one scope-and-methods textbook remarked, "theory is an imperfect and changing tool. Thus, if we have learned anything from the history of science, it is that history is a graveyard of scientific theories once considered useful."[28] The point was reaffirmed by James N. Rosenau, when he observed that "what we ascertain to be true is never a complete certainty," and therefore even what we call "the facts" are only "probability statements."[29]

Scholars who enjoy remunerative research grants, and perhaps even occasional consulting fees, are not likely to dwell upon the fact that, logically speaking, what they call scientific knowledge may be entirely mistaken. Still, behavioralists did commit themselves in principle to the inevitability of tentativity, and this tenet was forcefully expressed, for example, by Eulau, author of many testaments to the new outlook. Eulau stipulated that a behavioralist must constantly remind himself that all which he holds true may at any time be proved false.[30] He must therefore remain entirely open-minded and ready to believe in new, if also temporary, truths. This was the skepticism, according to Eulau, which distinguished behavioralists from earlier political scholars, those who, when speaking of science, envisioned it as an exercise in certainty.[31]

The Importance of Method

From testability, falsification, and tentativity, Popper moved to the putative importance of scientific methods over results, and this fourth point also appeared in behavioralism. For example, when Truman discussed science, he spoke of methods rather than results. To this end he cited Ernest Nagel, a philosopher of science, to the effect that the "scientific method is the persistent critique of arguments, in the light of tried canons of judging the reliability of the procedures by which evidential data are obtained, and for assessing the probative force of the

28. David H. Everson and Joann Poparad Paine, *An Introduction to Systematic Political Science* (Homewood, Ill.: Dorsey, 1973), p. 142.

29. *The Dramas of Politics: An Introduction to the Joys of Inquiry* (Boston: Little, Brown, 1973), pp. 18–19.

30. *The Behavioral Persuasion in Politics*, p. 10.

31. "The Behavioral Movement in Political Science: A Personal Document," *Social Research* (March 1968), p. 20.

evidence on which conclusions are based."[32] Kirkpatrick took the same view when he said that science is "a body of systematic and orderly thinking about a determinate subject matter."[33] Again, there was no mention of results. Apparently, what behavioral political scientists did deserved to be called science not because of their accomplishments, whatever these might be, but because the work was "modeled after the methodological assumptions of the natural sciences."[34] In this sense, political scientists were seen as potential novitiates for a larger vocation, if only they would adopt appropriate habits. In the words of one enthusiast, "Science is a method for acquiring knowledge and not knowledge itself. Those who employ the method and abide by its rules are players of the game, whatever their field."[35]

The Scientific Community

The right scientific method was crucial, to both Popper and the behavioralists, because it leads research toward maximally reliable conclusions. In both the physical and the social sciences, there can be no guarantee that investigators will uncover startling new facts or develop vital new information. But scientific method, properly employed, can at least reduce the margin of possible error inevitably attaching to all beliefs, and thus expand the scope of acceptable knowledge, whence the behavioral opinion that science is commendable for providing "a systematically articulated and comprehensive body of maximally reliable knowledge claims."[36]

Why was reliability so important? Popper had noted that the diverse personal origins of all scientists may bias their work, and that this bias raises the problem of the sociology of knowledge. Eulau agreed, and therefore held that the real "task of [scientific] method . . . is not to eliminate all subjectivity . . . but to maximize intersubjectivity."[37] Or, as Gregor phrased the same conclusion, "Without reliability argument and deliberation cannot proceed," and "rationality itself is . . . abandoned."[38] Thus if political scientists would only adopt the principles and procedures of science, patiently checking each other's propositions, the discipline could come to constitute a scientific community, with reliable results, in the Popperian style.

32. Ernest Nagel, *The Structure of Science* (New York: Harcourt, Brace and World, 1961), p. 13; cited in David B. Truman, "Disillusion and Regeneration: The Quest for a Discipline," *American Political Science Review* (December 1965), p. 871.
33. "The Impact of the Behavioral Approach," p. 71.
34. Easton, "The Current Meaning of 'Behavioralism,' " p. 9.
35. Rosenau, *The Dramas of Politics*, p. 121.
36. Gregor, *An Introduction to Metapolitics*, p. 21.
37. Eulau, "Comment on Professor Deutsch's Paper," p. 182.
38. Gregor, *An Introduction to Metapolitics*, p. 23.

Extensions of Popperian Science

And so the major articles of behavioral faith—the initial dichotomy, testability, falsifiability, tentativity, the importance of methods, the link between reliability and the scientific community—conformed to Popper's understanding of science. There were, in addition, two more behavioral convictions about science that deserve note. As they appeared in the discipline's writings, these two had no precise analogue in Popper's work. They were Popperian in kind, however, for they represented a logical extension of his view as developed by those trying to practice science, in contrast to Popper, who only wrote about it.

Building Blocks of Science

The first quasi-Popperian tenet may be called the "building block" idea of science. Because the world, both physical and social, is large and complicated, scientific researchers try to learn about it by first studying small bits and pieces of the whole. Accordingly, scientific inquiry may be defined as the process of acquiring a reliable fact here and another there, with the intention of putting them together occasionally to construct some broad understanding of reality. As David Easton made this point, "Only by . . . chopping the world up into manageable units of inquiry . . . can political science . . . [acquire] reliable knowledge."[39] In the process, "seemingly remote, often minute details, about scales, indices, specialized techniques for collecting and analyzing data and the like, these details are the building blocks of the edifice in which more reliable understanding occurs."[40] This means all scientists should use the scientific method on a little of this and a little of that, with some discovering facts and others evolving improved techniques for discovering further facts. As a collectivity, the scientific community will thus gather information that, in effect, constitutes building blocks from which structures of theory and generalized knowledge can be constructed.

Now it is a fact of scientific life that most researchers work on minor enigmas, either because they lack the genius for attacking people's largest problems or because money, staff, and laboratory facilities are in perpetually short supply. Behavioralists therefore needed the building-block notion because impressive results did not immediately appear when they of necessity worked on small matters, or, in Popper's words, when they engaged in piecemeal research. Perhaps the circumscribed discoveries of ordinary chemists and biologists spoke for themselves, but there were always people who charged that the assembly of bits and pieces of social information, however scientifically achieved, lacks co-

---

39. "The New Revolution in Political Science," *American Political Science Review* (December 1969), p. 1054.
40. Ibid.

herent direction and therefore leads to no more than a meaningless sample of insignificant odds and ends. In *Knowledge for What?* (1939), Robert S. Lynd wrote that social research lacking an overall and thoughtful objective may become like "the ditty bag of an idiot, filled with bits of pebbles, straws, feathers, and other random hoardings."[41] Eulau argued, to the contrary, that research projects about small matters must not be judged trivial until scientists have first considered how all of them will fit together as a larger picture of reality. That is, "An empirical discipline is built by slow, modest, and piecemeal cumulation of relevant theories and data."[42] Only when a great many pieces of the mosaic are available can they be weighed against one another, the valuable ones brought to the fore, and relevantly chosen pieces used to construct a complete contribution to knowledge.

Standing alone, the building-block notion was not very convincing. At bottom, it simply claimed that separate building blocks resulting from scholarly research are important because they may eventually be brought together as components for more inclusive edifices of scientific knowledge. But even if such blocks were not random elements, the combinations built from them might still contribute nothing of value to general knowledge. In other words, the synthesizing propositions that science builds up out of smaller bits of evidence might themselves collectively form no configuration of great consequence, but instead remain structures strewn haphazardly across the landscape of human consciousness.

Straight Lines of Knowledge

Because the building-block theory was weak, behavioralists reinforced it with a second quasi-Popperian concept, which may be called the "straight line" view of knowledge. This view emerged when they spoke as if scholars once knew really very little about the nature of man and society, whereas scientific research now steadily produces knowledge to the point where we do know more and more about what concerns us. In graphic terms, the idea was that science is engaged in an upward, straight-line progression from ignorance to a higher plane of learning and understanding. Thus the straight-line view assures us that adherence to the scientific method must lead eventually to cumulative and useful knowledge instead of only scattered propositions that add nothing to our understanding of the world. For a very clear example of the straight-line vision, we have Easton's contention that "Each transition, from philosophy to natural and moral philosophy, to moral and natural science, then to the social sciences, and now to behavioral sciences, signals a stage in a truly linear movement in the nature and assumptions about our understanding of man in society."[43]

41. (orig., 1939; Princeton, N.J.: Princeton University Press, 1970), p. 183.
42. *The Behavioral Persuasion*, p. 9.
43. "The Current Meaning of 'Behavioralism,' " p. 13.

The link between the building block and the straight-line notions of science was revealed in a passage from Karl Deutsch's work. "The truth," he wrote, "may reside not so much in any one kind of data, or in the result of any one technique."[44] That is, the structures of knowledge which scholars build from small research findings may indeed stand isolated and insignificant. Deutsch continued, however, to claim that "truth may be thought of as a relationship between different streams of evidence. A statement . . . contains the more truth the larger the part of the information contained in it which will have to be included in any successor statement to it, reformulated or revised, by which the original statement will have to be replaced in the light of new evidence."[45] Here, Deutsch was asserting that while every lesser discovery or finding may be of slight value, new and important truths will emerge from the relationships among minor accomplishments of the scientific method, and thus knowledge in its totality will progressively expand. So viewed, science can be relied upon to increase our understanding of any subject to which it is applied. Thus the assertion that "We know more about politics than Plato could ever conceive. We know more about politics, in fact, than did our teachers. It seems equally evident that our students will know more about politics than we."[46]

One must sympathize with the professional frustration that lay somewhere behind the straight-line notion. Political scientists have long been uncomfortably aware that students of the natural sciences spend very little time learning about the origins of knowledge in their respective fields. Potential young biologists, for example, do not first intensively study Aristotle, then move on to luminaries such as Harvey, Darwin, Mendel, Pasteur, Watson and Crick, and finally arrive at the most up-to-date formulas and equations. The study of politics, in contrast, traditionally started with Greek thought and, by progressing slowly through history and the great books, left relatively little time for strictly modern events and analytical techniques. It was, professionally speaking, a program of learning cluttered with so many antiquarian relics as to dismay those who aspired to scientific status. The eagerness of behavioralists to jettison some of their discipline's standard fare was therefore perhaps only slightly exaggerated by Glendon A. Schubert in 1969, when he discounted "traditional political science education" by comparing it to physics. "Physics has been able to incorporate concepts of specific gravity without requiring every student in a first-year lab course to climb into a bathtub," said Schubert. "That small residue of the work of *any* scientific generation that has relevance to the on-going work of the profession is retained; but most of what gets done becomes, mercifully, forgotten."[47] If only

44. "Recent Trends in Research Methods," p. 158.
45. Ibid.
46. Gregor, *An Introduction to Metapolitics*, p. 275.
47. "The Third Cla't Theme: Wild in the Corridors," *PS* (Fall 1969), p. 596.

political science could do the same. As George E. G. Catlin remarked, surely the time had come to move beyond an "endless academic gnawing of the small bones of Kant."[48]

The Behavioral Persuasion

With behavioralism appearing in the political science discipline after World War II as a form of Popperism, it is appropriate to refer to the new approach to political inquiry as "the behavioral persuasion," especially as this term was employed by Eulau in a book widely read by political scientists and their students.[49] Eulau used this term to suggest that he and his colleagues had in mind much more than a series of abstract rules of procedure for political analysis. Rather, they envisioned themselves as spokesmen for a very broad and deep conviction that the political science discipline should (1) abandon certain traditional kinds of research, (2) execute a more modern sort of inquiry instead, and (3) teach new truths based on the findings of those new inquiries. What all this meant is clear from what we know about the nature of the mid-century liberal matrix of discourse. Since behavioralists were basically liberal, like most political scientists, they could be expected to repeat Popper's example, doing their work in such a way as to reject ideological speculation and to highlight the virtues of existing political arrangements within American society. And this was precisely what happened, when members of the new school turned their attention to practical research and worked out some of the features of what was truly a persuasion, rather than merely a set of technical recommendations. The first step was to take a stand on the issue of political theory.

The Decline of Political Theory
From the very beginning, behavioralism gave an added impetus to what political scientists still call "the decline of political theory." In the late 1940s and early 1950s, even as membership in the discipline expanded, there was a marked decrease in the number of political scientists willing to devote their professional attention and energy to traditional—that is, philosophical—political theory. By 1956, political theory had so far fallen in favor that Peter Laslett regretfully announced its demise.[50]

In the broadest sense, what happened was a logical reflection of the point of view summed up in the initial dichotomy. It was not that philosophical matters

48. "The Function of Political Science," *Western Political Quarterly* (December 1956), p. 815.
49. See note 20, above.
50. "Introduction," in Peter Laslett, ed., *Philosophy, Politics and Society*, First Series (Oxford: Basil Blackwell, 1956), p. vii.

were deemed unimportant in principle, but that there seemed no way of dealing with them scientifically. In terms popular at the time, scholars increasingly accepted the proposition that a difference in kind separates facts and values. In Arnold Brecht's study of this dilemma, the modern world sees that scientists can use the scientific method to produce "intersubjectively transmissible knowledge"—a phrase indicating ideas that are patently true and therefore acceptable to everyone regardless of particular prejudices.[51] Here was the knowledge that Popper and behavioralists sought, and which is accepted as reliable by any scientific community. However, the scientific method works well only when applied to things that have tangible existence, that is, to facts. The consequences were severe for political values, which are the very stuff of traditional political theory. Because they entail loosely defined concepts such as justice, liberty, freedom, equality, and so forth, they are doomed to remain in the nonscientific realm.[52]

It follows that political studies, no matter how carefully pursued in a scientific way, may help us to achieve the ends people cherish, but they cannot prove which ends we should espouse.[53] Men of different backgrounds and faith will always entertain conflicting opinions about such matters, and political theory will therefore always be plagued by its origins, that is, by the sociology of knowledge. Here was a fact of life that seemed inescapable, especially for those scholars who knew something of linguistic theory. They knew, as Thomas Weldon had pointed out, that the very terms embodied in traditional political theory have no intrinsic meaning but only serve to label whatever men seek to define; in which case, various men will use the same labels—such as "justice"—to describe the different things they hold dear, and there is no avoiding multiple connotations when such terms are employed by several parties.[54]

So long as the alternative conclusions of a host of traditional political theories, such as those expounded by Aristotle, St. Augustine, Thomas Hobbes, John Locke, Jean Jacques Rousseau, and Karl Marx, remain matters of opinion rather than intersubjectively transmissible knowledge, no absolute moral beliefs about a good society, from those of the Bible, the Declaration of Independence, the Communist Manifesto, or the most recently interviewed man-in-the-street,

51. *Political Theory* (Princeton, N.J.: Princeton University Press, 1958), pp. 106f., 114f., and passim.

52. Ibid., p. 322.

53. Alfred Cobban, "The Decline of Political Theory," *Political Science Quarterly* (September 1953), p. 335.

54. As he put it, in *The Vocabulary of Politics* (Baltimore: Penguin, 1953), pp. 18–19, "The central doctrine taken for granted by all classical theorists is . . . that words have meanings in the same sort of sense as that in which children have parents. . . . [whereas in fact] words have no meanings in the required sense at all; they simply have uses."

can be proven more true than any others. Yet as David Easton observed, men who agreed that no eternal truth could be found in the great books were prone to evince a relativistic and unprofitable form of "historicism."[55] This occurred when some political scientists taught political theory as mere intellectual history. It was as if acquainting their students with an array of well-known writings and thinkers from Plato onward, while endorsing none of their conclusions, constituted the essence of teaching political theory itself. An implicit lesson of such teaching was that there is no persuasive way to choose among the great political ideals of the past and to say that any one of them embodies a true prescription for what men need in a good society. Indeed, in a world fascinated by scientific standards of proof and truth, merely to present ideas as the product of particular historical circumstances is to suggest that, as times change, the truth in those ideas diminishes.

Another lesson conveyed by the same sort of teaching was that, to the extent many "great books" of Western civilization now appeared empty of enduring truth, the void was a result of time-bound error. And so historicism in intellectual history went hand in hand with a tendency to highlight various "mistakes" made by prominent thinkers living in more primitive and superstitious times. By modern standards, the most common mistake was to jump to ethical conclusions from factual premises. Thus Leo Strauss, who believed that there really is something eternally true in the literature of political theory, complained that many modern political scholars are unable to appreciate the special validity of nonscientific moral teachings, and that this failing explains why many of their textbooks on political philosophy "will [repeatedly] give examples from Plato, Aristotle, Locke, Hume, or Rousseau and will show when and where these famous men committed a [scientific] blunder every ten-year-old child now knows how to avoid"—the error of inference from facts to values.[56]

Historicism did not stop with the notion that our predecessors had nothing worthwhile to say about politics. According to Alfred Cobban, this ethical uncertainty led some political theorists to conclude that, since specific moral standards from a particular era cannot be proved true, they should not be applied to current events in order to judge our acts but should be replaced by new morals drawn from the total panorama of history itself, so that the past may still instruct us.[57] Both Popper[58] and Cobban regarded this view as a most dangerous form of

55. Easton, *The Political System*, pp. 234–54.

56. "Political Philosophy and the Crisis of Our Time," in George J. Graham and George W. Carey, eds., *The Post-Behavioral Era: Perspectives on Political Science* (New York: McKay, 1972), p. 227.

57. "The Decline of Political Theory," pp. 333–34.

58. See Karl Popper, *The Poverty of Historicism* (orig., 1957; New York: Harper and Row, 1961).

historicism, which can produce lasting devotion to fixed ethical principles even while denying that they can be found in the annals of ordinary philosophy. And so Cobban joined Popper in condemning a reliance on history for encouraging some theorists to emulate Hegel and Marx by praising the historical accomplishments of certain nations as a demonstration of their culture's worth, even though the same culture might have gained its success by aggressive war or some other clearly immoral course of action. Here was the sort of systematic but invalid inference that behavioralists associated with what they called ideology.

The Rejuvenation of Political Theory

The basic idea was twofold—that speculative theory is fruitless, and hence the first sort of historicism, and that it can also be dangerous, and hence the critique vis-à-vis historicism of the second variety. In either case, behavioral attention turned away from such endeavors in the hope of finding a different form of political analysis that could be pursued more usefully. Oddly enough, this superior sort of analysis, in their view, turned out to be something still called political theory, for even as leading behavioralists refused to work in the old realm of theory, they believed that their new work constituted a rejuvenation of what they chose to call political theory. Some confusion on this point was caused by overworking the term at issue, for when behavioralists spoke of political theory they gave it a new and significant meaning.

According to Neil McDonald and James Rosenau in 1968, work on traditional political theory within the discipline of political science had long constituted an academic field, which they wrote of as "Political Theory" with capital letters.[59] Within this field, scholars, researchers, and students alike had long busied themselves with explaining the immediate nature of political things, philosophizing about their ultimate nature, and creating or commenting on ideologies. Plainly, explanation and philosophy and ideology had engaged the attention of classical theorists such as Aristotle, Rousseau, and Marx, who usually mixed them up inextricably within comprehensive general outlooks on politics. The same three concerns were not all included, however, within what McDonald and Rosenau called "the conception of political theory that was generated by the postwar behavioral revolution in political science."[60]

Postwar behavioralists decided that "political theory" was a way of executing political inquiry rather than a substantive area of study—an activity and not a field. As such, McDonald and Rosenau set it apart from "Political Theory" and spelled it with lowercase letters, to indicate that the former was a general and

59. "Political Theory as Academic Field and Intellectual Activity," in Marian D. Irish, ed., *Political Science: Advance of the Discipline* (Englewood Cliffs, N.J.: Prentice-Hall, 1968), pp. 26–27.
    60. Ibid., p. 30.

speculative manner of studying political things that could be applied to constitutional law, international relations, local government, voting behavior, legislative politics, and a host of other subjects constituting fields unto themselves within academic political science departments.[61] According to McDonald and Rosenau, this view of political theory helps to explain why, in the behavioral era, political scientists worked on, and spoke of, a wide variety of political theories, including democratic theory, empirical theory, systems theory, international relations theory, roll-call theory, and so forth, in addition to the traditional matters still lodged in the field of Political Theory. All of these behavioral theories were alike, and predictably so, in that they were equally concerned with explanation to the exclusion of philosophy and ideology.

In fact, political theory as a behavioral activity rather than a long-standing field was no more nor less than the whole of behavioralism itself, obscured by a borrowed name. McDonald and Rosenau implied as much, perhaps unintentionally, when they described the non–Political Theory theorizing in terms that are now familiar to us as a shorthand expression for behavioralism. Political theory as an activity, they said, means "explaining what *is* rather than evaluating what *ought to be.*"[62] Or, as Lasswell and Kaplan had expressed the same thought earlier, "Theorizing, even about politics, is not to be confused with metaphysical speculation in terms of abstractions hopelessly removed from empirical observation and control."[63]

Whatever identity existed between the new political theory and the whole of behavioralism, it received an authoritative statement in David Easton's behavioral call-to-arms, *The Political System* (1953). Easton argued that a lack of explanatory speculation was the most urgent problem confronting the discipline in his time.[64] Political science, he said, had failed to amass reliable knowledge up to the 1950s because practitioners could not yet grasp the significance of even such political facts as they had collected. Any collection of facts about politics is either explicitly or implicitly ordered by some political theory, Easton claimed.[65] Yet insofar as the facts known to political science had been ordered by scholars who, until the 1950s, had carelessly mixed them with values, the same facts told little that was significant

61. Ibid., pp. 27f. For example, see Harry Eckstein, "Political Theory and the Study of Politics: A Report of a Conference," *American Political Science Review* (June 1956), p. 476, "all types of political inquiry involve the construction of *theory*, implicit or explicit, and . . . the title of 'political theory' has been unjustifiably appropriated by the historians of political thought." Cf. John Plamenatz, "The Use of Political Theory," in Anthony Quinton, ed., *Political Philosophy* (New York: Oxford, 1967), pp. 18–19, "By political theory I do not mean explanations of how governments function; I mean systematic thinking about the purposes of government."

62. Ibid., pp. 39–40.

63. *Power and Society*, p. x.

64. *The Political System*, chs. 1–2, pp. 3–63, and passim.

65. Ibid., pp. 53–54.

about the political world. After all, the traditional theories that linked such facts were, in Easton's opinion, flawed by unreliable philosophical preconceptions. There was need instead, he argued, for carefully examining both the existing facts and those the discipline would collect in the future, in the light of scientific procedures for assessing their significance. This new kind of theorizing would produce reliable political knowledge and therefore constitute proper theorizing about politics, even though it might fail to proceed in the manner of what had formerly and traditionally passed for political theory.

In terms similar to those of Easton, David Truman also endorsed political theory as an activity rather than a field. "In noting a revived interest in theory," he wrote, "I refer to the creation, development, or application of theory and to 'theorizing,' or the readiness to draw inferences from a set of data to the class of events to which they belong." Truman was so convinced of this enterprise's efficacy that he eventually concluded that "the choice is only between implicitly, internally inconsistent, and hopelessly inadequate theory, on the one hand, and explicit, logically defensible, and reasonably adequate theory, on the other."[66] In a similar vein, Gabriel Almond praised "the system concept," which he considered central to the behavioral notion of theorizing. It "represents a genuinely important step," he said, "in the direction of science. It is a step comparable to the ones taken in Enlightenment [eighteenth-century] political theory over the earlier classical formulations."[67]

Behavioral Democracy

In 1969, Sheldon S. Wolin, a political philosopher, severely criticized the behavioral preference for political theory as distinct from Political Theory. Referring to behavioral investigations into political matters ranging from legislative activity to bureaucratic intrigues to voter preferences, Wolin observed that "a wide variety of theories [now] exists for the political scientist to choose from. To call them political theories [in the behavioral manner] is, in the language of philosophy, to commit something like a category mistake. Systems theories, communications theories, and structural-functional theories are unpolitical theories. . . . They offer no significant choice or critical analysis of the quality, direction, or fate of public life."[68] As Wolin contended, various parts of the behavioral enterprise offered no truly political theories in his sense of the term. Yet those endeavors did provide the wherewithal for a comprehensive evaluation of American democracy, since the most common conclusions of behavioral research were regularly taken to

66. "Disillusion and Regeneration," p. 870.
67. "Political Theory and Political Science," *American Political Science Review* (December 1966), p. 875.
68. "Political Theory as a Vocation," ibid. (December 1969), p. 1063.

add up to an explanation of how the nation's institutions functioned at least adequately. And if behavioral observers such as Seymour Martin Lipset* were willing to call America "the good society" in action,[69] their view of the nation's politics could not have been entirely apolitical.

The comprehensive behavioral understanding of American politics was achieved by following a Popperian line of professional procedure. When its practitioners insisted that the main business of political science would henceforth be empirical and practical, they were taking the first step that Popper had recommended, whereby a certain kind of political analysis was read out of the realm of respectable inquiry and then largely ignored as useless to the affairs of realistic people. But the movement away from Political Theory was only the first of two steps constituting Popperism. The second was to employ the scientific method in "piecemeal social research" that would somehow benefit humanity. This second step was also taken by behavioralists, via their efforts at the new and explanatory political theory. As it turned out, theory about one particular subject was considered especially urgent. Before World War II, scientific discoveries had raised serious questions about both the rationality and the morality of democratic politics. Popper's answer to such questions was his concept of "institutional democracy," which would function as efficiently as possible under conditions where no one could be certain whose morals were best. What behavioralists faced, then, was the challenge of showing that the sum total of existing political institutions, practices, and habits in America did constitute such an institutional democracy. This they proceeded to demonstrate, on the basis of many pieces of research which, in effect, constituted small pieces of knowledge, "building blocks," from which a general understanding of democracy emerged.

The Empirical Basis of Democracy

In logical order, the first element of the new behavioral canon on democracy rested upon a decision about what evidence could be considered relevant to the subject. On this point, a Popperian stance was taken when, as Henry B. Mayo put it, political scientists decided that the "validity" of democratic principles can be "established by empirical investigation."[70] In other words, the researcher is not expected to decide in advance what democracy ought to be, and then to see if his political environment matches that ideal. Such a course of inquiry would only encourage him to begin his work with metaphysical speculation, of the type favored by ideologues and the old Political Theory. Behavioral researchers, to

69. Seymour Martin Lipset, *Political Man: The Social Bases of Politics* (Garden City, N.Y.: Doubleday, 1960), p. 403.

70. "How Can We Justify Democracy?" *American Political Science Review* (September 1962), p. 559.

the contrary, preferred to start empirically, to look at the world, see which countries are commonly called democratic—such as England and the United States—and then study them to find out how they work in a way deserving of that name. As James W. Prothro and Charles H. Grigg carried this point into action, "Our research design was based upon the major assumption that the United States is a democracy. Taking this point for granted, we prepared an interview schedule around the presumably basic principles [beliefs held by citizens] of democracy."[71] Here was the way to explain what goes on in real democracies, as opposed to what Machiavelli called "imaginary republics."[72]

Anti-Absolutism

As for what really happens in existing democracies, it will be recalled that there had been some prebehavioral feeling—such as that reflected in Deweyism—that absolute moral convictions can be dangerous in politics. Moreover, if in principle the need for such convictions was inescapable, one then confronted a philosophical problem of deciding which values to espouse. As early as 1942, Carl J. Friedrich* addressed the issue of moral beliefs and concluded that "what binds a free people together is not an agreement on fundamentals, but a common way of acting in spite of disagreement on fundamentals."[73] In a real-world democracy such as America, Friedrich observed that what obtained was agreement on procedural ideas rather than on solutions to specific problems.

This important aspect of institutional democracy was confirmed by the empirical investigations of the new political theory. Prothro and Grigg, for example, asked respondents to give their opinions concerning two sets of propositions. The first contained abstract statements, such as: "Public officials should be chosen by majority vote." The second contained more specific statements, such as: "If a Communist were legally elected mayor of this city, the . . . people should not allow him to take office." A clear pattern of opinion was revealed, with 94 to 98 percent of the respondents agreeing in their answers on abstract matters, while 21 to 80 percent agreed with regard to specific issues.[74] Since the respondents were, by definition, democratic citizens because America was, by stipulation, a democracy, these figures meant that democracy runs well on the basis of procedural consensus rather than by recourse to dangerous, because absolute, moral faith.

71. "Fundamental Principles of Democracy: Bases of Agreement and Disagreement," *Journal of Politics* (May 1960), p. 282.

72. Nicolo Machiavelli, *The Prince* (Baltimore: Penguin, 1961), ch. 15, pp. 90–92.

73. *The New Belief in the Common Man* (Boston: Little, Brown, 1942), p. 181.

74. "Fundamental Principles of Democracy," pp. 282–85.

Tolerance

Having concluded that devotion to fixed beliefs was inadvisable, by the early 1940s liberals decided that the true virtue of a democratic society must be "tolerance," or willingness to accept the fact that anyone can err and that everyone should therefore be guaranteed the right to express opinions in an attempt to persuade the majority to adopt them as a temporary basis for government policy. Dewey, Herring*, and Popper all spoke, each in his own way, of the need for citizens to display, in their public behavior, that skepticism and open-minded receptivity to new ideas which characterized the scientific temperament. In the new political theory, the very devotion of most Americans to abstract generalities could be viewed as evidence of tolerance, for they agreed upon how to proceed in politics, how to let every citizen have his or her say. In the works of Truman and Dahl, therefore, tolerance was seen as a crucial element of democratic behavior, softening the letter of the law with a spirit of decency and moderation. Accordingly, Truman praised widespread devotion to what he called "the rules of the game," which Americans believe require that there be "fair dealing" with all individuals.[75] And Dahl wrote favorably of "the democratic creed," popularly entertained and calling for procedural impartiality and flexibility via majority rule, individual rights, and so forth.[76]

The Dangers of Equality

It was not enough to remain at a high level of generalities and say that American democracy worked well because it was rooted in broad convictions as to procedure. Political scientists also had to confront the concrete results of living with such convictions, and some of those results did not square well with the hopes and expectations shared by men of good will, including liberals. Thus there was no escaping the fact that American society suffered important manifestations of inequality, that some people were rich even while others were poor, some powerful and others weak, some educated and others ignorant, some skilled and others unskilled, that some were socially acceptable while others faced discrimination. The problem, then, was how to commend an institutional democracy which, however fine in theory, led to notable degrees of inequality. What was the sense of it all? And might not radical critics—from native populists to foreign adversaries—deserve more attention for the arguments they persistently made on behalf of greater equality and social justice in America?

The new empirical theory developed by behavioralists dealt with great disparities in the distribution of resources and rewards by emphasizing that some

75. *The Governmental Process* (New York: Knopf, 1951), pp. 512f.
76. *Who Governs? Power and Democracy in an American City* (New Haven: Yale University Press, 1961), pp. 316f.

measure of inequality had highly desirable effects upon American society as a whole, in spite of what burdens it might impose upon those individuals adversely affected. They acknowledged that members of the elite have more than their share of money, leisure, education, and good health, and that it is the few, rather than the many, who wield most of society's political power. But they also argued that people who are relatively privileged are more likely than the masses to support democracy itself, in which case the existence of elites and their exercise of great power are somewhat desirable, first impressions notwithstanding.

Thus Seymour Martin Lipset wrote descriptively of what he called "working-class authoritarianism" and pointed out that the poorer strata of Western society were most likely to support Communist parties and least likely to endorse liberal and democratic principles such as civil liberties and internationalism.[77] Herbert McClosky drew the same conclusion, and argued on the basis of survey research that "the uninformed, the poorly educated, and . . . the less intelligent" people of America are the ones most likely to be conservatives, whom he defined as "the most hostile and suspicious, the most rigid and compulsive, the quickest to condemn others for their imperfections or weaknesses, the most intolerant, . . . the most inflexible and unyielding in their perceptions and judgements."[78] And when David B. Truman wondered aloud in 1959 about "the capacity" of the American political system "to survive," he was hopeful that the well-to-do, the knowledgeable, the informed, and the interested—the elite as represented among politicians, lawyers, media, corporations, unions and churches—would maintain the rules of procedure necessary for democracy on the grounds of "consequences" rather than "transcendental doctrine."[79]

The Efficacy of Apathy

In Truman's lexicon, "consequences" referred to effective results, whereas "transcendental doctrine" hinted at dangerous ideological impulses. It was as if behavioral studies combined to show that lower-class people simply do not fit the requirements for good citizenship according to Dewey and Popper, that they are insufficiently pragmatic, open-minded, skeptical, and tolerant, from which it followed that there is a certain social utility in the relative weakness of the disadvantaged as compared with the usual power of the well-to-do. On this score, underlying behavioral composure concerning elites was a notion of rationality congenial to the new liberal matrix. From the behavioral point of view, there could be no denying that many men are less rational than liberals once thought.

77. *Political Man*, pp. 87–126, but esp. p. 92.

78. "Conservatism and Personality," *American Political Science Review* (March 1958), pp. 27–45, but esp. pp. 35, 37.

79. "The American System in Crisis," *Political Science Quarterly* (December 1959), pp. 481–97, but esp. pp. 481, 491.

In addition, however, behavioralists held that there should be no overlooking a corollary to this reality, for empirical research showed some people to be more rational than others, more able to understand political issues and to act upon them intelligently. Here was a point to be thoroughly appreciated, because careful investigations also registered the fact that real world democracies, as opposed to utopian fancies, operate on the basis of high participation by elites, with their superior political knowledge, and low participation by nonelites, who might impair the political process with their undemocratic attitudes.

And so behavioralists found a significant link between inequality and "apathy," a general term used to characterize the mental state of people in democratic countries who did not bother to vote or to inform themselves about political matters. Apathy perforce diluted whatever amount of political power and influence the nonactive might have had to begin with. Yet some scholars maintained, as one put it, that "apathy in a democracy is a good thing."[80] As they saw it, there should be no brief for denying political rights to any people so as to exclude them from political participation. Nevertheless, so long as civil rights are formally guaranteed and all citizens are free to exercise them equally, we should take some comfort from the fact that people whose opinions are most likely to be "misguided"[81] are also the most likely to do nothing about them. At the very least, according to the champions of apathy, a low level of political activism by the politically passive leaves most of the molding of public policy to others of a higher political character, say, to those who can take a "global point of view."[82] Then too, a generous amount of political apathy throughout the nation, for which we have mainly to thank the lower class, means that some voters are always available to be mobilized in support of new and popular causes, thereby lending to American politics a degree of flexibility lacking in totalitarian competitors—notwithstanding their 99 percent voter turnout.[83]

None of these explanations of inequality, elitism, limited rationality, or apathy, should be taken to suggest that behavioralists were indifferent to the fate of the poor or the oppressed. But writing with a heavy awareness of the history of nondemocratic regimes and the events of World War II, mainstream scholars did tend to emphasize the value of any factor that contributed to moderation, compromise, gradual reform, and domestic tranquillity generally. Inequality and apathy should eventually be reduced, they believed, but both should be treated

80. Morton Grodzins, *The Loyal and the Disloyal: Social Boundaries of Patriotism and Treason* (orig., 1956; New York: Meridian, 1966), p. 245.

81. Herbert McClosky, "Consensus and Ideology in American Politics," *American Political Science Review* (June 1964), p. 376.

82. Philip E. Converse, "The Nature of Belief Systems in Mass Publics," in David E. Apter, ed., *Ideology and Discontent* (New York: Free Press, 1964), p. 247.

83. Dahl, *Who Governs?* pp. 305–10f.

with care. Dahl was apparently pleased to see progress in the struggle against racial inequality, which had long entailed formal denial of civil rights and therefore violated the tolerant notion of fair play.[84] And as to apathy, Robert E. Lane* recommended that more political participation be encouraged together with increased education and personal income, so that the latter resources would influence the character of the former act, to the benefit of all.[85]

The First Question

All this was very well as far as it went, to explain with some satisfaction various aspects of democratic politics. But if elites do rule, reasonable as that may be, should there not be some way of restraining them when the need arises? Popper had assumed that democrats must create some mechanism of control over the strong because he believed all men, including a nation's leaders, are necessarily fallible. For this reason he called upon modern scholars to ask how political institutions "may be set up so that bad or incompetent rulers can be prevented from doing . . . damage."[86] Merely to ask the question was to imply that checks and balances must go into the makeup of "institutional democracy."

It is not surprising that behavioralists, whose logic and political stance so closely resembled those of Popper, also repeated his choice of questions. What they discovered, or what their empirical research confirmed, was that many people do not bother to vote, that those who do are often ill-informed, and that a relatively few people make most of the polity's most important decisions. Given these relevant facts, how did America's democracy control its rulers? Or, as Robert A. Dahl and Charles E. Lindblom* rephrased the Popperian query, here was "the First Problem" of politics, "the antique and yet recurring problem of how citizens can keep their rulers from becoming tyrants."[87]

The Role of Groups

Empirical political theory explained that within an ever-present environment of civil rights for all citizens, two main devices, built into the American system of elite rule, led to control over the relatively powerful few. First, there was an elaborate realm of group politics. The function of political interactions in such a realm was highlighted by scholars who remarked upon the absence of independent groups in totalitarian societies. Hannah Arendt, for example, showed how both the Soviet Union and Nazi Germany deliberately destroyed or neutralized

84. Ibid., pp. 293–96.

85. *Political Life: Why People Get Involved in Politics* (Glencoe, Ill.: Free Press, 1959), pp. 327–57.

86. Karl Popper, *The Open Society and Its Enemies*, 4th ed. (orig., 1945; New York: Harper and Row, 1963), vol. 1, p. 121.

87. *Politics, Economics and Welfare* (New York: Harper and Row, 1953), p. 273.

parties, classes, churches, unions, and other groups, leaving individual citizens socially atomized, cut off, with no loyalties or perspectives or interests other than those of the ruling class and the state.[88] Morton Grodzins[89] and William Kornhauser[90] worked with the same historical examples, and their writings helped to impress upon American scholars the importance of maintaining pluralism—a host of competing power centers—in an open society.

For political scientists, David B. Truman offered the most complete statement of a group theory in *The Governmental Process* (1951).[91] Truman first noted how evidence of the presence and influence of groups had accumulated in many small research works, and then he advanced a thoroughly democratic explanation as to how they served American society and why they should be permitted to continue to do so. As Truman saw it, people are animated by many diverse concerns and, through the exercise of civil rights, can express those interests via groups of like-minded others. Fortunately, those groups are characterized by what Truman called "overlapping memberships."[92] By this he meant that each person has many interests and can join many groups, with the result that any one group member's ideas are always moderated and restrained by the ideas of people in the same group who have conflicting interests in other groups. The sum total of groups in America works, then, so as to present powerful but moderate demands to political rulers, which they can ignore only at great electoral danger to themselves. There could be no doubt, as the evidence on elites showed, that only a few people would actually exercise power even in a democratic state. But so long as the realm of group politics is nourished by the existence of civil rights and frequent elections, Truman's theory showed that it could constitute an important institutionalized control over the powers that be, whereby the "active minority" is impelled to represent the "inactive majority."[93]

Political Parties

In the judgment of behavioralists, the second device that operated in America to restrain rulers was the two-party system. They saw democratic political parties as vehicles serving the group level of politics, somewhere between the masses and the elites. Parties were thus available to aggregate the interests and the votes of

88. Hannah Arendt, *The Origins of Totalitarianism*, 2nd ed. (New York: Meridian, 1958), esp. pp. 305–40.

89. *The Loyal and the Disloyal*, esp. pp. 69–81.

90. *The Politics of Mass Society* (Glencoe, Ill.: Free Press, 1959).

91. (New York: Knopf).

92. Ibid., pp. 156–67, and passim.

93. Michael Rogin, "Nonpartisanship and the Group Interest," in Philip Green and Sanford Levinson, eds., *Power and Community: Dissenting Essays in Political Science* (New York: Vintage, 1970), p. 112.

any number of citizens, whether they would join the party individually or as groups with clearly defined axes to grind. As Austin Ranney* observed, research showed that such parties did not rest upon widespread participation in decision making. Indeed, the actual state of affairs embodied a great deal of apathy instead. But the point was that parties did furnish a means of control over government, and that was a virtue even where citizens for one reason or another were not actively involved in the everyday course of public affairs.

Truman himself described parties as congeries of groups, and Samuel Lubell agreed. In his book, *The Future of American Politics* (1952), Lubell likened the majority party to the sun, and the minority party to the moon, and said that men see the smaller party in the light of the larger sphere's accomplishments or failures.[94] For Lubell, the two parties were constantly acquiring, holding, or losing the allegiance of various groups in the voting population, in competition with one another and therefore eager to serve the interests of voters who, by joining the party or staying with it, could assure a winning margin in the next election. Mayo commended this same American party system for offering choices to democratic citizens, which totalitarian governments do not, and he very explicitly described the operation of the two-party system as "one which institutionalizes popular control of policy-makers."[95]

The Analogy to Science

The mid-century liberal matrix, in both its Deweyian and Popperian versions, suggested that true understanding of democracy must rest upon an analogy between science and society, that is, between a scientific method for seeking the truth and a political method for making decisions, between a scientific community of scholars checking each other's work and a political community of citizens assessing each other's interests. Assuming that the starting conception of science was correct, occasional references to this analogy reinforced a conviction that political systems functioning along similar lines must be desirable.

Mainstream Political Science

Forward-looking political scholars in the postwar era took the parallel between science and society almost for granted, and they assumed that its implications constituted a powerful argument on behalf of existing liberal institutions. Thus Quincy Wright* observed in 1950 that science rests upon a philosophy of "nominalism and relativism." It was a typical Popperian definition that sounded almost bland by that time. Continuing from this stipulation, Wright went on to con-

94. (New York: Harper and Brothers, 1952), pp. 198–205.
95. "How Can We Justify Democracy?" p. 556.

clude that "science resembles [democratic] politics. Both are pragmatic and relativistic." There was the analogy. It followed that "Absolutists like Hitler and Stalin seek to eliminate politics by subordinating all parties to one,"[96] which was Wright's way of agreeing with Dewey and Popper that adherence to fixed truths fails the test of effective results. And finally, we have Wright's notion that "To liberals, a continuous competition of ideas in a free marketplace of discussion" is the ideal toward which democracy should strive.[97] Of course, that makes sense via the comparison to science and the contrast to Nazism and Stalinism.

Perhaps the most elaborate version of the scientific analogy appeared in Thomas Landon Thorson's *The Logic of Democracy* (1962).[98] Thorson definitely believed that the efficacy of science demonstrates the desirability of democracy, and he began his explanation of "the logic" of this situation by noting that science aims to find out "how the world is."[99] Since knowledge gained by science is not certain, however, he went on to assert that scientists must be determined not to "block the way of inquiry."[100] Then came the analogy. Political acts are also taken with regard to the way the world is. Yet they suffer the same fallibility as do scientific endeavors, and therefore we are "obligated to construct a decision-making procedure that will leave the way open for new ideas and social change."[101] As Thorson put it, the commanding principle of democracy is "Do not block the possibility of change with respect to social goals."[102] In his opinion, therefore, and according to behavioral political theory generally, a fully flexible political system must be democratic, based on popular sovereignty, political equality, individual political rights, and majority rule.[103] Thorson thus offered a prescription for institutional democracy fully compatible with the realities of American politics as revealed by empirical research.

The Second-Best Utopia

An inherent weakness in the analogy between science and democracy was that whatever science might reveal about the world, it could say nothing conclusive about how we should live there. Popper himself was perfectly aware of this situation as it must affect people's understanding of their surroundings. "In the

96. "Political Science and World Stabilization," *American Political Science Review* (March 1950), p. 5. [Nominalism is the philosophical doctrine that general or abstract words do not stand for objectively existing entities but are only names assigned to individual physical particulars which alone have objective existence.]
97. Ibid., p. 3.
98. (New York: Holt, Rinehart).
99. Ibid., p. 119.
100. Ibid., p. 121.
101. Ibid., p. 139.
102. Ibid.
103. Ibid., pp. 140–43.

case of a scientific theory," he wrote, "our decision depends on the results of experiments. . . . But in the case of a moral theory, we can only confront its consequences with our conscience."[104] Behavioralists, too, recognized the problem, and they admitted that even while democracy is as commendably open as science, "it does not answer all the questions of political philosophy, and certainly not the greatest of all—those concerned with 'final' or 'ultimate' ends."[105] There was, however, some comfort to be taken from the fact that even if democratic procedures cannot lead us automatically to answers about how we should live, they are available to help us correct our perceived mistakes. The argument along these lines came in two parts, which we may draw together from the works of two scholars.

When Gabriel A. Almond compared American to non-American political systems, he concluded that the "Anglo-American" form of polity rested upon bargaining and compromise that to a "Continental European" might seem "sloppy," with neither logic nor clarity.[106] But Almond went on to argue that Anglo-American regimes were in practice superior to others precisely because, as Thorson would argue, they resembled a scientific community. As Almond put it, the Anglo-American polity, by which he meant the arrangements which fall within the category of institutional democracy, has "some of the characteristics of a laboratory; that is, policies offered by candidates are viewed as hypotheses, and the consequences of legislation are rapidly communicated within the system and constitute a crude form of testing hypotheses."[107] The key word here was "testing," for in the second part of this line of argument David Spitz pointed out that the capacity for testing is actually the means for reversing error.[108] And so even if democratic procedures cannot lead us to any sort of promised land, they can assure the opportunity for resuming our journey on a felicitous road if we stray too obviously from it.

What finally emerged in the work of Almond and Spitz was a second-best sort of rationale for liberal democracy. One could not prove that America is the perfect society, but it did enjoy a political system that "provides the necessary mechanism for its own correction."[109] The logic had been familiar to political scientists at least since Charles Beard* told the story of democracy's leaky old scow, which couldn't keep your feet entirely dry, but wouldn't sink either. In the post–World War II era, this point seemed especially convincing when linked to

104. *The Open Society*, 2, p. 233.
105. Mayo, "How Can We Justify Democracy?" p. 559.
106. "Comparative Political Systems," *Journal of Politics* (August 1956), p. 398.
107. Ibid.
108. *Patterns of Anti-Democratic Thought*, 2nd ed. (orig., 1949; New York: Free Press, 1965), pp. 294f.
109. Ibid.

Cold War realities that served as a constant backdrop to scholarly research and teaching. There was, for example, the illustration offered by Ignazio Silone in *The God that Failed* (1950),[110] a collection of recantations by former Communists in several Western countries. "Liberty," said Silone, "is the possibility of doubting, the possibility of making a mistake, the possibility of searching and experimenting, the possibility of saying 'no' to any authority." It was a respectable Popperian view. "But that," replied one of the directors of the [U.S.S.R.] State publishing house, "that is counter-revolution." Here was a Stalinist conclusion justifying severe political repression. Such stories were particularly instructive to a nation locked into confrontation with regimes installed by force and maintained, regardless of their errors, by the same instrument.

The Revised Perspective

Some final points of empirical political theory deserve mention, for it is important to note that even while behavioralists were devoted to American democratic practices, they justified their affections on grounds somewhat different from the ideals of earlier liberals. In fact, they were especially enthusiastic about the benefits that democracy conferred on the American polity as a whole—a sort of G.N.P. approach—whereas earlier liberals had seen the virtues of the system mainly in individual terms. Therefore, behavioralists were willing to tolerate a good deal of inequality, apathy, ignorance, and so forth, whereas John Stuart Mill, the greatest of all nineteenth-century Anglo-American liberal thinkers, was impatient with precisely such conditions. In his opinion: "The worth of the state, in the long run, is the worth of the individuals composing it; and a State which postpones the interests of their mental expansion . . . will find that with small men no great thing can really be accomplished; and that the perfection of machinery to which it has sacrificed everything will in the end avail it nothing, for want of the vital power which, in order that the machine might work more smoothly, it has preferred to banish."[111]

Mill in fact agreed with traditional liberals who believed that men possess, or are capable of acquiring through education, a capacity for reason, and this is why he held that government must do all it can to promote the development of that capacity. But as we have seen, this liberal faith in men's rationality could not be defended against the discoveries of science. It was therefore eventually dodged by arguing that, even where men are less rational than once expected, they can be brought together politically in ways that permit many ideas to be expounded

110. In Richard Crossman, ed., *The God that Failed* (New York: Harper, 1949), esp. p. 90.
111. *On Liberty* (orig., 1859; New York: Library of Liberal Arts, 1956), pp. 140–41.

and tested until useful policies are proposed and executed. In the behavioral era this accommodation to irrationality, at first carried out through an elegant side-step, finally achieved explicit articulation in some detail.

The behavioral shift away from the old perspective, and the reasons for it, were succinctly outlined by the liberal economist Joseph A. Schumpeter. In his *Capitalism, Socialism and Democracy* (1942), Schumpeter observed that in eighteenth-century philosophy, democracy was defined as "the institutional ar-rangement for arriving at political decisions which realizes the common good by making the people itself decide issues through the election of individuals who are to assemble in order to carry out its will."[112] Here was what may be called the "mandate theory" of democracy, for it assumed that a nation's citizens—or, to be more exact, a majority of them—can knowingly decide what they want and then instruct representatives as to how to attain it. This theory ultimately became untenable, Schumpeter argued, when discoveries about limited human rational-ity showed that phrases such as "the common good" cannot be defined precisely, that "the people" are neither knowledgeable enough nor skillful enough to decide what is good for them and to express their opinions forcefully to govern-ment officials. And so there simply cannot be an intelligible mandate, in the traditional sense of that term. The best that can be attained is popular control in the event that rulers are patently tyrannical or outrageously mistaken.

In the light of this scientifically determined reality, Schumpeter offered a new and empirical definition of democracy. Based on consideration of the facts in existing democratic states, he suggested that the democratic method in politics is embodied in "institutional arrangements for arriving at political decisions in which individuals acquire the power to decide by means of a competitive struggle for the people's vote."[113] In contrast to the mandate theory, we may call this second definition the "process theory" of democracy, on the grounds that the perceived key element is a special process that assures some measure of popular control but no particular instruction to governors.[114]

The process theory of democracy comported well with those considerations that went into the mid-century liberal matrix and, as a reflection of that frame of reference, it was adopted into behavioral political science after a classic study of voting published by Bernard Berelson and several colleagues in 1954. Like Schumpeter, Berelson found that citizens were often indifferent to politics, that many were uninvolved, that some were progressive in their views while others were conservative, that some were in favor of individualism and some were for

112. 3rd ed. (New York: Harper and Row, 1950), p. 250.
113. Ibid., p. 269.
114. See David M. Ricci, "Democracy Attenuated: Schumpeter, the Process Theory, and American Democratic Thought," *Journal of Politics* (May 1970), pp. 239–67.

collectivism, that some were tolerant and others were not. To judge by the evidence, there was no longer reason to say that citizens are, or can be, "rational" in the sense that the term connotes some uniform ability to think in a way which will bring diverse people to agree upon common answers to political questions. Berelson concluded that if men are not rational, there is something seriously wrong, either with American society or with the liberal philosophy that assumes such men to be present in that society.[115] And this led him to the further conclusion that the liberal set of ideals was at fault. Paradoxically, even though citizens are not up to the standards set by liberal philosophy, the democratic political system is empirically sound, for it produces a considerable measure of stability, economic prosperity, and social progress.[116]

Building upon voting studies such as that by Berelson, and having Schumpeter's definition of democracy at hand for briefly stating their point, many behavioralists discarded the idea that there can be a mandate flowing directly from an informed and alert citizenry up to their government. Instead, they saw democratic policy as resting upon a tangle of complicated pressures, from the lower class and the upper class, from the rich and the poor, from the informed and the uninformed, from the tolerant and the intolerant, all operating either as individuals or as groups. This, at least, was the situation as it obtained in those countries known to be democratic, where the conditions of life seemed, on the face of things, more commendable than those in totalitarian states. In a book-length study of democratic practices in five countries, Gabriel A. Almond and Sidney Verba summed up the discipline's approval of no-mandate regimes when they concluded that an explanatory theory of democracy—in the sense of descriptive political theory as advocated by behavioralists—must conform to the facts as they exist.[117] Primary among those facts was that "rational-activist" citizens, in the phrase used by Almond and Verba, are relatively rare even in England or America. Judging from democracy's success in those countries, however, large numbers of rational-activists do not constitute the sine qua non of a free society, and real-world democracy can operate satisfactorily when elites, groups, the masses, pressures, attitudes, rights, and rules combine to form a "civic culture."[118] Nowhere is political life as simple as earlier liberals had supposed. On the other hand, neither constant confusion nor intractable complexity should give rise to civic despair.

115. Bernard R. Berelson, Paul F. Lazarsfeld, and William N. McPhee, *Voting: A Study of Opinion Formation in a Presidential Campaign* (Chicago: University of Chicago Press, 1954), pp. 311–13.

116. Ibid., pp. 322–23.

117. *The Civic Culture: Political Attitudes and Democracy in Five Nations*, abr. ed. (Boston: Little, Brown, 1965), pp. 339–40.

118. Ibid., pp. 337–74.

The New Citizenship

With appropriate extensions, the revised perspective helped political scholars to fulfill their professional obligations with regard to teaching good citizenship. It will be recalled that before World War I, the political science discipline had taken upon itself responsibility, within the universities, for teaching about the political devices and behavior that are necessary to sustain a good society. After that war, the conflict between scientific research findings and liberal convictions concerning desirable public life became apparent, and practitioners were forced to admit that they had very little to say, scientifically, in support of the nation's political system. Their devotion to it did not wane, however, and after World War II, in an intellectual climate represented by the new liberal matrix, political scientists reaffirmed their responsibility for citizenship training.

In the late 1940s, the American Political Science Association conducted a survey of more than two hundred and fifty colleges and universities offering undergraduate and graduate degrees in political science, in which data was gathered concerning typical courses, methods of instruction, and pedagogical objectives. The published report, entitled *Goals for Political Science* (1951), concluded that "Amongst political scientists in the United States, training for intelligent citizenship is the predominant interest and emphasis."[119] In a later survey volume, based on data compiled for the National Academy of Science and the Social Science Research Council, Heinz Eulau and James G. March echoed the earlier report and announced in 1969 that "education for citizenship" was one of the major goals of the discipline. According to Eulau and March, "By far the largest investment of time and effort by political scientists is in teaching and in political education," where research is commendable for informing "the textbooks that support the discipline's teaching mission" and for assuring that what they convey is "valid, reliable, and relevant."[120]

Continued commitment to teaching good citizenship was therefore evident, but the objective itself was not easy to define. As *Goals for Political Science* reported, "the difficulty" lay in "deciding what citizenship means and how best to go about producing it."[121] Now this was not a chance predicament, since American democrats, with no absolute aims firmly in mind, could only envision good citizenship in terms of moderate and decent behavior—a style of life—rather than as a list of specific steps to take in pursuit of preordained ends. Then too, after World War II some scholars warned that the "creation of good citizens" was not a matter to be dictated precisely, even if exactitude in such matters were

119. American Political Science Association, Committee for the Advancement of Teaching, *Goals for Political Science* (New York: William Sloane, 1951), p. ix.

120. *Political Science* (Englewood Cliffs, N.J.: Prentice-Hall, 1969), p. 8.

121. *Goals*, p. ix.

possible. There was always some danger, after all, that education toward that end might turn into "indoctrination," a reprehensible practice of totalitarian states.[122] Still, recent history indicated that democracy needed a very special sort of citizens, because authoritarianism, as in Nazi Germany, could come into being where men and women are no more than patriotic and law-abiding. And so political scientists were likely to define good democratic citizenship in terms of a capacity for independent judgment, for staying well informed, for taking an interest in public affairs, and for applying to political issues a commonsense notion of tolerance and fair play.

People who do enjoy this capacity do not necessarily acquire it through deliberate training—that is, indoctrination. But they may gain the requisite skills and outlook by taking some person or special group of people as an ideal example, what sociologists might call a "role model." Thus political science teachers, whose work may display great intellectual integrity and vigor, are capable of affirming important liberal values and indirectly making good citizens. And so, instead of various recipes for good citizenship—a bit of this and a pinch of that—one finds, in post–World War II political science, that practitioners went about their work as if the results of scholarly research would speak for themselves. Textbooks did not include sections entitled "good citizenship," but teachers did acquaint their students at every opportunity with the findings of behavioral research, thereby explicitly passing the message that democracy is a complicated business and implicitly indicating that good democratic citizens will let awareness of this complexity shape both their behavior and expectations accordingly. In the sense that expressions of professional judgment constituted, in effect, lessons on what democratic citizens should know and take into account when they act politically, we may take two "teachings" as typical of the behavioral persuasion. These concerned parties and progress.

The Report on Parties

In 1950, the APSA's "Committee on Political Parties" published a report entitled *Towards a More Responsible Two-Party System.*[123] This report was not an official document of the Association, and therefore its contents did not represent the opinion of the discipline as a whole. Nonetheless, the Committee aimed at a wide audience, hoping that lay readers would first accept its work as an important professional statement with regard to good citizenship and then adopt its major recommendations, calling for important structural reforms. For all the attempt at

122. Louis Hartz, in "Goals for Political Science: A Discussion," *American Political Science Review* (December 1951), pp. 1001–05.

123. American Political Science Association, Committee on Political Parties, *Towards a More Responsible Two-Party System* (New York: Rinehart, 1950).

advocacy, however, the report's basic view of American politics was not entirely accepted even by the authors' professional colleagues. Leading behavioralists found it unconvincing, and its recommendations found no prominent place in their teaching during the behavioral era.

As a central thesis,[124] the report claimed that the American two-party system operated as "two loose associations of state and local organizations, with very little national machinery and very little national cohesion." As a result, neither major party was equipped, when in power, to produce a government that held together on the basis of party program. And because of this, "Party responsibility at the polls . . . [tended] to vanish." With party platform vague as to goals, voters could not know just what their vote supported. Moreover, the nation's domestic and foreign policies suffered for having "to deal piecemeal with issues that can be disposed of only on the basis of coherent programs." To improve this situation, the Committee recommended a long list of reforms,[125] including biennial party conventions, regional party meetings, two-year party platforms, committees for party leadership in both houses of the Congress, four-year terms of office for Congressmen, equal size for congressional districts, direct election of delegates to national party conventions, and a national election-day holiday to stimulate voter turnout. If the lines of authority and responsibility were not made clearer to the public, said the Committee, the executive branch of government would grow dangerously strong, apathy might cause the major parties to distintegrate, and third parties might step into the breach with well-defined but narrow-minded policy proposals.[126]

The report was received unenthusiastically by many political scientists then rising to professional prominence, and their criticisms of it revealed the extent to which they were inclined to teach that existing political institutions required nowhere near as much reform as the report recommended. For example, while conceding that neatness and order were lacking in American political life, as the report claimed, Austin Ranney pointed out that democracy, in the United States at least, is predicated upon two conflicting principles, of majority rule and minority rights.[127] The problem with these two principles, each admirable in its own right, was that where one is fully realized, some sacrifice must be made with regard to the other. That is, where the majority decides, a minority may be trampled; whereas if minorities can uphold their interests in any event, the majority may fail to enact policy on behalf of the public as a whole. As Ranney observed, given the nation's sympathy for competing interests, large and small, it

124. Ibid., p. v.
125. Ibid., pp. 5–11.
126. Ibid., pp. 13–14.
127. *The Doctrine of Responsible Party Government* (Urbana: University of Illinois Press, 1954), pp. 160–62f.

followed that American parties could never be rebuilt as neatly as the report on the two-party system seemed to believe.

Criticism of the two-party report appeared from time to time in various postwar studies of parties and voters,[128] but the full weight of behavioral dissatisfaction with the report was summed up only in 1971, when Kirkpatrick wrote a retrospective essay designed to show how evidence contradicting the report had accumulated in the 1950s and 1960s. Kirkpatrick relied heavily on behavioral terms of reference. For example, he noted that the report hoped for increasing intervention by ordinary citizens in party affairs, so as to provide delegates and representatives with useful instructions concerning public policy. According to Kirkpatrick, though, research on political behavior demonstrated that most people are not capable of informed and sustained political participation. As he concluded, "The cumulative impact of voting studies on the Committee [on Political Parties] model of the responsible party doctrine is, quite simply, devastating."[129] Along the same lines, Kirkpatrick held that the report had advanced "a theory of democracy which conceives mass participation in policy decisions as crucial (choice among those competing for the right to rule is not enough)."[130] But to expect more participation rather than rule by elites, as we have seen, was to reject Schumpeter's process model of democracy. Kirkpatrick was therefore right in Schumpeter's camp when he said that the report had mistakenly accepted "the mandate theory" of representation.[131] And finally, Kirkpatrick complained that the theory was faulty for positing, too optimistically, a "rational-activist conception of citizenship."[132] It was a charge that came straight from Almond and Verba's work on the civic culture. In sum, Kirkpatrick accused the report of special pleading, whereby a particular set of moral principles had been incorporated into a document purporting to be based on the facts. In his opinion, the report's authors had slighted scholarly and scientific standards of research, and in the process ignored political realities that contradicted their thesis.[133]

Incrementalism
To some extent, the two-party report was a throwback to the days when liberals had routinely believed in the postulates of rationality and responsible govern-

128. For citations on this point, see Gerald M. Pomper, "Toward a More Responsible Two-Party System? What, Again?" *Journal of Politics* (November 1971), pp. 916–40.

129. Evron M. Kirkpatrick, "Toward A More Responsible Two-Party System: Political Science, Policy Science, or Pseudo-Science?," *American Political Science Review* (December 1971), p. 972.

130. Ibid., p. 966.

131. Ibid., p. 967.

132. Ibid.

133. Ibid., pp. 979–85.

ment. Consequently, it was so much at odds with scientific research findings as to be more ignored than explicitly criticized in the heyday of behavioralism. But while by inattention they disavowed a traditional view of good citizenship, behavioralists were at the same time especially heedful of whatever combinations of competing interests can actually be achieved in a democratic society, and of how such combinations may be fostered most efficiently. In this regard, a notion of serendipitous incremental change, rather than deliberate and long-range planning based on popular participation and consent, became the hallmark of modern political science teachings.

One early example of enthusiasm for incremental change came in *Politics, Economics and Welfare* (1953), by Robert A. Dahl and Charles E. Lindblom.[134] Here, concepts from the new liberal matrix were plainly and forcefully expressed, with frequent references to Karl Popper and his book *The Open Society.* Human irrationality was admitted, if somewhat overstated, in the assertion that "like Winnie-the-Pooh, he [man] is an animal of very limited brain."[135] From this "obvious limitation" on our capacity for intelligent thought, elaborated with suitable references to Freud and psychological problems such as compulsion, rationalization, and repression, Dahl and Lindblom went on to observe that circumstances and surroundings must also be taken into account when men seek to act. It followed that, where our talent for understanding is small and social pressures are great, the most efficient course of action must consist of "incrementalism," which Popper had called "piecemeal social engineering."[136]

By incrementalism, Dahl and Lindblom meant a series of policy adjustments starting from the basis of existing policy, recognizing its advantages and disadvantages, and continuing in small steps via calculated risks, where immediate additions to old policy will not at once achieve all goals but at the same time will not unduly invite unforeseen consequences. Here was a process of social choice aimed at avoiding the temptations of "utopian thinking" that masquerades as "rational calculation,"[137] and designed instead to proceed on the basis of cautious steps forward whose results we can, given our limitations, predict fairly well. To this end, said Dahl and Lindblom, students of politics should search out and cultivate those procedures and institutional devices that constitute aids to the necessary sort of policy calculation. They themselves spoke of discussion, codification, quantification of comparable values, sampling, delegation of choices to experts, and science itself, as aids to calculation for incremental social choice.[138] Their teaching on this subject defended American society largely as it was,

134. See n. 87, above.
135. Ibid., p. 60.
136. Ibid., p. 82.
137. Ibid., p. 86.
138. Ibid., pp. 65–88.

enjoying institutional democracy and receiving occasional recommendations from various social scientists regarding the probable consequences of different feasible social programs.

The behavioral era produced many more writings on the subject of incremental change, some of which we shall discuss in a later context. For the moment, it is enough to note only the derivative concept of "disjointed incrementalism," a term that summed up the discipline's mainstream teachings very usefully. In *Strategy of Decision* (1963), David Braybrooke and Lindblom argued that there were two ideal decision-making procedures, neither of which could work in a real-world democracy such as America. The first was the "rational-deductive" scheme, under which men start by establishing certain values as their goals, then ascertain the facts and estimate the consequences of alternative actions, and finally decide on the optimal social policy.[139] This decision-making ideal will never be implemented in public affairs because, as we know from scientific research, men will not agree from the outset as to which values are to be pursued. For Braybrooke and Lindblom, the second possible model for decision making was the "welfare-function" ideal, where values do not have to be specified in advance but where men express "direct preferences among various possible [existing] states of affairs in society. . . . Such preferences . . . [consist of] reactions to all the features of each state of society that might be subject to preference."[140] But this scheme is also doomed to failure, or so we are told by modern research findings. For even when they are not required to agree on fundamental principles of long-range moral strategy, men are unable to combine their short-run desires into a simple and attainable hierarchy of collective preferences. As a result, their immediate notions of what to choose from existing circumstances clash as inevitably as their ultimate goals, which means that the "welfare-function" scheme is as impossible to realize in practice as the "rational-deductive" ideal.

What actually obtains in America, according to Braybrooke and Lindblom, is a process of decision-making best known as "disjointed incrementalism."[141] On the one hand, small policy steps are taken without reference to unattainable consensus on grand objectives: this is the factor of incrementalism. On the other hand, a great many political actors—from voters to interest groups to parties to bureaucrats—must be consulted before anything gets done: here is the disjointed quality of the process as a whole. To understand this process as being the best that reality permits, is to learn that good citizenship does not rely on a checklist of specific and necessary acts but consists mainly of making the best of the

139. David Braybrooke and Charles E. Lindblom, *Strategy of Decision* (Glencoe, Ill.: Free Press, 1963), pp. 9–12.
140. Ibid., pp. 12–16.
141. Ibid., pp. 83–102.

American situation, of keeping options open, of supporting pluralism of groups and ideas, and of otherwise contributing to a maximally efficient process for gaining information and combining it with a host of interests to produce moderate and effective policy.

The Marxian Connection

Of course, one great post–World War II lesson on good citizenship had been learned by the entire nation, and it centered on the undesirability of Marxian perspectives and policies. This was a matter that received direct treatment in political science courses on subjects such as "comparative government" and "modern ideologies," where an extensive anticommunist literature came into existence during the behavioral era.[142] It was also an affair that the profession touched upon obliquely, however, in the sense that typical political science outlooks, as expressed in the behavioral persuasion, contradicted the Marxian position even where specific Marxian tenets of science and analysis were not denounced explicitly. In terms of the larger place held by political science in American life, and from what we have seen of the mid-century liberal matrix into which behavioralism fitted so comfortably, this anti-Marxism was perfectly logical, as the discipline maintained its customary support for liberal sentiments shared with Americans beyond the groves of academe.

There was, for example, the behavioral insistence on empirical research defined as inquiry into men's circumstances and capacities. On the basis of data generated by such research it seemed clear that, even where democracy flourishes, few citizens are capable of the sort of rational calculation and persistent activism postulated by earlier theorists of democracy. And so behavioralists did not hesitate to conclude that human character, in our time at least, does not warrant a thorough reconstruction of society in the hope that all citizens will subsequently attain equality of abilities and influence over public policy.

This approach to political analysis, and its logical conclusion, were anathema to Marxism. Marxists start from a presumption that empirical reality is no more than a reflection of whatever shape the existing society chooses to assume. It follows that to study people as they exist under capitalism will only reveal their nature as it emerges stunted and warped by the struggle for private profit, which engulfs people who must engage in free enterprise. For Marxists, the findings of research into human behavior under such circumstances should not be accorded even temporary truth value. They tell us nothing about what sort of society is

---

142. For example, A. James Gregor, *A Survey of Marxism: Problems in Philosophy and the Theory of History* (New York: Random House, 1965), and George Lichteim, *Marxism: An Historical and Critical Study* (New York: Praeger, 1961).

appropriate to man's real nature, which is a function of his essential, rather than historical character. This character is summed up in the Marxian concept of "species man"—a phrase indicating that human capacities and needs flow from irrevocable membership in a species, rather than from the particular society in which we live—and Marxists hold, as an axiom of unalterable truth justifying radical political policies, that people are fundamentally more rational and capable than current evidence reveals.

Even where political scientists did not disparage Marxism by name, the foregoing comparison shows how deeply a rejection was built into the very structure of conventional scholarly procedure. Simply to teach political science according to the modern professional canon was to come close to demonstrating an anti-Marxian approach to political questions, where answers hostile to the Left were the inevitable outcome of an enterprise that political scientists offered to their students as the uniquely scientific and therefore solely reasonable thing to do. In this respect, Marxism suffered the faults of any effort at "Political Theory" as a form of political philosophy. Thus when that realm was discounted because it encouraged speculative thinking of all kinds, the Marxian concept of species man was made to appear suspect for contradicting the weight of empirical evidence. Insistence on such notions automatically relegated their advocates to a place in the category of "ideologues," whose work was not so much challenged as disregarded. Quincy Wright predicted as much when he said in 1951 that, after a "general education in political science. . . . It is hard to see how a political scientist can be either a Nazi or a Communist."[143]

Insofar as the actual functioning of a democratic society was concerned, behavioral research had much to say about groups, parties, and elites—the rich and the poor, the apathetic and the active—and about how all these can operate together in a pluralistic society where many power centers sustain the process of disjointed incrementalism. The main assumption underlying the analysis was this: there is no set of ends so patently true as to justify perpetuating a particular public policy indefinitely, therefore all people are entitled to speak out concerning their interests and how these might be advanced together with those of others. If the assumption is true, the enormous variety of political actors in a pluralistic society is necessary in order to bring all interests to light and to make them available for inclusion in the final compromises that constitute desirable policy.

In Marxian terms, this syllogism was entirely invalid. Marxists believe, instead, that all noncommunist societies are divided into social classes, where one stratum rules and the other, or others, is subordinate. They therefore hold that the competition of elites, parties, and groups in America is no more than an

143. "Political Science and World Stabilization," pp. 7–8.

internal affair of the ruling class, where the eventual compromise of expressed interests serves the needs of that class alone and leaves the objectives of other classes unsatisfied. The underlying assumption of the Marxian syllogism here was diametrically opposed to that of mainstream political science. The Left is convinced that there exists a set of ends which can be specified irrespective of the immediate interests of individuals, and that it is by this standard that the acts of government should be judged democratic or not. Yet if this assumption is valid, public policy must be accorded support for its substance rather than for its origin in an open and competitive society. And that was the claim which, in behavioral eyes, left the way clear for ideologues to insist on rule by men with a special talent for reading the lessons of history and recognizing therein the course which, alone among all others, will produce an ideal society. Rather than judge American democracy by whatever standards such men might propose, political scientists preferred to use the test of effective results on real-world political systems. As Dahl concluded in 1970, although "polyarchy [democratic plural-ism] shows up badly compared with unrealized ideal forms [such as Marxist models of future democracy], it looks very much better when it is compared with other political systems that have actually existed up to the present. In particular, [polyarchy looks good] when it is placed alongside rival political forms that have been tried out in this century—waves of the future that swept the people overboard."[144]

The Prevailing Optimism

In retrospect, the behavioral era in political science appears to be a time of optimism. The great challenges of an economic depression and a world war had been dealt with successfully just before the era began. Moreover, while issues such as the Vietnam War and civil rights were beginning to receive national attention, in their early stages such matters seemed capable of satisfactory resolu-tion within the democratic framework. Going into the mid-1960s, then, behav-ioral writings on institutional democracy—as a complicated compendium of checks and balances, groups and individuals, activism and passivity—dovetailed neatly with what was being said in many intellectual circles. In *The Democratic Prospect* (1963), philosopher Charles Frankel proclaimed that the basic analogy between science and democracy was sound, and that the virtue of an open society lay not so much in its particular policy but in the fact that "it permits second thoughts" to be expressed through elections, thereby controlling rulers and protecting the public against "errors so fatal that there is no peaceful way out

144. Robert A. Dahl, *After the Revolution? Authority in a Good Society* (New Haven: Yale University Press, 1970), pp. 140–41.

or back."[145] For the country as a whole, such sentiments seemed quite reasonable. They were probably all the more persuasive for being confirmed by the continuing totalitarian example, which suggested that whatever ills a free society might suffer, they could not compare to those imposed by a patently repressive regime. Historical generalizations are always risky, but it may be fair to say that John F. Kennedy expressed the spirit of the age when he declared, in Berlin in 1963, that "Freedom has many difficulties and democracy is not perfect, but we never had to put a wall up to keep our people in."[146]

The Knowledgeable Society

Two essays by Robert E. Lane deserve special mention for the way in which, even as they partook of the larger optimism, they also indicated where political science might make its professional contribution to the good times then underway and yet to come. In "The Politics of Consensus in an Age of Affluence,"[147] and in "The Decline of Politics and Ideology in a Knowledgeable Society,"[148] Lane argued that modern Americans were slowly but surely moving into an age of affluence and reconciliation. Solid progress was already evident, in Lane's view, to the extent that class cleavages were softening, that religious harmony was spreading, that demands for racial equality were being met, and that personal satisfactions in life were growing steadily.

Lane's thesis offered a very special explanation of where the pattern of improvement was coming from. As he put it, most of the progress could be attributed to a decline in social, political, and economic friction occasioned by an increase in both the sum of available scientific knowledge and the uses to which it was put in informing public opinion and shaping governmental action. The marked influence of such knowledge caused Lane to describe America as "a knowledgeable society." This was a state, in Lane's terms, wherein people seek knowledge properly, that is, scientifically, and, in place of sheer power or electoral advantage, make it the basis of public policy. In the political vocabulary common both to behavioralism and the times, Lane saw knowledge as the opposite of ideology, and to the extent that the former rather than the latter will guide people in their understanding of social needs, we shall all profit. With regard to contemporary history, Lane saw signs of knowledge-laden decisions in many realms of political behavior. For example, more government employees than ever before were being hired under merit procedures instead of by patronage appointment, government expenditures were increasingly tailored to standards devised by impartial officials of agencies such as the General Services Administration, the Office of Economic

---

145. (New York: Harper and Row), pp. 174–76.
146. Quoted in Theodore C. Sorenson, *Kennedy* (New York: Harper and Row, 1965), p. 601.
147. *American Political Science Review* (December 1965), pp. 874–95.
148. *American Sociological Review* (October 1966), pp. 649–62.

Opportunity was trying to deal objectively with deep-seated and complex problems of poverty, and research institutions such as universities and the Rand Corporation were generating statistics and other data to be applied in resolution of numerous issues on the public agenda.

Lane's essays provide instructive insight into two key perspectives entertained by many political scientists in the behavioral era. First, there was an assumption concerning knowledge, that it accumulates to our benefit. As Lane himself observed, knowledge creates a certain disequilibrium in society, for where people come to see that existing conditions can be changed, pressure usually builds up or someone to make such changes.[149] Reflecting the optimism of his times, Lane seems to have assumed that change would go in the right direction, toward more desirable circumstances. In this sense, he belonged to a profession that held, implicitly at least, that more science is better science, that modern knowledge is by and large salutory. It was the fifth liberal postulate all over again, with the pre–World War II contradictions between science and democracy either discounted or forgotten.

Second, Lane's view of modern America rested on an assumption concerning the valuable role that professional social scientists, including political scientists, can play in the nation's public life. Here, the key was a notion that knowledge constitutes a force for progress even where a pressure group or ideological impulse does not exist to urge reform in the same policy area. As a general phenomenon of modern life, there were the research institutions and the government agencies, churning out vast quantities of statistical data and interpretive theory. For specific cases where this new knowledge contributed to public policy, Lane pointed to the realms of policy concerned with poverty, crime, and health.[150] The clear message was that to the extent American democracy still did suffer from imbalances of power, with some people having more and others less, the world of higher learning could by its scholarly efforts help to create an ongoing consensus taking into account any interests that, in the world of unadorned power, might be overlooked, however temporarily. In effect, what Lane offered was an up-to-date version of the late nineteenth-century vision, where growing interdependence could best be analyzed by professionals, to the benefit of all.

The Imperative of Myth

Since optimism, for science in general and for political science in particular, was the hallmark of behavioralism in its halcyon days after World War II, it is befitting that we conclude this chapter by noting how shaky the grounds for confidence were. It all rested, in fact, on a terribly fragile relationship between

149. Ibid., pp. 661–62.
150. Ibid.

myth and reality, which concealed an intractable problem in democratic theory based upon scientific discoveries. Even Schumpeter, who stripped his definition of democracy down to a Newtonian balance between competing elites, observed that democratic devices will function successfully only within a context of convictions and habits that lead to moderation and responsibility.[151] In short, democracy in the real world cannot be reduced to a free-for-all struggle for influence and advantage without producing extreme disparities of cost and benefit for various sectors of the citizenry. It followed, as Schumpeter pointed out, that the mechanisms of democracy produce tolerable results only when deeply embedded in a culture that encourages men to work together smoothly, to accommodate to the needs of others, and to compromise at least some of their own interests on behalf of the greater good.

In *The Symbolic Uses of Politics* (1964), by Murray Edelman,[152] and in *The Civic Culture* (1965), by Gabriel Almond and Sidney Verba,[153] this sociological side of the democratic method was directly confronted. But what all three authors discovered was that, in a purely empirical and scientific sense, the necessary beliefs were erroneous, mistaken, illusory, incorrect, or invalid by any other name. It was their common finding then that in an enormously complex modern society, where decision making is usually centered in large organizations, and where information bearing on social problems may be so technical as to defy popular comprehension, most people are powerless to participate in shaping public policy. Elections may still be held, but real control over the course of America's destiny lies mainly in the hands of those who manipulate public opinion and electoral campaigns, or who reserve the resources for acting to intricate bureaucratic or professional collectivities, which simply do not respond quickly, if at all, to expressed voter sentiment.

For Edelman,[154] where democratic procedures do not fulfill the function of controlling rules, their real job must be to provide the public with symbolic gratifications; that is, elections are for expressing discontent, for articulating enthusiasm, for enjoying political involvement, and, in some overarching sense, for legitimating the democratic regime by giving it an appearance of popular support.[155] All these are necessary, he thought, if democratic rulers are to possess sufficient authority to enact laws that will be obeyed. But the voters, who provide their potentates with this authority, actually do so in a mistaken belief that ballots both instruct the government and control it where necessary. And so, Edelman

151. *Capitalism, Socialism and Democracy*, pp. 290–95.

152. (Urbana, Ill.: University of Illinois Press).

153. See n. 117, above.

154. I do not mean to imply that Edelman was a behavioralist, only that his work on political symbols highlighted a particular empirical reality.

155. *Symbolic Uses of Politics*, p. 3.

concluded, running a real-world democracy rests squarely upon this misunderstanding, upon a "myth" that enables most members of the community to continue to believe things that political scientists have already demonstrated to be false.[156]

Almond and Verba reached a similar conclusion. In their analysis, the power of elites must be checked if democratic regimes are to be moderate and effective. Voting studies had shown that citizens are neither sufficiently active nor competent enough to perform this service. It was a fact, however, that most citizens had not yet received word of their empirical irrelevance. And so they continued to participate in politics regardless of how little their efforts mattered. It was also true, fortunately, that elites were still ignorant of the findings of voting studies. As a result, they restrained themselves in the mistaken belief that voters can punish leaders at the polls. In the long run, according to Almond and Verba, the double error was all to the good, since the public continued to do what it should, while the nation's rulers refrained from doing all that they might. In effect, both sides to this equation were dependent upon "the democratic myth of citizen competence," whereas scientific political research indicated that there was no substance to that myth in modern times, if ever in history.[157]

It was an ironic situation. Institutional democracy, the excellence of elites, the efficacy of apathy, the role of groups, the function of parties, the importance of tolerance, the rules of the game, the democratic creed, the analogy to science, the open society itself—operating together, these parts of the behavioral vision could work only if the general body of citizens failed to understand what was going on around them, both with regard to the nature of political procedures and to the substance of public policy. At the same time, the discipline of political studies was bent on telling the public just how much, according to the latest scientific research, its fondest expectations for the political system were actually unfounded. Perhaps professional teachings to that effect were not, by themselves, sufficiently persuasive to undermine public faith in the so-called democratic myth. But in the decade from approximately 1965 to 1975, events in the real world would very forcefully indicate to American citizens something of how their polity really functioned, and then the old-time tension in political science—between scientific findings and scholarly support for democracy—would return to the fore, where it had reigned in prebehavioral years.

156. See ibid., p. 18, for components of the myth.
157. *The Civic Culture*, pp. 337–74.

6

The Decade of Disillusionment

During the 1960s, the mid-century liberal matrix began to lose some of its apparent validity. A host of optimistic ideas had earlier come to prominence together with enormously impressive events in the real world—including the Great Depression, the rise of fascist dictatorships, World War II, the Cold War, and post–World War II affluence—and in important intellectual and political circles these had engendered a mood of confidence that lent credibility to the matrix's basic concepts. As the 1960s gave way to the 1970s, later events produced an exactly opposite reaction. The civil rights movement, the Vietnam War, urban riots, political assassinations, disclosures about the CIA, the student rebellion, the rise of the New Left, the drug culture, the feminist revolt, antiwar demonstrations, Earth Day, the Watergate affair, the oil embargo, large-scale unemployment together with intractable inflation: these affairs, and many more, crowded upon the historical stage, all the while suggesting pessimistic lessons unreflected in the liberal matrix. As a result, many Americans came to suspect both their country's theory and its practice of democracy.

We must remember that the political science enterprise never stands alone but always works within (1) the immediate framework of a university setting and (2) the wider environment of public thinking concerning liberal democracy. Under these circumstances, it was to be expected that within the community of political scholars, there should develop much dissent concerning the way in which the discipline was, or was not, fulfilling its social obligations in a time of widely perceived crisis. In the process, behavioralism as an approach to political inquiry was severely faulted, and many practitioners, among them scholars originally committed quite strongly to the behavioral point of view, concluded that a new professional stance was required. In consequence, there was much talk about ushering in a "postbehavioral era." All of this took place against a backdrop of disillusionment, which can best be understood by first analyzing the collapse of that overall consensus within which behavioralism had seemed eminently sensible.

The Counterculture

From roughly 1965 to 1975, an enormous quantity of critical writings, expounding a great many strands of social, economic, and political thought, combined to challenge the post–World War II liberal matrix. Some were advanced by men and women seeking to overturn the existing order, while others were offered by people dedicated to preserving liberalism but fearful of trends they believed would cause that civilization to destroy itself. In light of this common opposition to the status quo, even where ultimate objectives differed, the term *counterculture* will serve as well as any to label the arguments expounded, in opposition to conventional liberalism, by men such as Herbert Marcuse, Paul Goodman, Erich Fromm, C. Wright Mills, Robert Pirseg, Noam Chomsky, Theodore Roszak, Charles Reich, and Robert Paul Wolff. These arguments were complex, and to examine them together is necessarily to do violence to the purity of notions advanced separately by various authors. The exercise is nevertheless useful at least for revealing their main and common objective, which was to foster the conviction that comprehensive rethinking of democratic realities and expectations was long overdue. In this sense, although they brought to bear diverse perspectives and looked forward to a wide range of results, there really were an impressive number of people determined to join battle with what one political scientist called "usual politics."[1]

The Political Process

To begin with, critics of the existing order insisted that the political process be reformed so as to represent adequately the interests of all citizens. In earlier years, some scholars had maintained that political groups articulate such interests satisfactorily, while elites serve them, more or less faithfully, when decisions are to be made. Large events of the 1960s and 1970s cast long shadows on both notions. Persistent racial discrimination, for one, seemed to indicate that minority groups were permanently disadvantaged in American politics, and protracted war in Southeast Asia implied the inability of national security elites either to discern the country's interest accurately or to pursue it effectively. In addition, attention focused upon bureaucracy, which did not figure prominently in political thought of the immediate post–World War II era, but which became more

1. George D. Beam, *Usual Politics: A Critique and Some Suggestions for an Alternative* (New York: Holt, Rinehart and Winston, 1970).

and more annoying, and even ominous, as government expanded and citizen dissatisfaction with officials and regulations grew apace. Then there was the wretched example of Watergate, an obvious case of wrongdoing in high places, resolved neither by the energetic leadership of prominent statesmen, nor by the persistent lobbying of organized interests, but by the fluke discovery of recording tapes that no one in public office could safely ignore.

Against this backdrop of urgent and painful events, counterculture critics rejected the comfortable vision of democratic pluralism, according to which pressure groups, elites, bureaucrats, the White House, and other familiar political actors worked together fairly well, serving themselves but at the same time promoting the public interest. To the contrary, C. Wright Mills wrote that America's real decision makers were drawn from a "power elite," which superficially seemed to represent a wide range of citizen interests but in fact brought forward influential people who shared common social and ideological beliefs that they implemented in order to maintain the existing order unchanged.[2] It was, in effect, a theory which challenged Schumpeter's reassuring notion that there is not one elite but many, among whom intramural conflicts permit various conglomerations of voters to exercise some control over the powers that be. Another far-reaching attack on the elite theory of democracy came from Herbert Marcuse, who argued that even if today's masses *could* organize in opposition to the elites, they *would not*. For Marcuse, pluralism was a one-dimensional affair, where the competing institutions of American life—the parties, the corporations, the unions, the local governments, the churches, and more—concurred "in solidifying the power of the whole over the individual," whether that person belonged to the elite or the masses.[3] By this he meant that we are all products of a complex technological civilization, where getting and spending are a way of life leading to entrenched poverty, racial discrimination, economic imperialism, and military adventurism, and where an occasional reform appearing on the political agenda of pluralism poses no threat to the great and impersonal forces which underlie and sustain that civilization. In short, Shumpeterian democracy, of the process sort, can only make sense if voters enjoy some capacity for forming an independent judgment of their own interests.[4] But if their very thinking is shaped by the society in which they live, then their occasional preference for this or that set of rulers will only reflect the needs of society in the largest sense, rather than the requirements of those individuals and groups whom the social order is intended to serve. It followed, in the opinion of Marcuse and many other critics, that there is no point in extolling the virtues of a pluralistic political process

2. *The Power Elite* (New York: Oxford University Press, 1956).
3. Herbert Marcuse, *One-Dimensional Man* (Boston: Beacon, 1964), p. 50.
4. Ibid., p. 6, and passim.

within which, as a result of advertising, public relations, and educational indoctrination, people cannot direct their thoughts and efforts toward building a radically new society—one that might be, rather than one that is.[5]

Incrementalism

If we are to understand why imbalance in the political process could lead so moderate a critic as Theodore J. Lowi to predict "the end of liberalism,"[6] we must appreciate the sense of urgency that pervaded many works of dissent in this era. In the liberal matrix, political pluralism was made to appear as an adjunct of the open society, wherein a vector of clashing forces produced small and praiseworthy policy changes under various names, such as "piecemeal social engineering" or "incrementalism," always assuming that egregious errors can be corrected and the damage contained. Counterculture critics were dubious of such concepts, seeing in the political and economic trends of their day reason for denying the notion that partial policy reforms would produce long-run benefits, or that there would be time enough to correct the sort of potentially disastrous errors that were possible in modern America.

There was, for example, the overriding question of what to do about nuclear weapons and atomic power stations. With regard to the former, continuation of superpower confrontation held out the threat of worldwide holocaust, while as to the latter, related risks of nuclear mishap and waste disposal threatened to create extremely dangerous local pollution. In both cases, it appeared that incremental adjustments to existing policies were unlikely to avert larger threats.[7] In either area, therefore, the perceived danger of a single fundamental mistake was enough, for some observers, to disconfirm the reassuring idea that, under the reign of political pluralism, errors can over time be corrected.[8]

Just as incremental decision making seemed inadequate for the Bomb and its offspring, so, too, small steps appeared incapable of dealing properly with racial discrimination and the environment. Progress in race relations was painfully slow, and many people said that the delay perpetuated distressingly low levels of black income, education, employment, and housing. To blacks themselves, the costs of gradualism were obviously high. The slogan "Freedom! Now!"

5. Ibid., pp. 209–10.

6. *The End of Liberalism: Ideology, Policy, and the Crisis of Public Authority* (New York: Norton, 1969).

7. See the critique of Herman Kahn's notion of nuclear "escalation"—an incremental strategy—in Philip Green, *Deadly Logic: The Theory of Nuclear Deterrence* (Columbus: Ohio State University Press, 1966), pp. 165–84f.

8. J. William Fulbright, *The Arrogance of Power* (New York: Random House, 1966), p. 4: "The stakes are high . . . when for the first time in human history, a living generation has the power of veto over the survival of the next."

became a plain-spoken way of saying that small changes were not enough, and that mistakes made today would never be corrected satisfactorily in the stunted lives of their victims. Martin Luther King, Jr., made the same point when he explained to whites why—a century after the Emancipation Proclamation— blacks just "can't wait" any longer for racial justice and equality.[9] Coincidentally, it was a phrase that underscored similar sentiments among those fearful of incipient ecological disaster. In the Club of Rome's widely read report, *The Limits of Growth*, existing trends in population growth, consumption of natural resources, food production, and industrial pollution were extrapolated, whereupon it seemed clear that unless policies in both developed and underdeveloped countries were drastically revised, then war, or famine, or disease would inevitably deal with the results.[10] As in the case of nuclear hazards, at least some ecological problems were viewed as so perilous that, unless radical reforms were quickly effectuated to resolve them, the disorderly drift of policies built on a contemporary base might cross over thresholds beyond which errors are irreversible. But if that is the case, why laud political pluralism and institutional democracy, which may be on the way to producing an unlivable society, or none at all?

Absolutism and Tolerance
In opposition to the product of that balance of forces which had been endorsed by mainstream intellectuals after World War II, counterculture writers presented their arguments in terms that contradicted several axiomatic concepts of the mid-century liberal matrix. For example, there was much talk about the need for extremely firm guidelines to public behavior, even though scholars of the Dewey-Popper tradition had explicitly denounced absolute standards as dangerous. Many radicals protested that existing democratic institutions had done little on behalf of extraordinarily urgent ends, and, at least with regard to civil rights and the Vietnam War, went on to recommend outright disobedience to the law of the land. In justification, they said that men and women must be human beings before they are citizens; that there is a higher law to which our actions must conform, else what have we learned from the Nuremberg Trials?[11] This sort of uncompromising devotion to truth and justice—variously perceived, of course—informed the notion, common to the era, of "nonnegotiable demands." It also fueled the frustration of people like Noam Chomsky, who held that to debate certain issues—such as the war—in conventional terms was implicitly to concede some justice to one's opponents and therefore to lose a portion of one's

9. *Why We Can't Wait* (New York: Harper and Row, 1964).
10. Donella H. Meadows, *The Limits to Growth: A Report for the Club of Rome's Project on the Predicament of Mankind* (New York: Universe Books, 1972).
11. See the letters of David C. King and Roger Hallem, in George F. Kennan, *Democracy and the Student Left* (Boston: Little, Brown, 1968), pp. 27, 68.

humanity.[12] That moderation and mutual adjustment have a place with regard to some issues, the counterculturists did concede. But they also held that there are matters of supreme importance which must be pursued by citizens of unyielding vision and virtue, whose commitment will be an example to us all. As Robert Paul Wolff made this point, mankind's greatest achievements are attributable to men such as Socrates, who refused to adopt the "moderate" opinions of his day.[13]

One way of encouraging support for absolute principles was to revise the concept of tolerance that postwar liberals had strongly endorsed. On this attitude, considerable agreement reigned among the critics of pluralist democracy, who demanded that modern society be resisted for its tendency to make "the unthinkable become thinkable and the intolerable become tolerable."[14] Logically, this demand flowed from faith in the existence of an absolute truth, for once that verity is known, tolerating other ideas, ipso facto errors, makes no sense. Marcuse therefore argued that "the telos of tolerance is truth," in which case those certain of the way to a better society may feel justified in maintaining that the contemporary social order suffers from "policies, conditions, and modes of behavior which should not be tolerated because they are impeding, if not destroying, the chances of creating an existence without fear and misery."[15] The persuasive power of this theoretical distillation of counterculture discontent was heightened, no doubt, by constant reference to real-world situations, such as saber-rattling by nations possessing thousands of nuclear bombs.

The Calculus of Needs
Intolerance of the intolerable was sometimes expressed by the counterculture in terms of irreducible human needs that could not be accommodated within the liberal matrix. According to the conventional liberal view, no human desires can be judged superior to all others, and therefore everyone must be permitted to express his or her own sense of needs and interests, with public policy based on the sum total of those expressions. In one of the early works of social criticism adopted by counterculture enthusiasts, Erich Fromm pointed out the flaw in this syllogism. The concept of mental health, he said, is meaningless if defined only in terms of one's adjustment to society, for the same society may be so deficient with regard to human requirements and simple decency that, in reality, that society is pathological and the individual is sane.[16]

When Fromm and others developed this notion, they argued that careful

12. *American Power and the New Mandarins* (New York: Pantheon, 1969), p. 9.
13. *The Ideal of the University* (Boston: Beacon, 1969), p. 122.
14. Theodore Roszak, *The Makings of a Counterculture: Reflections on the Technocratic Society and Its Youthful Opposition* (Garden City, N.Y.: Anchor, 1969), p. 47.
15. Herbert Marcuse, "Repressive Tolerance," in Robert Paul Wolff, Barrington Moore, Jr., and Herbert Marcuse, *A Critique of Pure Tolerance* (Boston: Beacon, 1965), pp. 81, 90.
16. *The Sane Society* (London: Routledge and Kegan Paul, 1956), pp. 20, 72.

consideration of man's true nature will reveal his real needs—for love, for economic security, for creative work, for a sense of identity with the community, and more—and that these basic elements of life must serve as the benchmark against which a nation's practices and institutions will be measured. Above all, public policy should not be predicated upon people's expressed wants, because these are conditioned by complex forces within a technological civilization and reflect its needs rather the well-being of its citizenry. Many avenues of approach led to this conclusion, but none exceeded economic theory in elegance and precision. For one thing, economists contributed the notion of "effective demand." John Kenneth Galbraith, for example, popularized the notion that an "affluent" society, spurred by advertising and the profit motive, can satisfy fleeting fancies even while failing to provide enough public goods—such as roads, schools, bridges, clean air and water, parks, etc.—which are among the essential amenities of life.[17] Other economists extended this idea, showing how a nation's Gross National Product may constantly grow, apparently enriching people with plentiful goods and services, yet all the while never providing real contentment for those who aspire to keep up with the Joneses, who are at the same time trying to stay ahead of the Smiths.[18] We must somehow scale down our aspirations, an economist might say, in order to attain them in limited measure and prosper together.[19] This sort of economic analysis suggested to counterculturists the inference that political demand may be faulted for promoting the satisfaction of people's felt desires rather than their real needs. Election results notwithstanding, then, a critic could conclude that "So long as social deprivation exists [sanctioned by public policy electorally condoned], we do not 'need' cars that become obsolete, vacation trips to Europe, electric dishwashers, supersonic planes, or even television entertainment. We not only do not 'need' them, we cannot afford them."[20]

The Importance of Character
Because counterculture theorists suspected the way in which human needs and wants were currently defined and served by established institutions, some of them decided that social reform must rely on the proper development of human character rather than on present forms of collective behavior. It was a contention advanced frequently in critical writings. As Theodore Roszak said, "building the good society is not primarily a social, but a psychic task."[21] Or, as the Students for a Democratic Society proclaimed in their famous "Port Huron Statement" of

---

17. *The Affluent Society* (Boston: Houghton Mifflin, 1958).

18. E. J. Mishan, *The Costs of Economic Growth* (New York: Praeger, 1967); and Fred Hirsch, *The Social Limits to Growth* (Cambridge, Mass.: Harvard University Press, 1976).

19. E. F. Schumacher, *Small Is Beautiful: A Study of Economics as if People Mattered* (New York: Harper and Row, 1973).

20. Charles Reich, *The Greening of America* (New York: Random House, 1970), p. 164.

21. *The Makings of a Counterculture*, p. 49.

1962, "Loneliness, estrangement, [and] isolation . . . cannot be overcome by better personnel management, nor by improved gadgets, but only when a love of man overcomes the idolatrous worship of things by men."[22]

The interesting point here was that, whereas post–World War II liberals had argued that flaws in American democracy should be corrected by efforts to reform "institutional democracy"—tinkering with great political mechanisms such as the corpus of civil rights laws—counterculturists were more likely to prescribe a substantial infusion of virtue, something which, in their aversion to absolutes, champions of the liberal matrix tended to discount. And thus two widely read counterculture works made the plea for virtuous character their central message. In *The Greening of America*, Charles Reich argued in favor of a new mentality, called "Consciousness III," designed to liberate all Americans from obedience to standards laid down by various experts in thrall to industry, bureaucracy, and the professions since the New Deal. Men of the new outlook, claimed Reich, would use the technology of the corporate state, but would bend it to true human needs, for beauty, togetherness, and peace rather than war.[23] In a similar vein, in *Zen and the Art of Motorcycle Maintenance*, Robert M. Pirseg explained that the key to better living would emerge from an individual pursuit of "quality."[24] Tracing human confusion over this subject back into Greek philosophy, Pirseg held that technological progress and organizational efficiency must be softened by an appreciation of the pure excellence possible in all endeavors, from art to motorcycle maintenance. Like Reich, Pirseg refrained from considering how political and economic structures might be reformed in the present. He maintained, instead, that a good society will take shape as the "end product" of a process whereby correct social values are discovered and internalized by individuals who will first infiltrate and then subvert today's public institutions.[25]

The New Community
In some cases, counterculture critics spoke of immediately reforming institutions rather than eventually conquering them by default, when virtue would triumph even without a blueprint for reconstruction. On such occasions, they were likely to advocate fashioning intimate forms of collective life, serving both to protect their members momentarily and to suggest attractive alternatives to life within the reigning organizational giants. They had this in mind when they recommended "building communities" of "love and respect, where there can be enduring friendships, children, and . . . honorable and enjoyable labor."[26] As a

22. "Selections from the Port Huron Statement," in Robert A. Goldwin, ed., *How Democratic Is America? Responses to the New Left Challenge* (Chicago: Rand McNally, 1971), p. 6.
23. *The Greening of America*, pp. 217–63.
24. (orig., 1974; New York: Bantam, 1979), esp. pp. 190–294.
25. Ibid., p. 267.
26. Roszak, *The Makings of a Counterculture*, p. 201.

result, there was some support for the creation of "communes," often detached from the mainstream of technocratic life. There was also, however, an aspiration to transform, through enthusiastic collective efforts, the existing political framework into "a democracy of individual participation" that would provide some benefits of purposeful identity without entirely abandoning the advantages to be derived from complex political structures.[27] This notion of "participatory democracy," which assumed a widespread capacity for that political activity which behavioral research held to be either impossible or impractical, contained within itself various counterculture views. Among these was the idea of absolute human needs, to be spelled out by people free to perceive those needs as a result of proper character formation. These, in turn, would supersede the expression of mere wants incrementally aggregated and articulated by existing institutions, with the whole system being somehow intolerant of practices too dangerous to try out even temporarily.

The University Connection

Right or wrong, the critics helped to create an enormous shift in national sentiment, from an era of general optimism to one in which pessimism was more the rule. In the process of giving voice to that pessimism, critics of the existing order managed repeatedly to cast doubts on concepts vital to the liberal matrix. These included reliance on existing political groups and elites, admiration for the two-party system, respect for electoral decisions based on effective demand, acceptance of policies formulated and executed via incrementalism, a high regard for ethical relativism and a consequent rejection of moral absolutes, praise for tolerance, and the general notion of democracy based upon familiar institutions rather than purposeful virtue. Current events lent credibility to much of the critique, even though it is improbable that many people accepted it entirely, with regard to all public issues or with respect to every point of theoretical explanation.

The Call for Substantive Rationality
As a matter of bottom-line anxiety in the new era, there lurked the very old problem of substantive versus functional rationality, raised long ago by Karl Mannheim. It will be recalled that the tendency of large organizations is to foster functional rationality, to direct their members, both collectively and individually, toward reacting more or less efficiently in the light of immediate conditions while failing to consider what might constitute substantively reasonable behavior with regard to the sum total of our circumstances, now and in the future. In these terms, counterculture critics claimed that there was an irrational dimen-

27. "Selections from the Port Huron Statement," p. 7.

sion to the existing order, that even where some signs of reason were perceptible they represented mostly functional rather than substantive adjustments to reality. This is what Fromm had in mind when he called for a "sane society," which would put an end to modern workplaces that alienate both workers and managers, and which would establish instead small communities to provide creative toil and rewarding friendships.[28] It is also what Marcuse envisioned when he criticized technocratic society for turning "crimes against humanity"—such as nuclear proliferation and brinksmanship—"into a rational enterprise,"[29] and for permitting instruments of public relations, advertising, and education to promote an outlook on life so one-dimensional as to prevent people from recognizing or acting upon visions of a better world. The difference between the two, Reich highlighted in his example of an automobile executive, a man who works to maximize profits in a large corporation and therefore cannot recommend that society produce fewer cars in order to shift resources into the creation of public housing and other urban amenities. The car-maker's dilemma was clear-cut: "As long as he is in his role, he cannot act or think responsibly within the community. Outside his role, if there is any outside, he is virtually powerless, for his power lies in his role."[30] It was a classic illustration of the conflict between functional and substantive rationality, between the short-run gain and the long-run loss, the limited view and the wider perspective. Chomsky made the same point in relation to America's involvement in Vietnam. "No doubt," he said, "[Secretary of Defense Robert] McNamara succeeded in doing with utmost efficiency [prosecuting the war on the basis of 'effective political demand'] that which should not be done at all [in the objective terms of substantive reason]."[31]

Scholarly Responsibilities

For the world of higher education, the emphasis on substantive rationality was especially challenging because it had long been taken for granted that universities would provide impartial and objective guidance—substantive rationality—for society at large. Here, America's perception of interdependence came back to haunt the very professionals who had benefited from it to rise in social status and authority. If, as it now seemed, modern society was no more than an interlocking compendium of large institutions and closely related issues, where the price of one item in South Succotash could affect the supply of another in Podunk, then who else but scientists, in their natural or social variety, were competent to make sense of the whole? And so universities, whose function could be defined as providing the information and speculation necessary for coping with social com-

28. *The Sane Society,* esp. pp. 321–43.
29. *One-Dimensional Man,* p. 52.
30. *The Greening of America,* pp. 116–17.
31. *American Power,* p. 126.

plexity, were faulted for not doing their job properly. Some said that scholars did too little, remaining aloof from the nation's urgent problems, and others said they did too much, eagerly serving the interests of those in power. Whichever the complaint, a standard of substantive rationality was postulated, either explicitly or implicitly, and then applied sharply to academic activities.

Thus when Clark Kerr offered his encomium to the world of higher education in 1963 he argued, in the same spirit as Robert Lane, that modern society is served well by men who will increase the fund of knowledge, wherefore the "multiversity" plays a useful role by tending to society's needs as those arise. In this way, Kerr explained and justified the steady growth of American universities in recent generations, as additional departments, schools, faculties, and research institutes came into being in response to social demand. It was an image made to order for counterculture critics. Robert Paul Wolff summed up their general objection when he pointed out that making provision for such needs takes into account only "effective or market demand," which is to respond to "wants" rather than true "needs."[32] For example, a university might expand its engineering school in order to train more technicians, but the objective reflects no inherently worthwhile impulse and yields to the expressed demand for a multi-billion-dollar space program rather than society's need for inexpensive housing. The moral of this story, for Wolff, was that Kerr in effect endorsed "the goals and values of whoever in America has the money to pay for them," rather than formulating an independent assessment—substantively rational—of the nation's needs and acting accordingly.[33] The same sentiment unleashed student demonstrations against university support for the ROTC, and against Institute for Defense Analysis contracts with campus scholars. A similar theme ran through the attack upon social scientists who published professional articles developing a rationale for Washington's program of forcibly relocating hundreds of thousands of Vietnamese villagers in order to weaken their allegiance to the Vietcong.[34]

Some academicians answered this sort of criticism by recommending a plague on both houses, by rejecting both Kerr and Wolff in favor of the idea that universities should be neutral with regard to immediate public issues. In the opinion of men like Harvard's Adam Ulam, it was the function of university scholars to pursue learning "for its own sake," on the grounds that eventually some of the knowledge thus produced would help society to make its way in a complicated world, while some of the habits of scholarship acquired by students would foster calm and level-headed citizenship.[35] In the meantime, critics

32. *The Ideal of the University*, pp. 36–39.
33. Ibid., p. 40.
34. See Chomsky's critique of Samuel Huntington in *American Power*, pp. 42–43.
35. *The Fall of the American University* (London: Alcove, 1972), p. 179. Along the same lines, see Robert Nisbet, *The Degradation of the Academic Dogma* (New York: Basic Books, 1971).

should stop politicizing the campus, which occurs when they try to place the university's authority behind specific and inflexible opinions as to how particular social problems should be resolved.

When Princeton's George Kennan made this argument, it was typically rejected on the grounds that issues such as the Vietnam War were too urgent, and their implications too easily grasped, to justify delaying a resolution while ivory-tower research proceeded.[36] Responses like this reflected the common counterculture notion that universities were, by their very nature, intended to be critical rather than neutral. This contention came in two parts. On the one hand, as Chomsky put it, intellectuals are charged with an overall social responsibility "to speak the truth and to expose lies." This was why university scholars were required, at a minimum, to help students see through government propaganda, media bias, and the propensity of some intellectuals "to offer their allegiance, not to truth and justice, but to power and the effective exercise of power."[37] On the other hand, going even beyond the unmasking of falsehood and deception, it was said to be the task of scholarship to suggest alternatives to some social opinions conventionally held. As one dissenting anthropologist complained, it is not enough to speak the truth with regard to "such very limited subjects as . . . prescriptive marriage systems, kinship terms, or the Tzental words for 'firewood.' " Discussion of those matters evades a crucial question: "Who is to evaluate and suggest guidelines for human society, if not those who study it?"[38]

As with so many other issues of the day, the debate on universities generated many opinions but did not end conclusively. Participants meanwhile found themselves taking a closer look than ever before at the nature of scientific communities, those professional entities that cut across more than two thousand colleges and universities in the land. In a sense, here was the counterculture's penultimate challenge to American scholars, where not only the substance of the liberal matrix came into question but also the right of scholars to participate in the formulation and explication of such matrices, now and in the future. Hundreds of student demonstrations, many entailing the forcible occupation of campus buildings and the strident enunciation of "nonnegotiable demands," in effect announced that, for certain audiences at least, little persuasive force remained in whatever arguments university scholars were accustomed to making for the special validity of their teachings. As a result, many political scientists in the late 1960s and early 1970s began very carefully to reassess what their discipline was doing in the halls of academe. Was it serving society as well as Robert Lane, for

36. See the letter by David Cane in Kennan, *Democracy and the Student Left*, pp. 51–52.

37. Chomsky, *American Power*, pp. 313–14.

38. Kathleen Gough, "World Revolution and the Science of Man," in Theodore Roszak, ed., *The Dissenting Academy* (New York: Vintage, 1968), p. 138.

example, had seemed to think in 1965 and 1966? Because America still lived in an age of science, it was inevitable that such professional soul-searching would raise questions about the nature of knowledge, the way it is produced in scientific communities, and the benefits that people may expect from it consequently. Ironically, these were questions the likes of which Popperism had come to resolve a generation earlier.

Protest within Political Science

Counterculture dissent offered a critique of society at large and then moved against the universities for their support of, or failure to oppose, the status quo. This double indictment was brought directly to the attention of political scientists in 1967, when several hundred members of the APSA organized the Caucus for a New Political Science at the Association's annual meeting that winter. The Caucus insisted that APSA conventions be deliberately organized so as to highlight research on, and stimulate discussion of, urgent public issues including the Vietnam War, race relations, poverty, women's rights, and the environment. To this end, the Association quickly expanded its convention programs in order to permit an unprecedentedly large number of papers to be read and an extremely wide range of topics to be considered.[39] The Caucus also viewed the APSA as a professional organization dominated by conventional opinions,[40] and therefore it ran candidates for national office against scholars picked by the Association's nominating committee. Some of these candidates were eventually elected to the national Executive Committee, but no candidate backed solely by the Caucus won the office of APSA President. And finally, the Caucus prodded the Association to create committees to deal with various rigidities inside the discipline itself. As a result, by 1971 there were active committees for studying the status of women, blacks, and Chicanos in the profession, for formulating and administering professional ethics, and for assessing undergraduate instruction.

All of this activity spearheaded by the Caucus contributed to the discipline's turn away from pure behavioralism to what became known as "post-behavioralism." One may search in vain within Caucus writings, however, to find a set of common principles that can be said to characterize the new approach to political

39. In 1968, the national convention program listed 86 panel sessions; for 1970, the number had risen to 156.

40. See especially Alan Wolfe, "Practicing the Pluralism We Preach: Internal Processes in the American Political Science Association," *Antioch Review* (Fall 1969), pp. 353–74; and Theodore J. Lowi, "The Politics of Higher Education: Political Science as a Case Study," in George J. Graham and George W. Carey, eds., *The Post-Behavioral Era: Perspectives on Political Science* (New York: McKay, 1972), pp. 11–36.

inquiry.[41] In fact, there is no satisfactory way of summarizing in their totality the beliefs that Caucus members entertained concerning what should be done either in American society as a whole or within political science as a learned discipline. This is so because the Caucus was less a circle of scholars constituting a unified school of thought than it was a floating faction riding the currents of discontent—inside and outside of political science—whose ranks over the years included practitioners as diverse as Daniel Moynihan, David Easton, Leo Strauss, Alan Wolfe, Philip Green, Henry Kariel, Theodore Lowi, Michael Walzer, Morris Janowitz, H. Mark Roelofs, Charles McCoy, and Howard Zinn. Consistent with the mood of the era, these men were obviously impatient with politics and policy as usual. But it is equally true that they differed among themselves with regard to the content of whatever proposals they suggested for political reform and new public policy.

Post-behavioralism, then, appeared on the political science scene as a phenomenon whose name—like that of the counterculture—indicated a shared determination to leave something definite behind rather than a common notion of the direction in which the discipline should move forward. The irresolution of it all was revealed as early as 1969, when David Easton offered the term *post-behavioralism* to his colleagues. He observed that post-behavioralism constituted a "pervasive intellectual tendency" to rethink the nature of the profession, and he claimed that its "battle cries are *relevance* and *action.*"[42] Now clearly, in the late 1960s and early 1970s, the discipline was seized by some measure of commitment to the idea that scholarly research should be relevant to specific social issues. But which issues would those be, and who would define their significant features? It was also true that many practitioners, themselves citizens worried about various issues, were willing to call for research leading to amelioratory action. But which action would they recommend, from among the very large spectrum of nostrums available? To such questions, "post-behavioralism" could offer only eclectic responses.

As to what they *did not* want for their discipline rather than what they *did*, post-behavioralists took their cue from that "rethinking" of the nature of the

41. Many tenets are conveniently collected in Philip Green and Sanford Levinson, eds., *Power and Community: Dissenting Essays in Political Science* (New York: Random House, 1969); Marvin Surkin and Alan Wolfe, eds., *An End to Political Science: The Caucus Papers* (New York: Basic Books, 1970); and Graham and Carey, ibid. For an inadvertent reflection of the difficulty of defining the characteristic content of post-behavioral work, see Leon H. Hurwitz, *Introduction to Politics: Traditionalism to Postbehavioralism, Theory and Practice* (Chicago: Nelson-Hall, 1979). Hurwitz devotes 111 pages to behavioralism, which was in vogue for appoximately 25 years, and only 9 pages to the post-behavioral era, which Hurwitz himself credits with more than a decade of popularity.

42. "The New Revolution in Political Science," *American Political Science Review* (December 1969), p. 1051.

profession which Easton had noticed. Here, there was a reflection of counterculture sentiment in the air when some Caucus members advanced the idea that political scientists should together take a stand with regard to public affairs, that the discipline had a moral responsibility for seeking "the kinds of truth that would serve justice and humanity by questioning existing arrangements."[43] Heinz Eulau undoubtedly spoke for many practitioners when he opposed this notion, arguing that the APSA is "a subtle and fragile social mechanism" whose "members differ a great deal among themselves," and for that reason the Association and its journals should not be used as forums for the exposition of views calculated to solve particular national problems.[44] What made Eulau's argument less than totally convincing to Caucus members was their conviction that most practitioners were fairly united with regard to political opinion, that there was a sense in which the discipline in its behavioral incarnation presented society with certain specific teachings of a collective thrust. Indeed, Caucus members doubted that the scientific community run by political scholars was quite as open as that envisioned by the Popperian version of behavioralism, and this doubt led them to recommend that if the discipline were actually leaning in any direction, it might as well tend to be on the side of beauty and virtue or, in the argot of the age, in favor of "relevance" and "action."

The Theory of Scientific Revolutions

There were a great many post-behavioral complaints to the effect that political science in the behavioral era was more of a "closed" than an "open" community, and more likely to generate useless than useful knowledge concerning social issues of great urgency. In this sense, professional unease paralleled the counterculture notion that substantive rationality was somehow lacking all over America, that absolute values were denigrated and intolerable situations tolerated, both in the fashioning of public policy and in the work carried on by university scholars.[45] In chapters 7 and 8, we shall explore some of these complaints, which were far-ranging and diverse. By way of introduction, it is worth noting that, in toto, they gained credence within the discipline because, in the late 1960s, the Popperian model of science came under attack from a theory of scientific revolu-

43. Christian Bay, "For an American *Political* Science Association," *PS* (Summer 1968), p. 37.
44. "Report of the President," *PS* (Fall 1972), p. 438.
45. Christian Bay, "The Cheerful Science of Dismal Politics," in Roszak, *The Dissenting Academy*, p. 224: "our profession's persistent failure [is] to develop canons of *substantive* as distinct from *formal* rationality. 'Rationality' has come to be defined in terms of selection of means to given ends, rarely to the selection of ends."

tions expounded by Thomas Kuhn.[46] When that happened, the clash between ideas associated with the former and those of the latter provided a new context of speculation about science, which supplied much of the technical justification for practitioners eventually to abandon behavioralism's overall creed.

Scientific Progress

The underlying theme of Kuhn's work was an analysis of the nature of scientific progress. Karl Popper had intimated that knowledge will slowly but surely pile up when men use the right investigative method, and he had portrayed the scientific enterprise as a process that would generate a great deal of such knowledge. This, in fact, was the ultimate justification for science, that it could, unlike philosophy or theology or astrology or phrenology, produce an endless stream of valuable learning for the benefit of mankind. In complete contrast, Kuhn offered a theory of science that rejected the conventional devotion to method. Speaking historically, he called attention to many great scientists who had "persistently violated accepted methodological canons."[47] The lesson to be learned from their performance was clear to Kuhn: science had made great strides in spite of the fact that the investigative technique described by Popper was often ignored or unknown to leading scientific lights. It was this reality that led Kuhn to reject method as a sine qua non, and to look for other causes that might explain the progress of science. Eventually, he decided that advance in this realm may be described in a theory based on the concepts of paradigms, normal science, anomalies, and scientific revolutions, and this is the theory he set forth in 1962.

Paradigms, Normal Science, and Anomalies

Throughout history, according to Kuhn, groups of men have entertained divergent sets of beliefs about the nature of reality, the problems it poses, and the proper way to investigate those problems. Kuhn referred to every such set of beliefs as a paradigm.[48] Usually, as in the case of religious paradigms, it proved difficult to demonstrate conclusively that the paradigm of one school of thought was intrinsically valid or even superior to that of any other. With respect to what is called science, however, there arose, from time to time, a school of thought whose explanatory "achievement was sufficiently unprecedented to attract an

46. *The Structure of Scientific Revolutions*, 2nd ed. (orig., 1962; Chicago: University of Chicago Press, 1970).

47. "Reflections on My Critics," in ibid., p. 236.

48. On the various phenomena embraced by the term "paradigm," see Margaret Masterman, "The Nature of a Paradigm," in Imre Lakatos and Alan Musgrave, eds., *Criticism and the Growth of Knowledge* (Cambridge: Cambridge University Press, 1970), pp. 58–59. See also Kuhn, "Reflections on My Critics," pp. 176–90.

enduring group of adherents away from competing modes of scientific activity."[49]
That is, the conformity of thought that prevailed within one group spread, until
it became the dominant paradigm for most of those who called themselves
scientists. At that point, so great a number of teachers, researchers, and laymen
accepted the conventional wisdom that there came into being a widespread
conviction that only *their* understanding of the physical universe reliably represented the truth about the world.

A paradigm restricts the attention of its enthusiasts to those facts that alone
seem relevant to events of interest to the scientific community. In contrast, when
different schools of thought work without a common paradigm, they argue
incessantly about which facts to study and what various principles are demonstrated by the facts in question. The difference is crucial, for where attention is
focused rather than scattered, normal science can flourish. In Kuhn's words,
"normal science means research based firmly upon one or more past scientific
achievements, achievements that some particular scientific community ac-
knowledges for a time as supplying the foundation for its further practice."[50]
Proceeding in this manner, great advances in knowledge are made, for many
puzzling matters come to be understood better than ever before, as the original
paradigm is sharpened, measured against the real world, and tested again and
again.

Unfortunately, even though paradigms are enormously productive in a time
of normal science, they are never entirely successful because none has ever
succeeded in explaining everything that happens in nature. In fact, scientists
have always been aware of what Kuhn called "anomalies," where "nature has
somehow violated the paradigm-induced expectations that govern normal
science."[51] For the most part, scientists usually bypass and ignore most anomalies and thereby avoid being continually distracted by them. While there is no
logical reason for such complacency, the sociological solidarity of the scientific
community, built as it is upon the habitual and convenient collective acceptance
of a paradigm, ordinarily fosters a common feeling that most anomalies are
simply not important enough to warrant extensive concern or investigation.

But there comes a time in the life of every paradigm when more and more
scientists become alert to the imperfections of their work. Many are then provoked to explore areas of anomaly rather than matters comfortably contained
within the guidelines of normal science. When this happens, puzzle solving
gives way to problem solving. The former activity is a confident search for

49. *The Structure of Scientific Revolutions*, p. 10.
50. Ibid.
51. Ibid., pp. 52–53.

solutions that are believed to exist, although as yet undiscovered, within the established paradigm; the latter effort may be defined as a restless inquiry into matters that are problematical precisely because their solutions cannot be assumed to exist according to the existing paradigm.[52] Once begun, the debate over anomalies continues until the existing paradigm is substantially modified or another adopted to take its place.

Scientific Revolutions

Kuhn used the term *scientific revolution* to describe what happens when the scientific community accepts a new paradigm. As he viewed the history of science, it consists of a series of such revolutions, each one wrenching normal science, for a time accepted, into a new and different understanding of natural things and the forces that govern them. Immediately obvious in all this is how little a scientific revolution, however described by Kuhn, has to do with the scientific method as defined by Popper and the behavioralists.

Kuhn argued that new paradigms are accepted via a process that differs significantly from the technique of first falsifying beliefs and then replacing them with propositions deemed tentatively and temporarily true. According to his theory, scientific debate on patent anomalies starts with a suspicion that the old paradigm is partly wrong. This means, of course, that the old paradigm is still partly right.[53] And when a new paradigm is proposed, it is so crudely formulated that it is not, and cannot be, entirely persuasive. After all, *if* the new paradigm is accepted, it will *later* be refined and improved during a period of normal science. But at the moment of its inception it is not so thoroughly elaborated as to be clearly and obviously true.

So it was, for example, that the Copernican cosmology appeared on the scientific scene, not yet graced with the Newtonian laws of motion, and at a time when the Ptolemaic cosmology was considered weak but not entirely invalid as a guide to cosmic events.[54] The Copernican cosmology was nevertheless accepted, with all its imperfections. With such shifts of allegiance in mind, Kuhn generalized that every scientific revolution succeeds by joining a little falsification of the old paradigm with a little verification of the new. Paradigm change thus depends on a blurred combination of negative and positive impulses that does not resemble

52. Kuhn did not use the term "problem solving" as it is used in the text above, but the term serves as a convenient complement to "puzzle solving," which he did use. See Thomas Weldon, *The Vocabulary of Politics* (Baltimore: Penguin, 1953), pp. 77–83, who defined "puzzles" as matters that permit foreseeable solutions, while "problems" are situations whose solution is unforeseeable and perhaps never to be found.

53. *The Structure of Scientific Revolutions*, pp. 146–47f.

54. Ibid., pp. 154–55.

"the methodological stereotype of falsification by direct comparison with nature."[55] Indeed, the notion of falsification as a hallmark of scientific progress is
flatly contradicted by the fact that every old paradigm held sway even though
known anomalies, while being disregarded, gave the lie to at least part of it.

In sum, Kuhn was not sure why scientists accept a new paradigm, but he
was convinced that this acceptance should be regarded as a sociological event
rather than a methodological step, and that in each major instance it was influenced by a combination of contemporary mentalities and the available facts. He
therefore described the historical process in terms usually applied to nonscientific
changes of opinion or conviction. Indeed, he called paradigm change a kind of
"conversion." Thus, much as when individuals convert from one religious faith
to another, a scientific "conversion experience" is not dependent upon "proof or
error."[56] As Kuhn saw it, a scientist somehow surveys all his impressions of the
subject at hand, and then decides to transfer his "allegiance"[57] to a new view of
the matter. His change of heart is at least partly an act of "faith,"[58] for at the
moment of paradigm change, there can be no conventional proof that the new
paradigm is really superior to the old. Something is mysterious here, and it can
be summed up in the phrase "gestalt switch," which Kuhn also used to describe
the transition from one set of perceptions to another.[59] The world may be the
same after the paradigm change as before, but the scientist who accepts the new
paradigm will perceive and judge that world differently. It is as though the old
paradigm teaches that half a glass of water is a glass half full, while the new
paradigm suggests that the glass is half empty instead.

Two Problems for Behavioralism

At the most obvious level of analysis, Kuhn's work expressly rejected the Popperian and behavioral description of science as an enterprise definitively marked by
elements of method—by empiricism, falsification, tentativity, and so forth. In
consequence, those who were attracted to Kuhn's theory were led to believe that
behavioralists erred by misconstruing science, by holding it to be something it is
not. What science truly is, though, according to Kuhn, projected a challenge to
conventional political science far more serious than that conveyed by merely
questioning its standard terms, and in this respect Kuhn carried intellectual
history beyond the point that Popper had reached. Whereas Popper had created a
formula that he hoped would distinguish between science and nonscience, so as

55. Ibid., p. 7.
56. Ibid., p. 151.
57. Ibid.
58. Ibid., p. 158.
59. Ibid., pp. 111–15.

to confer great authority on the former, the new theory seemed to suggest that, even after an enterprise has been identified as scientific, it would be a mistake to place unlimited confidence in it. For Kuhn, science was highly commendable for its tangible achievements. Still, once we understand its true nature, any discernible scientific activity should remain dubious precisely insofar as it is scientific, a product of human consensus embodying the biases of its practitioners and/or their age.

To put the matter into a very broad perspective, Kuhn raised once again the problem that Mannheim had labeled the sociology of knowledge. Mannheim had hoped that knowledge untainted by the sociological origins of its discoverers could be gained within the community of intellectuals, and Popper had, in effect, transferred this role to the community of scientists, where scientific method would purge their testable hypotheses of distortions flowing from the personality or social background of each researcher. Now Kuhn seemed to be saying that paradigmatic conceptions of reality are adopted even by scientists on grounds that are not entirely objective, in which case it was quite likely that any specific scientific community, such as political science, might conduct its affairs in such a way as to permit influence to factors that tend to produce one range of findings and belief rather than another. Even giving the discipline of political studies credit, then, for acting in the behavioral era as a scientific community, critics in the late 1960s and early 1970s were able to charge, in the light of Kuhn's new theory, that its joint endeavors suffered from the sociology of knowledge on at least two grounds.

The Problem of Quality

There was, to begin with, the problem of quality in behavioral work. Behavioralists essentially agreed to statements like this: "The behavioral and social sciences . . . can help us survive current crises and avoid them in the future, provided that these sciences continue to make contributions of two kinds: first, in increased understanding of human behavior and the institutions of society; and, second, in better ways to use this understanding in devising social policy and the management of our affairs."[60] The suggestion is that behavioralism offers society a uniquely valuable "input" because, unlike what other political actors have to offer, the findings and opinions of behavioral scientists are firmly grounded in the scientific way they pursue their work. In the 1960s, Truman, Almond, and Easton clothed this basic claim with a measure of Kuhnian rhetoric by arguing that behavioralism, as a sort of working paradigm, could enable political scien-

60. This passage comes from a National Academy of Sciences Report entitled *The Behavioral and Social Sciences: Outlook and Needs* (Englewood Cliffs, N.J.: Prentice-Hall, 1969), p. 1. The report was endorsed by Heinz Eulau and James March, eds., *Political Science* (Englewood Cliffs, N.J.: Prentice-Hall, 1969), p. 3.

tists to stop wasting time and energy arguing over first principles.[61] From this point of view, it was incumbent upon the discipline to accept behavioralism and thereby foster the efficient practice of normal science, under whose reign scholarly attention might be drawn powerfully and productively to research that would bring forth new knowledge of the political world. In terms of the interplay between Mannheim, Popper, and Kuhn on the sociology of knowledge, here was a claim that political science, as a scientific community, could overcome the influence of its practitioners' origins and produce a body of knowledge reflecting objective and useful truth.

This claim emerged, however, at a time when dissenting political scientists were wondering how deeply the normal science research of behavioralists would ever delve into the nation's most pressing social problems, for, as Robert Engler observed, "Questions as to why the channels [of political power] do not always seem responsive to mass needs tend to go unasked [in political science writings]."[62] To such critics, Kuhn's theory not only gave little support to the notion that behavioral work is powerful and productive, but cast serious doubts on that very notion. This reality was highlighted by Sheldon S. Wolin in 1968 and 1969;[63] later, similar comments came from other critics of behavioralism.[64] Wolin agreed with the leading behavioralists that behavioralism could be regarded as a sort of scientific paradigm, but he reminded them that paradigms are conventional outlooks which, in Kuhnian terms, are restrictive.[65] As Kuhn observed, no paradigm manages to explain all in the world that needs explaining. Yet the sociological solidarity of scientists is such that they come to accept as true—via conversions, gestalt switches, transfers of allegiance, and acts of faith—their own paradigmatic understanding of reality, even though it is necessarily partial and subjective. In this sense, every scientific community that works within a paradigm is always confined within a limited view of the world, according to the particular selection of facts which it recognizes.

Wolin concluded that the discipline could not profit from accepting behav-

61. See David B. Truman, "Disillusion and Regeneration: The Quest for a Discipline," *American Political Science Review* (December 1965), pp. 865–73; Gabriel A. Almond, "Political Theory and Political Science," *American Political Science Review* (December 1966), pp. 869–79; and Easton, "The New Revolution in Political Science," pp. 1051–61.

62. "Social Science and Social Consciousness: The Shame of the Universities," in Roszak, *The Dissenting Academy*, p. 199.

63. See his "Political Theory as a Vocation," *American Political Science Review* (December 1969), pp. 1062–82, and his "Paradigms and Political Theories," in Preston King and B. C. Parekh, eds., *Politics and Experience* (Cambridge: Cambridge University Press, 1968), pp. 125–52.

64. See the many references to Kuhn and behavioralism in Green and Levinson, *Power and Community*. See also Philip L. Beardsley, "A Critique of Post-Behavioralism," *Political Theory* (February 1977), pp. 97–111.

65. "Political Theory as a Vocation," esp. pp. 1064–65, 1069–77.

ioralism as a controlling paradigm, precisely because orthodoxy would only produce knowledge of limited quality. Instead, he recommended a renaissance in the vocation of political theory, renewed efforts to read, analyze, appreciate, extend, and build upon, the great political philosophies of yesterday. He spoke of those philosophies as "epic theories,"[66] by which he meant that every epic political theory constitutes a distinct and paradigmatic way of appraising the political world.[67] To Wolin, no single such paradigm was, or could be, in itself a complete explanation of the world about us. To best understand the political world, then, political scientists should try to grasp the sum total of the partial and limited truths that are offered, sometimes separately, by all political paradigms, including those of the past. The resulting compendium of insight, wisdom, and understanding went by the name of "tacit knowledge" in Wolin's argument, which was one way of rejecting the confines of any particular strand of political thought, including the behavioral strand.[68]

The Problem of Quantity

Wolin showed why, even if they are scientific, behavioral opinions about politics may be no more valuable than those of any other school of thought. Yet this was not the only area where Kuhn's theory of science failed to support a behavioral claim. There was also what may be called the problem of quantity in regard to behavioral research findings. There were plenty of behavioral findings, in the sense that large numbers of behaviorally oriented books and journal articles attested to no problem of absolute quantity. There was, however, a shortage of concrete, complete and unquestionably useful findings. Not a few dissidents pointed out that behavioral research after World War II often neglected the most pressing social and political questions of the day. Lewis Lipsitz, for example, reported that out of 924 articles in three leading political science journals from 1959 to 1969, only one dealt with Vietnam and only 6 percent "deal with policy analysis 'in the broadest terms.' "[69] Jack Walker analyzed a decade's worth of articles in five major political science journals up to 1970 and found virtually no writings on powerful bureaucracies such as the Department of Justice, the Federal Aviation Agency, the Ford Foundation, or the Institute for Defense Analysis.[70] Even David Easton, in response to pleas for more relevant behavioral work, conceded that "in the decade from 1958 to 1968, [the APSR] published

66. Ibid., pp. 1078–79.
67. "Paradigms and Political Theories," pp. 139–40.
68. "Political Theory as a Vocation," pp. 1070–71f. Wolin borrowed the term "tacit knowledge" from Michael Polanyi, *Personal Knowlege* (New York: Harper and Row, 1964).
69. "Vulture, Mantis, and Seal: Proposals for Political Scientists," in Graham and Carey, *The Post-Behavioral Era*, p. 184.
70. "Brother, Can You Paradigm?" *PS* (Fall 1972), pp. 419–22.

only 3 articles on the urban crisis; 4 on racial conflicts; 1 on poverty; 2 on civil disobedience; and 2 on violence in the United States."[71]

The general explanation for this state of affairs was that useful knowledge in the natural sciences took centuries to accumulate. Thus, according to Easton, the physical sciences were "centuries ahead" of the social sciences in "theoretical and factual maturity."[72] One had no real reason, therefore, to expect the application of scientific methods to produce useful political knowledge more quickly, in a period of time reaching back only to World War II and the rise of behavioralism. As for specific arguments, there was recourse to the two behavioral tenets noted in chapter 5, that science proceeds slowly but surely on the basis of building blocks, in a more-or-less straight line. We should note, however, that neither of these tenets found support in Kuhn's work. How was this so?

As Kuhn would have it, most scientists understand very little of the history of science. Like Molière's bourgeois gentleman who did not expect to be told that he had been speaking "prose" for much of his life, scientists would be surprised to hear that they think in terms of paradigms, at least while engaged in professional activities. Kuhn used the term paradigm to describe orthodox thinking in general, rather than to label any particular bundle of ideas that is handed about openly in an intellectual marketplace, there to be accepted or rejected like a tangible commodity. In the history of science according to Kuhn, no scientist sees paradigmatic bundles of ideas carried around like mental baggage. He simply absorbs some ideas and, unless influenced by reading Kuhn's book, proceeds without recognizing their collective impact on his perception and curiosity.

Because scientists are unaware that they think in terms of paradigms, it follows that they do not understand the nature of scientific revolutions, where one paradigm is exchanged for another. According to Kuhn, this second failing causes scientists to write textbooks which systematically misrepresent the nature of scientific progress. A general reading of such textbooks leads both novitiates and laymen alike to believe that scientific progress is "linear or cumulative."[73] This belief is fostered by treating "experiments, concepts, laws, and theories of current science" almost "seriatim." These same conventional books also nourish the linear, or cumulative, illusion by making it appear as if, "in a process often compared to the addition of bricks to a building, scientists have added another fact, concept, law, or theory to the body of information" collected in the text.[74] Thus readers of textbooks are led to believe that scientific discoveries have been

71. "The New Revolution in Political Science," p. 1057.
72. *The Political System: An Inquiry into the State of Political Science*, 2nd ed. (orig., 1953; New York: Knopf, 1971), p. 59.
73. *The Structure of Scientific Revolutions*, p. 139.
74. Ibid., p. 140.

made in somewhat logical order, with more discoveries waiting in line for future revelation.

Perhaps reading standard scientific textbooks encouraged behavioralists to believe that their kind of social science could change into what natural scientists held natural science to be. But Kuhn saw the process of all scientific advance in a different light, and he rejected both the building block and the straight line analogies. As he saw it, scientific history consists of a series of scientific revolutions, one following another in no particular order at all. True, each successive innovation increases understanding of some natural phenomena, but every time there is a paradigm change, some old mysteries are left behind unresolved and some new problems are revealed as so important that they require extended investigation. The dictated investigations then lead to entirely new speculations and inquiries, which eventually again cause so much dissatisfaction and ferment as to provoke the birth of still another paradigm. From all of this, Kuhn concluded that the scientists of each paradigm generation find themselves working on problems—in his term, puzzles—unknown within older theories and paradigms.[75] It followed that work in one generation did not necessarily serve as a building block for work in another, and there is no reason to believe that a continual line of inquiry is consciously maintained from one paradigm period through a second and on to a third. To make the point graphically, Kuhn implied that the scientific road is not a broad highway where travelers press on, slowly but surely, in order to reach some perceived destination on the horizon. It is, instead, a crooked and winding path, meandering haphazardly across the intellectual landscape, with each twist and turn marked by a paradigm change and a new direction for research and concern.[76] If this was in truth the path that behavioralists had chosen for themselves, there was little reason to believe that their work would lead to any place or thing in particular, regardless of how carefully and faithfully they were to employ the scientific method.

The Co-optation of Kuhn's Theory

The response of leading behavioralists to the Kuhnian challenge was an attempt to fit their discipline into the framework of forward-looking theory by accepting the notion of paradigms. They spoke, therefore, as if the community of political scientists should accept as its paradigm a single approach to political inquiry— say the notion of systems theory,[77] or behavioralism itself[78]—whereupon the

75. Ibid., pp. 140–41.
76. Kuhn himself described scientific progress as movement without a goal. See ibid., pp. 171–72.
77. Almond, "Political Theory and Political Science," p. 875.
78. Easton, "The New Revolution in Political Science," p. 1053.

practice of normal science, energetically pursued within the guidelines of that overall view of reality, would produce a growing stock of useful and reliable knowledge about politics. The sort of attack carried out against behavioralism by Wolin indicated, however, that, as Albert O. Hirschman put it, "the search for paradigms," if successful, would actually constitute "a hindrance to understanding."[79] Since this quickly became clear, the original accommodation to Kuhn's ideas soon yielded to a different attempt to defuse their radical implications. In this fall-back position, so to speak, it was conceded that many great scientists have made discoveries even while unaware of the subtle complexities of proof and disproof known to the scientific method. Yet this fact did not necessarily demonstrate that Kuhn had accurately gauged the difference between revolutionary and normal science. For Kuhn, the canons of scientific method do not govern when scientists decide to switch paradigms, although the same rules may guide the patient puzzle-solving that is carried on during a period of normal science. To all of this, Kuhn's critics responded that even if paradigms do emerge from creative impulses which defy logical analysis, they are in fact judged by a rigorous process of scientific tests.

Popper himself never disputed the contention that scientific discoveries may be sparked by unpredictable forces such as social change, intuition, revelation, and the like, totally apart from any system of scientific method. He insisted, nevertheless, that once such a discovery is made, its acceptance or rejection by the scientific community has nothing to do with any collective state of mind similar to that which induced the discovery in the first place, Rather, it is accepted or rejected like any puzzle-solving piece of scientific work, on the basis of rigorous empirical tests and comparison with other work.[80] As one philosopher of science described the distinctions that are pertinent here, Kuhn was not sufficiently alert to the differences between "generation" and "evaluation" of scientific theories, between the "context of discovery" and the "context of justification," between "theoretical creation" and "theoretical test."[81] The real issue concerns "not the psychology of the paradigm originator, but the public procedures of evaluation by which new paradigms are assessed."[82]

Protagonists for behavioralism in political science often repeated this argument. A. James Gregor, for example, maintained that intuition or an act of faith may produce a new and paradigmatic impression of reality, meaning there surely must be a role for idiosyncracy in science. After the new outlook is idiosyncratically created, however, it may be transformed into an effective explanatory

79. "The Search for Paradigms as a Hindrance to Understanding," World Politics (April 1970), pp. 329–43.
80. "Normal Science and Its Dangers," p. 57.
81. Israel Scheffler, Science and Subjectivity (Indianapolis: Bobbs-Merrill, 1967), pp. 67–71f.
82. Ibid., p. 79.

theory, and at that point scientists would have to be unreasonable not to accept it. In other words, while there may be a "logic of discovery" which is not very logical, there is also a "logic of justification" which is available and persuasive to reasonable men.[83] Arthur S. Goldberg made this same point when he wrote that science consists of both creating and checking hypotheses about the nature of the world. The latter involves the scientific method, and the former flows from a mysterious thought process called "retroduction."[84] Philip H. Melanson concurred, and held that "it is not the source of insight that determines scientific quality, but, rather, the epistemic procedures that follow it"—that is, science is still a matter of techniques used to check our ideas, which may come from anywhere, anyhow.[85] Martin Landau, who very explicitly explored the links between Mannheim, Popper, and Kuhn, concluded that there can be no such thing as "immaculate perception." Still, our subjective views can be put to "the test of independent and impartial criteria," and we may thereby neutralize human factors that would otherwise determine the shape of knowledge.[86]

The net effect of this line of reasoning was to co-opt Kuhn's sociological insight by using his terms to reiterate the central importance of scientific techniques. If what Popper and the behavioralists said about Kuhn was true, it defused the most radical elements of his theory. Thus the co-opters agreed with him that paradigms are shared outlooks playing an important role in shaping and guiding day-to-day science, but they claimed that such broadly accepted views are not widely adopted until they have been intensively and publicly tested. In other words, scientific orthodoxies do exist, but none of them are unreasonable. Yet if this is the case, a scientific community of scholars retains its crucial Popperian function of compensating for the subjective origins of its members via an application of objective standards for evaluating any claim to new knowledge. For behavioralists, at least, this line of reasoning was agreeable because, by commending the scientific method, it justified their personal preference for continuing behavioral work as usual. Insofar as political science as a collective endeavor was concerned, it could be said that, having demonstrated the soundness of Popper's theory, the discipline should do its best to act in accordance with the requirements of that theory, thereby performing a valuable and distinctive function side by side with the other scholarly disciplines that seek knowledge of social affairs.

83. *An Introduction to Metapolitics* (New York: Free Press, 1971), pp. 32–34.
84. 'Political Science as Science," in Howard Ball and Thomas Lauth, Jr., eds., *Changing Perspectives in Contemporary Political Analysis* (Englewood Cliffs, N.J.: Prentice-Hall, 1971), pp. 47–48.
85. *Political Science and Political Knowledge* (Washington, D.C.: Public Affairs Press, 1975), p. 132, and passim.
86. *Political Theory and Political Science: Studies in the Methodology of Political Inquiry* (New York: Macmillan, 1972), pp. 44–45.

The Shift to Policy Studies

There remained the embarrassing fact of so much political science research failing to foresee the rise of great public issues, and failing to comment usefully on those it had addressed. Co-opting Kuhn was therefore only the first response of mainstream scholars to the era of disillusionment. The second was to recommend that political scientists put more of their efforts than ever before into what were called "policy studies." In general, the idea was that behavioral research had concentrated, until the mid-1960s, on the "input" side of political life. Thus, leading practitioners had primarily studied great institutions such as Congress and the political parties and had considered how they were designed to receive and assimilate expressions of political interest, which in turn flowed from the efforts of individuals and pressure groups to make powerful and effective statements of their needs. But times had changed, according to advocates of a turn to policy studies, and the press of urgent political issues, such as the Vietnam War, racial discrimination, women's rights, environmental pollution, and so forth, made it imperative that political scientists should initiate intensive investigations into what might be called the "output" side of political affairs. As Austin Ranney made this point, now was the time to pay less attention to the "processes" whereby political decisions are taken and to focus more on the "content" of those actually made.[87] Or, in the words of Richard I. Hofferbert, "To focus upon policy as an object of study is to focus on the 'product' side of the political equation. Instead of being concerned primarily with what affects government, or with what goes on inside political institutions, we are primarily interested in what comes out of the process."[88]

Scholars who accepted the challenge of policy studies were surely responding positively to Easton's notion that "relevance" should become one of the hallmarks of political research in the "post-behavioral" era. Of course, there was no guarantee that research along the recommended lines would produce clear and unequivocal recommendations for new or reformed public policies, although that was always a possibility, indeed a goal to be desired. Still, after behavioralists had been faulted for ignoring major social issues that came to the fore during the 1960s, it seemed reasonable to argue that direct study of public policies and how they touched upon such issues would at least produce data that could serve as the basis for intelligent and informed public debate. Thus Thomas Dye held that "there is an implied assumption in policy analysis that developing scientific knowledge about the forces shaping public policy and the consequences of policy designs is itself a socially relevant activity, and that such

87. "The Study of Policy Content: A Framework for Choice," in Austin Ranney, ed., *Political Science and Public Policy* (Chicago: Markham, 1968), p. 3.
88. *The Study of Public Policy* (Indianapolis: Bobbs-Merrill, 1974), p. 7.

analysis is a prerequisite to prescription, advocacy, and activism. In short, policy analysis might be labeled the 'thinking man's response' to demands that social science become more 'relevant' to the problems of our society."[89] For the discipline as a whole, increased attention to public policy could even be described as serving the long-standing goal of citizenship training. As William A. Welsh observed, citizens must make "intelligent judgments about political issues," and these should be based on "reliable information about public affairs," which political scientists will provide.[90]

And so a great many political scientists were encouraged to inquire after and teach about various aspects of public policies, and a mounting number of professional publications presented the results of their research. In the process, two significant realities were revealed. On the one hand, what seemed to be an interest in something specific, that is, an object labeled "public policy," very quickly turned into concern for so wide a range of political phenomena as to make summarization of the new efforts virtually impossible.[91] As enthusiasts themselves conceded, public policy required extremely broad definition. Dye, for example, candidly suggested that "Public policy is whatever governments choose to do or not to do."[92] It was a formulation which, however justifiable, covered an enormous range, from everything concrete that touches upon government action, to everything intangible that might induce or impel government to refrain from movement at all. Hofferbert agreed with Dye, that it is not only what officials do but also what they do not do that constitute government policy. As he observed, "anything in society can be considered a public policy because public officials allow it to exist."[93]

Yet if public policy is a reflection of "anything in society," it will be very difficult for political scientists to decide which particular aspects of our world they might investigate for being crucial elements of the policy process. And so, with regard to political actors who help to create and maintain public policy, it was the opinion of Charles E. Lindblom that, "To understand who or what makes policy, one must understand the characteristics of the participants," including "ordinary citizens, interest-group leaders, legislators, legislative leaders, party activists, party leaders, judges, civil servants, technical experts, and business-managers."[94] Or, to suggest the enormously broad spectrum of political actions, rather than merely actors, which might legitimately be brought within the scope of research into public policy, we have the items enumerated by

89. *Understanding Public Policy* (Englewood Cliffs, N.J.: Prentice-Hall, 1972), p. 6.

90. *Studying Politics* (New York: Praeger, 1973), pp. 23–24.

91. See the attempts at summarization in "The Place of Policy Analysis in Political Science: Five Perspectives," *American Journal of Political Science* (May 1977), pp. 415–33, esp. p. 424.

92. *Understanding Public Policy*, p. 1.

93. *The Study of Public Policy*, pp. 6–7.

94. *The Policy-Making Process*, 2nd ed. (Englewood Cliffs, N.J.: Prentice-Hall, 1980), pp. 2–3.

Charles O. Jones, who held that the "basic elements of the policy process" include perception, definition, aggregation, organization, representation, formulation, legitimation, application, administration, reaction, evaluation, appraisal, resolution, and termination.[95] Given such a wide range of matters which political scientists properly might investigate as bearing on public policy, it is no wonder Lindblom concluded that "to understand policy making one must understand all of political life and activity."[96]

In fact, the discipline's move to policy studies did not so much discover a new realm for professional inquiry as it offered an alternative name for the old realm, the world of politics in its various dimensions. Such a ploy is quite unremarkable, for people often improve the appearance of a familiar thing by assigning it a more attractive name. President Reagan, for example, while committed in 1982 to not raising "taxes" but compelled to redress enormous budget deficits, began to speak of the need to generate "revenue enhancers." Where such consistency with regard to underlying realities is likely, it is not surprising that the second significant reality of policy studies consisted of their continuing devotion to scientific techniques of the sort developed by the discipline's mainstream since World War II. Easton had foreshadowed as much when he declared in 1969 that putting more efforts into research on immediate problems "need not be considered a threat to behavioral research but only an extension of it necessary for coping with the unusual problems of the present epoch."[97]

Basic textbooks on policy analysis agreed with Easton. Thus Jones wrote of how a concern for the policy process would supersede the earlier behavioral interest in various institutional affairs without substantially altering the discipline's devotion to behavioral research techniques per se.[98] As if to demonstrate Jones's point, Dye recommended that policy studies be carried out via any one of six "analytic models"—which he listed as the systems model, the elite-mass model, the group model, the rational model, the incremental model, and the institutional model—most of which had been devised during the behavioral era.[99] Confronted by a good deal of this sort of prescription, John G. Gunnell correctly contended that, whereas the shift to policy studies may have enabled mainstream political scientists to grapple more directly with certain issues widely deemed important to society, the same shift did not necessarily dictate a revision in "the basic assumptions about the character of social scientific theory."[100] In a

95. *An Introduction to the Study of Public Policy* (Belmont, Cal.: Wadsworth, 1970), p. 11.

96. *The Policy-Making Process*, p. 5.

97. "The New Revolution in Political Science," p. 1055.

98. *Public Policy*, pp. 3–4.

99. *Understanding Public Policy, passim.*

100. "Political Science and the Theory of Action: Prolegomena," *Political Theory* (February 1979), p. 76.

remark that could have been directed against Dye specifically, Gunnell pointed out that, even though recent critics of political science had plausibly challenged all of the discipline's standard research devices and conceptual schemes, "Political scientists tend to see no fundamental problem in applying, for example, a little personality 'theory,' some notions of collective choice from economics, a dose of organization 'theory,' and some brands of systems analysis."[101]

The Outstanding Question

In short, the 1960s brought the nation face to face with a host of social, economic, and political issues, which led to complaints that the prevailing understanding of American democracy, as embodied in the mid-century liberal matrix, was largely invalid. Eventually, criticism focused on America's great universities for somehow failing in their duty to help society deal with such issues. Along the way, disaffection spread to specific learned disciplines, including political science. At this point, a new theory of what science was all about, propounded chiefly by Thomas Kuhn, was applied to political studies in order to explain why that scholarly community must fall short of doing its job. To counter the charges, leading political scientists tried to show how, in theory, the discipline could be both Kuhnian and socially productive at the same time. They continued by advocating the study of public policy as an immediate and patent fulfillment of the discipline's obligation to serve a democratic society by producing relevant knowledge for use in public discussion of urgent political issues. In practice, they worked as if research into public policy could fruitfully be conducted in the same way that other inquiries had been conducted in the past, in the scientific mode advocated by political science since World War II.

It will be some time before we acquire the historical perspective necessary for judging the phenomenon of policy studies. It is not too early to suspect, however, that, less than constituting a significant contribution to the development of political science as a discipline, the move to policy studies was more a case of pouring old wine into new bottles. Nothing can detract from the practical value of many works produced by that enterprise, which have special merit for shedding light on particular policy questions of our time. Yet it is also true that, compared to previous research projects, the new were not very different in principle from the old and took as their main original feature an emphasis upon matters of common concern. We may then ask whether or not more of the same was really sufficient in light of the charges that had been raised between, roughly speaking, 1965 and 1975. This is a question to which the discipline eventually delivered a negative answer.

101. Ibid., p. 83.

The Community of
Political Scholars

7

Politics, Publishing, Truth, and Wisdom

In late 1979, Leon Epstein, then president of the American Political Science Association, spoke to the discipline about political parties but refrained from developing "generalizations of the kind that distinguished earlier presidential addresses on the nature and responsibility of political science." It was difficult, said Epstein, "to offer general advice now that political scientists identify with increasingly specialized subjects and employ more disparate methods."[1] This parenthetical aside, coming from an unimpeachable source, pinpointed an important fact of professional life in the post-behavioral era: Members of the discipline were increasingly unable to choose among proffered ideas and to certify some of them so authoritatively as to persuade practitioners to work along common lines. Such vocational incoherence, literally a failure to cohere, reflected the inability of political scientists to behave as a scientific community in the Popperian sense of that term, as behavioralists had long claimed they would behave. And this failure complemented a paradoxical ambivalence among practitioners, when most political scholars continued to execute studies that were technically proficient, as in the area of policy studies, even while lacking confidence in the ultimate efficacy of their collective efforts.

Technique without Vision

What was the nature of this ambivalence? One thing is clear: the enterprise of policy studies made maximum sense if one ignored the theory of scientific

1. "What Happened to the British Party Model?" *American Political Science Review* (March 1980), p. 9. See also John C. Wahlke, "Pre-Behavioralism in Political Science," ibid. (March 1979), p. 13: "political behavior research . . . exhibits . . . a near-total lack of consensus about what are the main topics for research, and the main subdivisions of the field."

revolutions or concluded that its radical implications were invalid. Any more positive regard for Kuhn's work would have implied that policy research was likely to suffer the same faults attributed by critics to earlier behavioralistic inquiry; that is, that findings in the fashionable mold might shed an occasional ray of light on some important matters but that, collectively, they would not constitute a particularly useful body of knowledge concerning the political world.

Yet what of the mainstream position with regard to Kuhn? Oddly enough, it came to rest in the peculiar happenstance that the co-opters did not get down to facts but made their case mainly out of terminological exercises. In fields of knowledge such as physics and biology, there may be tangible evidence for distinguishing between revolutionary and normal science; that is a controversial matter which historians of natural science have been debating for two decades. But with regard to the social sciences, and for political science in particular, parties to the debate on Kuhn tended to dwell less on the facts than on the precise meaning that might be imputed to terms in Kuhn's lexicon.[2] For instance, was a paradigm *this?* or was it *that?* and what exactly did Kuhn mean by "normal science" or "anomaly?" While asking questions of this sort, writings about Kuhn among mainstream scholars rested upon abstractions quite removed from the discipline's work and teachings over the years, whereby his theory's most challenging implications were not so much contained as they were bypassed. As a result, the discipline was left with a body of commentary on Kuhn that was internally consistent but imperfectly persuasive.

To judge from the way in which political scientists viewed their own efforts in the post-behavioral era, the co-optation of Kuhn was quite unconvincing. On the one hand, the content of published works revealed that many scholars continued to employ behavioral techniques in their research,[3] while surveys of professional preferences indicated that most practitioners still favored a scientific style over any other.[4] This sort of evidence led Bernard Susser to conclude that, in the

2. For examples of the terminological debate over Kuhn's theory, see Jerone Stephens, "The Kuhnian Paradigm and Political Inquiry," *American Journal of Political Science* (August 1973), pp. 467–88; Philip L. Beardsley, "Political Science: The Case of the Missing Paradigm," *Political Theory* (February 1974), pp. 46–61; John S. Nelson, "Once More on Kuhn," *Political Methodology* (Spring 1974), pp. 73–104; Terrance Ball, "From Paradigms to Research Programs: Toward a Post-Kuhnian Political Science," *American Journal of Political Science* (February 1976), pp. 151–77; and Michael Kirn, "Behavioralism, Post-Behavioralism, and the Philosophy of Science: Two Houses, One Plague," *Review of Politics* (January 1977), pp. 82–102. See also the exchange between Beardsley and Kirn in *Political Theory* (August 1975), pp. 323–28.

3. See the figures in James L. Hutter, "Quantification in Political Science: An Examination of Seven Journals," *Midwest Journal of Political Science* (May 1972), pp. 313–23.

4. See the figures in Walter B. Roettger, "The Discipline: What's Right, What's Wrong, and Who Cares?" paper delivered at the 1978 Annual Meeting of the American Political Science Association (August 1978), pp. 10–15.

post-behavioral era, "Precision and verifiability continue to be valued scholarly traits."[5] On the other hand, many practitioners judged the flow of scientific works to have lost its progressive thrust. Here is what Henry S. Kariel had in mind when he complained that, while the descriptive power of behavioral science is impressive, "it does not allow us to come to terms with our ideals."[6] It was therefore a sign of the vocational times that, in the 1970s, no one succeeded in publishing a comprehensive and widely acceptable work explaining how bits and pieces of political science research, such as the outpouring of policy studies, could be brought together by the community of scholars in comprehensive and useful form.

The Sociology of Political Science

In sum, the discipline reacted to a decade of disillusionment by remaining loyal to behavioral techniques while at the same time losing faith in the larger professional outlook which we have called the behavioral persuasion. Yet if the terminological debate failed to co-opt Kuhn and sustain optimism with regard to political science's shared character, the facts of vocational life within political science must of themselves have induced pessimism with regard to the discipline's collective capacities. Unfortunately, we are not well situated to draw firm conclusions as to how that pessimism set in, and for which particular reasons. The last decade may well contain signs indicating the onset of a long-term failure of nerve in the community of political scholars. But too few years have passed to permit members of the discipline to winnow out key writings and ideas which, by withstanding the test of time, may one day stand revealed as having caused that irresolution. Moreover, lack of confidence in the behavioral vision was actually a "non-event," logically difficult to analyze. That is to say, most practitioners do *not* now believe in the mid-century liberal matrix, but this does not mean that they *do* believe in something else. The result is a negative reality that may have many implicit causes, as opposed to a positive commitment whose immediate sources are fewer and more explicit. Once again, only the long-run perspective will eventually illuminate our present situation.

Given the difficulties of interpretation to date, the current state of ambivalence in political science may best be appreciated by treating the post-behavioral era less chronologically and more analytically than our account of the discipline so far. This may be done by considering post-behavioralism via an "ideal type" of argument, where one reflects upon the essence of post-behavioralism rather than

5. "The Behavioral Ideology: A Review and a Prospect," *Political Studies* (September 1974), p. 288.

6. *The Promise of Politics* (Englewood Cliffs, N.J.: Prentice-Hall, 1966), p. 19.

upon its manifestations as they consecutively appear.[7] An exposition of this sort is not literally accurate, in the sense of being derived from specific sources that state its component parts clearly, for attribution and citation. It is also not entirely valid, to the point of being endorsed in every detail by all those scholars who no longer expect great things from their collective enterprise. Nonetheless, such an approach can serve to illustrate the kind of case that might be made by any number of today's practitioners, were they to attempt what they have not yet done, which is to bring order to some of the many available reasons for wondering whether their individual scientific efforts will together provide knowledge leading to the maintenance of a good and democratic society.

An ideal-type explanation of political science's current outlook may be distilled from a host of complaints that practitioners are prone to express, sometimes in private conversations and occasionally in print. In their totality, these recall some of the matters touched upon when we considered the nature of learned disciplines in chapter 1, for their overall thrust reflects the fact that political scientists are more than ever aware of the sociology of political inquiry and how it can militate against a scholarly community's attempts to provide useful and objective knowledge of social affairs. This awareness flows from dissatisfaction with the discipline's small success at dealing with urgent events in the real world, and from recognition of considerable validity attaching to some of the criticisms leveled against mainstream political studies by dissenters such as those who supported the Caucus for a New Political Science. To demonstrate these sentiments, I have selected for examination a number of matters that provoke concern and unease because they entail sociological factors that prevent the discipline from fulfilling ends which, formally at least, many practitioners hope it will serve. This chapter will consider professional definitions of politics, the imperatives of publishing, the search for truth, and the teaching of wisdom, while chapter 8 will pass on to the quest for laws of political behavior, the case of community power studies, and the challenge of critical theory. Within the political science community, opinion on such matters adds up, if not always systematically and elegantly, to a nagging suspicion that the discipline is merely marking time.

Definitions of Politics

Political science's vocational predicament starts with how, as a scholarly discipline, it defines the object of its learned attentions. The age-old definition of politics, which underlay the classic college curriculum even before political

---

7. On "ideal types," see Hans H. Gerth and C. Wright Mills, eds., *From Max Weber: Essays in Sociology* (New York: Oxford University Press, 1946), pp. 59f., 294, 323f.

studies emerged as a distinct discipline, came from Aristotle. Deferring to a commonsense notion that politics touches upon every aspect of public life, and that rulers must deal with whatever important matters a society may encounter, Aristotle defined politics very broadly. Various other sciences may deal with knowledge of particular affairs, he said, but politics "ordains which of the sciences should be studied in a state, and which each class of citizens should learn and up to what point they should learn them; and we see even the most highly esteemed of faculties to fall under this, e.g., strategy, economics, rhetoric."[8] In our terms of a Temple of Science, Aristotle had in mind that politics constituted the Temple's roof, which was in some sense a master science over all the lesser realms of knowledge to be found in the Temple's columns. This conception of politics has always enjoyed some support within the community of political scholars, such as when Woodrow Wilson, speaking as president of the APSA, held that "nothing which forms or affects human life seems to me to be properly foreign to the student of politics."[9] Along similar lines, James K. Pollack and Peter H. Odegard, both serving as APSA presidents long after Wilson, argued that political science is "the integrating and synthesizing discipline,"[10] and that it must be "blind to the barriers" which nowadays separate various social sciences.[11]

It is a fact of modern university life, however, that the reputation of great educational institutions rests on their ability, or presumed capacity, for delivering scientific knowledge where, in the modern view, that knowledge is specialized rather than general. And therefore when universities came to prominence in America, as we have seen, each discipline took upon itself responsibility for one column within the Temple of Science, whilst none made a very clear-cut claim of tenancy on the roof. It could hardly have been otherwise, there being no way that any group of scholars could absorb all the knowledge developed by all the scientific communities working in the world of higher learning; a single column of the Temple, figuratively speaking, was all that most scholars were capable of knowing. Moreover, it is the nature of organizations, as we have noted, to seek control over some area of expertise and then maintain their authority by rejecting the claims of other people to expertise in the same realm. For this reason, if any discipline were to attempt to sit, figuratively, on the Temple's roof and comment, from there, on matters jealously guarded by other disciplines, its practitioners would surely be labeled dilettantes and ignored by practitioners of the more specific sciences.

8. *Ethica Nicomachea*, trans. David Ross (London: Oxford University Press, 1925), Bk. 1, §1094.

9. "The Law and the Facts," *American Political Science Review* (February 1911), p. 2.

10. Pollack, "The Primacy of Politics," ibid. (March 1951), p. 15.

11. Odegard, "Variations on a Familiar Theme," ibid. (December 1951), p. 964.

In time, then, it was bureaucratically inevitable that the Aristotelian definition of politics would be renounced by political scientists seeking to portray their discipline as one legitimate scholarly enterprise among others, by enterprising practitioners who would understand that, in the general scheme of things incorporated into higher education, political science must erect a column of its own within the Temple of Science. The discipline's writings came to be marked, therefore, by frequent indications of envy toward those who, like the economists, have managed to take "a particular aspect of the complex social whole" for their province and avoid dissipating intellectual energies by trying to analyze all of social reality.[12] In recognition of the obvious need, an APSA report in 1962, entitled "Political Science as a Discipline," stated flatly that "Political science has its own area of human experience to analyze, its own body of descriptive and factual data to gather, its own conceptual schemes to formulate and test for truth."[13]

Behavioral Definitions of Power

Even as political science came to dwell within a university environment and accept its prescription for scientific research, however, no clear idea emerged of what political scientists were actually studying, as distinguished from those subjects handled by other disciplines. Yet absent such a definition, no one could say for sure why the work of political scientists on any particular public question should be more authoritative than that of, say, philosophers, economists, sociologists, or even journalists. A possible solution to the problem was suggested in 1904, when Frank Goodnow addressed his colleagues as the APSA's first president and stipulated that "Political Science is that science which treats of the organization known as the state."[14] This notion presented difficulties, including the fact that "the state" as commonly understood does not exist in every society— such as among nomads, or in primitive tribes—at all times.[15] Political scientists therefore eventually sought to characterize politics more accurately by rallying to the suggestion that "power" should be the target of political science research. And so, after World War II, Harold Lasswell held that "the science of politics" is "the science of power."[16] Or, in another formulation, Lasswell and Abraham

---

12. Frederick M. Watkins, "Comments on Professor Van Dyke's Paper," in James C. Charlesworth, ed., *A Design for Political Science* (Philadelphia: American Academy of Political and Social Science, 1966), pp. 29–30.

13. *American Political Science Review* (June 1962), p. 417.

14. "The Work of the American Political Science Association," *Proceedings of the American Political Science Association*, vol. 1 (1904), p. 37.

15. Henry Jones Ford, "The Scope of Political Science," ibid., vol. 2 (1905), p. 200.

16. *The Language of Politics* (New York: G. W. Stewart, 1949), p. 8.

Kaplan suggested that "Political science is concerned with power in general,"[17] where "the political process is the shaping, distribution, and exercise of power."[18]

This definition of politics had the serious institutional shortcoming of laying exclusive claim to a phenomenon appearing in many nonpolitical realms. For example, economists are interested in control over markets, and sociologists want to investigate religious sanctions. To lay down a more effective boundary line between political science and other scholarly endeavors, David Easton suggested that his colleagues continue to deal with power, but that they confine their efforts to a particular kind of it. He therefore offered the idea that "political life consists of those actions related to the authoritative allocation of values,"[19] where by "values" he meant the desired conditions of life. In choosing the phrase "authoritative allocation," Easton portrayed public affairs as entailing political decisions which, while based on power broadly speaking, enjoy a capacity for overriding decisions flowing from lesser power. Assuming the existence of such a power hierarchy, wherein political decisions are categorically superior to all others, it follows that political scientists should be professionally responsible for examining the actors and institutions who produce decisions of ultimate force for local, national, or international communities. In technical terms, Easton held that "political life" is "a system of interrelated activities," which "influence the way in which authoritative decisions are formulated and executed for a society."[20] This was his formulation of a "systems theory," within which the "political system" was cast as an adjunct of the larger system of community life and where politics was viewed as a subsystem of the whole which, for purposes of scholarly research, could be isolated and studied as effectively as economists cordoned off and then analyzed the subsystem of prices, supply and demand, and economic choice.[21]

By postulating a realm of political activity separate from all others, Easton in effect created a Temple column that could henceforth be occupied exclusively by the discipline of political science. He then called upon his colleagues to concentrate their efforts on formulating general ideas and hypotheses about the political system, so called, in order that around such shared notions the community of political scholars would eventually build up a compact and consistent body of political knowledge as its contribution to human welfare. Concentration

17. *Power and Society: A Framework for Political Inquiry* (New Haven: Yale University Press, 1950), p. 85.

18. Ibid., p. 75.

19. *The Political System: An Inquiry into the State of Political Science*, 2nd ed. (New York: Knopf, 1971), pp. 143–44.

20. David Easton, "An Approach to the Analysis of Political Systems," *World Politics* (April 1957), p. 384.

21. *The Political System*, p. 97.

of scholarly efforts along the recommended lines would lead to important breakthroughs in our understanding of public life, he said, and these were necessary because unless practitioners are able to achieve "a more reliable picture [of politics] than the insight of the well-informed layman . . . the existence of a special political discipline will indeed take a good deal of explaining."[22]

Easton's description of the political system was modified into a "structural-functional" definition of political life, when scholars such as Gabriel A. Almond and James S. Coleman suggested that politics be viewed as an enterprise fulfilling certain necessary tasks for entire societies. As they put it, all societies manage, most of the time, to maintain internal and external order, and they do this via social devices which Almond and Coleman saw as political structures. It followed, in this view, that every society, from the most modern to the most primitive, must have political structures of some kind, even if, at the primitive end of the scale, these do not much resemble the American Congress or other modern institutions.[23] In light of what must be done to maintain public order, it seemed plain to Almond and Coleman that the political structures of any society must handle the various "functions" of "integration and adaptation (both internally and vis-à-vis other societies) by means of the employment, or threat of employment, of more or less legitimate physical compulsion."[24] In other words, all political systems will provide for "political socialization," "leadership recruitment," "interest articulation," "interest aggregation," and "political communication," as well as the traditional political tasks of making rules or laws, applying them, and judging their application.[25]

Building like Easton upon the idea that a political system can be located among other social systems, Almond and Coleman offered their definition of politics to the discipline as a framework within which to pose related hypotheses and test their validity. With time, they hoped, unified knowledge would accumulate from collective efforts along such lines, and a useful understanding of political life would emerge.[26] There can be no doubt, then, that the functional approach to political studies was designed both as an objectively true definition of politics and as a bureaucratically serviceable instrument for concentrating political scientists' efforts so as to produce knowledge that would redound to the profession's credit. As Almond and Coleman themselves put it, the functional

22. Ibid., p. 42.
23. Almond and Coleman, eds., *The Politics of the Developing Areas* (Princeton, N.J.: Princeton University Press, 1960) pp. 11–12.
24. Ibid., p. 7.
25. Ibid., p. 17.
26. Ibid., p. 64.

approach was offered as "a major step forward in the nature of political science as a science."[27]

Shortcomings of the Behavioral Approaches

These behavioral definitions of politics had the virtue of characterizing their subject so narrowly as to delineate a province of inquiry which the political science discipline could claim for its own. In this sense, such definitions were functionally rational for serving the interest of the scholarly community within its larger environment. Of course, what serves a single institution does not necessarily contribute to the pursuit of wider goals. This sociological reality was recognized by practitioners who repeatedly charged that Easton, Almond, Coleman, and their supporters failed to supply objective criteria for a comprehensive study of the subject at hand, which was everything that belonged to politics in the real world no matter how leaders of a learned discipline might hope to define the essence of politics succinctly. Over the years, these charges gave rise to an extensive critical literature, which cannot be summarized briefly.[28] Roughly speaking, however, they fell into two categories, pertaining to factual and to ethical shortcomings of the systems theory and the functional approach.

As a matter of empirical reality, for example, both of the behavioral conceptions seem to assume that a political system maintains itself over time. We are prepared to recognize this actuality from our commonsense perception of the underlying continuity of political entities such as "France," or "Great Britain."

27. Ibid., p. 4.
28. For some interesting examples of this literature, see Paul F. Kress, "Self, System, and Significance: Reflections on Professor Easton's Political Science," *Ethics* (October 1966), pp. 1–13; Peter Leslie, "General Theory in Political Science: A Critique of Easton's Systems Analysis," *British Journal of Political Science* (April 1972), pp. 155–72; Reid R. Reading, "Is Easton's Systems-Persistence Framework Useful? A Research Note," *Journal of Politics* (May 1972), pp. 258–67; John D. Astin, "Easton I and Easton II," *Western Political Quarterly* (December 1972), pp. 726–37; Eugene F. Miller, "David Easton's Political Theory," *Political Science Reviewer* (Fall 1971), pp. 184–235; J. S. Sorzano, "David Easton and the Invisible Hand," *American Political Science Review* (March 1975), pp. 91–106; Robert E. Dowse, "A Functionalist's Logic," *World Politics* (July 1966), pp. 607–22; Martin Landau, "On the Use of Functional Analysis in American Political Science," *Social Research* (1968), pp. 44–75; A. James Gregor, "Political Science and the Use of Functional Analysis," *American Political Science Review* (June 1968), pp. 425–39; Jerone Stephens, "The Logic of Functional and Systems Analyses in Political Science," *Midwest Journal of Political Science* (August 1969), pp. 367–94; Alexander J. Groth, "Structural Functionalism and Political Development: Three Problems," *Western Political Quarterly* (September 1970), pp. 485–99; Stanley Rothman, "Functionalism and Its Critics: An Analysis of the Writings of Gabriel Almond," *Political Science Reviewer* (Fall 1971), pp. 236–76. For responses by Easton and Almond, see David Easton, "Systems Analysis and Its Classical Critics," *Political Science Reviewer* (Fall 1973), pp. 269–301; and Gabriel A. Almond, "Slaying the Functional Dragon," *Political Science Reviewer* (Fall 1973), pp. 259–68.

Yet what do we really mean by "France" or "Great Britain"? The history of any political entity suggests that neither the systems theory nor the functional approach can tell us very much about its key characteristics, because the normal condition of such entities must be known before we can tell if a specific act or actor is functional or dysfunctional, system-supporting or system-destroying, with regard to their continued existence.[29] It is clear, however, that in the real world "France" has "persisted" over the last two centuries while moving back and forth from democracy to authoritarianism.[30] What are we to make of such different responses at various times to the constant functional requirement of maintaining identity? Apparently the same functions can be served by a broad range of structures, in which case behavioral political theory offers no particular way of predicting which structure will, or should, triumph.[31]

To criticize along these lines is to point out that neither the systems theory nor the functional approach does a good job of limiting the number of things that political scientists must study, because if political life can be maintained over time by a very great variety of institutions and processes, almost anything can be considered relevant to public life and important in the study of politics. To take a recent example, the realm of politics in Iran is now seen as inextricably linked to at least one other realm of human affairs, since religious authority is now capable of influencing both the choice of Iran's public leaders and their subsequent behavior. Looked at this way, neither the systems approach nor the functional notion offers much more than an elaborate vocabulary for putting labels on a great many phenomena and claiming that some of them may be called political science's own. Exactly which these last are, and which among them are important, or significant, or necessary, or conclusive, or definitive, or fundamental, are matters that neither definition of politics seems capable of addressing effectively.

While empirical criticisms suggested that behavioral research programs could not avoid being too broad and indiscriminate, the ethical critique took an opposite tack, saying that the discipline had been induced to narrow its focus so sharply as to ignore a host of matters belonging legitimately to political thought and speculation. On this score, Christian Bay spoke for many Caucus members and the overall counterculture position. In general, he argued that the study of politics must take into account the aim of building a just community, according

29. A. James Gregor, "Political Science and the Uses of Functional Analysis," pp. 432–33; Groth, "Structural Functionalism and Political Development," pp. 490–91.

30. France is used as a historical example for testing the functional approach in W. G. Runciman, *Social Science and Political Theory* (Cambridge: Cambridge University Press, 1963), p. 117.

31. Carl G. Hempel, "The Logic of Functional Analysis," in Hempel, *Aspects of Scientific Explanation* (New York: Free Press, 1965), pp. 311–13.

to man's best hopes and aspirations. More specifically, he spoke of paying more attention to "some conception of human welfare or the public good," where men's true needs rather than mere wants are the criteria for deciding what constitutes a normal and desirable society.[32] It was a misnomer, Bay declared, for behavioralists to claim that the visible stuff of public life is somehow the sum total of politics. Rather, we should concede that most public life deserves no more than the title of "pseudopolitics," an affair "concerned with either the alleviation of personal neurosis or with promoting private or private interest-group advantage"—this as opposed to "politics," a matter of satisfying the basic needs of society "according to some universalistic scheme of priorities, implicit or explicit."[33] Yet "it is our obligation as political scientists," Bay argued, "to teach the principle of good politics,"[34] the rules and standards by which a good society may be devised and maintained.

Taken together, the two sets of charges against behavioral definitions of politics left the discipline in a quandary. On the one hand, they indicated that political science still lacks a clear and concise notion as to the very subject of its concern. The impact of arguments to this effect is necessarily unsettling in a bureaucratic sense, because they suggest that no concept yet exists for drawing together research results attained by separate scholars in the learned community and thereby facilitating the expression of definitive professional statements about politics. On the other hand, there are arguments which claim that political science in the conventional mold has already led to an undesirably narrow focus of concern. Such arguments strike a sensitive nerve among practitioners who believe that, regardless of professional strictures, politics touches upon just about everything, as it is and as it should be. Scholars of this mind fear that America's current difficulties may overwhelm the nation without political science offering advice aimed at realizing men's highest aspirations for social life, at what Henry Kariel called "the promise of politics."[35] In Bay's terms, they are afraid that, given the range of problems besetting the country, behavioralism is simply not "substantively rational."[36]

There does not seem any way out of the definitional dilemma. To narrow the scope of political studies is functionally rational for the discipline, and so there will always be practitioners who feel uneasy when this goal remains un-achieved. But to widen the definition back to Greek proportions, as Bay recom-

32. "Politics and Pseudo-Politics: A Critical Evaluation of Some Behavioral Literature," *American Political Science Review* (March 1965), pp. 40, 48–51.

33. Ibid., p. 40.

34. Christian Bay, "For an American *Political* Science Association," *PS* (Summer 1968), p. 36.

35. See n. 6, above.

36. "Politics and Pseudo-Politics," p. 41.

mended,[37] would in effect place political scholars up on the Temple's roof and leave them without professional authority at all, since such authority is accorded today only to experts with specialized knowledge. The intractable paradox of it all was summed up by Leonard J. Fein when he observed that, if man is indeed a political animal in the Aristotelian sense, "then nothing human is alien to political science." Yet if every aspect of human existence may rightfully be considered a matter for political scholars to investigate, Fein continued, against what finite and manageable quantity of political knowledge can the discipline measure professional competence and noteworthy teaching about politics?[38]

The Imperatives of Publication

Even if a satisfactory definition of politics were available to the discipline, political science would still find itself in difficult straits. After all, complementing any description of a professional boundary is the way scholars work within it. On this score, members of the political science community investigate politics, well defined or not, according to certain very problematical imperatives of publication. Research findings in a scientific community must be published, else how can knowledge accumulate and understanding advance? Yet, for political science, at least, the very mechanics of this enterprise are rooted in sociological tendencies that make intellectual progress difficult if not unlikely.[39]

The Knowledge Market

The conventional view of scientific knowledge is that society needs more and more of it, in order better to utilize natural and social resources and thereby attain a healthier and more wholesome life. This knowledge is produced in scientific communities that can be said to resemble markets, where goods are offered for sale to potential customers. Thus, scientific researchers (or "sellers") submit new ideas for publication to scholarly journals, where their acceptance (or "purchase") indicates that these researchers are highly regarded by the community, since journal editors and referees (or "buyers") are scholars of repute who would not certify a manuscript for publication unless it were commendable according to the discipline's lights. Accordingly, the status of "scientist" is earned in exchange for an offering of knowledge, when a scholar's ideas are accepted by his intellectual peers. But how do some scientists acquire a higher standing than

37. Christian Bay, "Thoughts on the Purposes of Political Science Education," in George J. Graham and George W. Carey, eds., *The Post-Behavioral Era: Perspectives on Political Science* (New York: McKay, 1972), p. 97.

38. "Teaching Political Science," *PS* (Summer 1969), p. 306.

39. For contrast to the description of publishing about to be offered in the text, see J. H. Hexter, "Publish or Perish—A Defense," *The Public Interest* (Fall 1969), pp. 60–77.

others? In every scientific community, there will be an informal understanding that publishing outlets are ranked in terms of disciplinary excellence, so that to achieve publication in the best journals, as opposed to the more commonplace, signifies a more substantial addition to the knowledge enjoyed by one's colleagues. Presumably, the discipline accords differential prestige to such contributions when they serve unequally toward maintaining repute for the entire community, whose professional task it is to provide knowledge for use in society at large.

Such is the theory of markets for scientific knowledge among scholars.[40] Difficulty arises because markets in practice do not always produce desirable outcomes, or because, as counterculturalists would say, "effective demand" does not always foster the production of human well-being. In the case of scholarly publications, it is an obvious peculiarity of market behavior that the immediate quantity of publications often counts for more than their absolute quality. Thus when Albert Somit and Joseph Tanenhaus surveyed political scientists in 1964, they discovered that among "attributes contributing to career success," the quantity of a scholar's publications was most important, while their quality was ranked fifth.[41] Yet if professional advancement depends more on the amount of one's writings than on their intrinsic worth, there can be no assurance that the sum total of political science research findings, as published, are enhancing human welfare and not merely occupying library shelf space. Articles and monographs aside, one book editor of a leading journal estimated that close to five thousand volumes on political subjects were submitted to his journal for possible review each year.[42] He did not venture to guess how many of them significantly advanced our understanding of public life.

The Tendency to Specialize
Quantity of publication becomes important to career success for reasons that are deeply rooted in vocational reality. Thus political scientists who aspire to advance professionally try to make scholarly contributions that can quickly earn them recognition. And within large organizations, one way of getting ahead is to invent

40. On the structure of scientific communities, see Norman W. Storer, *The Social System of Science* (New York: Holt, 1966); Michael Mulkay, *Science and the Sociology of Knowledge* (London: Allen and Unwin, 1979); Warren O. Hagstrom, *The Scientific Community* (New York: Basic Books, 1965); and Jerome R. Ravetz, *Scientific Knowledge and Its Social Problems* (New York: Oxford University Press, 1971).

41. *American Political Science: A Profile of a Discipline* (New York: Atherton, 1964), p. 79. By 1976, the quantity of a scholar's publications ranked second to the school at which his doctorate was taken. On this point, see Roettger, "The Discipline," p. 28.

42. See the estimates in Nelson W. Polsby, "Report of the Managing Editor," *PS* (Fall 1971), p. 541.

something not yet being provided by any other member of the organization.[43] It follows, in scholarly communities, that one tends to develop research projects which break ground that others have not tilled before, to stake out small areas of inquiry that other scholars have not yet invaded and conquered for their own. There is, therefore, a propensity constantly to refashion the scope of political science into smaller and smaller realms of expertise, so that some scholars can quickly stand forth as patently competent with regard to subjects that other scholars have somehow overlooked. Accordingly, the number of fields and sub-fields within political science has steadily increased over the years, a matter of disciplinary fragmentation that suddenly became visible when the *APSA Biographical Directory* for 1968 listed twenty-seven subfields,[44] and when the same publication, updated for 1973, listed over sixty subfields.[45]

As rapidly as realms of research multiply, they do not outnumber the ways in which they are investigated. As A. James Gregor pointed out, "Hardly a year passes that fails to find a new, oft-times exotic, research method or technique added to the armarium of political inquiry. . . . Anyone who cannot negotiate Chi squares, assess randomization, statistical significance, and standard deviations is less than illiterate; he is preconscious."[46] Some practitioners of course view frequent changes of technique as the cardinal requirement for a truly scientific understanding of political life, on the grounds that constant refinement of a profession's tools will help to produce a more impressive end product. On the other hand, sober reflection indicates that, just as it is functionally rational for the aspiring political scientist to develop a heretofore unexplored field, so too there is good cause to devise techniques that go beyond those currently in use. That is, apart from any immediate efficiency which newer techniques may bring the discipline as a whole, authorship in this area constitutes a claim to expertise, to presumed scientific contribution beyond that previously achieved by one's colleagues.

And so, as subfields multiply and as research techniques proliferate, political scientists are, as a rule, less and less able to judge the quality of works by their colleagues, except for those few working on precisely the same problems and with exactly the same devices. In 1935, Frederick A. Ogg, the managing editor of the *American Political Science Review*, was able to read and evaluate most of the manuscripts submitted to that journal.[47] By 1977, Nelson W. Polsby, hold-

43. Anthony Downs, *Inside Bureaucracy* (Boston: Little, Brown, 1967), p. 267: "Climbers are strongly motivated to invent new functions for their bureaus, especially functions not performed elsewhere."

44. 5th ed. (Washington, D.C.: APSA, 1968), p. xii.

45. 6th ed. (Washington, D.C.: APSA, 1973), pp. v–vi.

46. *An Introduction to Metapolitics* (New York: Free Press, 1971), p. 3.

47. "Report of the Committee on Policy," *American Political Science Review* (February 1935), p. 128.

ing the same office, conceded that no editor could "judge the quality of manu-scripts over the full range of concerns that political scientists write about."[48] Surveys within the discipline show that Polsby actually gave voice to a widely shared sense of professional limitations. Thus practitioners say that journals are the most effective device—better than conventions or books—whereby their community disseminates new knowledge among its members.[49] And they consis-tently rank the *APSR* as their best journal in terms of prestige.[50] That is, an article in the *APSR* presumably transmits more important knowledge than an article published elsewhere. Moreover, practitioners say that, among all jour-nals, they are most likely to read the *APSR*.[51] Yet less than half of the *APSR* readers claim to read even 25 percent of the journal's articles, and only one-fifth of all practitioners report that the *APSR* is the journal they read most, with the vast majority of other journals attracting the first attention of no more than 5 percent of all practitioners.[52] These figures reveal that not many political scien-tists deem their discipline's leading journal to be especially relevant to their particular interests; of those who do so, few read very much of it; for the most part, practitioners are so specialized that they congregate to various lesser jour-nals in notably small audiences; that, in short, most members of the discipline read the work of their colleagues hardly at all. The conclusion is inescapable: when a scholar knows that his associates are unlikely to judge the quality of his work by reading it directly, he will seek to publish frequently, in hopes of making at least the length of his publications list impressive.

The Prevalence of Jargon

The great majority of political scientists must be unaware of the figures on journal readership. As parties to the phenomenon, however, they cannot help but notice at least one immediate cause of antipathy, which is a prevalence of jargon. Even if practitioners today all wanted to read a wide range of the disci-pline's published products, it is unlikely that many of them would understand most of what their colleagues write. To the contrary, persistent failure to com-municate is reflected in the contemporary scholarly habit of reading only the introductions and conclusions to published works, leaving unexamined the cen-tral parts, which consist of very specialized and technical explanations as to how various authors get from the beginning to the end of their research. For political

48. Nelson W. Polsby, "Editorial Comment," ibid. (December 1971), p. 960.

49. William C. Baum, et al., "American Political Science Before the Mirror: What Our Journals Reveal about the Profession," *Journal of Politics* (November 1976), pp. 897–98.

50. Roettger, "The Discipline," pp. 18–20.

51. Thomas E. Mann, "Report on a Survey of the Membership of the American Political Science Association," *PS* (Fall 1974), p. 384.

52. Ibid.

studies, this practice is so widespread that one commentator, faithful to the notion of "keeping up" with the latest technical terminology, has deplored such skimming and recommended a number of statistical textbooks that he says will help political scholars to decode the latest scientific jargon. [53]

Jargon enjoys a formal theoretical rationale in that an effective science can exist only where the ambiguity of everyday terms is avoided by a technical vocabulary which enables scientists to speak precisely and effectively about the complex world of nature and society. For political science in particular, David Easton long ago argued that the way traditional political questions are framed makes them difficult to answer, for the very words used suffer from vagueness, emotional biases, and preconceived ethical judgments. [54] A standard scope and methods textbook is therefore likely to draw up a list of traditional words and recommend that political scientists gradually replace them with new ones in the profession's discourse. Among the old would be words like "absolutism," "justice," "nation," "patriotic," "rights," "society," and "tyranny." Among the new would be "attitude," "conflict," "cross-pressure," "game," "interaction," "pluralism," "socialization," and "valuation." [55]

Notwithstanding formal justifications, the primary reason why political science spawns more and more new terms for describing public life has little to do with a calculated desire to transform political studies into an analogue of, say, physics. It is not at all clear, after all, that the accomplishments of the physical sciences can be duplicated in the study of society, because we cannot be sure that social phenomena are unambiguous enough to be labeled briefly and accurately, thenceforth to be studied effectively. We can speak fairly intelligibly about "political parties," for example, and know more or less what we mean. But a leading textbook is unable to define them precisely, [56] and an authoritative journal article finds them involved in so many political events and processes that there seems no way of saying that a political party is anything in particular. [57]

Thus the major impetus for ceaselessly creating new terminology in political science has less to do with the substance of science than with the form of organized enterprise. As Max Weber observed, bureaucrats seek to gain power by secrecy, and clothing knowledge with jargon is therefore a way of excluding

53. Michael Margolis, "The New Language of Political Science," *Polity* (Spring 1971), pp. 416–26.

54. Easton, *The Political System*, pp. 44–47.

55. The lists of words, old and new, may be found in Ralph M. Goldman, *Contemporary Perspectives on Politics* (New York: Van Nostrand, 1972), pp. 15–17.

56. See Maurice Duverger, *Political Parties*, rev. ed. (New York: John Wiley, 1959), who offers no explicit definition of parties but uses a comparative approach that describes, for purposes of demonstration, what are called parties in several countries.

57. Avery Leiserson, "The Place of Parties in the Study of Politics," *American Political Science Review* (December 1957), pp. 943–54, but esp. p. 948.

outsiders from access to it; in the case of Persian treasury officials, he noted, the clerks actually invented a secret script so as to maintain control over financial affairs.[58] Yet if organizations tend to generate jargon to protect the interests of their members, then even while individual political scientists may be frustrated by professional jargon, their colleagues will have no great collective incentive to seek its demise. If this functional rationality serves some larger purpose, as it does in the realms of natural science, so much the better. But the two purposes are not necessarily linked, and jargon can flourish even where substantive rationality fails to emerge. Such may be the case with political science, as individuals tend to specialize and build their professional reputations at least partly on the basis of appearing to get a grip on something no one else has successfully grasped.

Examples from the literature abound, and are not confined to particular fields. For instance:

> A model is a guide to theory, but no model is itself a theory. Only an imaginative observer can generate theoretical propositions using the bare bones of models. Models are no sure path to explanation of specific historical events but are guides to possible explanations. Every case is a different combination of factors and thus no model will automatically explain a case.[59]

> The problem is that the schema, at least in the form presented, cannot logically deliver the theoretical benefits claimed for it because certain epistemic prerequisites are absent: (1) clear and testable distinctions between dependent and independent variables, (2) a theoretical framework positing predications or generalizations directly relevant to understanding the *how* and *why* of political development beyond an intuitive, descriptive exposition or a mere association of traits, and (3) "statements of theory" that are not analytically barren or tautological. Without these components all that remains is classification via a descriptive model that cannot explain.[60]

> Each procedure will be discussed in relation to an essential step on the long road to international relations theory. Thus "regional factor analysis" will be proposed as a method for testing the universality of different con-

58. Weber is cited on this point in Ralph P. Hummel, *The Bureaucratic Experience* (New York: St. Martin's, 1977), p. 143. The original passage may be found in Gerth and Mills, *From Max Weber*, p. 233.

59. Erwin C. Hargrove, *The Power of the Modern Presidency* (Phildelphia: Temple University Press, 1974), p. 123.

60. Philip H. Melanson, *Political Science and Political Knowledge* (Washington, D.C.: Public Affairs Press, 1975), pp. 56–57.

cepts, indicators, and data aggregations; "covariance analysis" will be presented as a means of discovering nonadditive explanations relating independent and dependent conceptual variables; and "confluence analysis" will be suggested as a feasible way of taking apart, putting together, and deductively testing systems of causal generalizations about international relations.[61]

. . . the theorist must resist the temptation to depict the iron cage [Max Weber's metaphor] from the abstract freedom of the thinking subject and refuse the mythical notion of the iron cage as an "empty society." That is, [John] Scharr must resituate man, as a real historical subject, in that iron cage which as a "bad totality" tends to impose the Medusan view of social reality "only in the form of objects, results, and already given facts," i.e., only in its reified mediations.[62]

In the interest of clarity, the related terms "interpretation," "exegesis" and "commentary" will be used in specialized ways in the discussion. "Interpretation" and "interpretative inquiry" connote the enterprise of understanding phenomenal meaning and significance, usually textual meaning and significance. "Exegesis" refers narrowly to the explication of textual meaning. "Commentary" refers to writing about the history of political theory, regardless of orientation.[63]

Members [of society] could not possibly recall the whole history transmitted to each generation, even if it were desirable or necessary. Retrieval is always selective. What a person recalls will hinge on those rules governing the ways in which he scans his memory, the criteria of appropriateness used to make selections from the information retrieved, and the rules regulating the way he goes about synthesizing and reorganizing the knowledge recalled for immediate use. . . . The rules themselves constitute part of the available resources necessary for handling feedback response.[64]

Some political scientists have struck back against the use of jargon. Lee C. MacDonald, for example, argued that much of it serves only to imply that political science is more scientific than it really is. The unwarranted pretense of

61. Hayward R. Alker, Jr., "The Long Road to International Relations Theory," *World Politics* (July 1966), p. 628.

62. Herbert G. Reid and Ernest Yanarella, "Political Science and the Post-Modern Critique of Scientism and Domination," *Review of Politics* (July 1975), pp. 300–01.

63. Deborah Baumgold, "Political Commentary on the History of Political Theory," *American Political Science Review* (December 1981), p. 929.

64. David Easton, *Systems Analysis of Political Life* (New York: Wiley, 1965), p. 458.

such literary excesses could be demonstrated, he thought, by reducing the East-
onian passage quoted above, about recall and feedback, to the simple statement
that "Habit affects memory and people remember from history what is useful for
them to remember."[65] Few political scholars have been so totally unforgiving of
jargon as John Stuart Mill, however, who wrote that whatever Hegel published
on metaphysics was "sheer nonsense," and that "conversancy" with the German
philosopher "tends to deprave one's intellect."[66] What usually obtains instead is
weary resignation to the inevitable, and only rarely will an elder statesman of the
discipline, such as Lindsay Rogers in 1958, risk saying openly that he has
decided not to bother trying to stay abreast of developments along these lines,
because "life is too short."[67]

The Lack of Sustained Judgments

So long as there are scholars bent on attaining reputation, there will be more
publications, more specialization, more refinements of technique, and more
jargon. We may therefore expect that the stock of political knowledge, rather
than gaining strength and utility from additional research findings, will instead
become increasingly fragmented and confused. In this sense the mechanics of
publication, for political scholars at least, make the certification of sustained
judgments unlikely.[68] It would be unfair to accuse only the publication system
for this condition in political studies, since in the twentieth century there are
wider causes as well. Still, there are at least two reasons why the imperatives of
publication currently make discipline-wide commitment to broad precepts difficult to attain.

To begin with, a great many publications are the work of younger scholars
rushing to achieve higher rank and tenure. Thus a report from 1962 showed that
eleven of thirty-three articles in three successive issues of the *APSR* were written

65. "Myths, Politics and Political Science," *Western Political Quarterly* (March 1969),
p. 147.

66. Cited in Lewis S. Feuer, *Ideology and the Ideologists* (New York: Harper Torchbooks,
1975), p. 76. See also the attack on "the Schoolmen," in Thomas Hobbes, *Leviathan* (orig., 1651;
Oxford; Basil Blackwell, 1960), p. 51: "What is the meaning of the words, *The first cause does not
necessarily inflow any thing into the second, by force of the essential subordination of the second
causes, by which it may help it to work.* They are the translation of the title of the sixth chapter of
Suarez, first book, *Of the concourse, motion, and help of God.* When men write whole volumes of
such stuff, are they not mad, or intend to make others so?"

67. "Political Philosophy in the Twentieth Century: An Appraisal of its Contribution to the
Study of Politics," in Roland Young, ed., *Approaches to the Study of Politics* (Evanston, Ill.:
Northwestern University, 1958), p. 191.

68. Note the early recognition of this point in Logan Wilson, *The Academic Man: A Study in
the Sociology of a Profession* (orig., 1942; New York: Octagon, 1964), p. 219: "Disinterested activity
and the slow ripening of long-term projects become well-nigh impossible as situational pressures
[publishing] call for quick results."

by scholars aged thirty-five years or younger, with sixteen additional articles coming from scholars between the ages thirty-five and forty-five, people still intent on professional advance.[69] In the field of political studies, however, in contrast to what happens in physics and mathematics, one needs time to reflect in order to understand the complexities of life and society. Therefore most work published early in a political scholar's career is necessarily immature when compared with, say, that of Immanuel Kant, who would have failed to achieve tenure in an American university today since he published nothing much until the age of fifty-seven, when he brought out *The Critique of Pure Reason*.[70] As a result, political science journals are full of works lacking perspective, which bombard practitioners with seemingly important notions—if not important, why are they published?—that rarely present considered judgments linked to long-term and sustained inquiry. A great many bits and pieces of research are thereby certified as reputable by the publication system, but they generally shed little light, in a principled and systematic way, on political reality. And only very rarely does an author help us to separate the wheat from the chaff by repudiating his own work at the moment of publication, telling us that it constitutes a "rather sterile exercise" as compared with some other inquiry which he has decided to pursue after the original work was accepted for publication.[71]

The second reason why the publication system discourages long-term commitments relates to the discipline's sheer size and human diversity. Research, experimentation, and publication are supposed to increase the fund of political knowledge but actually become destructive of sustaining large ideas because, whenever a political scholar advances one, someone else will challenge it in order to advance his own reputation. The result is almost mathematically predictable. For total confusion, we need only a sufficiently large number of potential challengers, working on a great many small parts of political life. Where that situation obtains, individual pieces of research will add up to an impenetrable mass of limited findings of such intrinsic inconsistency that even when large-scale coherence might be desirable as the basis for public policy, it will be impossible to draw the pieces of knowledge together and use them effectively.[72]

69. Harvey C. Mansfield, "Toward a Definition of Editorial Policy for the Review," *American Political Science Review* (March 1962), p. 132.

70. Lewis Coser, *Men of Ideas* (New York: Free Press, 1970), pp. 281–82, uses Kant's career to illustrate the problem of aspiring academicians who do not let their scholarly plans mature.

71. See the footnote marked with an asterisk in William R. Caspary, "The 'Mood Theory': A Study of Public Opinion and Foreign Policy," *American Political Science Review* (June 1970), p. 536.

72. The intellectually corrosive effect of many scholars constantly challenging each other's ideas is examined, with many specific examples where contradictory policy recommendations ensue, by Henry J. Aaron, *Politics and the Professors: The Great Society in Perspective* (Washington, D.C.: Brookings Institute, 1978), passim, but esp. pp. 155–56f.

The Search for Truth

In short, publishing engenders a certain measure of intellectual chaos. This phenomenon may be understood further in the light of the responsibility political scientists bear for discovering the "truth," which is a matter of large and significant realities rather than small points of indisputable fact. Here, the problem is not so much how the mechanics of publishing lead to the appearance of bits and pieces of fragmentary knowledge, but the way in which the content of those pieces tends to be shaped, undesirably, away from the traditional ends of scholarly endeavor.

Thinking and teaching in Western society have long been the province of men dedicated to the search for truth in the widest sense, even where they might differ as to its content. Examples abound. In ancient Greece, Plato used *The Republic* to portray Socrates, himself an exemplary seeker after truth, as saying to Glaucon that genuine philosophers are "Those whose passion it is to see the truth."[73] In modern times, Julien Benda charged European intellectuals with treason to civilization for foresaking the truth and endorsing national interests with their writings,[74] while Karl Mannheim hoped that the same intellectuals might detach themselves from social ties completely so as to serve humanity by pursuing the truth objectively.[75] And Barrington Moore, speaking for the counterculturists in America, insisted that the job of intellectuals is not to speak for any particular doctrine or ideal but "to find and speak the truth, whatever the political consequences may be."[76]

Scientists and the Truth

Modern science inherited this tradition of searching for the truth as it grew out of classical fields of knowledge. Indeed, according to historians of science, commitment to the quest developed into a ruling ideology among scientists, from the days when their work came to be distinguished from theology and moral philosophy.[77] Thus Charles Darwin, as an early case in point, concluded his essay on human evolution, *The Descent of Man*, with the disclaimer that "we are not here concerned with hopes and fears, only with the truth as far as our reason

73. Plato, *The Republic*, trans. and introd. by Francis M. Cornford (New York: Oxford University Press, 1945), chapter 19, p. 183.

74. *Betrayal of the Intellectuals* (orig., 1928; Boston: Beacon, 1955).

75. *Ideology and Utopia: An Introduction to the Sociology of Knowledge* (New York: Harcourt, Brace, 1936), pp. 136–46.

76. "Tolerance and the Scientific Outlook," in Robert Paul Wolff, Barrington Moore, Jr., and Herbert Marcuse, *A Critique of Pure Tolerance* (Boston: Beacon, 1965), p. 78.

77. Jerome K. Ravetz, *Scientific Knowledge and Its Social Problems* (New York: Oxford University Press, 1971), pp. 17–20.

allows us to discover it."[78] From the natural sciences, this tradition passed into social inquiry, including the field of political studies. John W. Burgess, for instance, announced that his School of Political Science at Columbia University, dedicated to scientific scholarship, would foster the "progressive development of truth" as a replacement for conventional beliefs based on religious authority.[79]

In more recent times, both mainstream political scholars and their critics have reaffirmed, albeit in different terms of reference, this commitment to truth. One account of modern political analysis concluded, therefore, that, while behavioralism must be understood as an enterprise committed to the vocation of science, that enterprise itself is marked by "the attraction of seeking after truth."[80] Faithful to this commitment, Robert A. Dahl argued that political theory "in the grand manner" is inadequate because it "can rarely, if ever, meet rigorous criteria of truth." It followed, he said, that political research must seek to achieve truth via "testability," else political theory will remain on a par with "literary criticism."[81] Those who deprecated the behavioral approach rejected Dahl's prescription with regard to particular techniques but agreed with him that truth is the main objective of political studies. To this end, Christian Bay held that "All scientists must share a concern for truth as an overriding value."[82] Similarly, Leo Strauss called upon his colleagues to investigate the underlying reality of human nature so that men might transcend their immediate surroundings "by pursuing true happiness, not by pursuing happiness, however happiness may [for the moment] be understood."[83]

Novelty versus the Truth

Spoken agreement to seek the truth does not guarantee that political scientists will search it out, for the scientific communities, and especially their publication systems, must respond to other imperatives as well. We know, after all, that collective activity involves both manifest and latent functions. Thus if the pursuit of truth is a manifest function of science, as so many practitioners agree, there must be latent functions which science also serves, such as providing employment and prestige for members of the scientific community. It follows that, as

78. *The Descent of Man* (New York: Heritage, 1972), p. 619.

79. *Reminiscences of an American Scholar* (New York: Columbia University Press, 1934), p. 203.

80. James Steintrager, "Prediction and Control versus the Narcissus Trance of Political Science," *Polity* (Spring 1971), pp. 315–16.

81. "Political Theory: Truth and Consequences," *World Politics* (October 1958), pp. 95, 97–98.

82. "Political Science Education," p. 93.

83. "Political Philosophy and the Crisis of Our Time," in Graham and Carey, *The Post-Behavioral Era*, p. 242.

they publish in order to serve those functions, practitioners will do so mainly in ways which avoid drawing down upon the collective enterprise criticism that would make continued service of such latent functions problematical or impossible. Here is the spur to ingrained caution that angered Hans Morganthau and drove him to insist that his colleagues tell the truth about politics even though doing so would inevitably offend the established powers.[84]

The institutional view reminds us that scholarly pursuit of the truth can be influenced by, or may yield entirely to, many factors. Among these is a tendency toward seeking novelty rather than the truth. Novelty has an important role to play in scientific progress, because useful scientific truths are often new. However, novelty is also forced upon all scientists as a form of self-advertisement, since elaborating the obvious engenders boredom whereas highlighting the unusual attracts favorable attention.[85] Under the circumstances, there exists the possibility that in some fields of science, where many basic truths are fully known, the emphasis on novelty will detach itself from social utility and come to constitute little more than its own reward.

A considerable gap between truth and novelty seems to have materialized in the field of political studies. Even without the aid of science, we know that there are political facts which are true in the sense of persisting importantly over time. Many of these have already been discovered and summed up in popular sayings, such as that "every man has his price," or that "nations have interests, not friends." As a matter of civic education, it might seem reasonable to believe that repeated lessons based on such maxims would help bring both citizens and officials to understand much of what they need to know about public life.[86] However, a political scientist who seeks to advance professionally can make only

84. "The Purpose of Political Science," in Charlesworth, *A Design for Political Science*, pp. 73–74f.

85. Wilson, *The Academic Man*, pp. 206–07.

86. According to Ravetz, *Scientific Knowledge and Its Social Problems*, pp. 375–77, such maxims—or, in his terms, aphorisms—rather than laws of behavior are the most conclusive sort of knowledge likely to emerge from an "immature" science such as political science. Of course, Ravetz meant aphorisms conforming to solid learning and erudition. He therefore did not suggest that political scholars should expound all those folk sayings that have, over the years, gained some measure of credence. Ravetz also did not discuss the difficulties that would confront scholars seeking to draw up lists of truly valid maxims, while in real life so many plausible adages contradict one another. For example, regarding public affairs, we might easily teach that "He who hesitates is lost," whereas it is also prudent to remember to "Look before you leap." In political science literature, the classic discussion of such conflicting maxims appeared in Herbert Simon, *Administrative Behavior: A Study of Decision-Making Processes in Administrative Organization*, 2nd ed. (New York: Macmillan, 1957), pp. 20–35. The difficulties involved in choosing maxims do not seem to me insurmountable and, at any rate, my point in the text is simply that, for professional reasons, it is not likely that political scholars would spend much time expounding such truths even if an acceptable list were available.

limited publication use of such truths. Once they are enunciated in the profession's literature, if at all, they must be superseded by something new, lest the author be accused of failing to make an "original" contribution to knowledge in his chosen area of inquiry.

It is not surprising, then, that political scientists who are sensitive to vocational reality will pursue novelty in their scientific work. Doctoral students, for example, are given to understand that the discipline expects them, in the image of science, to write dissertations that will "evidence a capacity to do original, if not creative work."[87] And older practitioners, who have attained the doctorate but still aspire to prove themselves, will take note when the community's leading journal expresses a preference for provocative new items in place of follow-up articles that offer refinements and elaborations of an earlier work.[88] A specialized journal, not to be outdone, may even inform its readers plainly, if unwittingly, that it is guided less by a firm notion of enduring truth than by a careful eye to scholarly fashion. For example, in 1978 the editor of *Political Theory* wrote that, "In keeping with current vogues," article manuscripts commenting on "[Robert] Nozick outdrew [John] Rawls by 11 to 3."[89]

Distortions of the Truth

Even if the tendency for novelty to outweigh truth could be overcome, only the naive would expect that, as the phrase has it, "the whole truth and nothing but the truth" would then appear. Instead, there are a host of factors which, separately or in combination, make research into public life very likely to reveal only a part of what is really there. There is, significantly, the matter of getting a grant to do the research in the first place. A great many publications are based upon investigations that require time-consuming library research, well-staffed survey interviewing, and elaborate computer processing of raw data. This is why standard accounts of the rise of behavioralism agree that the movement was facilitated by research funds made available through the Survey Research Center at the University of Michigan, by the Center for Advanced Study in Behavioral Sciences at Palo Alto, California, and by agencies of the Social Science Research Council such as the Committee on Political Behavior and the Committee on Comparative Politics.[90]

Yet where research grants become increasingly necessary for scholars who

87. "Political Science as a Discipline," p. 420.
88. Mansfield, "Toward a Definition of Editorial Policy," pp. 134, 136.
89. Benjamin R. Barber, "From the Editor," *Political Theory* (May 1978), p. 147.
90. Robert A. Dahl, "The Behavioral Approach in Political Science: Epitaph for a Monument to a Successful Protest," *American Political Science Review* (December 1961), p. 765; and Heinz Eulau, "The Behavioral Movement in Political Science: A Personal Document," *Social Research* (March 1968), p. 15.

try to publish and advance professionally, financial considerations may turn both investigative techniques and resultant findings away from the truth. This is because research projects tend to be devised in harmony with the sort of techniques that can gain support rather than with the intrinsic significance of a political question or issue. A reputable political scholar may contend that researchers first choose a problem and only afterward select methods of investigation so as to marshal data bearing on that problem.[91] But a survey of his colleagues shows more than 70 percent of practitioners believing that "Much research in political science is undertaken simply because the projects lend themselves to research by a fashionable tool or because financial support can readily be secured."[92] Their realism matches that of Daniel S. Greenberg, who parodied such vocational propensities by inventing the fictional character of Dr. Grant Swinger, Chairman of the Board of the Center for the Absorption of Federal Funds. Dr. Swinger and his associates studied the feasibility of building a T.C.L.A., or Transcontinental Linear Accelerator. According to their plan, "It would commence in Berkeley [California] and terminate in Cambridge [Massachusetts] and thereby pass through at least 12 states, which means that 24 senators and about 100 congressmen could reasonably be expected to support it."[93]

Apart from the attraction of fashionable techniques, the identity of grantors may introduce selectivity into research projects. Very little is known about this sort of selectivity, for it is difficult to examine grant proposals that have been rejected to see how different they might be from those that were accepted. Still, common sense suggests that a measure of deference for grantor interests must result in many research projects and findings which do not necessarily serve truth in the widest sense. As the Vietnam War grew in scope and intensity, for example, critics complained that university budgets were so heavily supported by federal funding as to discourage faculty researchers from arriving at unorthodox conclusions even where investigative techniques were brilliantly innovative.[94] In the field of defense spending, this indifference to larger goals was easily condemned, as in Tom Lehrer's immortal verse about physics research: " 'Once the rockets are up, who cares where they come down? That's not my department,' says Wernher von Braun."[95] For political studies, Theodore J. Lowi referred to

91. Heinz Eulau, "Segments of Political Science Most Susceptible to Behavioristic Treatment," in James C. Charlesworth, ed., *The Limits of Behavioralism in Political Science* (Philadelphia: American Academy of Political and Social Sciences, 1962), p. 32.

92. Somit and Tanenhaus, *American Political Science*, pp. 14–15.

93. *The Politics of Pure Science: An Inquiry into the Relationship Between Science and Government in the United States* (New York: New American Library, Plume Books, 1967), p. 29.

94. J. William Fulbright, *The Arrogance of Power* (New York: Random House, 1966), p. 41.

95. "Wernher von Braun," *Tom Lehrer's Second Song Book* (New York: Crown, 1968), p. 43. Von Braun made rockets for Germany during World War II and for America in the postwar era.

the same problem when he observed that scholars who endeavor to answer questions posed by clientele, such as grantors, engage in a process which is "inherently conservative" because the agenda of their inquiry is set by the clients rather than an unbridled pursuit of objective excellence in political science.[96]

Even if political science grantees were willing, on the whole, to use the most unfashionable techniques to investigate the most controversial issues, and thereby demonstrate indifference to the preferences of their benefactors, they would be hard pressed to grasp the whole truth of any matter touching upon public affairs. What can be done, for instance, about skewed data? In the early 1970s, political scientists began to think about devising "social indicators" that would be as useful and informative as the "economic indicators" interpreted by economists for society. They soon realized that government supplies most of the statistics that social scientists work with, yet those statistics do not provide all of the information which might be relevant to social problems, depending on who is defining the problem.[97] Ralph Nader complained, for example, that government does not in any systematic way keep track of corporation crimes, such as price fixing, stock swindles, embezzlement, adulteration of goods, illegal kickbacks, false advertising, and so forth.[98] Consequently, there were no data. Yet to use the available figures on violent crime as an index of social pathology in America would be to imply that certain groups in society constitute *the* problem that social policy must deal with, even though more may be stolen through *haute finance* than through pilfering and petty robbery. Alternatively, even where data are not absent but widely disseminated, they are sometimes inherently biased. This is the case with statistics reaching the public domain from private groups rather than government collection agencies. It is well known that the Department of Energy generates little original data on oil supplies and reserves but uses figures supplied by the oil industry. How to arrive at the truth concerning the nation's energy situation under such circumstances is not at all clear.

Other obstacles to arriving at political truth include "pseudo-events," government secrecy, and official lies. Heinz Eulau once held that "The analysis of political group behavior . . . promises rich returns once small groups like legislative committees, administrative bodies, or party councils allow themselves to be systematically studied",[99] but they probably never will. In large part, political

96. "The Politics of Higher Education: Political Science as a Case Study," in Graham and Carey, *The Post-Behavioral Era*, p. 32.

97. Peter J. Henriot, "Political Questions about Social Indicators," *Western Political Quarterly* (June 1970), pp. 235–55, passim.

98. "Introduction" to Morton Mintz and Jerry S. Cohen, *America Inc.: Who Owns and Operates the United States* (New York: Dial, 1971), pp. xi–xix.

99. *The Behavioral Persuasion in Politics* (New York: Random House, 1963), p. 34.

actors of this sort seek to create what may be called "pseudo-events," which are happenings such as news conferences, interviews, information "leaks," background stories, televised election debates, and more, all standing in "ambiguous" relation to reality but designed to keep officials favorably on view via sympathetic coverage in the news media.[100] Some scholars will be taken in by pseudo-events, judging ubiquity to be a sign of validity. Against those who refuse to be misled by such "counterfeit happenings," public officials may react defensively by stamping their recorded deliberations "secret" or "confidential."[101] Thus, only much later will historians be able to unearth even that fraction of the truth which exists among government records.

To make matters worse, political actors may avoid registering any grounds for their decisions at all. Daniel Ellsberg revealed a case of this sort when he wrote of electoral considerations that figured importantly in presidential decision making for the Vietnam War, but which were nowhere written down, in secret or otherwise.[102] And then, of course, after all other efforts at obfuscation fail, there is the occasional official lie, as admitted by Arthur Sylvester when, as assistant secretary of defense, he proclaimed in 1963 that "when the nation's security is at stake, the Government has the right, indeed the duty, to lie if necessary to mislead an enemy and protect the people it represents."[103] This sort of distortion, when discovered, justifies speculation that many commonly accepted "truths" already uttered by public officials, and the basis for scholarly research, may be false to begin with. The Nixon presidency commenced, for example, with the robust promise that "Truth will become the hallmark of the Nixon Administration."[104] Before it ended, the president's official spokesman proved so unreliable that James M. Naughton of the *New York Times* described him as "a Pinocchio puppet whose nose does not grow when he fibs."[105]

100. Daniel J. Boorstin, *The Image: Or What Happened to the American Dream* (New York: Atheneum, 1962), pp. 7–45.

101. On the Kafkaesque system of classifying government documents, see David Wise, *The Politics of Lying* (New York: Vintage, 1973), pp. 79–171.

102. *Papers on the War* (New York: Simon and Schuster, 1972), pp. 75–77, 89, 94, 102.

103. See the testimony by Sylvester in the *Congressional Record*, Senate (June 24, 1963), 89 Congress, 1st Session, p. 859.

104. Herbert Klein, White House Communications Director, in "Nixon Reported Offering Cabinet Post to Democrat," *New York Times* (November 26, 1968), p. A 35.

105. Quoted in Wise, *Politics of Lying*, p. 278. The vocabulary of social science is usually too oblique to convey the truth about untruth directly, and therefore an appreciation for the role of lying in politics is most easily gained from nonacademic works. See Barbara W. Tuchman, *The Guns of August* (New York: Dell, 1963), p. 20, for a colloquial description of General Karl von Bulow, commander of the German Second Army on the Western Front in 1914. "Bulow had no principles; he was so slippery, lamented his colleague Admiral Tirpitz, that compared to him an eel was a leech."

The Effects of Untruth

An annoying price paid for the premium on novelty is what C. Wright Mills would have called "a trained incapacity" for seeing the overall shape of society, which is an affair of great and complex institutions enduring through time. There is danger, he wrote, that we will confuse "precision" with "truth," as if a great many exact pieces of knowledge, offered without any particular interpretation, can tell us something important about the larger reality in which we and they exist.[106] In such a view, it does not much matter that the items of precise knowledge are true, merely in contrast to not being false. Anyone, for example, can safely predict that Americans will elect a president in 1988; for the most part, this is a small and unremarkable truth. The real problem is not to distinguish between true and false, but "to select from among all the truths which can be known those which ought to be known."[107] That is, facts of the human condition must be discovered, but they also must be ordered so as to tell us something *significantly* true about public life. Yet the tendency to novelty in political research does not seem to point in that direction at all. In the words of counter-culturalist Robert M. Pirseg, " 'What's new?' is an interesting and broadening eternal question, but one which, if pursued exclusively, results only in an endless parade of trivia and fashion, the silt of tomorrow."[108]

The Loss of Wisdom

Truth in the largest sense is surely more than just bits and pieces of knowledge. It is instead a two-level phenomenon, partly a matter of collecting the facts and partly a judgment as to which ones are important in relation to wider considerations. Justice, for example, which Aristotle deemed the most important of political truths, he defined as part legal and part natural, that is, somewhat a matter of observing legislated rules and somewhat a function of promoting the intangible but proper order of human existence.[109] In ordinary language, the truth in this two-level sense is something inherently desirable and often goes by the name of "wisdom," as when the Book of Proverbs says that "Wisdom is better than rubies,"[110] or that "Wisdom is the principal thing; therefore get wisdom; and with all the getting get understanding."[111] The question is, what-

---

106. C. Wright Mills, *The Sociological Imagination* (New York: Oxford University Press, 1959), pp. 72–73.

107. Hans J. Morgenthau, *Scientific Man vs. Power Politics* (Chicago: University of Chicago Press, 1946), p. 166.

108. *Zen and the Art of Motorcycle Maintenance* (New York: Bantam, 1974), p. 7.

109. *Ethica Nicomachea*, bk. 7, §1134.

110. Proverbs 8:11.

111. Proverbs 4:7.

ever happened to wisdom in the study of politics, and in the estimation of modern political scientists?

The Relation of Knowledge to Wisdom

The ancients understood that knowledge, or sheer information, was a precondition for the achievement of wisdom. They also believed, however, that some special force must temper the mere acquisition of knowledge, so that men may become wise in the sense of being able to distinguish soundly between the trivially and the significantly true. With regard to men of little faith, St. Paul even expressed this conviction in terms that critics could apply to entire academic disciplines today. "They are continually learning," he said, "but can never attain knowledge of the truth."[112]

In general, classical writers spoke of wisdom as something generated by four forces, separately or in combination. These were religious revelation, experience, age, and reason. For example, revelation might be the cardinal factor leading to insight into the eternal nature of things. We are admonished to read the Holy Scriptures because, as the Gospel according to St. John says of the world, "In the beginning, there was the Word [of God]."[113] Similarly, Ecclesiastes preaches that "the beginning of wisdom is reverence for God."[114] Alternatively, or in tandem, experience and age may provide wisdom concerning man's character and capacities, and so the Book of Job contends that "With the aged there is wisdom, and in length of days there is understanding."[115] Much the same theme underlies Plato's essay on *The Laws*, where a Nocturnal Council of rulers is led by elders of the community.[116]

Reason as the source of wisdom was also cited in ancient writings, and it eventually became a signally important term for discussions of wisdom in the modern world. In contrast to early Jewish and Christian theologians, the Greeks made much of men's capacity to achieve wisdom through a faculty for reasoning. Plato and Aristotle, among others, strove to pick and choose rationally among the contradictory facts of social life and the confusing myths that portrayed gods quarreling among themselves while issuing conflicting commands to mere mortals. The idea was that true understanding of the good life, based on a reasonable assessment of human capacities and requirements, and leading to a well-ordered state, might be developed by at least a few philosophers and statesmen. Many other people, however, by virtue of their power to reason, could affirm this vision

112. 2 Timothy 3:7.

113. John 1:1.

114. Ecclesiastes 12:13.

115. Job 12:12.

116. *The Laws*, trans. R. B. Bury (Cambridge: Harvard University Press, 1926), vol. 2, bk. 12, p. 509.

and carry it into practice.[117] Under the Romans, the notion of wisdom as growing mainly out of reason expanded into an elaborate theory of natural law, where the uniform principles of human nature were to be discovered by individual thinkers, such as Cicero, or distilled from a corpus of legal precedents gathered over time, such as in Justinian's *Digest*.

The assumption that reason can fathom the nature of man and therefore generate wisdom grew more appealing as Western Christian orthodoxy splintered in the Protestant Reformation and as science challenged the persuasive power of theology generally. During the Enlightenment, many political philosophers based their work on a presumption that the natural world is made by God for our edification. As Rousseau said, why believe "That God should go in search of Moses [revelation] to speak [via nature] to Jean Jacques Rousseau?"[118] Having committed themselves to analyzing life according to the dictates of reason, the same thinkers then turned to the public as if all were capable of rational cogitation. Thus Thomas Paine, who was active in both the American and the French revolutions, said in his aptly entitled *Common Sense* that "I offer nothing more than simple facts, plain arguments, and common sense: and have no other preliminaries to settle with the reader, than that he will divest himself of prejudice and prepossessions, and suffer his reason and his [sympathetic] feelings to determine [the truth] for themselves."[119]

The Retreat of Reason

The goal was a polity inhabited by reasonable citizens and governed by equitable policies, and the common understanding of that objective was shared so widely that, throughout the nineteenth century, many social theorists agreed on what they meant by a "rational society." In this sense, men such as Marx, Durkheim, Mosca, and Weber were all "participants in a single debate about the possibility of putting into practice the principles proclaimed earlier by the French Revolution."[120] Little by little, however, the goal came to seem less and less attainable as

117. See the assumption, in Greek philosophy, of a "rational or noetic element" in all people, in James L. Wiser, "Political Theory, Personal Knowledge, and Public Truth," *Journal of Politics* (August 1974), pp. 664f.

118. Quoted in Carl L. Becker, *The Heavenly City of the Eighteenth-Century Philosophers* (New Haven: Yale University Press, 1932), p. 46.

119. Howard Fast, *The Selected Work of Tom Paine and Citizen Tom Paine* (New York: Modern Library, 1945), p. 18. See also Thomas Jefferson's letter of May 8, 1825, in which he recalled to Henry Lee that the Declaration of Independence was intended "to place before mankind the common sense of the subject in terms so plain and firm as to command their assent." The letter is excerpted in Edward Dumbauld, ed., *The Political Writings of Thomas Jefferson* (New York: Liberal Arts, 1955), p. 8.

120. Barrington Moore, Jr., *Political Power and Social Theory* (New York: Harper and Row, 1965), p. 113. A rational view of man's natural condition was common even to many nineteenth-

an extension of man's unique abilities and character, because these were increasingly viewed as imperfectly rational. Thus the very definition of human nature changed with time, to denote a smaller and smaller talent for reasoning. Political theorists of the Enlightenment wrote about *homo philosophicus*, Jeremy Bentham spoke of *homo economicus*, and Karl Marx placed *homo faber* at the center of history. All of these were *homo sapiens*, but the successive substitutions of one term for another suggested movement toward regarding man's mental powers as increasingly marginal to his main activity in life.[121] Then came Sigmund Freud, who saw the irrational as constantly impinging upon man's capacity for achieving full reason. One term in the Freudian lexicon, "rationalization," even indicated that, just when people think they are behaving reasonably, a seemingly coherent explanation for their acts can mask a completely irrational motive. From Freud's time onward, we are prone to think of human beings as creatures less inclined to reflect soberly on their needs than to react unthinkingly to their impulses.

It was within the context of this waning confidence in humanity's power to reason that Karl Mannheim, following the work of great European sociologists seeking to come to terms with Marxism, defined the capacity for cogitation in terms of functional and substantive rationality. As against wisdom in the traditional sense, Mannheim argued that most men and organizations can achieve no more than a shortsighted adjustment to immediate circumstances, while only a few people are capable of appraising their places in the totality of events and moral challenges that surround everyone. As we have already noted, Mannheim hoped to bridge the gap between functional and substantive reasoning by relying on a special community of thinkers free from social ties and therefore capable of overcoming the bias of immediate interests. The more recent version of his ideal may be found in a popular notion of scientific communities, composed of men and women no more rational than Freud had assumed, but working in such a way as to make their collective judgment of new ideas and theories inherently impartial.

Many political scientists eventually agreed that scientific work can be rational even though scientists are not. As the behavioral era began, their conception was summarized by Francis G. Wilson, who observed that most of his colleagues wished to be rational and therefore took as their ideal the methods of

century political thinkers who had little sympathy for the principles of the French Revolution. For example, see John C. Calhoun, proslavery senator from South Carolina, in his *Disquisition on Government* (orig., 1853; New York: Liberal Arts, 1953), p. 3: "In order to have a clear and just conception of the nature and object of government, it is indispensable to understand correctly what that constitution or law of our nature is in which government originates."

121. Max Mark, "What Image of Man for Political Science?" *Western Political Quarterly* (December 1962), pp. 593–94.

natural science. According to this ideal, they believed that "A respectable social scientist is an empiricist; he is a pragmatist or an instrumentalist; he is a willing heir of the tradition of positivism; in morals he is a relativist; and his definition of values is operational.[122] In this Deweyite-Popperian scheme of things, there could be little enthusiasm for traditional political theory, which took for its goal "truth in the sense of political wisdom," that is, truth as an understanding of human nature and the sort of public life people should lead, individually and collectively.[123]

And so political philosopher Leo Strauss could insist that human beings are endowed with "speech or reason or understanding. Therefore the proper work of man consists of living thoughtfully . . . in accordance with the natural order of man's being. . . . One may therefore call the rules circumscribing the general character of the good life 'the natural law.' "[124] And he could further argue that unless social scientists will subscribe to the imperatives of this natural law, "we can be or become wise in matters of secondary importance, but we have to be resigned to utter ignorance in the most important respect."[125] And he could even say that to become wise only on matters of secondary importance was to achieve "retail sanity" at the price of "wholesale madness," which is a dichotomy very similar to Mannheim's twin notions of functional and substantive rationality.[126] But Strauss's protests were to no avail. Heinz Eulau rejected the old-time, two-level approach to wisdom on behalf of the behavioral mainstream when he said that men's attitudes and acts are the proper subject of political analysis, whereas human nature is something that social scientists must leave to philosophers.[127] And David Easton set aside natural law as a guide to conduct because, in his opinion, it lacks specific answers to specific issues and implies the necessity of government by an educated elite rather than by elected officials ruling with reference to popular will.[128]

The Rationalist Postulate

When wisdom through reason was judged incapable of discovering man's basic nature and ascertaining the moral guidelines for creating a good life and the just

122. "Generalists versus Specialists in Social Science—Discussion," *American Political Science Review* (June 1950), p. 383.

123. This definition of traditional political theory comes from David Kettler, "Political Science and Political Rationality," in David Spitz, ed., *Political Theory and Social Change* (New York: Atherton, 1967), p. 75.

124. *Natural Right and History* (Chicago: University of Chicago Press, 1953), p. 127.

125. Ibid., p. 4.

126. Ibid.

127. *The Behavioral Persuasion*, pp. 133–34.

128. David B. Truman, "The American System in Crisis," *Political Science Quarterly* (December 1959), pp. 485–86.

society, post—World War II relativists in political science developed a form of inquiry that dealt directly with the question of rationality. This was rooted in models of rational man, sometimes called theories of social choice or of rational decision making. Their point of departure was the notion that, even were it possible definitively to choose the right moral standards, total rationality is unattainable because (1) men cannot know all of the alternative courses of action available to them in the present, and (2) they must of necessity remain ignorant as to how a particular course of action will affect the future.[129] Thus even if people were to understand how, in principle, they ought to behave so as to achieve a substantively rational life, they could not know, in practice, what sort of behavior, from day to day, would surely lead to that end. This is what James G. March and Herbert A. Simon had in mind when they said that "From a phenomenological viewpoint we can only speak of a rationality relative to a frame of reference; and this frame of reference will be determined by the limitations on the rational man's knowledge."[130]

Assuming that substantive rationality is impossible, rationalist theorists went on to define real-world social choice as a matter of doing the best we can within our limitations. With regard to research procedure, the first step was to accept as given people's desires, rather than to assess their intrinsic merit.[131] The second step was to explore the parameters of rational action in terms of how effectively the subjects manage to use whatever means they possess in order to gain the ends they posit for themselves. Here was the strategy of inquiry that Anthony Downs endorsed when he stipulated, in his work on democracy, that "the term rational is never applied to an agent's ends, but only to his means. This follows from the definition of rational as efficient, i.e., maximizing output for a given input, or minimizing input for a given output."[132]

Starting from a basic axiom that "the representative or the average individual, when confronted with real choice in exchange, will choose 'more' [utility] rather than 'less,' " theorists of social choice were able to formulate elaborate models of how democratic institutions in America probably work.[133] They claimed, for example, that political leaders and parties do not actually stand for any principle of public or collective interest, but instead shape their expressed views on public affairs with an eye to how many votes they will acquire as a

129. Simon, *Administrative Behavior*.

130. *Organizations* (New York: Wiley, 1958), p. 138.

131. Sidney R. Waldman, *Foundations of Political Action: An Exchange Theory of Politics* (Boston: Little, Brown, 1972), p. 21.

132. *An Economic Theory of Democracy* (New York: Harper, 1957), p. 5.

133. James M. Buchanan and Gordon Tullock, *The Calculus of Consent: Logical Foundations of Constitutional Democracy* (Ann Arbor: University of Michigan Press, 1962), p. 18.

result. The main thing, in this view, is to win office, whereupon that office may be used as a way to more of the things in life that the officeholder and his constituents desire and will enjoy.[134] If this notion of democracy as a ceaseless quest for political power rather than community welfare is correct, it means that firm commitment to political principles, rather than enthusiasm for playing the political game flexibly, is the opposite of rational political action or, in a word, irrational. The point is true but not necessarily indicative of a systemic flaw, for rationalist theorists also claimed that, even where political actors seek narrow and personal ends, a democratic electoral system will compel them to serve the interests of many other people in order to gain and maintain power.[135] In that event, a democratic society can accommodate a great deal of indifference and even hostility to common ends, since its institutions will act, as a visible hand, to channel private impulses in the direction of public needs. As Downs put it, "The behavior of voters may be ignorant but that is not equivalent to its being irrational."[136]

The Public Interest

As a result of this kind of analysis, some political scholars who championed rationalist theories took a new view of speculation concerning "the public interest." This phrase had traditionally connoted political wisdom as a matter of discovering and implementing principled guidelines to public life. Woodrow Wilson, for example, argued long ago that "Our search is for the common interest," which must be "something more than a mere sum of the parts."[137] Clearly he had his sights fixed on a reality transcending the immediate desires of ignorant voters and opportunistic politicians. Leo Strauss had similar aspirations when he reminded his colleagues that "According to the old political science, there is necessarily a common good, and the common good in its fullness is the good society and what is required for the good society."[138] Again, there was the notion that men should seek wisdom in the sense of overarching and balanced insight into human affairs. But political scholars committed to the rationalist postulate disagreed with the Wilson-Strauss presumption that a truly rational understanding of human affairs is possible to achieve. They therefore decided either to revise the traditional definition of the public interest or to abandon that term entirely.

The revision occurred when the public's expressed wants, including those

134. Downs, *An Economic Theory of Democracy*, pp. 28, 295.

135. Buchanan and Tullock, *The Calculus of Consent*, pp. 19–20.

136. *An Economic Theory of Democracy*, p. x.

137. "The Law and the Facts," p. 6.

138. "An Epilogue," in Herbert J. Storing, ed., *Essays on the Scientific Study of Politics* (New York: Holt, Rinehart and Winston, 1962), p. 323.

born of ignorance, were held to add up to the community's collective interest. Arguments to this effect appeared very early in the behavioral era when David Truman observed that something similar to the traditional goal of a public interest will emerge as pressure groups attenuate their demands in the electoral and administrative arenas, thereby producing catchall compromises that constitute policy serving the needs of the entire community.[139] Rationalist theorists restated the same idea and believed that it was even more persuasive for being rephrased in their rigorous analytical terms. Thus we have a typical rationalist formulation from Gordon Tullock, who noted that the "higher goal" of real-world communities is always based on statements of preference made by some individuals in contrast to the desires articulated by others, in which case we are entitled to conclude that "the state (like the market) has no goal 'higher' than the carrying out of the desires of the people" who compose it.[140]

The tendency to abandon discussion of the public interest entirely came as a corollary of the idea that public policy as it *is* may be labeled the public interest as it *ought to be*. Some political scholars searched through existing policies, which they saw as rooted in a compendium of conflicting private interests, and announced that they were unable to discover a truly public interest, in the traditional mode, located anywhere in the empirical realm of politics. Nor were they able to find public officials who, while buffeted in office by expressed interests, were able to formulate, even in theory, a line of policy that could serve the entire community in some ideal sense. Not finding the thing itself, therefore, and not being able to describe it in the abstract, rationalist theorists could conclude that "the public interest makes no operational sense."[141] In such a vein, Frank Sorauf spoke for many of his colleagues when he suggested that "the public interest" was so ambiguous a phrase that the discipline could easily stop using it, whereupon, like society offenders in *The Mikado*, it "never would be missed."[142]

The Uses of Rationalist Theory

While analyzing political behavior as a matter of rational use of means rather than proper selection of ends, rational theorists explicitly abandoned the search for wisdom in their work. William H. Riker, for example, observed that "traditional methods . . . can produce only wisdom and neither science nor knowledge. And while wisdom is certainly useful in the affairs of men, such a result is a failure to

139. David B. Truman, *The Governmental Process* (New York: Knopf, 1951), pp. 501–35.

140. Gordon Tullock, *Private Wants, Public Needs: An Economic Analysis of the Desirable Scope of Government* (New York: Basic Books, 1970), pp. 32–33.

141. Glendon Schubert, *The Public Interest: A Critique of the Theory of a Political Concept* (New York: Free Press, 1960), p. 211.

142. Frank Sorauf, "The Conceptual Muddle," in Carl J. Friedrich, ed., *The Public Interest* (New York: Atherton, 1962), p. 190.

live up to the promise in the name of political science."[143] Yet as against the Aristotelian prescription for what political thought and teaching must embrace, including the special form of truth known as wisdom, political science work on social choice and rational decision making suffers serious shortcomings.

Some of these are easily illustrated. For one thing, how can we compare leaders such as Abraham Lincoln and Joseph Stalin? If whatever people do is no more than a visible attempt to fulfill personal desires, and if there is no valid rule of wisdom for judging those desires to be better or worse in the overall scheme of things, then according to rationalist theory there can be no significant difference between what was done by the American president and the Russian dictator, except insofar as one might have been more "rational" than the other in "efficiently" pursuing his quest for "utility."[144] In real life, however, we know very well that there were enormous differences between these two men, variances that had nothing to do with efficiency and everything to do with the ways in which they served their respective nations. Surely these variances must be assessed if political knowledge is to be relevant, broadly speaking, to human existence. For another thing, there is certainly more to political life than self-interested gain. Were we to start from the premise that men and women always act in public so as to maximize their private satisfactions, we would inevitably overlook a great deal of important political behavior. Using a rationalist postulate, it would appear that piecework incentives will make American business and the all-volunteer army equally efficient. It is widely known, however, that whereas individually tailored corporate salaries may spur imaginative administration, army units built upon personal rewards rather than patriotism and small-group cohesion will fight poorly when soldiers' lives are at stake.[145]

Some advocates of the rationalist approach concede that public affairs and civic sentiment entail an important measure of "altruistic concerns," whereby some people express "demands for and expectations of justice for others as well as for themselves." A rationalist scholar may even note that such concerns and expectations constitute "one of the most important problems confronting social science."[146] But since there is no way that the rationalist approach can deal with such matters scientifically, they are left for other scholars to address. As against

143. William H. Riker, A *Theory of Political Coalitions* (New Haven: Yale University Press, 1962), p. viii.

144. The contrast between Lincoln and Stalin is an extrapolation of the position taken by Russell Kirk, in "Segments of Political Science Not Amenable to Behavioristic Treatment," in Charlesworth, ed., *The Limits of Behavioralism*, p. 55.

145. See the critique of Pentagon personnel practices during the Vietnam War, in Richard A. Gabriel and Paul L. Savage, *Crisis in Command: Mismanagement in the Army* (New York: Hill and Wang, 1978).

146. Waldman, *Foundations*, pp. 57–59.

this stance, Allan Bloom has argued that "students and citizens in general have an instinctive awareness . . . that politics has to do with justice and the realization of the good life." We should conclude, in his view, that the discipline of political science must accept responsibility for giving instruction with regard to political ends and how to achieve them.[147]

Notwithstanding the severe shortcomings of any rationalist approach, the American Political Science Association chose William Riker, the discipline's foremost rationalist theorist, as its president for 1983. Riker's election may be interpreted as confirmation of the claim that such theories constitute the twentieth century's fourth great scientific revolution in the organized study of politics.[148] Without challenging the accuracy of this count to four, which depends on how one classifies behavioralism and its chief variations, there can be no doubt that rationalist theories bring the discipline beyond the ideas advanced by systems theory and the functional approach. Yet just as the earlier behavioral strategies for analyzing and describing politics enjoyed a certain institutional virtue, so also rationalist theories presumably supply the discipline with at least some collective benefits. And indeed there is a measure of functional rationality in the rationalist view of political things, in two important senses having to do with professional difficulties that the approach manages to avoid.

For example, the alternative to basing political science upon the study of expressed interests is to fashion a scale of people's true needs versus their immediate wants. This is the sort of rule that philosophers of natural law seek as "a standard with reference to which we can judge the ideals of our own as well as of any other society,"[149] and whose absence, in the days of the counterculture, provoked Michael Rogin to complain that when everyday "desires" are equated with fundamental "needs," the "public interest" cannot be calculated except as the sum total of short-term fancies.[150] In 1969, Sheldon S. Wolin called upon the discipline to judge politics in terms of such a scale, when he argued that "political science" and "political wisdom" depend upon different kinds of knowledge. The former, he said, aspires to empirical and testable propositions, while the latter pursues knowledge that "inheres" in intuition, faith, historical sensibility, acquaintance with past political theories, and more.[151]

147. "Political Science and the Undergraduate," in Vernon Van Dyke, ed., *Teaching Political Science: The Professor and the Polity* (Atlantic Highlands, N.J.: Humanities Press, 1977), p. 118.

148. Ronald Rogowski, "Rationalist Theories of Politics: A Midterm Report," *World Politics* (January 1978), pp. 296–97.

149. Strauss, *Natural Right*, p. 3.

150. "Nonpartisanship and the Group Interest," in Philip Green and Sanford Levinson, eds., *Power and Community: Dissenting Essays in Political Science* (New York: Random House, 1969), pp. 114–15.

151. "Political Theory as a Vocation," *American Political Science Review* (December 1969), pp. 1070–71, 1075, 1077.

From the institutional point of view, Wolin's appeal was extremely problematical. The knowledge that provides wisdom, or the sense of what is "appropriate to a subject," Wolin called "tacit knowledge."[152] He was convinced it could be achieved by political theorists who would steep themselves in the study of the past as well as the present, in philosophy as well as current events, so that their "political understanding" would be enhanced, even if it remained untested in the modern fashion.[153] But can a scholarly discipline, in the bureaucratic sense, openly admit that its work is flawed for not paying sufficient attention to wisdom? After all, specific knowledge is a bureaucratic source of power and prestige, and this means that most organizations worthy of the name will define their work in such a way as to exclude outsiders from a claim to expertise on whatever subject the organization takes for its own. Yet if values are acknowledged as a central concern of political studies, almost anyone—from banker to housewife—might qualify as an expert of sorts, and the discipline would virtually certify outsiders as competitors for its turf.

So Wolin favored the pursuit of "tacit knowledge," while Henry S. Kariel declared that only "unaccredited prophets, poets, seers, preachers, and metaphysicians" had predicted America's contemporary crisis in authority.[154] And a satirical article in *PS* implied that the discipline would learn more about Congress from muckraker Ralph Nader than from professor Ralph Huitt.[155] Yet to honor the political acumen of outsiders such as Nader would be to undermine the profession's claim to special competence, and we must therefore conclude that Wolin, Kariel, and critics with a similar point of view may have been substantively right but functionally wrong. As Austin Ranney observed, "If all we can offer is common sense or a passion for social justice, then we have no claim to and will not receive any special attention not paid to any other citizen enjoying these admirable but widely diffused assets."[156] Indeed, if wisdom were to reign as an ultimate goal for political studies, one cannot be sure that the discipline would survive in its present form. As a rule, every community of scholars is characterized by some common intellectual baggage, from shared techniques to familiar readings. In this regard, a discipline requires some intellectual coherence if it is to deserve being called a discipline at all. But if graduate students were set loose to search for wisdom, they might not find any particular sort of it "inhering" in the millions of far-ranging volumes contained in a good university library. Ergo, Arnold Rogow's

152. Ibid., p. 1071.
153. Ibid., p. 1077.
154. "Possibilities," in Graham and Carey, *The Post-Behavioral Era*, p. 125.
155. Arthur Clun, "The Ralph Ratio: A Value-Laden, Scientific Method for Selecting Texts in American Government," *PS* (Winter 1975), p. 30.
156. "The Study of Policy Content: A Framework for Choice," in Ranney, ed., *Political Science and Public Policy* (Chicago: Markham, 1968), p. 17.

somewhat bitter observation that "Prestige if not survival itself, some argue, depends on our becoming less literary, less impressionistic, less political, and more scientific."[157]

To begin with, then, rationalist theories are functionally rational for offering political science a column, figuratively, in the Temple of Science, safe alongside the columns of other disciplines that dwell in American universities. A second point of functional rationality relates to the substance of political science's column, in the sense that this particular discipline is devoted to a liberal tradition outside the world of higher education, a tradition which suggests that political scholars had best leave the subject of wisdom alone. Rational models of man serve liberalism by obviating the need for gaining agreement to principles of collective decisions even as they speak of social choice, by saying that people may be left free to make up their own minds as to whatever course they might wish public policy to take. The liberal tradition says very little about wise and proper directions for public policy, and has even insisted on the separation of church and state so as to deny public force to certain strong claims of wisdom with regard to the shape of a good society. What liberalism offers, instead, is a vague but comfortable notion that reason will prevail, that people will be rational enough to decide what their community needs and reasonable enough to work together so as to fulfill those needs. Thus even when Popper wrote of an "open society," he highlighted the efficacy of a proper framework for decisions rather than the perfection of a particular social policy, stressing the institutions whereby interests would be expressed and balanced rather than the programs by which society would be served and maintained. In this sense, a theory of rational social choice can very usefully explain why liberal democracy as a system must remain flexible, such as when Albert O. Hirschman argued that democratic organizations should seek a balance between loyalty, voice, and exit, between constituents supporting, dissenting within, and quitting their respective organizations.[158] Such theories serve the larger requirements of liberalism when they avoid suggesting that America needs more preaching of absolute standards, or a rational citizenry more numerous than the number of informed voters who presently inhabit the country. Talk in that vein would dangerously resemble Marxism, a point to which we shall return in chapter 8.

157. "Comment on Smith and Apter: or, Whatever Happened to the Great Issues?" *American Political Science Review* (September 1957), p. 772.

158. *Exit, Voice, and Loyalty: Responses to Decline in Firms, Organizations, and States* (Cambridge, Mass.: Harvard University Press, 1970). On the vogue of this book among political scientists, see Brian Barry, "Review Article: 'Exit, Voice, and Loyalty,' " *British Journal of Political Science* (January 1974), pp. 79–82.

The Vindication of Thomas Kuhn

The roof or a single column in the Temple of Science, quantity versus quality of publications, the propensity to specialize, the proliferation and endless refinement of techniques, rewards for novelty rather than the truth, distortions of the truth, the retreat of reason, the loss of wisdom, revising or abandoning the public interest—there is a certain logical progression from point to point in the ideal-type view of political science sketched thus far. Starting with the issue of a proper scope for the discipline's inquiries, as between the institution's need for a limited field and the larger need for studying politics in all of its ramifications, we found that no satisfactory definition of politics yet exists. We then saw that even if such a definition were to appear, the imperatives of publishing would encourage members of the discipline to produce fragments of knowledge that do not easily combine to tell us what we might want to know about the political world. Moreover, even if the number of discrete items in the corpus of political science knowledge were ever to become manageable, and if jargon and technique were somehow brought under control, there still could be no assurance that valuable information will emerge from scholarly research. This is because the discipline as yet lacks an organizing principle capable of helping practitioners to distinguish between the significant and the trivial in politics, the true from the merely not-false. Yet the absence of a guiding rule is ultimately related to the decline of rationality in general rather than to some failure of the political science discipline in particular. From this it follows that the discipline suffers a disability of society at large rather than some special vocational flaw given to academic repair.

These difficulties of defining politics appropriately, and of addressing issues of truth and wisdom effectively, suggest that sociological factors very materially affect the sort of product which emerges from research done by political scientists collectively, in their shared role as members of a scholarly community. The facts of the case, then, indicate that the radical implications of Kuhn's theory cannot be brushed aside, damaging as they are to the behavioral persuasion in its dimension of confidence for the larger efficiency of scientific inquiry. These are the facts, among others, which prevent the discipline from wholeheartedly accepting terminological arguments to the effect that Kuhn was really wrong on those points of his theory that lead to such implications. Jerone Stephens, for example, spoke for the co-opters when he announced that "What we must not do . . . is to take Kuhn seriously when he suggests that what scientists [including political scientists] learn and apply are values and not rules."[159] To the contrary, there are a great many values, some small and some large, involved in the process by which political scientists decide what sort of inquiries they will make and what findings they will certify and expound.

159. Stephens, "The Kuhnian Paradigm and Political Inquiry," p. 488.

8

Political Laws, Community Power, and Critical Theory

The sociological conditions touched upon in chapter 7 might be discounted, and their unwelcome implications overlooked, if the community of political scholars were capable of making discoveries about public life so unmistakably accurate as to stand out from the publication fray and earn recognition as useful contributions of knowledge for the benefit of mankind. After all, even if there is reason to suspect that collective scholarship will not systematically produce the right sort of knowledge, important findings may flow from ad hoc observations of the political world around us. Thomas Edison, for example, as a scientist was no great theoretician. But he did doggedly test thousands of materials before finding one suitable for use as an electric lamp filament, and the result was an impressive practical discovery that worked regardless of how attained. It follows that if political scientists were to make notable discoveries concerning public life, no matter how haphazardly or even accidentally, the limitations that collective scholarship impose could be considered an ancillary cost to be borne gracefully in return for the discipline's real work and achievements. Such discoveries have not been made, however, and there is the professional rub we must now consider.

The Search for Political Laws

Many practitioners writing on "scope and methods" for political scholars have adopted what historians of science call "the standard view of scientific knowledge."[1] It is a framework of assumptions about the scientific enterprise which includes the notion that natural and social phenomena can be described in

---

1. On the "standard view," see Michael Mulkay, *Science and the Sociology of Knowledge* (London: George Allen and Unwin, 1979), pp. 19–21.

systematic statements called "universal and permanent laws of nature."[2] In political science writings, the term *law* is often replaced by the word *theory*. However phrased, the goal is a measure of certainty that, if achieved, will relegate most of the discipline's peculiar sociological qualities to insignificance. And so David Easton argued that there are regularities in political behavior which can be "expressed in generalizations or theories with explanatory or predictive value."[3] Similarly, Fred M. Frohock held that "Science is concerned with establishing causal relations and general laws. To do this the social scientist must concentrate on systematic patterns of human conduct."[4] In slightly different terms, James N. Rosenau suggested that in political analysis, the "prime aim" is "to move up the ladder of generalization and construct theories that encompass and explain more and more of the phenomena that make up the universe of politics."[5] Likewise, Adam Przeworski and Henry Teune claimed that the "pivotal assumption" of political research is "that human and social behavior can be explained in terms of general laws established by observation."[6] A great many more passages bear the same message.[7]

The Lack of Examples

The problem with all this affirmation and reaffirmation of professional confidence is that more than a generation of intensive work aimed at the discovery of such laws did not produce any. In 1967, as resistance to behavioralism mounted, Andrew Hacker challenged the expectation that political analysis can assess the political world objectively, that it can discover laws of political behavior. As he put it, "At this time, it is hard to point to any 'findings' that have been accepted by the scholarly community."[8] Soon afterward, in discussions devoted to analyzing how far political science had come by the early 1970s, Robert Bierstedt noted that, from the social sciences in general, "We

2. Ibid., p. 20.
3. "The Current Meaning of 'Behavioralism' in Political Science," in James C. Charlesworth, ed., *The Limits of Behavioralism in Political Science* (Philadelphia: American Academy of Political and Social Science, 1962), pp. 7–8.
4. Fred M. Frohock, *The Nature of Political Inquiry* (Homewood, Ill.: Dorsey, 1967), p. 141.
5. *The Dramas of Politics: An Introduction to the Joys of Inquiry* (Boston: Little, Brown, 1973), p. 117.
6. *The Logic of Comparative Social Inquiry* (New York: Wiley, 1970), p. 4.
7. See those cited in Gabriel A. Almond and Stephen J. Genco, "Clouds, Clocks, and the Study of Politics," *World Politics* (July 1977), pp. 498–99, 502–03, 507–09. As a case in point, see also William H. Riker, "The Future of a Science of Politics," *American Behavioral Scientist* (September/October 1977), pp. 12–16f.
8. Andrew Hacker, "The Utility of Quantitative Methods in Political Science," in James C. Charlesworth, ed., *Contemporary Political Analysis* (New York: Free Press, 1967), p. 147.

have a great many taxonomies, but we have a dearth of causal propositions."[9] During the same discussions, Charles E. Lindblom made the same point in different terms, when he remarked that the social sciences have produced only a "few nomothetic propositions,"[10] which are statements "true of all times and all places."[11] And in an essay recommending directions for political inquiry to take in the future, E. W. Kelly found himself unable to predict what road the discipline would travel because "No large body of lawful knowledge exists" to guide the work of political scientists.[12]

Although direct admissions of failure are few and fragmentary, the nonexistence of political laws may be inferred indirectly from statements which purport to show that regularities of political behavior, or some large and significant truths about political life, have actually been discovered. Sometimes the inference is obvious, as when such statements are noticeably barren of evidence in support of their central contentions. For example, while claiming that "The growing success of the scientific enterprise in political science cannot be denied," David Easton cited no instances of this success.[13] Similarly, Martin Landau asserted that "whatever the pretension, extravagance, even foolishness, to be found in the last fifteen years of social scientific effort, it has produced results that warrant a substantial investment of our resources."[14] Which results? Or, consider Avery Leiserson's confident assurance that "the gains from clarification of assumptions underlying comparative [political research] work, . . . as well as the improved statement of methodological problems, pitfalls, and opportunities, can scarcely be denied."[15] Which gains?

To compliment political science on its success, then, is not necessarily to introduce facts that will convince. Yet on other occasions, when political regularities supposedly discovered by scientific inquiry are mentioned, they tend to be trivial or otherwise unimpressive. James N. Rosenau, for example, complained

9. "Conference Discussion II," in James C. Charlesworth, ed., *Integration of the Social Sciences Through Policy Analysis* (Philadelphia: American Academy of Political and Social Science, 1972), p. 160.

10. "Integration of Political Science and the Other Social Sciences Through Policy Analysis," in ibid., p. 12.

11. "Conference Discussion III," in ibid., p. 218.

12. "Political Science as Science and Common Sense," in George J. Graham and George W. Carey, eds., *The Post-Behavioral Era: Perspectives on Political Science* (New York: McKay, 1972), p. 192.

13. "The New Revolution in Political Science," *American Political Science Review* (December 1969), p. 1053.

14. *Political Theory and Political Science: Studies in the Methodology of Political Inquiry* (New York: Macmillan, 1972), p. 12.

15. "The Behavioral Approach," in Robert Connery, ed., *Teaching Political Science* (Durham: Duke University Press, 1965), pp. 60–61.

accurately that the field of foreign policy analysis suffered a dearth of scientific hypotheses.[16] By way of contrast, he referred approvingly to a collection of domestic political propositions in *Human Behavior: An Inventory of Scientific Findings*, by Bernard R. Berelson and Gary A. Steiner. Yet turning to the actual inventory which so impressed Rosenau, one discovers there were many "findings" of dubious value, such as that "In a modern democratic industrial country, with substantial social heterogeneity, political parties must appeal to a range of social groups in order to secure a majority."[17] This finding may be true of parties seeking an electoral majority and confronted by opponents pursuing a similar strategy based on broad-gauged appeals. It will be useless, though, as a predictor of party behavior where ideology is so highly regarded that purity of principle cannot be sacrificed on behalf of electoral success. Moreover, the same finding tells us little about party behavior in democratic states which use parliamentary procedures and whose political spectrum embraces several rather than merely two parties. When states of that sort permit the formation of government coalitions, they thereby encourage parties to adopt strategies aimed at achieving substantial electoral support rather than absolute majorities.

With regard to explicit claims advanced by political scholars, the case is no more persuasive. Ithiel de Sola Pool contended that research findings teach more about "citizen participation" than ever known before. But when it came time to describe what practitioners have learned from such research, Pool offered little that was compellingly persuasive. "We know," he said, "that a vested . . . interest in the results of the political process . . . increases politicization." In addition, "we know . . . that politicization is reduced if political participation is unpleasant or dangerous."[18] These are not laws such as those that earned for natural science the reputation it enjoys today. A random sample of regularities announced in the journal literature is equally uninspiring. For instance, Richard W. Boyd wrote in 1969 about his research on presidential elections and concluded, among other things, that "cross-pressures relate monotonically to voting defection—the greater the cross-pressures, the greater the likelihood of defection" to another party.[19] In plain English this means that when supporters of one party feel there is reason to vote for another, they may do so. It is not the sort of regularity that political scholars can take much pride in discovering, if indeed it

16. "Moral Fervor, Systematic Analysis, and Scientific Consciousness in Foreign Policy Research," in Austin Ranney, ed., *Political Science and Public Policy* (Chicago: Markham, 1968), pp. 199–200.

17. *Human Behavior* (New York: Harcourt, Brace and World, 1964), p. 417.

18. "The Public and the Polity," in Ithiel de Sola Pool, ed., *Contemporary Political Science: Toward Empirical Theory* (New York: McGraw-Hill, 1967), pp. 42, 44.

19. "Presidential Elections: An Explanation of Voting Defection," *American Political Science Review* (June 1969), p. 509.

were unknown previously. In 1974, Lloyd Jensen summarized a great many works on international relations and announced that "among the conclusions which would seem most relevant to policy-makers is the finding reported by several authors that actions [such as hostility, violence, and concessions] are reciprocated."[20] In real world diplomacy, however, such as during the Falkland Islands War of 1982, actions are sometimes reciprocated and sometimes not, for a great deal depends upon clashing objectives, variable circumstances, selective perceptions, and unique personalities. So much for the universal validity of Jensen's finding.

Quantitative Analysis and Comparative Politics

What causes the shortage of political laws even though political science is ostensibly devoted to their discovery? A typical textbook claims that "there is nothing in the subject matter of political science" that will prevent "the development of empirical theories and laws of politics."[21] The authors who wrote these words may have assumed that the social realm is tangible and objective, and that its laws are waiting to be discovered like America awaited Columbus.[22] But the world of human affairs is much more complicated than that, and even if social scientists were to imitate their natural brethren faithfully in habit and technique, it is likely they would fail to understand societies as precisely and as fruitfully as many parts of the natural world are comprehended by, say, physicists and biologists.

The difficulties that plague social science inquiry as compared with natural science research are enormous, and there is no way to treat them adequately here. Highlighting a few even briefly, however, will indicate how intractable they are. To begin with, there is the problem of numbers. Thomas Kuhn reminded his readers that the Social Science Research Building of the University of Chicago bears the inscription, attributed to Lord Kelvin, that "If you cannot measure, your knowledge is meager and unsatisfactory."[23] It is not surprising, then, that political scholars committed to scientific standards of research have often argued that empirical political theory must be based upon quantitative data, just as natural scientists use that kind of data in their work. This is what Harold Lasswell was saying when he advised his colleagues that "the first technical step in conducting research on trends is to take the 'key abstractions,' such as

20. "Quantitative International Politics," *Political Science Reviewer* (Fall 1974), p. 326.

21. M. Margaret Conway and Frank B. Feigert, *Political Analysis: An Introduction* (Boston: Allyn and Bacon, 1972), p. 33.

22. The comparison between discovering scientific laws and finding America is suggested by Mulkay, *Science and the Sociology of Knowledge*, p. 21.

23. "The Function of Measurement in Modern Physical Science," *Isis* (June 1961), p. 161.

'freedom' or 'shared power,' and to choose the most appropriate indices for each term."[24]

Unfortunately, such advice runs into the problem of using figures—such as electoral results, congressional committee votes, and socioeconomic indices—simply because they are available rather than because they measure what we are trying to understand. Thus L. S. Shapley and Martin Shubik suggested calculating the power exercised by legislators as a function of the frequency with which they voted in committee with the committee majority,[25] and Robert A. Dahl recommended estimating the power of Senators according to their yea or nay positions with regard to sixty-five roll call votes.[26] These were two sets of numbers readily available. Yet Shapley and Shubik had no way of accounting for the fact that some legislators may vote with the majority out of weakness rather than strength,[27] and Dahl could not say which senators were absolutely the most influential, because he did not weigh their votes in terms of each roll-call's importance to the nation or to particular senatorial constituents.[28] David Easton was therefore being realistically modest when he observed that the concept of a political system will not make sense until we are able to assign definite weights to the power of various actors and entities who make up a political equilibrium at any time.[29] Yet when Karl W. Deutsch tried to use quantitative data to prove that Nazi Germany was probably suicidal by 1937–38 and surely so by 1942, Hans Morganthau rightfully chided him for using figures which prove nothing about "moral stamina," or "political and military genius."[30] To make the point vividly, Morganthau quoted Frederick the Great of Prussia, who discounted mechanical efforts at measuring the international balance of power and asked: "How do you assess the influence which a mistress has upon a prince?" Mistresses aside, for surely Golda Meir had none, quantitative factors accounted for little when Israel under her leadership defeated both Egypt and Syria after halting a massive surprise attack at the outset of the October War of 1973.

Numbers are so difficult to employ usefully in political analysis that mainstream members of the discipline have frequently insisted on comparing impor-

24. "The Immediate Future of Research Policy and Method in Political Science," *American Political Science Review* (March 1951), p. 136.

25. "A Method for Evaluating the Distribution of Power in a Committee System," ibid. (September 1954), pp. 787–92.

26. "The Concept of Power," *Behavioral Science* (July 1957), pp. 209–14.

27. Francis D. Wormouth, "Matched-Dependent Behavioralism: The Cargo Cult in Political Science," *Western Political Quarterly* (December 1967), pp. 819–20.

28. Hacker, "The Utility of Quantitative Measurements," pp. 136–38.

29. *The Political System: An Inquiry into the State of Political Science*, 2nd ed. (New York: Knopf, 1971), pp. 284–89.

30. 'Conference Discussion on Methods," in James C. Charlesworth, ed., A *Design for Political Science* (Philadelphia: American Academy of Political and Social Science, 1966), p. 224.

tant political entities. David Easton, for example, argued that political studies will never be scientific if they cannot overcome the limitations of time and place by engaging in comparative research.[31] Deutsch shared Easton's sentiments when he observed that the more than 140 nations and states of the modern world provide potential comparative studies with a range of political experience "far beyond anything that Aristotle, Machiavelli, Montesquieu, Rousseau or Pareto could have included in their [prescientific] theories."[32] Both political scholars hoped that incisive comparisons would eventually reveal those regularities of political behavior so sought after by the discipline. The same expectation was shared by their colleagues, for when Albert Somit and Joseph Tanenhaus asked practitioners in 1963 to rank fields of research according to the "significance of current work" being done within them, the field of "comparative government" ranked first.[33] By 1976, "comparative government" was still highly regarded by practitioners, holding second place right behind the field of "American Government."[34]

While the case for comparing political things is fine in principle, it suffers serious shortcomings vis-à-vis the practical world of research, where such entities are extraordinarily difficult to compare. From the prosaic example of apples and oranges, even small children know that dissimilar objects do not come together easily to facilitate general conclusions, although they may belong to the same broad class of things such as fruits. Yet the same is true when a scholar tries to compare two political entities that are superficially alike, such as an American political party and an African political party. Yes, they are both parties according to common parlance. However, electoral success is a main goal of the former, whereas the latter may deal also with religion, marriage, dance, feuds, debts, land, birth and death, and more. Under the circumstances, two very different things are parading under the same name.[35]

The trouble does not stop there, for unless each analytical term is defined very precisely, we cannot know just what attributes of any political entity under investigation are being weighed and measured. Dahl had this point in mind when he observed that James Madison, in the "Tenth Federalist" essay, offered a brilliant argument about factions but defined the special quality of faction so

31. *The Political System*, pp. 31–35.

32. "On Political Theory and Political Action," *American Political Science Review* (March 1971), pp. 19–20.

33. *American Political Science: Profile of a Discipline* (New York: Atherton, 1964), p. 56.

34. Walter B. Roettger, "The Discipline: What's Right, What's Wrong, and Who Cares?" (paper prepared for delivery at the 1978 Annual Meeting of the American Political Science Association, New York City, 1978), p. 22.

35. A. C. MacIntyre, "Is a Science of Comparative Politics Possible?" in Paul G. Lewis and David C. Potter, eds. *The Practice of Comparative Politics* (London: Longman, 1973), pp. 224–25.

inexactly as to preclude our knowing when any particular group must be judged a faction or something else.[36] The same failure to define analytical terms also plagues modern comparative research. In the case of functional analysis, for example, political scholars would like to show how certain political institutions, such as the American Congress and the British Parliament, fulfill a variety of "functions" within their respective political systems. But unless the term function is defined more rigorously than it has been so far in the discipline's literature, so that it can denote very specific dimensions of human life, we cannot be sure that researchers will wind up measuring the same qualities from one society to the next, or from one situation to another in the same country.[37]

Experiments and Reality Checks

The difficulty with numbers and the problem of how to characterize political phenomena precisely enough to permit fruitful comparison from place to place and time to time, point to something baffling in the very stuff that political analysis seeks to understand, as opposed to the materials that natural scientists deal with in their work. Perhaps this is inevitable when we consider that political scholars usually confront a situation of *not* experimenting—of *not* dealing—with dogs and cats, proteins and microbes, incoming starlight and falling apples. Like many natural scientists, students of politics for the most part work in widely scattered universities and research laboratories. But the subjects of political research are not common items, conveniently found in many locations, or easily brought there, and presenting to researchers a fairly invariable appearance under predictable circumstances. Instead, political scientists must study public affairs wherever they occur, in enormous complexity and variation, with dimensions that are constantly changing, and with component parts that cannot be broken down separately and studied repeatedly. A congressional committee, for example, which is worth examining as an important factor in national politics, consists of both voting members and administrative staff, some of whom will be replaced even in the short run, and it cannot be appraised in isolation from the larger House to which it belongs, whose party composition and ideological mood keep changing as election follows election.

In short, the nature of their subject precludes political scientists from conducting experiments as do natural scientists,[38] even though most physical laws

36. A *Preface to Democratic Theory* (Chicago: University of Chicago Press, 1956), pp. 25–27.

37. Robert E. Dowse, "A Functionalist's Logic," *World Politics* (July 1966), p. 608.

38. This is apparently a long-standing reality. Thus *Webster's Universal Dictionary* (New York: World Syndicate Publishing Co., 1936) [original version, *An American Dictionary of the English Language*, 1828]), uses the following quotation from John Adams to illustrate how the word "experiment" may be used: "A political *experiment* cannot be made in a laboratory, nor determined

have been derived from, or confirmed by, such experiments. What obtains in political science is therefore a far cry from the precision and elegance with which natural scientists go about the work of checking and testing their colleagues' ideas. Writing about the impact of social and economic factors on voting behavior, for example, Glaucio Soares and Robert L. Hamblin noted that "the present investigation should be replicated many times if the phenomena [*sic*] of the alienated vote is to be understood."[39] But their investigation was not replicated, perhaps because of indifference to their work, but more likely because other scholars preferred to analyze different data, as it became available to them in other areas of the country. Similarly, David W. Adamany encountered a replication problem when he sought to consider the possible impact of partisanship in judicial decision making. Adamany was teaching at the University of Wisconsin, and he used data on the judges of that state because he had to do "on-the-scene research" and Wisconsin "was convenient."[40] He conceded, however, that there was no clear relationship between his work in Wisconsin and the possible validity of a hypothesis concerning judicial partisanship advanced on the basis of Michigan data by S. Sidney Ulmer and Glendon A. Schubert. In conclusion, Adamany could offer only the notion that there was "need for a more careful conceptualization and more rigorous testing" of the "provocative hypothesis" advanced by his Michigan colleagues.[41]

Where repeated experiments under controlled conditions cannot take place, a political scientist will endeavor to study something that he thinks is important, such as the administration of highway safety regulations by a state agency, even though no other political scientists are likely to study exactly the same phenomenon again, under the same conditions. And therefore the community of political scholars does not at all resemble that described by James D. Watson in *The Double Helix*,[42] where he and Francis Crick knew which other biologists were trying, in laboratories around the world, to determine the structure of DNA, a molecule present for experimental observation in all of those laboratories. Likewise, the realm of political science has nothing to compare to the case of T. D. Lee and C. N. Yang, who in October of 1956 published an article in the *Physical*

---

in a few hours." My attention was drawn to this citation by Rush Welter, *The Mind of America, 1820–1860* (New York: Columbia University Press, 1975), p. 23. On the importance of experiments in science, see James B. Conant, *On Understanding Science: An Historical Approach* (New Haven: Yale University Press, 1947), p. 24.

39. "Socioeconomic Variables and Voting for the Radical Left: Chile, 1952," *American Political Science Review* (December 1967), p. 1065.

40. "The Party Variable in Judges' Voting: Conceptual Notes and a Case Study," ibid., (March 1969), p. 61.

41. Ibid., p. 73.

42. *The Double-Helix: A Personal Account of the Discovery of the Structure of DNA* (New York: Atheneum, 1968).

Review suggesting certain experiments to demonstrate that in molecular structure, parity is not conserved.[43] Within months, researchers at the National Bureau of Standards successfully conducted the experiments and decisively disconfirmed the rule of parity in physics.[44]

The odd thing, then, is that political scientists actually have very little to do with checking, rechecking, confirming, or falsifying the ideas that colleagues advance, no matter how much these practices are talked about and recommended to the discipline. Practitioners themselves are aware of the discrepancy, because more often than not they agree that political scholars normally engage in studies where one investigator cannot replicate the findings of another.[45] Instead, because they are usually unable to bring disputed research objects into their own laboratories for testing, it is customary for political scientists who dispute the findings of others in their field to refute a far-away colleague's work by assailing its internal logic. That is, as a substitute for comparing research findings against real-world materials, which are usually unavailable for confirmation or refutation, critics frequently endeavor to find some mistake in an antagonist's course of argument. This strategy is so commonplace that practitioners have developed virtually a formula for "disproofs" along such lines. Brown might therefore say that Smith and Jones "have attacked a perennial issue in an imaginative manner. It seems to me, however, that they have made several errors in logic which detract considerably from their methods and conclusions."[46]

Even if it were possible to deal experimentally with identical political materials in widely separated laboratories, there is another sense in which the work of political scientists is not likely to generate the sort of laws that natural scientists have revealed. Here, the degree of proof is at stake. Because natural scientists again and again manipulate their subjects under controlled or predictable circumstances, they will occasionally offer an idea which, in relation to real-world phenomena, works so well as to appear unquestionably and definitively true. There is, in other words, in addition to laboratory results, an occasional "reality check" against which natural scientists may be fortunate enough to measure the validity of their ideas. What this check provides is a standard by which scientific notions can be assessed dramatically and persuasively, quite independently of their internal elegance and consistency, assuming that they enjoy these at all.

43. "Question of Parity Conservation in Weak Interactions," *Physical Review* (October 1, 1956), pp. 254–58.

44. Chien Shiung Wu, E. Ambler, R. W. Hayward, D. D. Hoppes, and R. P. Hudson, "Experimental Test of Parity Conservation in Beta Decay," ibid. (February 15, 1957), pp. 1413–15.

45. Somit and Tanenhaus, *American Political Science*, p. 21; and Roettger, "The Discipline," p. 9.

46. The quoted words are from David J. Schnall, in a letter to the editor, *American Political Science Review* (March 1975), p. 579.

When Allied physicists managed in 1945 to make an atomic bomb which *exploded*, the fact of that explosion, rather than theoretical debates as to its likelihood, proved conclusively that the ideas underlying the bomb's design—only some of them experimentally supported—were correct.

Reality checks would be very helpful to political scholars, for an occasional and unmistakable demonstration proving the accuracy of some of their research findings might cut through a great deal of verbal disputation and show once and for all that some regularity has been uncovered. But public life is too complex for its component parts to be isolated and worked on directly, as physicists did with elements of the atomic bomb, and the nation's leaders are too jealous of their prerogatives to permit political scholars to meddle in public affairs so powerfully as to push the course of events in any particular direction. The result is professionally ironic. There are times when people look upon the political circumstances surrounding them and draw persuasive conclusions as to underlying regularities. But when this happens, the chances are that political scientists will have contributed little to any dramatic demonstration that those conclusions are warranted. It is probable, for example, that many Americans who read David Halberstam's book *The Best and the Brightest* (1972)[47] took it as definitive proof that events in Washington and Saigon during the Vietnam War, constituting a sort of reality check, indicated the inadvisability of entrusting America's foreign policy to leaders drawn mainly from the nation's social and economic elite. Here was a contradiction of behavioralist teachings concerning the benign effects of elite rule in a democracy. But Halberstam was a journalist, and the research leading to his conclusions did not entail techniques that political scientists say are necessary for ascertaining the truth about politics. So the public may have learned a very persuasive lesson which most political scientists were not teaching and which, if asked, they might even have rejected as poorly grounded in scientific methods. It was an odd situation, as compared to the shifts of public opinion that natural science from time to time engenders.

Criteria of Adequacy

Where does all this failure to discover regularities leave the discipline of political studies? For one thing, practitioners are confused about which of their colleagues have made the greatest contributions to political knowledge, since no one seems to have enunciated a political law at all. In the 1963 survey conducted by Somit and Tanenhaus, where respondents were asked to name the top scholars of the discipline, and where one could offer as many names as he wished, V. O. Key received the highest score of mentions with 36 percent, while David B. Truman followed

47. (New York: Random House, 1972).

with 20 percent, and all others received less than 20 percent each.[48] The rankings prompted Somit and Tanenhaus to remark that there was a "curious lack of consensus in recognizing great contributors to political science,"[49] and Marian D. Irish expressed much the same sentiment in 1968 when she observed that "No one was nominated by majority vote, much less by acclamation."[50]

In technical terms, David Easton revealed what was problematic when he noted that political scientists have "difficulty in agreeing on the great discoveries, so undeveloped are our criteria of adequacy."[51] That is to say, political science does not confront a situation wherein its theoretical or technical apparatus, either conceptual or mechanical, is somehow flawed and needs only be repaired or improved. What obtains, instead, is a condition of uncertainty as to what sort of demonstrations would suffice to persuade us as to the validity of propositions advanced within the community of political scholars.[52] As Jerome R. Ravetz would say, the problem is a "systematic weakness" in the "materials" that political scientists must handle, to the point where no compellingly persuasive demonstrations of ideas advanced in the field take place.[53] In Ravetz's terms, political science remains an "immature field" when measured against the natural sciences, a field where hard and fast facts do not pile up but a "succession of leading schools" controls the discipline, each offering a fashionable interpretation of hypotheses that never get proved definitively.[54]

Journal Debates and Invisible Colleges

What in fact obtains in the political science community is a collegial system that does not satisfy the standard view of science at all. Propositions are rarely checked by one's critics via controlled experiments; they are usually discounted, instead, on the basis of logical and terminological arguments. And the occasional, powerful, fruitful, and unmistakably correct notion that might win widespread acclaim never materializes because, in the absence of collegial testing and retesting, reality does not operate as a nontheoretical, practical, and ultimately persuasive check upon the kind of hypotheses that political scholars tend to advance. As a result, various ideas endorsed by diverse members of the community circulate, somehow gaining more or less credence, in ways that are nowhere described in

48. *American Political Science*, p. 66.

49. Ibid., p. 75.

50. "Introduction: Advance of the Discipline," in Marian D. Irish, ed., *Political Science: Advance of the Discipline* (Englewood-Cliffs, N.J.: Prentice-Hall, 1968), p. 4.

51. "The New Revolution in Political Science," p. 1054.

52. On "criteria of adequacy," see Jerome R. Ravetz, *Scientific Knowledge and Its Social Problems* (New York: Oxford University Press, 1971), pp. 148–59.

53. Ibid., p. 369.

54. Ibid., p. 368.

the literature of political science. Indeed, avoiding the subject entirely is more the rule, as when Avery Leiserson, in his presidential address to the American Political Science Association in 1974, observed that "How the whole body of scientific associates decides on what is truth, or the correct way of ascertaining it, is a debatable, empirical question; I do not here attempt to describe or evaluate it."[55]

The process of certifying ideas that Leiserson neither described nor evaluated is marked by two central realities. The first is that practitioners tend to express their differences of opinion in journal debates which end inconclusively, if at all. Sometimes these rest upon a series of articles published over the years in several journals, where various authors take part in a continuing controversy as to what sort of research techniques may be employed on a particular subject and what they may prove.[56] Alternatively, journal debates may take place within the same journal, where a few related articles follow each other within a fairly short space of time,[57] or where a single issue of one journal will contain an article succeeded by another refuting central ideas advanced in the first.[58] In any case, the technique of countering one article with another is employed with regard to

55. "Charles Merriam, Max Weber, and the Search for Synthesis in Political Science," *American Political Science Review* (March 1975), p. 183.

56. For example, see the following articles, which comprise a portion of one such running dispute: Fred Kort, "Predicting Supreme Court Decisions Mathematically: A Quantitative Analysis of the 'Right to Counsel' Cases," *American Political Science Review* (March 1957), pp. 1–12; Franklin M. Fisher, "The Mathematical Analysis of Supreme Court Decisions: The Use and Abuse of Quantitative Methods," ibid. (June 1958), pp. 321–38; Fred Kort, "Reply to Fisher's Mathematical Analysis of Supreme Court Decisions," ibid., pp. 339–48; Glendon A. Schubert, "The Study of Judicial Decision-Making as an Aspect of Political Behavior," ibid. (December 1958), pp. 1007–25; S. Sidney Ulmer, "The Analysis of Behavior Patterns on the United States Supreme Court," *Journal of Politics* (November 1960), pp. 629–53; S. Sidney Ulmer, "Supreme Court Behavior and Civil Rights," *Western Political Quarterly* (June 1960), pp. 288–311; Harold J. Spaeth, "An Approach to the Study of Attitudinal Differences as an Aspect of Judicial Behavior," *Midwest Journal of Political Science* (May 1961), pp. 165–80; Glendon A. Schubert, "The 1960 Term of the Supreme Court: A Psychological Analysis," *American Political Science Review* (March 1962), pp. 90–107; Wallace Mendelson, "The Neo-Behavioral Approach to the Judicial Process: A Critique," ibid. (September 1963), pp. 593–603; Wallace Mendelson, "The Untroubled World of Jurimetrics," *Journal of Politics* (November 1964), pp. 914–22; Harold J. Spaeth, "Jurimetrics and Professor Mendelson: A Troubled Relationship," *Journal of Politics* (November 1965), pp. 875–80.

57. For example, James Q. Wilson and Edward C. Banfield, "Public-Regardingness as a Value Premise in Voting Behavior," *American Political Science Review* (December 1964), pp. 876–87; Raymond E. Wolfinger and John Osgood Field, "Political Ethos and the Structure of City Government," ibid. (June 1966), pp. 306–327; and James Q. Wilson and Edward C. Banfield, "Political Ethos Revisited," ibid. (December 1971), pp. 1048–62.

58. For example, see the *American Political Science Review* (June 1972), pp. 415–70; ibid. (September 1972), pp. 796–873; and ibid. (September 1974), pp. 951–1001.

traditional as well as behavioral fields,[59] thereby identifying it as a standard tool of the entire discipline rather than a special instrument applicable only to empirical issues that some scholars wish to treat by trial.

Such debates are seemingly Popperian for offering practitioners an opportunity to assess their colleagues' research claims and decide whether or not they are false. The normal strategy is therefore summed up when a writer remarks that his purpose is "to demonstrate that . . . [Professor X's] conclusions are at worst misleading and at best subject to serious qualifications."[60] Yet there is something odd about all of this "falsification," since, as we have already seen, it does not proceed as rigorously as the Popperian-behavioral ideal would seem to require. Neither the nature of the material nor the quality of terms make conclusive arguments possible, and the journals which publish such articles apparently judge each one to be equally worthy of serious consideration and credence, for they never indicate which is more correct than any other.

Worse still, when journal editors do comment on a specific article, their opinions are likely to underscore the judgmental difficulty. What can we conclude, for example, when an editor introduces an article on systems theory and international relations with these words? "Whether or not his [the author's] arguments are persuasive perhaps depends as much upon the initial commitments which the reader brings to the article as it does upon the arguments themselves."[61] In the natural sciences, hypotheses are not accepted as true simply because researchers and readers are compatible in outlook; as Popper said, one did not have to be Einstein's coreligionist to recognize the truth in his theory of relativity. It is not surprising, then, given the prevailing uncertainty, that a survey revealed more than four-fifths of political scientists to believe that there is often, or almost always, disagreement in their research field over "the validity of published answers to research questions in that area."[62]

While journal debates are inconclusive, the discipline has recourse to a second sociological device for certifying some ideas as true and others as false, and this is what may be called an "invisible college." As defined by Diana Crane, an invisible college is a "network of productive scientists linking separate groups of collaborators within a research area."[63] It is difficult to locate the boundaries of

59. Such as ibid. (March 1972), pp. 114–28, and ibid. (March 1975), pp. 162–70.

60. Jerry Hollenhorst and Gary Adult, "An Alternative Answer to: Who Pays for Defense?" ibid. (September 1971), p. 760. This article is a reply to Bruce Russett, "Who Pays for Defense?" ibid. (June 1969), pp. 412–26.

61. See the Editor's note for John J. Weltman, "Systems Theory in International Relations: A Critique," *Polity* (Spring 1972), p. 301.

62. L. L. Hargens, *Patterns of Scientific Research: A Comparative Analysis of Research in Three Scientific Fields* (Washington, D.C.: American Sociological Association, 1975), p. 18.

63. *Invisible Colleges: Diffusion of Knowledge in Scientific Communities* (Chicago: University of Chicago Press, 1972), p. 54.

such a group, and Crane suggested that many people in it may not even know one another formally.[64] What is clear, however, is that scientific communities do tend to divide up into circles of scholars who work on similar research problems using common techniques, where certain kinds of findings are considered truthful and reasonable and others are not, and where a fairly consistent understanding of the subject at hand is therefore shared by members of the group. Kuhn himself took note of such groups, which he referred to as "schools." He even said that were he to write *The Structure of Scientific Revolutions* again, he would place more emphasis on the importance of those schools and their common points of view.[65]

Political scientists are well aware that clusters of like-minded scholars operate within their discipline, although they may not call them invisible colleges. Thus one survey showed over 80 percent of political scientists agreeing that the schools exist, as compared with 36 percent of chemists and 18 percent of mathematicians.[66] It is in the nature of vocational log-rolling and professional courtesy, however, that their members are nowhere listed formally, and that clues to mutual understanding and shared perceptions must be gleaned from sources that are not designed to reveal invisible college networks directly. Book reviews are one place to look. For example, when Karl W. Deutsch reviewed William Kornhauser's *The Politics of Mass Society* (1958), he observed that it showed "no evidence of familiarity with such authorities as Daniel Lerner, Gabriel Almond, and James S. Coleman."[67] Authorities for whom? For a specific circle of political scholars, including Deutsch. Footnotes are another place to look. Thus Christian Bay asked rhetorically how political scientists can know that "development" means what the United States has done already. They know, he said, by "citing primarily each other's work," whereby a certain group has "produced quite an imposing consensus on the meaning of 'political development.' "[68] Again, the hand of an invisible college reveals itself indirectly.

In 1975, Robert T. Holt and John E. Turner analyzed the shortcomings of comparative politics research as it appeared in a series of seven books sponsored by the prestigious Social Science Research Council's "Committee on Comparative Politics."[69] In effect, Holt and Turner commented on the work of something

64. Ibid., pp. 13–14.

65. "Reflections on My Critics," in Imre Lakatos and Alan Musgrave, eds., *Criticism and the Growth of Knowledge* (Cambridge: Cambridge University Press, 1970), p. 252.

66. Hargens, *Patterns of Scientific Research*, p. 19.

67. Review of William Kornhauser, *The Politics of Mass Society* (1959), in *American Political Science Review* (March 1961) p. 149.

68. "The Cheerful Science of Dismal Politics," in Theodore Roszak, ed., *The Dissenting Academy* (New York: Random House, 1967), p. 221.

69. The seven books were all published by Princeton University Press. They include: Lucian W. Pye, ed., *Communications and Political Development* (1963); Joseph Palombara, ed., *Bureau-*

very close to what Crane had called an invisible college, for they pointed out that the Committee had sponsored numerous academic conferences and professional publications over the years, involving hundreds of scholars, and culminating in the seven books among others.[70] Among practitioners, it was clear that certain shared understandings of the nature of political development had emerged during all of this intensive interaction.[71] Yet taking the appearance of the seventh and summary volume, *Crises and Sequences of Political Development*, by Leonard Binder, et al., as an occasion to review these joint scholarly efforts, Holt and Turner decided that the goal of "theory development"—to discover laws of political behavior—remained unattained. In their view, practitioners in this working group within the discipline failed to achieve its objective because of the very difficulties we have just noted. For example, various books in the series used basic terms such as "political development" in different ways, said Holt and Turner, and some key terms, such as the "capacity" of a political system to cope with crises, were never defined precisely at all.[72] As a result, no testable hypotheses appeared in the seven books, authors did not really check one another's work, and, where confirmation or disconfirmation never took place, dramatically or otherwise, not a single conclusion drawn by any of the authors achieved the status of a theory, or law.[73]

The Repute System and Vocational Knowledge

The dilemmas that plague scholars searching for political laws unfold with a certain internal logic, as do so many other features of collective political scholarship. No laws of the requisite power stand revealed in political science writings. Nonetheless, the work of some scholars is highly regarded by their peers. Why is this so? Formally, the discipline employs a "repute system"—with journals, conventions, scholarly writings, and modern research apparatus—that looks something like what we might expect to find in any scientific community.[74] This set of institutional devices certifies some work as superior and other work as

---

cracy and Political Development (1963); Robert E. Ward and Dankwart A. Rustow, eds., *Political Modernization in Japan and Turkey* (1964); James S. Coleman, ed., *Education and Political Development* (1965); Lucien W. Pye and Sidney Verba, eds., *Political Culture and Political Development* (1965); Joseph Palombara and Myron Weiner, eds., *Political Parties and Political Development* (1966); and Leonard Binder, et al., *Crises and Sequences in Political Development* (1971).

70. "Crises and Sequences in Collective Theory Development," *American Political Science Review* (September 1975), p. 980.

71. Robert A. Packenham, *Liberal America and the Third World: Political Development Ideas in Foreign Aid and Social Science* (Princeton, N.J.: Princeton University Press, 1973), passim.

72. "Crises and Sequences," pp. 981, 992.

73. Ibid., pp. 987–88.

74. The term "repute system" comes from Philip H. Melanson, *Political Science and Political Knowledge* (Washington, D.C.: Public Affairs Press, 1975), pp. 95–98.

inferior, by granting to some ideas publication in highly ranked journals while others are accepted only by lesser journals or rejected for publication entirely. Yet in the case of political science, the acclaim accorded via the repute system comes more from a realm of effective association with colleagues than from a rigorous process of testing and retesting of hypotheses such as might occur in a community of natural scientists. The discipline's sociological qualities thereby outweigh the experimental and predominantly objective procedures that help natural scientists produce reliable findings when they work within their own, similar repute systems.

This point is illustrated when those conventional truths that circulate within the community of political scholars are called "vocational knowledge."[75] The very term implies that even though various understandings are shared by like-minded practitioners as they exchange ideas and research findings, one cannot be sure that this professionally certified knowledge holds true for the real world outside. In general, if a discipline's practitioners are divided by intractable disagreements, expressed through invisible colleges, the confrontation is a sign that the contested items of vocational knowledge are probably insufficiently convincing to gain widespread endorsement by intelligent men and women in society at large. Within the discipline of political science, such disagreement is revealed when journal editors admit that various fields in the study of politics are characterized by such fierce infighting among referees as to greatly influence their choice of manuscripts for publication.[76] The same disagreement is reflected in a rejection rate of 80 percent for political science article manuscripts, as against 24 percent for physics and 29 percent for biology.[77]

The Case of Community Power Studies

From the foregoing, we might conclude that in political science the search for laws, theories, hypotheses, or political regularities under any other name, must encounter the difficulties we have just reviewed, and that the discipline's repute system will surely turn out vocational knowledge which, in the absence of conclusive verifications or falsifications, bears no necessary relationship to a constant political reality. Yet as we have seen, if the search for political laws did succeed, it might overshadow the discipline's traditionally disappointing performance with regard to matters such as adequate definitions of politics, the propensity to specialize, the proliferation of jargon, distortions of the truth, a retreat from reason, the loss of wisdom, and so forth. Given the serious implications of

75. The term "vocational knowledge" comes from ibid., pp. 98–99.

76. Lindsay, *The Scientific Publication System*, p. 38.

77. Harriet Zuckerman and Robert Merton, "Patterns of Evaluation in Science: Institutionalization, Structure, and Functions of the Referee System," *Minerva* (January 1971), p. 76.

failure in this quest, then, we should reserve judgment on the discipline's ability to discover political laws until we move beyond general suppositions and expectations to examine how the course of research events within a particular field of political studies follows a script that reflects many of the sociological dimensions of professional life for political scholars. For this purpose, a convenient case in point is the realm of community power studies. From approximately 1950 to 1970, several schools of thought contended against each other in that realm, with some large ideas being accepted and others rejected, by one scholarly circle or another, in ways that bear upon the question of how new ideas are received by political scientists working together.

Approaches to Community Power

Elsewhere, I have written at length about the field of community power studies, and about how ideas were debated there by scholars trying to decide how power is distributed both in the American nation and in its local cities and towns.[78] Very briefly, there were three major schools of thought on this subject, known as "the reputational approach," "the positional approach," and "the decision-making approach." These labels referred to the alternative research techniques employed by each of the three schools, whereas in terms of their findings concerning the distribution of community power, the first two schools held that American communities are run somewhat selfishly by elites, and the third school argued instead that major community decisions are based more equitably on compromises reflecting the needs of many diverse interest groups.

Floyd Hunter initiated the reputational approach for studying power with his *Community Power Structure* (1953), where he reported on his investigation of the city of Atlanta, Georgia.[79] By asking various prominent citizens of the city to tell him whom they considered to be the most powerful local leaders, Hunter was able to draw up a list of forty people who, by reputation at least, made Atlanta's major decisions in banking, industry, trade, and land development.[80] The economic power of these forty was so great, Hunter claimed, that they dominated the other citizens who were active in public life, a larger group which Hunter called the political understructure, including civic organizations, trade unions, and political parties.[81] At the bottom of Atlanta's power structure, which was actually shaped like a pyramid, there remained the majority of ordinary men and women, for the most part powerless.[82]

---

78. David Ricci, "Receiving Ideas in Political Analysis: The Case of Community Power Studies, 1950–1970," *Western Political Quarterly* (December 1980), pp. 451–75.
79. (New York: Doubleday, 1953).
80. Ibid., pp. 13–59.
81. Ibid., pp. 81–86.
82. Ibid., pp. 223–54.

From this portrait of the facts of political power it followed, in Hunter's opinion, that the situation in Atlanta was not democratic. True, most municipal policies appeared to originate in the political understructure, but in reality the elite, consulting informally within itself in small cliques, first formulated policies beneficial to itself and only then transmitted them to the understructure for publicized approval.[83] In the total circumstances, Hunter concluded that despite elections, Atlanta would be truly democratic only if more and more citizens were to form groups, enter the understructure, bolster its resources, and challenge the power of the elite by acting in concert to advance their own interests.[84]

The Positional Approach

The leading exponent of the positional approach to community power was C. Wright Mills. In *The Power Elite* (1956), Mills emphasized the class characteristics shared by people who held leading positions in the most powerful institutions of American national life, in banking, law, politics, the military, and high society.[85] He observed that these people attended private schools, joined exclusive social clubs, enjoyed similar manners and pastimes, and married uncommon spouses; as a result, they evinced much the same outlook and interests. The elite worked in various realms of power, such as politics and industry. But the differing surroundings did not weaken their common upper-class sentiments, which continued to color the standards of all leaders regardless of formally different responsibilities in whichever realm they served.[86] Moreover, when a lower-class person rose to power by any means, he quickly acquired upper-class sentiments, thereby assuring that the harmony of outlook in leadership circles remained unbroken.[87]

Like Hunter, Mills took the facts of elite power to suggest an undemocratic situation, this time at the national level. He asserted that at the top of American society there existed a "power elite," with representatives entrenched in leading political, military, and business positions.[88] Because of their shared mentality, members of this elite formulated policies that served their own interests in preference to those of anyone else. In the power ranks directly below the elite, Mills found what he called "the middle level of power," an entity that embraced the day-to-day hurly-burly of politics, and which included national and local interest groups, state legislatures, regulatory agencies, and even most of the

83. Ibid., pp. 62–79.
84. Ibid., pp. 228–54.
85. (New York: Oxford University Press), pp. 30–197.
86. Ibid., pp. 284–85.
87. Ibid., pp. 141–46, 193–97, 235.
88. Ibid., pp. 269–97.

Congress.[89] As Mills saw it, the power elite was able to act through the president, a few key leaders in the Congress, and the moguls of the military-industrial complex, to influence and manipulate the middle level of power so effectively that that level exercised little authority except on minor issues. Below everyone else, Mills found the great mass of politically impotent citizens, whom he referred to as "the mass."[90]

The Decision-Making Approach

The third approach devised for studying community power was called the decision-making technique, and it was exemplified in Robert A. Dahl's book *Who Governs?* (1961).[91] Instead of checking by reputation or by institutional position to see who was most powerful in New Haven, Connecticut, Dahl insisted that only close examination of decisions already taken in a community can reveal the distribution of power there.[92] Consequently, he studied decisions made in New Haven for three realms of public policy: education, party nominations, and urban renewal. Using interviews, newspaper files, personal observations, and other data sources, Dahl found only a relatively few people who could accurately be called decision makers, among whom the mayor and his aides enjoyed dominant power with regard to each of the three issue areas.[93] The mayor's power, and that of other elected officials, rested on the support given to him by a collection of politically interested groups and individuals whom Dahl called "the political stratum," and these people were in turn constantly replenished by the great majority of citizens who on occasion chose to become politically active and leave their customary place in "the apolitical stratum" of society.[94]

Thus elected officials who either directly or indirectly represented all of New Haven's citizenry actually wielded more power than any economic or social elite, no matter how active upper-class people might have been in the city. And therefore by Dahl's estimate, New Haven was democratic.[95] More precisely, the city enjoyed a pluralist sort of democracy, where the political stratum, which Mills had dismissed as the middle level of power, and which Hunter had written off as the understructure of power, served as a composite sounding board for the expression of numerous interests and the application of broadly based political

89. Ibid., pp. 4, 31, 290–92.

90. Ibid., pp. 198–324.

91. *Who Governs? Power and Democracy in an American City* (New Haven: Yale University Press).

92. See Robert A. Dahl, "Critique of the Ruling Elite Model," *American Political Science Review* (June 1958), pp. 463–69.

93. *Who Governs?*, pp. 200–14.

94. Ibid., pp. 90–100.

95. Ibid., pp. 311–25.

pressures. In other words, even though only a few men and women seemed to make the key decisions in New Haven, they were constrained by democratic institutions to shape those decisions on behalf of the community as a whole.

The Logical Impasse over Methodology

These three major approaches to studying community power encouraged a great number of more and less notable studies in the 1950s and 1960s, plus a host of journal articles and books for or against various points of methodology and finding.[96] Despite very lengthy scholarly debate, however, it proved impossible to achieve consensus throughout the community of political scholars as to which method, study, model, or set of conclusions concerning power was unquestionably valid. As a result, by roughly 1970, the diverse research projects in this field, and their contradictory findings, had together created an impasse. On the one side stood a group of scholars who believed that American politics was generally elitist and unrepresentative; they cited evidence derived mainly from power studies similar to those of Hunter and Mills. On the other side stood those who asserted that American politics was by and large pluralistic and democratic; they presented as proof the facts revealed in studies such as those by Dahl.

From about 1950 to 1970, then, community power was a field wherein: (a) new ideas were offered to the community of political scientists, and (b) some ideas were accepted by virtually everyone, although not everyone accepted the same ideas. The central reality of it all is worth careful consideration. A number of ideas about power were certified by members of the community of political scholars. Why was this so? In fact, there was a time of widespread belief in opposing ideas, with congeries of scholars—in effect, invisible colleges—taking one position or another. Did the reign of belief, regardless of which ideas it entailed in specific cases, involve subjective or objective causes? Here is the major point at issue in Kuhn's theory. Behavioralists might agree with Robert A. Dahl, that whether an empirical proposition "is true or false depends on the degree to which the proposition and the real world correspond."[97] Or, in the terms of Jerone Stephens's distinctly anti-Kuhnian thesis, "What we must not do . . . is to take Kuhn seriously when he suggests that what scientists [including political scientists] learn and apply are [subjective] values and not [objective] rules."[98] But did the findings of men such as Hunter, Mills, and Dahl run a gauntlet of rigorous tests? Is that why they found schools of believers?

To ask these questions is to draw attention to a striking aspect of the debate

96. See Willis D. Hawley and James H. Svara, *The Study of Community Power: A Bibliographic Review* (Santa Barbara, Ca.: ABC-CLIO, 1972).

97. *Modern Political Analysis* (Englewood Cliffs, N.J.: Prentice-Hall, 1963), p. 8.

98. Jerone K. Stephens, "The Kuhnian Paradigm and Political Inquiry: An Appraisal," *American Journal of Political Science* (August 1973), p. 488.

on community power, for in fact only rarely did scholars go out in the field and investigate the same community that their antagonist studied, to see if "reality" in a specific case confirmed or denied his findings. Moreover, in the rare cases when a replication study was executed,[99] there is no evidence that it influenced the course of belief beyond strengthening the convictions of those already committed. Instead, most parties to the community power debate, lacking the time or the means to duplicate controversial studies, argued as if the findings of such studies were to be accepted or rejected on the basis of internal evidence. And so arguments were advanced that one study or another was persuasive because its methodology was logical and consistent, because it seemed reasonable to proceed in such a way. The stage was set for this sort of intellectual dueling as early as in 1954, when Herbert Kaufman and Victor Jones reviewed Hunter's *Community Power Structure* and asserted that "Hunter may . . . be right or wrong about the social structure of Regional City [Atlanta], but that is beside the point if his methods are faulty. Unfortunately, they are, and these shortcomings are probably more important than any chance accuracy in his conclusions."[100]

Parallel Arguments concerning Community Power

The point is that where logic and methodology, rather than empirical tests and persuasive facts, formed the basis of debate in this field, journal articles expressed the conflicting opinions of opposing invisible colleges without offering arguments that could conclusively demonstrate the validity of any particular position to an objective outsider. Indeed, in the relevant texts, there appeared a remarkable pattern of intellectual symmetry. On a great many questions of proof and disproof for new ideas in the field, those who argued for a specific idea employed exactly the same logic which they identified in their opponent's work and which caused them to argue against his idea. Similarly, those who found fault with a particular concept for its imperfect logical underpinning used the same logic when speaking in favor of their own ideas. Nevertheless, choices were made to accept one idea or another, for reasons that, by elimination, must have been subjective or, in wider terms, sociological.

For example, a persuasive criticism was leveled at Hunter's reputational technique. It was said that the opinions of local respondents were worthless, if only because no objective and intelligent criteria can be advanced to justify the selection of such respondents in the first instance. The question was asked: If

---

99. For example, David A. Booth and Charles R. Adrian, "Power Structure and Community Change: A Replication Study of Community A," *Midwest Journal of Politics* (August 1962), pp. 277–96, and M. Kent Jennings, *Community Influentials: The Elites of Atlanta* (New York: Free Press, 1964).

100. "The Mystery of Power," *Public Administration Review* (Summer 1954), p. 207.

Hunter was sufficiently informed about power in Atlanta to be sure his "judges" were truly knowledgeable on the subject, what need was there for polling them at all?[101] This was a telling point, for it revealed an apparent paradox, that the expertise of respondents can only be proved if a researcher has acquired in advance the information he seeks from those people themselves. Be that as it may, the fact remains that the sources of information used in decision-making research were no more reliable than reputational respondents, for the same logic applied to both. Decision-making researchers relied on interviews, books, newspaper articles, broadcasts, historical documents, and other conventional reports. All of these are actually secondary sources. But if all such sources, themselves no more than statements of information gathered by fallible men, may be inaccurate, slanted, or wrong, how was the investigator to evaluate them? He could compare the information supplied by different sources and thereby check them for internal accuracy,[102] but reputational researchers could similarly cross-check the answers of their respondents.[103] In the last analysis, even with the most painstaking of comparisons, all that can be said with certainty is that both the decision-making and the reputational techniques were capable of faithfully bringing to light an image of community power as it existed in the minds of local citizens, or some other representative cross section of the community.

In another example of logic-chopping rather than fact-finding, it was said that researchers who employed the reputational and positional methods usually failed to prove "cohesion" among the few decision makers they found in any community. Those methods could reveal decision makers per se, but they could not prove that those leaders represented only themselves rather than diverse, competitive, and democratic constituents.[104] Granted, both methods may fail to prove cohesion in that sense, for if it exists it may originate in forums inaccessible to researchers, in private luncheons, "smoke-filled rooms," or golf clubhouses after the eighteenth green. On the other hand, there was no way of proving that cohesion did not exist, that common understandings were not arranged out of sight of the researchers. How could a decision-making researcher be sure, for example, that Smith, the mayor of Gotham City, did not make a deal with

101. Robert A. Dahl, "Hierarchy, Democracy, and Bargaining in Politics and Economics," in Heinz Eulau, et al., eds., *Political Behavior* (Glencoe, Ill.: Free Press, 1956), p. 85.

102. In Dahl's New Haven study, Raymond Wolfinger was a participant-observer in City Hall for a year. In this way, the project was designed to have someone who could check interview data and other kinds of available information. See Dahl, *Who Governs?*, pp. 335–36.

103. See Robert O. Schulze and Leonard V. Blumberg, "The Determination of Local Power Elites," *American Journal of Sociology* (November 1957), pp. 290–96; and Robert E. Agger and Daniel Goldrich, "Community Power Structures and Partisanship," *American Journal of Sociology* (August 1958), pp. 383–92.

104. Dahl, "Critique of the Ruling Elite Model," p. 118; and Daniel Bell, "The Power Elite—Reconsidered," *American Journal of Sociology* (November 1958), p. 242.

Jones, the president of Gotham's First National Bank?[105] After all, decision-making research is based upon facts gained from public documents or statements, or from respondents directly, and both of these sources of data may fail to reveal deliberately clandestine matters. The 1967 revelations concerning illegal CIA activities highlighted the existence of such machinations, as did the later Watergate scandals.

Further complicating the matter of cohesion, Mills's work was interpreted as suggesting that if a researcher did not himself see instances of collusion, he could still justifiably say elitism existed, on the grounds that the shared class sentiments of all leaders will induce them, publicly or privately, to support policies favorable to their common interests. Hunter employed much the same approach in his work, contending that Atlanta's elite had economic interests strong enough to create a general background of consensus regardless of which specific matters the elite might consider. What is interesting here is the notion of common interests as a source of cohesion, seen or unseen, now or in the future. The logic of the conception was unassailable, especially when expressed in the form of conditional assertions; for example, if and when the upper class really feels threatened, it will coalesce and rally to its fundamental interests.[106] But if this is true, it means that the plainest facts of pluralism in America are misleading, for despite leaders periodically offering alternative policies to the people, elite power always stands apart waiting to be exercised in matters that count. Accordingly, it may be said that pluralism, such as it is, exists by sufferance of the elite.

Fortunately for decision-making researchers, the same irrefutable logic served to support a pluralistic view of who rules in America; they too made conditional assertions the key to their image of the structure of community power. Dahl's use of the concept of "indirect influence,"[107] for example, was actually a confident extension of the idea that something democratically important was happening even though it could not be seen. In his scheme of things, members of the "apolitical stratum" in New Haven were not normally active in politics. Even so, they wielded indirect influence because political leaders deferred to their interests for fear that passive citizens might someday vote against candidates known for disregarding those same interests. In short, if and when the

---

105. Wolfinger, who was assigned by Dahl to observe New Haven's mayor, "seldom lunched with him or accompanied him to private talks in offices outside city hall." See Raymond E. Wolfinger, *The Politics of Progress* (Englewood Cliffs, N.J.: Prentice-Hall, 1974), p. 4.

106. Mills implied this notion when he claimed that the truly significant national community decisions, the "big decisions," the decisions that reveal whether or not America enjoys democracy or suffers elitism, are those relating to foreign policy. In other words, on these decisions, the power elite is presumably protecting its interests by causing America to persist in capitalistic and imperialistic activities on the world stage. See *The Power Elite*, p. 22.

107. *Who Governs?*, pp. 105–06, 139–40, 159–65.

interests of the poor and the politically inert are really threatened, they can and will unite to protect themselves. And thus the parallel between elitist and plural-ist logic was complete. One could almost say that the power of elites persisted only because the masses willed it.

The Decline of Community Power Studies

Notwithstanding all of these efforts, nothing definitive emerged from the field of community power studies between 1950 and 1970. And so, when Kenneth Dol-beare summarized what had been learned during several decades of community power studies, he concluded that "the data would seem to suggest. . . . It might be. . . . we may speculate that. . . . Louis Hartz may have been right. . . . For the most part, voters. . . . It is possible that. . . . The concept of a 'majority will' or a 'public opinion' on an issue is elusive if not illusory. . . . the general implica-tion seems to be."[108] Nelson W. Polsby, one of Dahl's closest collaborators and consistent supporters, was equally reticent about concrete results when he offered a retrospective survey of the field in 1980. In the second edition of his *Community Power and Political Theory*, under the subtitle of *A Further Look at Problems of Evidence and Inference*, Polsby noted that the academic study of community power was less about real-world politics than it was about "the writings of scholars, and what they say they have found, and whether we ought to believe them or not, and why."[109]

Interesting studies of political power continued to appear in the 1970s and 1980s.[110] Still, as a field of research where common questions were asked, different answers were offered, and many practitioners followed the exchange of views even if they did not contribute to it themselves, the realm of community power studies gradually faded away after two decades of active work and scholarly interest. As we might expect, there were significant sociological dimensions to this decline. The repute system worked smoothly, offering many scholars continuing opportunities for publishing their ideas and advancing professionally. In the process, journal

108. "Power and Process in the Contemporary United States," in Kenneth M. Dolbeare, ed., *Power and Change in the United States* (New York: Wiley, 1969), pp. 244–51.

109. *Community Power and Political Theory: A Further Look at Problems of Evidence and Inference*, 2nd ed. (New Haven: Yale University Press, 1980), pp. xi–xii.

110. Among latter-day efforts, an excellent primary study is Frederick M. Wirt, *Power in the City* (Berkeley: University of California Press, 1974); an excellent secondary study is Kenneth Prewitt and Alan Stone, *The Ruling Elites* (New York: Harper and Row, 1973); an excellent theoretical essay is Jack H. Nagel, *The Descriptive Analysis of Power* (New Haven: Yale University Press, 1975); and an excellent radical essay is Lynda Ann Ewen, *Corporate Power and Urban Crisis in Detroit* (Princeton, N.J.: Princeton University Press, 1978). The most recent notable contribution is John Gaventa, *Power and Powerlessness: Quiescence and Rebellion in an Appalachian Valley* (Urbana: University of Illinois Press, 1980).

debates were conducted,[111] and invisible-college phenomena came into being.[112] However, quantitative equivalents for the object in question—power—were never produced,[113] and key terms were always variously defined.[114] Moreover, the nature of the research material did not permit controlled and repeatable experimentation, and therefore logical arguments came to the fore. In all, conclusive proofs or disproofs of the most common professional convictions about power simply did not materialize, and journal debates on the subject therefore probably never convinced anyone who was not predisposed in one direction or another. Finally, although knowledge did not accumulate, jargon did, to the point where latter-day journal debates were extremely complicated and closely argued.[115] As a result, most nonpartisans evidently decided that, since the field of community power had produced terminological chaos, the broad questions asked in that field were no longer worth considering.[116]

The bottom line is clear: No laws were discovered in the field of community power studies. Polsby said as much in 1980, perhaps unintentionally, when he concluded that political scientists still lacked "a firmly grounded set of empirical propositions" about the world of power.[117] The end result of this situation was

111. For example, Jack Walker, "A Critique of the Elitist Theory of Democracy," *American Political Science Review* (June 1966), pp. 285–95; and Robert A. Dahl, "Further Reflections on 'The Elitist Theory of Democracy,' " ibid., pp. 296–305.

112. For example, see Richard M. Merelman's review of Matthew A. Crenson, *The Unpolitics of Air Pollution: A Study of Nondecision-making in American Cities* (1971), in *American Political Science Review* (March 1973), pp. 216–17; and Nelson W. Polsby's review of G. William Domhoff, *Who Rules America?*, in *American Sociological Review* (June 1968), pp. 476–77.

113. The problem was highlighted as early as 1955, but never resolved. See James G. March, "An Introduction to the Theory and Measurement of Influence," *American Political Science Review* (June 1955), p. 434: "At present, there is lacking not only an immediately obvious unit of measurement [of influence] but even a generally feasible means of providing simple rankings."

114. For example, see the table of concepts offered in Peter Bachrach and Morton S. Baratz, "Decisions and Nondecisions: An Analytical Framework," ibid. (September 1963), p. 640, which attempts to distinguish between terms such as "power," "authority," "influence," "manipulation," and "force." These may be compared with the somewhat different definitions offered in Robert Bierstedt, "An Analysis of Social Power," *American Sociological Review* (December 1950), pp. 730–38. Given the field's lack of clarity with regard to central concerns, it is no wonder that Wolfinger concluded eventually that "power is not a very useful or interesting empirical concept." See his *Politics of Progress*, p. 9.

115. For one such debate, see Raymond E. Wolfinger, "Nondecisions and the Study of Local Politics," *American Political Science Review* (December 1971), pp. 1063–80; and Frederick W. Frey, "Comment: On Issues and Nonissues in the Study of Power," ibid., pp. 1081–1101.

116. To sense the exasperation that set in, see Arthur Clun, "The Post-Behavioral Revolution in Community Power: A Brief Note from a Frontier of Research," *PS* (Summer 1972), pp. 274–77. This satirical article reduced the work of pluralists and antipluralists to a few propositions, all well documented but inconsistent with one another.

117. Polsby, *Community Power and Political Theory*, p. xvii.

summed up in Thomas Dye's comment that "theory and conceptualization about power and elites is in such disarray in the social sciences . . . that it is really impossible to speculate about the theoretical relevance of our data on institutional leadership without generating endless unproductive debate."[118] Yet if "the theoretical relevance of our data" cannot be usefully discussed, then all that emerges from community power studies is an occasionally impressive work, whose findings never seem unquestionably capable of being fitted together with the findings of other studies in order to support firm and general conclusions. And that, of course, is a reality which contributes to the current mood in political science, where behavioral techniques are still popular but where confidence in their ultimate efficacy has declined over the last ten to fifteen years.

The Case of Critical Theory

In the case of community power studies, a specific field of research within the discipline of political science produced no laws of political behavior, but furnished much evidence to the effect that political scholars work collectively along lines that are more sociological than experimental. As a complementary lesson, it will be instructive to consider the case of "critical theory."[119] This approach to political inquiry is difficult to describe, since the scholars who expound and refine its basic tenets draw upon a wide variety of sources, ranging from Karl Marx and Friedrich Engels to Sigmund Freud, Søren Kierkegaard, Edmund Husserl, Georg Lukács, Maurice Merleau-Ponty, Alfred Schutz, Jurgens Habermas, Theodore Adorno, Herbert Marcuse, Max Horkeimer, and Erich Fromm. Still, there is considerable consistency to critical theorists' diverse explanations as to why, after a great many failures, the discipline should renounce its devotion to behavioral technique, sometimes called "positivism" by this school. [120] Moreover, in arguments that these dissident scholars have powerfully expounded for more than a decade now, there is great concern for many of the problematical aspects of political scholarship that we have already considered. Herbert G. Reid and Ernest Y. Yanarella, for example, correctly identified the crucial terms of debate within recent political science when they observed that practitioners in the 1960s tended to "devalue the writings of Kuhn (who is now seen as heretical or at the very least muddleheaded) while simultaneously elevat-

118. *Who's Running America?* (Englewood Cliffs, N.J.: Prentice-Hall, 1976), p. 217.

119. I am using the term *critical theory* as it is used broadly by Richard J. Bernstein, *The Restructuring of Social and Political Theory* (New York: Harcourt Brace Jovanovich, 1976). See also Max Horkheimer, *Critical Theory*, trans. Matthew J. O'Connell (New York: Seabury, 1972).

120. As in John G. Gunnell, *Philosophy, Science, and Political Inquiry* (Morristown, N.J.: General Learning Press, 1975).

ing the work of Karl Popper to the status of new orthodoxy."[121] And John G. Gunnell extended the same insight when he remarked that "the emphasis on policy analysis" pervading the post-behavioral era was closely linked to a denial of the sociological realities highlighted by men such as Kuhn. In Gunnell's view, it was this rejection which permitted mainstream political scientists "to see no fundamental problem in applying . . . a little personality 'theory,' some notions of collective choice from economics, a dose of organization 'theory,' and some brand of systems analysis to an examination of the same events," as if those events existed quite independently of our perception of them.[122] The question is, how did the discipline respond to criticism from this quarter, which in many respects fastened upon difficulties that were an inherent part of the community's professional life?

Scientific Laws, The Life-World, and Intersubjectivity

Critical theorists approach standard political inquiry from many directions, so one cannot say that their charges begin with any specific contention. Analytically speaking, however, the point of departure is a rejection of what they call "scientism," or the notion that scientific laws as produced in the style of natural science are the only form of real knowledge.[123] They contend, instead, that behavioral science—or positivism—falls short of achieving real knowledge because it cannot grasp all of the manifold dimensions of human life. From the critical point of view, Hwa Yol Jung stated the conditions for this failure when he commented that "The world is the comprehensive and inclusive horizon of all possible and actual experiences. This world contains innumerable realities, that is, as many as there are orders of experience."[124] If men see the world in different ways at different times and in different places, it follows that the limited objective data available to scientific analysis simply cannot be compressed into laws which will account for all that the world means to human beings.

In the vocabulary of critical theory, some of the world's enormous complexity is reduced to a commonly understood set of shared circumstances that surround the members of any human community, and which goes under the name of "the life-world," or *Lebenswelt*. In one description, this is "the prescientific,

121. "Political Science and the Post-Modern Critique of Scientism and Domination," *Review of Politics* (July 1975), p. 287.

122. "Political Science and the Theory of Action," *Political Theory* (February 1979), p. 82.

123. Herbert G. Reid and Ernest Yanarella, "Towards a Post-Modern Theory of American Political Science and Culture: Perspectives from Critical Marxism and Phenomenology," *Cultural Hermeneutics*, no. 2 (1974), p. 100.

124. "The Political Relevance of Existential Phenomenology," *Review of Politics* (October 1971), p. 540.

pretheoretical world that we immediately experience and inhabit in our everyday lives and at all times."[125] Most importantly, this is the realm of human action in any community, the realm of standard behavior and joint expectations that characterize those people who live in, say, a liberal society. From the fact that behavior in every particular human community exhibits a measure of respective conformity, it follows that each life-world must be comprehended by its individual inhabitants in fairly consistent ways. For critical theorists, this means that although people see their surroundings subjectively, there is a sense in which the same subjective perceptions are repeated in citizen after citizen. In the lexicon of critical theory, then, the life-world "is not the private world of an individual but is from the outset an intersubjective or socialized world."[126] Or, in another formulation, the life-world is "an intersubjective world of shared meanings, beliefs, and values."[127] Yet in positivist science these meanings, beliefs, and values—such as those that surround the individual act of voting, or the cooperative conduct of negotiations—do not register accurately, if at all, when conventional research techniques are applied to political inquiry. Hence the complaint that such research "occludes" significant parts of the life-world at every step. [128]

The Hermeneutic Circle and Antinomies

Critical theorists state these same points in various terms, as when they talk of a hermeneutic circle of events and the meanings that may be attributed to them. [129] Here, the basic idea is that the world does not exist in objective suspension but enjoys a quality of "meaningfulness" which men impute to its manifestations as they see fit. Accordingly, that meaning can only be understood when the world is considered as the sum of its related parts, whereas modern science and today's learned disciplines tend to divide reality up so that each discipline gets its own area to investigate, with men hoping to comprehend society as a whole on the basis of "combining data from all social disciplines."[130] By contrast, critical theorists contend that scholars must look at entire societies directly and comprehensively, since the bits and pieces of data acquired by separate learned disci-

125. Reid and Yanarella, "Towards a Post-Modern Theory," p. 116.

126. Hwa Yol Jung, "The Political Relevance of Existential Phenomenology," *Review of Politics* (October 1971), p. 542.

127. Reid and Yanarella, "Towards a Post-Modern Theory," p. 102.

128. Ibid., p. 116.

129. On the significance of meanings for political analysis, see Charles Taylor, "Interpretation and the Science of Man," *Review of Metaphysics* (September 1971), passim, but esp. pp. 10–17.

130. Robert A. Gorman, "Phenomenology, Social Science, and Radicalism: The View from Existence," *Politics and Society*, vol. 6, no. 4 (1976), p. 499.

plines are usually obtained via "conceptual frameworks" that tend to recognize only a limited range of facts while overlooking the larger meanings inherent in them.[131] The problem of selective perception is especially acute when modern researchers assume the validity of various dualities, or "antinomies," such as essence and appearance, fact and value, theory and practice, description and evaluation, and the knower and the known.[132] When research is conducted according to such categories of analysis and experience, entire dimensions of continuous social development and history are collapsed into a very limited view of human affairs. Once again, the meaning of things and events is difficult if not impossible to grasp.

Empiricism and Time

The comprehensive nature of hermeneutic reality is frequently ignored, according to critical theory, by the positivist insistence on strictly empirical research. As critical theorists see the situation, to the extent that such research dwells mainly upon "the facts," it assumes that they "have some existence, some inherency, beyond human cognition. Like atoms, which existed before they were seen, the facts of political life are assumed to be there, waiting for the magic bullet of a correct hypothesis to uncover them."[133] One trouble with this notion is that men see certain social "facts" as a function of how they judge their surroundings to have come into being. That is, there are important dimensions of historical time built into men's perceptions of society. Then, too, people not only live in the present with a residue of historical impressions and attitudes, but they live, individually and collectively, in parallel time streams that may not move at the same speed and therefore cause time-imposed residues to accumulate differentially from person to person and group to group.[134] If the world is viewed in this light, political research that slights the past, and that pays little attention to expectations for the future, will obscure rather than illuminate the reality of public life. Indeed, such research will inevitably misconstrue some of the great problems of modern society, such as protracted alienation, or the gradual breakdown of civility, both of which are enormously affected by historical experiences.[135]

131. John G. Gunnell, "The Idea of a Conceptual Framework," *Journal of Comparative Administration* (August 1969), pp. 140–76.

132. Reid and Yanarella, "Toward a Post-Modern Theory," pp. 105, 111.

133. Philip H. Melanson, *Political Science and Political Knowledge* (Washington, D.C.: Public Affairs Press, 1975), pp. 71–72.

134. Herbert G. Reid, "American Social Science in the Politics of Time and the Crisis of Technocorporate Society: Toward a Critical Phenomenology," *Politics and Society* (Winter 1973), pp. 201–43.

135. Reid and Yanarella, "Toward a Post-Modern Theory," p. 103.

Intentionality and Interests

The all-encompassing sweep of hermeneutic reality is also imperfectly understood when conventional researchers overlook the factor of human "intentionality."[136] According to critical theorists, men are conscious entities who respond knowingly to their environment, with the result that their actions are not automatic but constitute "motivated behavior." Yet the intentions that impel men to act entail such an array of passions and values that positivist researchers must lose sight of the political actor if they assume that this personality can be ruled by simple calculations of profit and loss, such as the pursuit of utility in an economic sense.[137] On the contrary, says Thomas A. Spragens, Jr., political behavior is so affected by numerous values that we will never comprehend public affairs if we do not reintegrate "empirical and normative theory into a spectrum."[138]

Critical theorists link the condition of intentionality to a wider notion that men have the capacity to intend that things will be other than they are at any given time. In this sense, "an adequate description of the present requires the use of concepts which reflect its existence in the tension between 'has been' and 'not yet.' "[139] To carry the conception even further, for critical theorists reality becomes "the totality of the not yet actualized potentialities within the present, the immediately given, and the work needed to transform the present into its full potential."[140]

The objective of such formulations is to suggest that standard political science severely limits our vision by paying too much attention to what citizens are thinking and doing momentarily, as if this subjective perception constitutes their interest even though living under other circumstances might cause them to aspire to conditions permitting more "human freedom and autonomy" than exist today.[141] In fact, according to Clarke E. Cochran, men's character is such that we must not, by concentrating on their present behavior, lose sight of "the future possibilities of order grounded in man's capacity for community."[142] In this sense, "man has neither fixed properties nor a predetermined future," but by making and remaking his world can achieve societies far more decent and just than those he has constructed so far. In short, like the counterculturists whom

136. Ibid., p. 106.
137. Jung, "The Political Relevance of Existential Phenomenology," p. 554.
138. *The Dilemma of Contemporary Political Theory: Toward a Post-Behavioral Science of Politics* (New York: Dunellen, 1973), p. 21.
139. Ibid., p. 102.
140. Jane Flax, "Critical Theory as a Vocation," *Politics and Society*, vol. 8, no. 2 (1978), p. 207.
141. Ibid., p. 205. See the critical conception of "interests" in Isaac D. Balbus, "The Concept of Interest in Pluralist and Marxian Analysis," *Politics and Society* (February 1971), pp. 151–77.
142. "The Politics of Interest: Philosophy and the Limitations of the Science of Politics," *American Journal of Political Science* (November 1973), p. 764.

we have already noted, critical theorists continually refer, via their own concepts, to the very vexing problem of true needs versus immediate desires, or to
people as they are today in contrast to what they are capable of becoming
tomorrow.

Truth, Wisdom, and Self-Reflection

All told, critical theorists offer a systematically elaborated notion that the social
world is very complicated, with facts and values, capacities and potentialities,
past and present and future, inextricably mixed together. Regardless of how their
objectives may be phrased in technical terms, the political understanding they
seek to achieve is clearly a matter of truth in the largest sense—concerning the
shape of a fundamentally good society and how to get there—rather than small
and empirically bounded research findings on the order of those produced by
standard professional research in the behavioral mode. It follows that this sort of
understanding can be defined, as we did in chapter 7, as a sort of wisdom which
penetrates into the heart of things. Henry S. Kariel therefore observed that a
critical approach may not produce "findings, conclusions, information, or general theories" as these are envisioned for conventional political studies, but it
should engender "a measure of wisdom—an increase in self-conscious empathy,
in managed compassion and governed openness."[143] David Kettler was thinking
along the same lines when he recommended that radical intellectuals should
offer counsel rather than expertise, where the former is linked to wisdom that is
inherently impartial as opposed to the latter resting on technical knowledge that
can be used for selfish ends.[144]

Now if behavioral contributions to knowledge do not add up to the requisite
and comprehensive political understanding, truth about public affairs must be
attained in a different fashion. Critical theorists therefore suggest that political
analysts will turn to a technique of self-reflection. This technique is only loosely
defined in the literature of critical theory. Its character is therefore best illustrated
by quoting directly from those who recommend self-reflection to all social scientists in general and to the community of political scholars in particular. The
basic idea was offered by the philosopher Jurgen Habermas, in his *Knowledge
and Human Interests* (1971), when he said that "The methodological framework
that determines the meaning of the validity of critical propositions . . . is established by the concept of self-reflection."[145] In like vein, Thomas Spragens told
his political science colleagues that "the condition of knowing something is . . .
a felicitous indwelling of the knower in the world."[146] Such indwelling requires

143. "Expanding the Political Present," *American Political Science Review* (September 1969),
p. 775.
144. "The Vocation of Radical Intellectuals," *Politics and Society* (November 1970), p. 48.
145. (Boston: Beacon), p. 310.
146. *The Dilemma of Contemporary Political Theory*, p. 146.

"a dialectic between a personal agent and an external reality upon which the person is contingent," where "relative epistemological transcendence" is achieved by a "critical recognition of one's own suppositions and their relationship to one's own historical contingency."[147] For much the same perspicacity, described somewhat differently, we have the claim of Robert A. Gorman concerning what he calls "the epistemological primacy of individual experience." In his words, only "what is perceived by a conscious individual adequately reveals what is."[148]

When subjective reasoning is compared with experimental procedures, as Popper realized, one quickly sees that individual opinions may be impossible to reconcile, for they may be as different as the separate people who entertain them. Both Spragens and Gorman recognized this potential difficulty. In Spragens's view, "Grounding knowledge in commitment does not equate it with subjective opinion," because we are all "responsible" to report as best we can.[149] Gorman admitted that "Scientific knowledge cannot be drawn from the objective world." He then added that "Intersubjective knowledge that can be validated exists, but it must be constituted individually by a successively purified consciousness, which can transcend subjectivity and merge with the absolute."[150]

Specialization and Jargon
The writings of critical theorists are generally unpopular with most political scientists, and survey reports indicate very little regard for the published contributions of "Left Radicals" such as Ira Katznelson, Herbert Marcuse, Ralph Miliband, James O'Connor, and Bertell Ollman.[151] It would be easy to attribute this rejection to technical factors we have already considered, such as the tendency toward specialization and the prevalence of jargon. There can be no doubt, after all, that the concepts of critical theory are extremely specialized, and therefore difficult for novices to grasp thoroughly. As Reid and Yanarella said, without a trace of irony, one cannot really understand phenomenology without perceiving "the complex, yet vital, distinction between the writings of the early [Edmund] Husserl and those of the later Husserl."[152] Yet getting acquainted with such distinctions is a full-time job that most political scientists are not about to undertake. In addition, mainstream practitioners shun critical theory because much writing in that field is incomprehensible except to enthusiastic disciples. Jargon is especially dense when critical theorists expound their own concepts, as when Jung quotes a colleague to the effect that "existential phenomenology

147. Ibid., pp. 145, 153.
148. "Phenomenology, Social Science, and Radicalism," p. 496.
149. *The Dilemma of Contemporary Political Theory*, p. 146.
150. "Phenomenology, Social Science, and Radicalism," p. 492.
151. Roettger, "The Discipline," pp. 26–27.
152. "Toward a Post-Modern Theory," p. 114.

makes the transition between transcendental phenomenology, born of the reduction of everything to its appearing to me, and ontology, which restores the question of the sense of being for all that is said to 'exist.' "[153] However, impenetrable language also shows up where critical theorists comment on something that should be intelligible in its own terms, as when Herbert S. Reid observes that "[Alexis de] Tocqueville appreciated the social and temporal consequences (intimately related) of the naive institutionalization of American life in terms of the subject-object dualism of the modern mechanistic world view."[154] Tocqueville himself was far more comprehensible than that.

The Rejection of Marxism

Ultimately, the antipathy to critical theory runs deeper than an irritated response to technical annoyances. Here, there comes into play the largest invisible college of all in American political science, the vast majority of practitioners who are dedicated, consciously or unconsciously, to a liberal rather than a Marxian view of human affairs. It is no secret of intellectual history that the critical perspective, in various manifestations, had its origins in disappointment with Western society for failing to produce a working class intent on ushering in socialist society, a failure that could be blamed for promoting fascist tendencies which threatened to propel liberal capitalism backward toward authoritarianism rather than forward to freedom.[155] Moreover, critical theorists do not hide the fact that their sympathies with regard to these events are rooted in Marxian categories of analysis, although they usually contend that works by the young and sensitive Marx are more instructive than those by later and more rigid thinkers such as Lenin.[156] Furthermore, the Marxian features of critical theory are really quite central, such as when the concept of "false consciousness" comes to the fore while we are asked to overlook what citizens think their interests are and to act instead in accordance with what some critical theoretician believes their "real" needs may be. And finally, critical theorists do nothing to conceal their conviction that political scholars should work at putting radical ideas into effect, should constantly question the liberal principles, behavior, and institutions that exist in America today.[157]

153. Jung, "The Political Relevance of Existential Phenomenology," p. 539.

154. "American Social Science," p. 204.

155. Martin Jay, *The Dialectical Imagination: A History of the Frankfurt School and the Institute of Social Research, 1923–1950* (London: Heinemann, 1973), chapter 2, "The Genesis of Critical Theory," pp. 41–85. See also William Leiss, "Critical Theory and Its Future," *Political Theory* (August 1974), pp. 330–49.

156. See the title essay in George Lichtheim, *From Marx to Hegel* (New York: Herder and Herder, 1971), pp. 1–49.

157. See the definition of "theorizing" in Gunnell, "Political Science and the Theory of Action," p. 98.

All of this is massively unacceptable to the community of American political scholars in their collective role. Yet the Marxian perspectives of critical theory are so fundamentally and totally antithetical to conventional political science thinking that individual practitioners tend more to ignore critical attacks than to comment on them directly. In this largest sense critical theory is regarded as an ideology and therefore slighted for much the same reasons that many liberal political scientists rejected ideology as they defined it after World War II.[158] Karl Popper had set the stage by attacking what he called "essentialism," or "the view, held by Plato and many of his followers, that it is the task of pure knowledge or 'science' to discover and to describe the true nature of things, i.e., their hidden reality or essence."[159] Taking much the same line, Lewis S. Feuer noted that when critical theorists seek such fundamental knowledge, they simultaneously deny to anyone else the means of impartially checking their claims with regard to the structure of society or the potential of its citizens. Thus if empirical evidence is brought to bear against their contentions, Feuer complained, scholars of the critical persuasion will enunciate some higher standard of truth so as to prevent disconfirmation of their convictions. As Feuer put it, "Mathematical science makes voyages to the moon possible; Einstein's theory of relativity enables one to predict the deflection of light during the sun's eclipse; but these achievements are not 'true' in the Marcusean 'dialectical logic'; there is a more 'concrete' reality, never specified but closer to the wishes of 'critical theory.' "[160]

Withal, critical theorists argue that this sort of reality must be described in their research and taught in the classroom, for they take instruction about politics to be a political act, meaning that public life as it exists in America must be subject to constant scrutiny—mostly unsympathetic—and students encouraged to seek reform. According to mainstream conceptions of scholarship, this view that classroom teaching must be deliberately political is an idea rooted in ideology, whose validity can neither be confirmed nor denied conclusively. Validation aside, however, in historical perspective the dangers of such a notion are quite clear. Evron M. Kirkpatrick, for example, charged that a politically inspired assault on conventional political science teachings, such as that recommended in critical theory, assails "the very foundations of the scholarly ethic: reason, objectivity, and freedom." According to his sense of the matter, "Nazis, Fascists, Communists, and assorted modern tyrants have denounced reason as

158. Thus the post–World War II practice of linking ideologies of the left and the right appeared in Ole R. Holstoi, "The Study of International Politics Makes Strange Bedfellows: Theories of the Radical Right and the Radical Left," *American Political Science Review* (March 1974), pp. 217–42.

159. Karl Popper, *The Open Society and Its Enemies*, 4th ed. (New York: Harper and Row, 1963), vol. 1, p. 31.

160. *Ideology and the Ideologists* (New York: Harper Torchbooks, 1975), p. 110.

enfeebling, objectivity as a sham, and defined truth as whatever served their purposes at the moment. . . . The attack and the accompanying activism may— if pushed far enough—threaten the very processes of rational debate that have made possible modern science and the modern university."[161] Kirkpatrick pressed the case against critical theory further than most practitioners would, since they tend to deprecate that view by disregard rather than by condemnation. Nevertheless, historical sensibilities do figure at least somewhat in the discipline's overall rejection of critical theory, as when Martin Landau observed that purposefully injecting partisan objectives into the teaching of politics would "return us to that period in American education which historians refer to as 'the theological era'— a time when the test of a theory was held to be the morality of the theorist."[162]

Reaffirmation of the Scientific Method

Landau's comment is particularly useful because it reminds us of the collective nature of political inquiry within higher education's long-term development, going back far into the nineteenth century. Against such a background, we should expect most practitioners to respond negatively to the central point of critical theory, which was the technique of self-reflection, regardless of how that technique may be linked to Marxian or quasi-Marxian objectives. As Austin Ranney expressed his colleagues' shared vocational interest, "our professional skills and utility depend upon the scientific quality of our special body of knowledge. Hence our primary obligation as scholars and teachers is to improve that knowledge."[163] But if this is true, many political scientists will be unable to see just how self-reflection can contribute to such knowledge.

Morton Kaplan, for example, enthusiastically praised the importance that Thomas Spragens attributed to studying the realm of political values. He confessed to little sympathy, however, for the way in which Spragens, as a critical theorist, insisted on intuitive knowledge as the key to comprehending that realm.

161. "From Past to Present," in Donald M. Freeman, ed., *Foundations of Political Science: Research, Methods, and Scope* (New York: Macmillan, 1977), p. 39.

162. "The Classroom and Political Science: An Essay on Political Theory," in Vernon Van Dyke, ed., *Teaching Political Science: The Professor and the Polity* (Atlantic Highlands, N.J.: Humanities Press, 1977), p. 72.

163. "The Study of Political Content: A Framework for Choice," in Austin Ranney, ed., *Political Science and Public Policy* (Chicago: Markham, 1968), pp. 20–21. Compare Ranney's view with that of Ben Agger, "Invisible Politics: Critique of Empirical Urbanism," *Polity* (Summer 1974), pp. 550–51: "It would be altogether better if we . . . became content with an unscientific critical theory of public reality and human experience and need. . . . Ultimately, social science needs to be made into a form of participatory democracy built on the ashes of scientific professionalism. . . . The elaborate paraphernalia of theory and method can be abandoned for the more direct language of body-politics and social poetry, changing scientism into a form of art and talk."

The problem, according to Kaplan, is that such knowledge does not facilitate the "public communication" which is "essential to the enterprise of science."[164] A similar hostility toward knowledge that is not "intersubjectively transmissable," in Arnold Brecht's classic phrase, was expressed by James Rosenau. In his view, the outcome of "the science game" is "public knowledge." And the game itself is to be played out "entirely in the open," where everyone is free "to point out flaws in the reasoning, data, and methods" employed by their antagonists, as opposed to other games such as journalism, where truth never becomes "independent of the compiler" but "must be taken on faith."[165]

In regard to "understanding," as self-reflection is sometimes called, the same resistance to critical theory appeared. From the critical theory point of view, John S. Gunnell wrote that real scientific explanation is rooted in variable circumstances, whereupon there can be no one, single test of scientific truth but only "a search for understanding or intelligibility," which varies from context to context.[166] A. James Gregor disputed Gunnell's thesis, saying that "By characterizing explanation as 'a search for understanding,' we have no reason to exclude from the reference class yoga exercises (done to 'enhance your understanding'), phrenology, tealeaf reading, crystal ball gazing," and so forth. If the truth flows from understanding, said Gregor, the real question is "who could *not* meet such loosely framed and porous criteria?"[167]

In the language of philosophical discourse, Gregor assailed critical theorists and rejected their work because it failed to provide for a "public test" of their teachings. In Gregor's terms, critical scholars rely too heavily on "indwellings," "pourings," and "relivings," while never telling us exactly how we can distinguish the "successful" from the "unsuccessful" of such understandings.[168] In more everyday prose, a similar point was made in the Broadway hit play *Jumpers*, by Tom Stoppard. "What makes you so sure that it *was* Miss Moore who shot McFee?" asks Archie, the vice chancellor of the university. "I have a nose for these things," replies Bones, the policeman. "With all the best will in the world, I can't give the Chair of Logic to a man who relies on nasal intuition," says Archie.[169]

164. See Kaplan's "Foreword" in Spragens, *The Dilemma of Contemporary Political Theory*, p. vi.

165. *The Dramas of Politics*, pp. 118–19.

166. "Deduction, Explanation, and Social Science Inquiry," *American Political Science Review* (December 1969), pp. 1238–46.

167. "Gunnell on 'Deductionism,' The 'Logic' of Science and Scientific Explanation: A Riposte," ibid., p. 1258.

168. A. James Gregor, *An Introduction to Metapolitics* (New York: Free Press, 1971), pp. 257–58.

169. (New York: Grove Press, 1972), p. 65.

Closing the Circle

The case of critical theory closes a circle of considerations, which I began to present in chapter 7, starting with a discussion of how political scholars are hard pressed to define the very nature of politics, and continuing with a description of various problems that arise from publishing and the search for truth and wisdom. The circle closes at this point because, logically speaking, the literature of critical theory comes to political science as a sequel to the discipline's failure to discover laws of political behavior. Consider the case of power, which remains enormously important to political scientists. Even while practitioners are unable to define the scope of their field precisely, they know very well that it has something to do with the exercise of political power—who wields it, and to what ends. [170] Yet the twenty-year-long professional attempt to locate and characterize power precisely was to no avail. Accordingly, there is a sense in which critical theory serves to explain why the failure was foreordained from the outset.

As critical theorists contend, scholarly research in the conventional manner cannot discover laws of political behavior so long as it remains inattentive to political factors that lie outside the bounds of standard scientific analysis. As an alternative to the ceaseless quest for such laws, critical theorists suggest a vaguely defined pursuit of self-reflection, whose conclusions would constitute exactly the sort of "wisdom" that mainstream political scholars have already rejected over the last several decades. Thus, even while critical theorists have highlighted significant weak points in common behavioral arguments concerning the nature of political inquiry and knowledge, the discipline's rejection of critical theory indicates the persistence of sociological factors that restrain the community of political scholars from forsaking their collective rationale in favor of one that reserves no special social role for that community as a whole. As we noted in chapter 7, anyone can be wise.

The paradoxical nature of this disciplinary status quo may be seen in Charles E. Lindblom's presidential address to the American Political Science Association in 1981. Lindblom spoke of two schools of thought, the first being "a conventional intellectual tradition in American political science," and the second an alternative view based on "dissenting Marxist and other radical thought on liberal or bourgeois democracy." [171] Throughout his essay, he highlighted the striking fact that, even where virtual unanimity on certain political beliefs appears in the first school, much of what it sincerely holds to be true has never been conclusively demonstrated. Although Lindblom did not say so explicitly, the

170. See David E. Apter, *Introduction to Political Analysis* (Cambridge, Mass.: Winthrop, 1977), p. 17, where Apter claims that political science's "key concern is with power—how it is shared through participation and representation, and how it is affected by growth and change."

171. "Another State of Mind," *American Political Science Review* (March 1982), p. 10.

problem was a shortage of patently true laws of political behavior that would support mainstream contentions as to the nature of existing democratic institutions. Rather than solid if tentative scientific truths, what actually existed were merely items of what we have called "vocational knowledge." And such knowledge, as Lindblom pointed out in his terms, may be widely endorsed even though never persuasively validated.

Confirming what we have seen of the mainstream response to critical theory, Lindblom noted the discipline's overall rejection of radical writings and ideas. He made no attempt to counter that response with a comprehensive argument proving critical theory's methodological and philosophical validity. On the contrary, he claimed that the radical model of democracy may be entirely wrong. What did intrigue him about radical thinkers, however, was their insistence on looking in some of the right places, politically speaking, in which case we would do well, without endorsing the critical approach as a whole, to try to check out their convictions on certain important questions. He was particularly impressed by radical devotion to studying how it is that some values come to be shared by all members of a society—what critical theorists might call the substance of a life-world—even though other values can better serve at least some citizens within the same society.[172] That is, he agreed with the radicals that potential conflicts between the advantaged and the disadvantaged may be foreclosed by consensus and therefore not appear empirically on the agenda of democratic politics, and he held that we should at least try to see why this happens rather than ignore what is apparently nonexistent.[173]

An unresolved dilemma may be discerned in Lindblom's address. While calling upon his mainstream colleagues to check hypotheses advanced by their unconventional opponents, he never did show how political scholars can, in acceptable scientific fashion, go about testing the critical theory notions he thought were so suggestive to begin with. He plainly refrained from recommending that such tests be carried out according to radical standards of research, for he was aware that those standards have not yet been applied in empirical work even by their enthusiasts.[174] It is also true, however, that nothing in his article demonstrated the methods of conventional inquiry to be superior. Indeed, Lindblom himself conceded that "mainstream views" are "unsubstantiated,"[175] and that "we have . . . found no solid ground for choosing the first approach [positivism] over the second [critical theory]."[176] But in that case, what is behavioral research really worth? If it has so far produced truths that are more vocational than

172. Ibid., pp. 19–20.
173. Ibid., p. 15.
174. Ibid., p. 16.
175. Ibid., p. 15.
176. Ibid., p. 14.

confirmed, why should we believe that the fault lies in the questions asked, the subjects studied, and the conclusions drawn, rather than in the testing process employed? In short, without intending to do so, Lindblom unwittingly demonstrated the typical confusion that reigns in political science during the post-behavioral era, when he assumed that technically proficient research can continue as usual, even though similar efforts failed to produce satisfactory results in the past. It is surely significant that he did not suggest a single experiment by which radical views might be tested, nor did he suggest any criterion of adequacy by which we might decide that such a test, once performed, has unquestionably confirmed or disconfirmed a hypothesis drawn from critical theory.

Conclusions

9

The Tragedy of Political Science

I began this book by explaining why we should consider the nature of political science as a collective entity rather than the sum total of what individual political scientists do, from time to time, poorly or well. In order to demonstrate the influence of communal, as distinct from personal, features of scholarship, I then proceeded to discuss various bureaucratic, professional and scientific dimensions of political studies. Now it is time for speaking of how to fashion a reasonable response to the discipline, in the light of institutional realities that can no longer be denied.

These realities suggest an obvious point of departure: any idea advanced in political science literature must be judged cautiously on its merits as the product of an organizational environment rather than accepted automatically because practitioners certify it as a valuable addition to our knowledge of public affairs. The question is, into what sort of context should we place such judgments in order to ascertain their larger meaning? That is, how shall we assess the social significance of political science's accomplishments, whatever we make these out to be? On this score, a second point of departure must be drawn from the concept of tragedy, defined in previous chapters as a clash of ideals, where firm commitment to one goal at the expense of others is likely to bring downfall and destruction upon its protagonist. It may be difficult to find precise analogies between the world of drama, where authors can tailor their creations to fit exacting standards of genre, and the world of social relations, where real people and institutions are so complex and distinct that they resist all effort at perfectly accurate classification. Still, the concept of tragedy, with its rich freight of connotations originating in literature rather than social science, provides a useful touchstone of reference for deciding where we are left concerning the character of political studies and what might be done about them.

What Is Really Happening?

Institutional realities indicate that the discipline will remain devoted to studying politics scientifically. More than a century ago, this commitment was proposed as the raison d'être for higher education, and as the years passed it grew into a driving force at those universities where political scientists today perform their work of research and teaching. There is no reason to believe that the nation's great learning institutions, and the departments of political science they contain, are about to abandon science for another road of knowledge.[1] Rather, from what we have seen, it seems fair to conclude that political science is actually the dependent variable of a larger entity, a small community that will continue to guard its prescribed place as one column among many within the modern Temple of Science.

Scholarship and Its Outcome

As in the past, where enthusiasm for scientific analysis reigns, it evokes widespread preference for political scholarship of a special kind, which entails what may be called descriptive empiricism. In this mode of analysis, practitioners aim at drawing an accurate portrait of political reality according to what can be discovered by scientific research techniques. These techniques vary, from searching for concrete data that will support a preconceived hypothesis, to expounding the facts of a case where even a straightforward account of what happened is considered valuable. But in any event, political scholars are strongly encouraged to touch base with tangible manifestations of human behavior so as to better understand public life.

Unfortunately, this sort of empirical work tends to highlight situations which seem undesirable as compared with various democratic expectations, in particular when research findings conflict with several postulates of freedom and equality embraced by the liberal tradition. I noted that propensity in chapter 1, when I briefly described a professional orbit summarized in this book's subtitle: *Politics, Scholarship, and Democracy*. First, certain subjects and events are rec-

---

1. Modern readers may need their historical memories refreshed on this point because, although prescientific scholarship suffered from grievous flaws, many of them are ignored or discounted by critics of social science today. For an extreme example of what used to obtain, see Herbert J. Muller, *The Uses of the Past* (New York: Oxford University Press, 1954), p. 232. Muller quotes Agnellus, the ninth-century bishop of Ravenna, who wrote biographies of the bishops who had already served in his post: "Where I have not found any history of these bishops, and have not been able by conversation with aged men, or inspection of monuments, or from any other authentic source, to obtain information concerning them, in such a case, in order that there might not be a break in the series, I have composed the life myself, with the help of God and the prayers of the brethren."

ognized as important to political life in America. These objects are then approached according to scientific guidelines laid down for all academics by pace-setting universities. Next, the findings produced by painstaking investigations are compared with democratic ideals and found wanting. At this point, practitioners begin the cycle all over again, hoping to produce a more satisfactory set of conclusions. In later chapters we saw how, in effect, political scientists traveled this road twice in the twentieth century. Thus, tension between research findings and the ideals of a free society grew slowly from 1900 to 1940 while political studies were becoming increasingly scientific. The ensuing crisis was resolved in the 1940s, with the rise of Popperism, and equanimity reigned, with some exceptions, during the heyday of behavioralism. In that era, the facts changed very little, but many practitioners accepted an optimistic interpretation of their larger significance. When this optimism waned during the late 1960s and early 1970s, the discipline found itself back where it had begun, confronting facts regarded as discouraging to a democratic people.

Descriptive empiricism continues to dominate political science today, with predictable results. Detailed findings from one research project do not necessarily agree with those of another, but many converge to deliver the somber message that America's institutions are not working well. For example, one study concludes that political parties are incapable of adopting coherent positions on the range of issues that presently concern voters,[2] while another suggests that bureaucrats are only occasionally able to devise rational policies that deliver benefits which satisfy public needs.[3] Alternatively, two researchers claim that bureaucrats should not be blamed for a catastrophic error such as the Vietnam War, since the Departments of Defense and State in that case did no more than execute a policy laid down by elected officials.[4] Yet to absolve leaders of responsibility, another well-known scholar argues that America became ungovernable when its citizens made so many demands on their rulers that the latter could not respond effectively.[5] And for the inveterate optimist who still believes that parties, bureaucrats, statesmen, and the public are all serving the country well, there looms the reincarnation of an old thesis, that big business is really running the national political show, operating openly or behind the scenes to advance its

2. Norman H. Nie, Sidney Verba, and John Petrocik, *The Changing American Voter* (Cambridge, Mass.: Harvard University Press, 1976).

3. George C. Edwards and Ira Sharkansky, *The Policy Predicament: Making and Implementing Public Policy* (San Francisco: Freeman, 1978).

4. Leslie H. Gelb and Richard K. Betts, *The Irony of Vietnam: The System Worked* (Washington, D.C.: Brookings Institute, 1979).

5. Samuel P. Huntington, "The United States," in Michael Crozier, Samuel P. Huntington, and Joji Watanuki, *The Crisis of Democracy* (New York: New York University Press, 1975), pp. 59–118.

interest at the expense of those pursued democratically by men and women in other walks of life.[6]

Unfulfilled Promises

As a strategy of inquiry, descriptive empiricism is tragically unbalanced. It does gather great amounts of sheer information about political life, which constitute a veritable who's who, and what's what, guide to much of the public world about us. But at the same time, it injects a measure of despair into political studies by highlighting the dreary or dangerous imperfections of democratic behavior. The risk here was foreshadowed by behavioralists themselves, when they observed that support for democratic government may be rooted in popular myths as to what sort of political practices characterize a free society.[7] Where the facts discovered by social science contradict such myths, what will replace them in our affections as a source of legitimacy for democratic government?

Science does not speak directly to the issue of creating and maintaining political legitimacy. If all goes well with scholarly research, or so the discipline's leaders intimate, popular misconceptions will be superseded by incisive and fruitful new political ideas, supplied by scientifically minded practitioners. That is, the cure for unease induced by scientifically revealed facts is . . . more science. Yet in reality, practitioners perpetuate the injury to faith by promising to undo the damage and then failing to carry out their pledge. In this respect, paradoxically, sound scholarship is persuasive enough to make men believe the worst of their polity, but insufficiently productive to reveal a certain way to create public harmony and well-being. Progress in political affairs will come about, mainstream scholars say, when they manage one day to amass a "cumulatively reliable body of knowledge" capable of preventing "errors of calculation on the parts of voters, office seekers, secretaries of state, etc."[8] Yet this knowledge, in the form of political laws, is something the discipline has never produced, for reasons we have reviewed at length.

In the standard view of political science, this last and vital point is insufficiently appreciated. Perhaps it is obscured by the many apologies that have been offered to explain why so few political laws have been discovered. Analytically, they begin with the notion that the sum of reliable knowledge will grow in conjunction with practitioners sharpening up their research tools, as when Heinz Eulau said relevant data will become more accessible as "instruments and tech-

---

6. Charles E. Lindblom, *Politics and Markets: The World's Political-Economic System* (New York: Basic Books, 1977).

7. See pp. 173–75 above.

8. Arthur S. Goldberg, "On the Need for Contextualist Criteria: A Reply to Professor Gunnell," *American Political Science Review* (December 1969), p. 1247.

niques of inquiry" are progressively developed.[9] Next comes the claim that knowledge of public affairs is indeed moving forward, if only by exceedingly small steps. This idea often appears in disclaimers that political scholars attach to their own research findings. For example, the conclusion to a prestigious journal article may sound something like this: "The technique . . . which has been presented here . . . must not be regarded as the final step in the gradual evolution of models in this area. It is to be hoped, however, that it will prove an aid to further progress in both substantive and methodological research."[10] Then too, practitioners occasionally assure us that scientific progress is just a matter of time. Robert A. Dahl was therefore able to note the shortcomings of community power research and then discount them by observing that "despite the fact that the attempt to understand political systems by analyzing power relations is ancient, the systematic empirical study of power relations is remarkably new."[11] Furthermore, if research findings, such as those on power, appear to be less patently true than plainly disparate in substance and implications, someone will always characterize the confusion as fruitful. Thus Lloyd Jensen claimed that contradictory findings concerning international relations "may cause some concern about the usefulness of quantitative studies, but it is out of such conflicts that new interpretations and conclusions are developed."[12]

As a final excuse, there is the argument that frequent instances of failure to formulate political laws do not conclusively prove that political regularities cannot be discovered in the future. This point is logically unassailable, because inductive proof based on examining actual cases can never extend to all future instances of any matter in question. In the analogy employed by Philip H. Melanson, "To conclude that social science lacks . . . theories because of [social] complexity is as useful as saying that one's automobile won't run because one doesn't know how to fix it."[13] In fact, though, as we have seen, discovering laws of political behavior is no more likely, objectively speaking, than in 1930 when Thomas H. Reed, reporting on behalf of the American Political Science Association's Committee on Policy, stoutheartedly paid his early-day respects to the discipline's scientific aspirations. "Far less has been done in formulating 'laws' upon the basis of observed phenomena in this field [of political studies]

9. "Segments of Political Science Most Susceptible to Behavioral Treatment," in James C. Charlesworth, ed., *The Limits of Behavioralism in Political Science* (Philadelphia: American Academy of Political and Social Science, 1962), p. 38.

10. Richard S. Katz, "The Attribution of Variance in Electoral Returns: The Alternative Measurement Technique," *American Political Science Review* (June 1973), p. 828.

11. "Power," in David L. Sills, ed., *International Encyclopedia of the Social Sciences*, vol. 12 (New York: Crowell Collier and Macmillan, 1968), p. 414.

12. "Quantitative International Politics," *Political Science Reviewer* (Fall 1974), pp. 329–30.

13. *Political Science and Political Knowledge* (Washington, D.C.: Public Affairs Press, 1975), p. 65.

than has been achieved in the natural sciences," said Reed, "but sufficient progress has been made to sustain the belief that great contributions to human welfare will result from research in political science."[14]

Tragedy, Good, and Evil

To restate the problem, tragedy lies in the fact that, even while mainstream practitioners strive without success to produce the reliable knowledge that might enable us somehow to change political behavior for the better, their work succeeds in carrying the discipline away from considering a great many intangible factors that can make democracy attractive and worth supporting. Let us recall that the first liberal postulate affirmed the moral equality of all human beings. This postulate of principle, rather than empirical fact, bespeaks an entire realm of ethics, values, rights, obligations, and expectations, which together foster powerful conceptions of fraternity and mutual interest designed to help men live decently together. American voters, for example, do not go to the polls just because they understand or misunderstand exactly how things work in Washington and because they believe, mistakenly, that their single vote will tip the balance in any electoral race. But they do come out on election day to participate in their community's affairs by expressing sentiments shared with friends and neighbors, and to exercise not just a civil right, but a civic duty that weighs, and justly so, upon all free men and women.

Science cannot deal with this realm of intangibles decisively. Wise men, on the other hand, have always insisted upon the social importance of moral commitments. Cicero, for example, defined a republic as a collection of men sharing a common devotion to natural law, equality, and legal rights, without which they might fashion only distinctly inferior forms of political union.[15] The same emphasis on shared values within the human community informed many social contract theories in the seventeeth and eighteenth centuries, and it was incorporated into the Declaration of Independence when Thomas Jefferson demanded political independence as a right based on divine equality. From there, communitywide ethical standards continued to inspire the college curriculum, where political science was taught as a branch of moral philosophy and judged by the notion that, as Francis Wayland put it, "a human action may be either right or wrong."[16]

To use Wayland's lexicon, no matter how important the moral framework of life may be, political science, as practiced scientifically, can pay very little

14. "Report of the Committee on Policy," *American Political Science Review* (February 1930), appendix, p. 2.

15. Marcus Tullius Cicero, *On the Commonwealth* (Columbus: Ohio State University Press, 1929), esp. bk. 1.

16. *The Elements of Moral Science*, 2nd ed. (Boston: Gould and Lincoln, 1872), p. 26.

attention to distinctions as basic as those between good and evil. Yet talking to citizens about how to attain the former and avoid the latter has long been a primary mission of those who care deeply about the foundations of social order. On this score, we have exemplars such as Plato and St. Thomas Aquinas, both of whom toiled, each in his own way, to formulate rules for living a good life as opposed to perpetuating a less desirable existence. In their disregard for such endeavors, mainstream political scholars break no new ground in professional ignorance of right and wrong, for the very enterprise of modern science, starting at least several hundred years ago, gradually removed God and transcendent purpose from the world of observable phenomena and thereby made questions of good and evil difficult for social scientists even to discuss, no less to resolve.[17]

At stake here is our ability to recognize that human beings often act in socially harmful ways, and our determination to curb their tendency to do so, even though it constitutes an unpredictable, even mysterious, force in political affairs. Science has difficulty in conceding that such a force exists.[18] If enough knowledge were available, scientists are prone to say, men's lives would be made easier, healthier, and happier. Surely there is some truth to this claim, because new knowledge has fueled notable progress in fields such as medicine, construction, communications, clothing, transportation, and agriculture. The Johns Hopkins University therefore expressed an understandable confidence in science's product when, as the nation's first great university, it took for its motto the Latin phrase *Veritas Vos Liberabit*, "The Truth Will Make You Free." Still, saying something confidently, no matter how often, does not necessarily make it so, and the only thing we can be sure of regarding the idea of progress via new knowledge is that entertaining the idea itself is functionally rational for scientists as a class, whose business it is to amass such knowledge. It is therefore natural for them to encourage us to believe that society will benefit for so long as science is generously funded, even though signs of social improvement are not always forthcoming in every sphere of life—such as those of war and peace.

In social studies, the scientific approach repeats its claims. And thus, in an early work on policy studies, Charles E. Rothwell suggested that "Our failure to perfect human relations results less from lack of trying than from not discovering how."[19] But are society's imperfections really a result of insufficient knowledge?

17. Alfred Cobban, *In Search of Enlightenment: The Role of Enlightenment in Modern History* (New York: George Braziller, 1960), chapter 8, "The Problem of Good and Evil," pp. 76–89.

18. William H. Riker and Peter C. Ordeshook, "A Theory of the Calculus of Voting," *American Political Science Review* (March 1968), p. 25: "The function of [scientific] theory is to explain behavior and it is certainly no explanation to assign a sizeable part of politics to the mysterious and inexplicable world of the irrational."

19. "Foreword" in Harold D. Lasswell and Daniel Lerner, eds., *The Policy Sciences* (Stanford: Stanford University Press, 1951), p. vii.

Or should we not attribute them, perhaps in large part, to greed, jealousy, spite, vanity, pride, hatred, and a great many other character traits that impel men to behave nastily? Only a relentless optimist would deny that such qualities of human nature are a common part of the social scene. Yet because they are intangible and their essence difficult to ascertain, most political scholars seem content to write them off, in Arthur F. Bentley's term, as "spooks" that cannot and should not be studied by social scientists.[20]

Not being subject to the same strictures as university-based scholars, Western theologians have investigated many harmful acts and labeled most of them sins, in copious variety. Catechisms vary from sect to sect, of course, but their main conclusion is generally the same: men sin against their fellows impulsively, regardless of how much knowledge they possess, and they must be restrained from doing harm to others by force of conscience rather than data, by the strength of authoritative ideas and not disembodied statistics. In this view of human affairs, unchecked passions, rather than insufficient information, constitute our greatest social problem.[21] That is exactly what Hans J. Morgenthau had in mind when, after World War II, he charged that scientifically minded political scholars are naive to think that "It is through lack of reason that evil came into the world."[22] Not so, said Morgenthau. Rather, "corruption and sin" continue to contaminate much of social life, and war, which is perhaps the greatest evil of all, becomes extremely difficult to abolish because it stems from forces "which have their roots in the innermost aspirations of the human soul."[23] Some years later, F. F. Ridley argued in much the same vein as Morgenthau when he attributed the horrors of modern war and brinksmanship to "wickedness or folly."[24] Not many political scientists would agree with Ridley, if he were entirely serious, that the Devil is to blame for such qualities. Nevertheless, the terms "wickedness" and "folly" can tell us a great deal about political reality, and how to talk about it constructively. Yet they are not the kind of terms most political scientists prefer to employ in political inquiry. And that reticence reflects our oft-noted dialectic between the promise of scientific inquiry and the needs of civilized intercourse.

The Small Conversation

Words such as "wickedness" and "folly," "good" and "evil," were read out of the discipline by David Easton, when he called upon his colleagues to abandon the

20. *The Process of Government* (Cambridge, Mass.: Harvard University Press, 1967).

21. This point is central, for example, in the theology of Reinhold Niebuhr. See especially his *The Nature and Destiny of Man* (New York: Scribner's Sons, 1949).

22. *Scientific Man vs. Power Politics* (Chicago: University of Chicago Press, 1946), p. 13.

23. Ibid., pp. 95, 195.

24. "If the Devil Rules, What Can Political Science Achieve?" *Government and Opposition* (Summer–Autumn 1980), p. 472.

traditional vocabulary of political theory because, in his opinion, it contained terms so ambiguous and provocative as to invite interminable and fruitless controversy.[25] We have seen how political scholars welcomed this notion, when they relegated old-style political theory to marginal importance within the discipline. It is therefore not surprising that, as I noted earlier, a standard textbook would eventually draw up a list of traditional words and recommend that political scientists gradually replace them with new ones in the profession's discourse. Among the old were words like "justice," "nation," "rights," "patriotic," "society," "virtue," and "tyranny." Among the new were "attitude," "cross-pressure," "conflict," "game," "interaction," "cognition," "socialization," and "system."[26] These then became substantive matters for the profession to discuss.

This kind of vocabulary became the basis for what may be called a small conversation. Small conversations take place in many learned disciplines, when members of a scholarly community speak mainly to one another, in language so specialized and full of jargon that it is largely unintelligible to the public or to their colleagues in other university departments across the campus mall.[27] In justification, practitioners seem to believe that they can profitably imitate the natural sciences. After all, even though ordinary citizens do not understand, say, the professional parlance of chemists, they do enjoy the outcome—from Corning Ware to miracle fabrics to the Green Revolution—of small conversations among the inventors of such things.

But can a purely professional vocabulary of politics, given the range of concerns it addresses, really come to grips with what everyone needs to know about public life? On this score, we may consider the personal credo of Lindsay Rogers, a prebehavioral political scientist: "Whatever we say must conform to the facts: so far we may be scientific. But when we elaborate on the facts? The House of Representatives has 435 members. Is it too large or too small? The average age is X, and twenty percent of the members are over x + y. Good or bad? Lawyers are the dominant occupation group. Welcome or regrettable?"[28]

Rogers assumed that there can be no retreat from science, that political scholars must never turn back from studying the real world with great care. What he added was an insistence that they weigh its significance according to standards

25. *The Political System: An Inquiry into the State of Political Science* (New York: Knopf, 1953), pp. 44–47.
26. The lists that contain these words, old and new, may be found in Ralph M. Goldman, *Contemporary Perspectives on Politics* (New York: Van Nostrand, 1972), pp. 15–17.
27. Clark Kerr, *The Uses of the University* (New York: Harper and Row, 1966), p. 43: "the intellectual world has been fractionalized . . . and there are fewer common topics of conversation at the faculty clubs" than ever before.
28. "Political Philosophy in the Twentieth Century," in Roland Young, ed., *Approaches to the Study of Politics* (Evanston, Ill.: Northwestern University Press, 1958), p. 206.

that men have commonly used in order to make sense of their lives. We should bear in mind that politics is by no means like chemistry. Ordinary people relate to chemists by their concrete artifacts, which may be used without being comprehensible. Political scientists, on the other hand, do not construct such artifacts. Yet even if they did, in democratic politics it is a matter of widespread participation in the formulation of the ultimate product that counts. For in a democracy it is the public which, through discussion and elections, must continually engage in the business of constructing new political artifacts—i.e., new policies, new institutions, new rights, new habits, and more. It follows that whatever special knowledge or insight political scientists acquire can be maximally useful only if transmitted to society as an intelligible element in the sort of debate that free men have always conducted on public affairs.

The Great Conversation

Through what sort of debate can political analysis contribute toward controlling passion and channeling human behavior into socially acceptable pathways? Surely the beginning of wisdom concerning decency, moderation, toleration, and other civilized virtues lies in a conversation much wider than that understood only within a single discipline, one that is therefore appropriately called a great conversation.[29] Its nature was summed up in the words of two Englishmen, writing almost two centuries apart:

> [Society is] a partnership in all science; a partnership in all art; a partnership in every virtue and in all perfection. As the ends of such a partnership cannot be obtained in many generations, it becomes a partnership not only between those who are living, but between those who are living, those who are dead and those who are to be born. Each contract of each particular state is but a clause in the great primeval contract of eternal society.[30] (Edmund Burke, 1790)

> [A civilization] may be regarded as a conversation being carried on between a variety of human activities, each speaking with a voice, or in a language of its own; the activities (for example) represented in moral and practical endeavor, religious faith, philosophic reflection, artistic contemplation and historical or scientific inquiry and explanation. And I call the manifold which these different manners of thinking and speaking compose, a conversation.[31] (Michael Oakeshott, 1962)

29. Robert M. Hutchins, *The Great Conversation: The Substance of a Liberal Education* (Chicago: Encyclopaedia Britannica, 1952).

30. *Reflections on the Revolution in France* (London: Dent and Sons, 1910), p. 93.

31. "The Study of 'Politics' in a University," in Michael Oakeshott, *Rationalism in Politics* (New York: Basic Books, 1962), p. 304.

Both Burke and Oakeshott held that society is the process by which many different kinds of people—to some extent vertically in time but also horizontally in space—communicate their thoughts to one another and thereby create and sustain a civilization. What this requires, in effect, is a great conversation, larger than any small conversations that members of particular social groups, such as professions, or learned disciplines, are accustomed to conducting among themselves. The goal of this large-scale dialogue is, in fact, for various groups to express diverse aesthetic, moral, and scientific opinions and somehow thrash them out on common grounds, in intelligible terms, so that a slowly moving consensus on truth and decency can be worked out and maintained over the generations, to serve as a framework of social cement binding members of the community to one another and enabling them to live good lives together. Withal, it is an intellectual enterprise intent on examining a great many facts by comparing them to canons of right and wrong, good and evil, sin and virtue, rights and obligations, just as Rogers said political scientists should.

To rephrase the matter, a great conversation relies very heavily on time-worn and emotional terms, many suffering from imprecise character but still carrying enough moral authority, by precedent, habit, experience, and spiritual commitment, to be capable of moving many people in the right direction much of the time. It is thus an extraordinarily wide-ranging affair, touching upon knowledge both stored up throughout history and newly achieved in manifold realms of learning today. And here we see the weakness of political science as an organized entity. Where can the discipline possibly stand with regard to a great conversation? Scientifically, that enterprise makes no sense. It is the roof of the Temple of Science all over again, even while political scientists collectively, for bureaucratic and professional reasons, are driven to work on research projects that enable them to stay within the confines of a single column of knowledge. The discipline as a whole cannot commit itself to any great conversation, so long as its members are to avoid the appearance of being scholars who, in a world dominated by science, lack expertise at anything in particular.

The Loss to Political Studies

As new terms develop within the discipline's small conversation, to crowd out the old, some practitioners may sincerely believe that only with the new nomenclature can they think constructively about politics. But the words we normally use to describe public affairs carry their power to sway from the fact that different generations have understood them in certain ways. This is the chilling message in George Orwell's anti-utopian novel, *1984*.[32] No society can be more decent and free than its terms of political discourse permit, he argued. Consequently, in

32. (New York: Harcourt and Brace, 1949).

his tale, if words are dropped from everyday language about politics, citizens will be unable to think clearly about the things those words stand for. When "justice," "equality," and "democracy" are lost to ordinary speech, the people who speak the language of what words remain, which Orwell called "Newspeak," will fail to comprehend, much less demand and uphold, the extraordinary political heritage embodied in statements such as: "We hold these truths to be self-evident, that all men are created equal, that they are endowed by their Creator with certain unalienable Rights, that among these are Life, Liberty and the pursuit of Happiness. That to secure these rights, Governments are instituted among men, deriving their just powers from the consent of the governed"[33] (Declaration of Independence, 1776).

Unfortunately, these are exactly the sort of terms—Creator, Rights, Liberty, etc.—that contemporary political science feels impelled to remove from its small conversation, with enormous impact on the substance of what remains. It may sound innocuous when a political scientist advises us to say "interest group" instead of "pressure group," so as to rid our vocabulary of various preconceptions conveyed by the latter phrase.[34] But what will teachers of politics, for example, do to inspire pride and enthusiasm in democracy when they no longer have a professionally acceptable way to explain the vital connotations of those traditional words—such as "duty," "virtue," and "dishonor"—which Pericles used in a funeral oration to hearten his countrymen more than two thousand years ago? "And when Athens shall appear great to you, consider then that her glories were purchased by valiant men, and by men that learned their duty; by men that were sensible of dishonor when they came to act; by such men as, though they failed in their attempt, yet would not be wanting to the city with their virtue, but made unto it a most honorable contribution"[35] (Thucydides, c. 406 B.C.).

The Tragic Vision
At least part of political science's predicament here must be recognized for what it is, the symptom of a much wider malaise that weighs upon many publicists and scholars in the modern world. The situation can be illuminated by some basic connotations of literary tragedy. As we have seen, tragedy involves a situation entailing a clash of ideals leading to downfall and destruction. Yet analytically speaking, this is only one half of a theatrical tragedy. If the play is to be meaningful, we must bring to its dramatic action some confidence that man is endowed with an ability to learn from adversity. Either we must expect the

---

33. This passage is quoted in ibid., "Appendix: The Principles of Newspeak," p. 313.
34. Goldman, *Contemporary Perspectives on Politics*, p. 16.
35. *The Peloponnesian War* (Ann Arbor: University of Michigan Press, 1959), vol. 1, p. 113.

protagonist to ennoble his character through suffering, or we must anticipate that onlookers will appreciate the protagonist's mistakes and try to moderate their own choices when confronted by painful alternatives. This second, and hopeful, half of tragedy we may call the "tragic vision."[36]

It is a fact that the great tragedies of classical Greece and Elizabethan England were inspired by an optimistic view of man's capacities, a buoyant faith that was expressed in words such as "love," "honor," and "glory," so as to convey to theater audiences a sense of the extraordinary accomplishments that are within our grasp even during difficult times.[37] Explicit expressions of this faith abound in the repertoire of tragedy. Thus a powerful choral ode in *Antigone* calls out that "Wonders are many in the world, and the wonder of all is man," after which the ode continues to catalogue a great many remarkable achievements of statecraft, agriculture, animal husbandry, and seafaring.[38] Similarly, Hamlet speaks with awe of human abilities: "What a piece of work is a man! How noble in reason! How infinite in faculty! In form and moving, how express and admirable! In action, how like an angel, in apprehension, how like a god! The beauty of the world! The paragon of animals!"[39]

In our era scientific research into human behavior—in fields from psychology to sociology to anthropology to political science—has cast grave doubts on the validity of the tragic vision. If human actions and motivations flow from irrational and unreliable impulses linked to various sorts of personal and collective compulsions, the affairs of even well-known men and women can hardly inspire us as they might have in the past. In this regard, political scientists and scientifically minded scholars in other disciplines share a propensity to speak of public affairs in terms far removed from those that once seemed adequate to explain what men knew of their lives. There is, though, a further reason for abandoning the traditional discourse. It has to do with the quality of modern life, and on this score, scientific perceptions may actually be the lesser enemy of a vibrant and persuasive tragic vision.

George Steiner, in *The Death of Tragedy* (1961), argues that horrifying recent events prevent serious thinkers from talking confidently about honor, duty, glory, and the like. What exalting sentiments can such words inspire when measured against the excesses of public conduct in this century? As Steiner observes, the "political inhumanity" of this age, whereby seventy million people were killed between 1914 and 1945, "has demeaned and brutalized language

36. See Richard B. Sewell, *The Vision of Tragedy* (New Haven: Yale University Press, 1959).

37. See Joseph Wood Krutch, *The Modern Temper* (New York: Harcourt, Brace and World, 1957), pp. 115–43, esp. 126.

38. Sophocles, *Antigone*, lines 330–40, in L. R. Lind, ed., *Ten Greek Plays* (Boston: Houghton Mifflin, 1957), p. 89.

39. William Shakespeare, *Hamlet*, act 2, sc. 1, lines 295–301.

beyond any precedent. Words have been used to justify political falsehood, massive distortions of history, and the bestialities of the totalitarian state." As a result, "Because they have been used to such base ends, words no longer give their full yield of meaning."[40] But that is not all. Having glimpsed the archetype of human depravity—pure evil in the Nazi death camps—we are now trapped in a terrible paradox of having to defend freedom and democracy, such as they are, by threatening to rain down atomic destruction upon our enemies and thereby risk annihilating the entire human race.[41] The Greeks thought their civilization was incomparably grander than barbarism. Can we admire our own culture if it takes us to the nuclear brink? Under the circumstances, if political scientists have grown away from interpreting Pericles to their students and colleagues, it is really no wonder.

Can Something Be Done?

In sum, political studies suffer from overemphasizing science while paying insufficient attention to the realm of morals, where men may be impelled to behave well and inspired to resist wrongdoing. It remains to ask, How should we deal with political science? In a moment, I will show that the answer to this question carries a prescription for action that comes in several parts. By way of introduction, it will be helpful to turn once again to the concept of tragedy in order to establish a context within which that answer can most usefully be expressed. Here, two points are worth bearing in mind.

On the one hand, we must not press the analogy between literary tragedy and the condition of political science too far. In theatrical drama, a situation embodying a clash of ideals gives rise to action that leads to the protagonist's downfall and destruction. In the case of political science, this conflict is certainly present. But the protagonist is still alive, and some would go so far as to say he is well. How can this signify tragedy? In fact, it is reasonable to conclude that the price of professional prosperity in one realm is a failure to perform the discipline's social duty in another. In this sense, the cost of political science's commitment to science may be regarded as what economists would call an "external diseconomy," a burden falling on someone outside the productive and profitable enterprise.[42] External or internal, however, the cost of a tragic choice is there, and in this case at least some of it is borne by political scientists themselves. As citizens of a society increasingly hard pressed to find inspiration in its historic

40. (London: Faber and Faber), p. 315.

41. Reinhold Niebuhr, *The Irony of American History* (New York: Scribner's Sons, 1952), pp. 1–2.

42. See E. J. Mishan, *The Costs of Economic Growth* (Harmondsworth, Middlesex, England: Penguin, 1967), pp. 82–86.

ideals and to nourish devotion to them, even political scientists are occasionally aware that a bargain of some sort has been struck by their discipline—although to call it Faustian would perhaps be pushing the analogy too far.[43]

On the other hand, and more importantly, we need not wield the analogy to tragedy too timidly. The institutional realities of political science make it very unlikely that the discipline will, as a collective entity, abandon its commitment to science. Yet, if this is true, we confront a situation in real life remarkably similar to tragedy on the stage, where our protagonist is driven by forces of character into making a choice that cannot be prevented by the best of impartial advice. It is a condition that political scholars as social scientists will have difficulty appreciating.[44] After all, the scientific outlook encourages us to regard life as a set of circumstances susceptible to technical solutions. These are what science offers, on the basis of its research, and they are the source of its reputation and status. As a result, most political scientists will read a scholarly book such as this one with the expectation, conscious or otherwise, that its final chapter must offer some recommendation for solving whatever problem its earlier chapters identified. The concept of tragedy reminds us, to the contrary, that some situations in life require not technical repair, but the courage and insight to moderate our aspirations in order to escape falling into a choice that produces terrible consequences. Literary scholars are accustomed to studying such dilemmas, and do not expect them to be resolved easily, if at all. As one authority on the subject remarked, "More pliant divorce laws could not alter the fate of Agamemnon; social psychiatry is no answer to Oedipus."[45] We therefore need to recognize political science's predicament as very definitely analogous to tragedy, and that recognition will help us to realize that there is very little we can do about it.

The Worth of the Organization
Assuming that the tragic condition of political science reflects institutional imperatives which will endure indefinitely, let us recall the question: How should we deal with political science? In many respects, this question, with different terms of reference, is already familiar to members of modern society. After all, the particular learned discipline at hand is a large organization like many others, going about its work according to guidelines that enjoy some overall justification but at the same time promote functional rationality so persistently as to lead

43. See the original version of the Faust story in Irving Ribner, ed., *Christopher Marlowe's "Doctor Faustus": Text and Major Criticism* (New York: Odyssey Press, 1966).

44. There are few references to tragedy in political science writings. But see Glenn Tinder, "Transcending Tragedy: The Idea of Civility," *American Political Science Review* (June 1975), pp. 547–60.

45. Steiner, *The Death of Tragedy*, p. 8.

many practitioners away from the substantively rational needs it is supposed to serve. The first thing to do about political science, then, is to conclude that, to some extent, we have seen this problem before. Big Government, Big Business, Big Agriculture, Big Labor—what might be called Big Political Science has something in common with all of these, and it should be approached similarly. That is, we do not call for the abolition of government, business, agriculture, or labor just because they are big. Rather we try to exploit the benefits generated by their economies of scale, even while avoiding the costs imposed by their size.

As to size, thousands of political scientists work in academic departments scattered throughout the nation's colleges and universities, and in various national and regional networks of professional contact—such as associations, conventions, journals, and occasional symposia—which members of those departments choose to establish and maintain. On the whole, modern societies derive great benefits from having large numbers of intellectuals based in universities.[46] Most important, universities provide a milieu that permits scholars to detach themselves from the immediate needs of their day and to think in terms of far-ranging and long-standing truths, both physical and social. The world of higher education cannot assure that great or even useful ideas will come forth from the academy, because genius is an item that appears unpredictably rather than on command. Still, by providing steady salaries and academic tenure, with adequate time for conducting serious inquiries into a very wide range of subjects, America's universities enable a large group of men and women to seek the truth about a great number of things. That is a service which learned disciplines could hardly provide if their members were employed entirely by government, as in the Soviet Union, or if their practitioners worked mainly on behalf of commercial interests, as in American advertising.

The second thing to do about political science, then, is nothing or very little, at the level of its communitywide institutions. If political science did not exist in its present shape, it would have to be reinvented to provide a flexible and independent framework within which political thought at universities could take place. Practitioners therefore need not campaign together in an attempt to take over the American Political Science Association and subsequently refashion the scholarly community along completely new lines. Of course, some structural reform here and there might be appreciated, via a change in the program of events at the American Political Science Association's annual convention, for instance, and some recasting of substance might be welcome, as in a revised balance by fields among articles accepted for publication in leading scholarly journals. Nevertheless, there is great virtue in the overall shape of this discipline, as there is in all others, and we should try to build on that bedrock of available utility.

46. Lewis Coser, *Men of Ideas* (New York: Free Press, 1965), pp. 275–93.

The Need for Deception

The alternative to large-scale reform of political science is that practitioners will seek, more or less individually, to confront the discipline and to do their own work more effectively. In that event, a third response to political science must follow this rule: on the plane of personal engagement, whoever wants something desirable from an organization must consciously reject the undesirable products that come along with it. Organizations tend to press us to accept whatever they certify as worthwhile, both in action and belief. We have seen, though, that what an institution calls true is shaped, over time, more by its own needs than by those of society at large. It follows that we must constantly scrutinize what organizations say or offer to us, and we must judge their product by standards of common sense and good taste which can arise only outside the bureaucratic bounds of functional rationality.[47]

The classic exploration of this theme appeared in *The Organization Man* (1956) by William H. Whyte, Jr. Corporations supply work and financial reward, he observed, on condition that their employees demonstrate devotion to attitudes that serve the institution rather than individual needs—a triumph of what we have called functional over substantive rationality. In order to safeguard and promote the private lifestyles of people who prefer human rather than corporate ideals, Whyte recommended that people seeking to join large organizations should cheat on the personality tests administered as a precondition of employment in such places of work. This cheating should take the form of applicants deliberately answering test questions so as to give the appearance of possessing a bland and innocuous character, even though they do not.[48] In Whyte's opinion, deception in a good cause is preferable to letting workers be screened out of jobs for responding honestly and expressing their convictions fearlessly. Both probity and courage rank high on any scale of human virtues, but they are not necessarily the social graces sought by large organizations.

The Dilemma of Students

In a word, the operative steps against political science must entail some form of deception, whereby people who turn to the profession in order to acquire political knowledge must somehow give the appearance of accepting what the discipline prescribes as true and useful even while rejecting a good deal of the same product as unimportant and even misleading. Students may find this deception

---

47. Robert N. Kharasch, *The Institutional Imperative: How to Understand the United States Government and Other Bulky Objects* (New York: Charterhouse, 1973), p. 209.

48. Whyte, *The Organization Man* (New York: Simon and Schuster, 1956), "How to Cheat on Personality Tests," pp. 449–56.

difficult to practice. Coming to a political science department in search of enlightenment, they cannot afford to jeopardize their career plans, whatever those may be, by failing to strive for good grades according to whatever standards the department may enforce. Under the circumstances, required introductory courses will expose students to vocational knowledge in books that speak of what political science is according to professionally sound, but unrealistic, accounts. This version of truth they must resist internally, even while embracing outwardly its particulars. Later, in more advanced and elective courses, some unconventional viewpoints may be discussed. Still, students must read faithfully whatever works are assigned in such courses, and they must produce acceptable answers for all examination questions. Once again, many professionally attractive ideas must be weighed, with some being privately rejected even while they are publicly endorsed.

A student's mechanical encounter with political science can be fairly easy, for he has only to study the discipline's works carefully and endorse their substance loyally in term papers and examinations. The larger difficulty lies in discriminating between what actually to accept and what secretly to reject. At a time when students are only beginning to acquire the intellectual and practical experience necessary for judging the ideas expounded in typical political science courses, how can they decide which of those ideas are true and significant? Lacking much of the wherewithal for informed resistance, all that most students can do is to conform outwardly to the discipline's demands, while maintaining an inner skepticism based on recognizing that professional political knowledge should always be measured, if only later in life, against the widest possible background of human needs and convictions. Such skepticism will deepen and mature if students use their spare time to read history, a useful corrective to the notion that political life is a matter of predictable behavior that can be explained by laws based on average qualities and quantities. On such readings I shall say more in a moment.

A Strategy for Professors

The other large group of people who must continually deal with the collective impact of political studies are professors of political science. In their pursuit of knowledge these professors are, in effect, advanced students. It follows that they too, like beginners, must look askance at what political science certifies as worth learning. But having acquired more education and experience than their students possess, teachers are consequently far better equipped to play the game of deception by deciding which items of information and insight within the corpus of disciplinary writings and ideas are really true and significant.

For professors bent on achieving substantive rationality and passing it on to students, the term "robinhooding" will serve to suggest a strategy of resisting certain intellectual trends encouraged by organized political inquiry.[49] As a term for action of a special sort, robinhooding implies taking from the rich and giving to the poor, or exploiting a large and powerful patron in order to serve interests that are small and weak. Robinhooding against learned disciplines is thus a matter of bending the organization's needs to one's own, of finding some objective that is intrinsically worthwhile and making it appear to conform in some sense to the concerns of the institution.

As *Ecclesiastes* tells us, there is a season for all things, and political scientists should therefore resort to whatever forms of robinhooding will fit the changing times. At the outset of one's teaching career, it is advisable to display unexceptional qualities of professional competence, expressing sound opinions and publishing unremarkable writings. This tactic will help young scholars to gain tenured rank at some university, thereby turning to good advantage the discipline's power within academe to determine who, including themselves, will be guaranteed freedom to speak the truth about political life. In other words, don't start by rocking the boat, but do maneuver to take control of a position enabling its occupant to teach ideas that are intrinsically important, even though beyond the scope of disciplinary objectives. Once a base of operations has been secured, boldness becomes more feasible. Now is the time to seek research funds under various subtle pretenses, whereby inherently significant matters are disguised so as to make them appear worthy to some sponsor. By obtaining such grants, a resourceful professor can make possible the research that adds to his understanding of politics. Then he can share the new knowledge with students, safe from outside interference. Of course, the academic schemer may have to publish some of his findings in a form that encourages sponsors to continue awarding the grants. But with tenure safe in hand, he can also afford to write up some of his thoughts in plain English, which the discipline's journals will not reject on principle so long as he manages to inject here and there a note of novelty that will disguise their wisdom.

The System of Scholarly Authority

Both students and teachers can overcome their natural reluctance to dissemble by bearing in mind just what they will practice deception upon. As presently constructed, the discipline of political science purveys a notion that political scholars work as a community of scientists, who produce findings that should be considered valuable because they have been certified as true by a system of scientific publications and objective referees. Not to belabor the point, this

49. Used in a narrower sense than in the text above, the term "robinhooding" appears in Peter H. Rossi, "Researchers, Scholars and Policy Makers: The Politics of Large Scale Research," in Robert S. Morison, ed., *The Contemporary University: U.S.A.* (Boston: Beacon, 1967), p. 125f.

notion is erroneous. A great deal of truth in political science writings there may be, but it is there because they sometimes accord well with political phenomena and not because they are certified as true. The only absolute certainly here is that political scholars do not perform scientific experiments in the commonly understood sense of that phrase, and their work therefore cannot be checked for accuracy and validity according to the usual meaning of those terms. And what this signifies is that, all vocational exaggeration aside, political science operates on the basis of scholarly, rather than scientific, authority.

Where scholarly authority certifies political science writings, we have a right to reject the notion that those writings are automatically credible. Indeed, there is no intellectual obligation to accept them at all, unless we trust the authorities who approved them for publication. When we have no special reason to extend such trust, it is time to begin asking if a specific work enjoys qualities not always rewarded by the scholarly repute system. Do we know, or believe, that a particular author is honest? Can we rely on the accuracy of his reporting? Are we sure that he pays attention to the substance of things rather than frills? Has he a sense of history? Did he therefore consider the continuing context within which his subject came into being and continues to exist? Is he a good judge of character? Does he understand the kind of people whose political behavior he investigates? And finally, is he concerned with decency and human welfare? Or is he a technician, who cares only about resolving matters that do not deserve our attention?

In his essay "Civil Disobedience," Henry David Thoreau argued that it is morally necessary to stand up to the power and influence of government, a very large organization, and he encouraged would-be resisters by reminding them that "Any man more right than his neighbors, constitutes a majority of one."[50] When applied to learned disciplines, Thoreau's axiom suggests that where the magisterial weight of scientific truth is unavailable, each scholar should decide for himself the worth of divergent opinions, policies, and standards that come to his attention. Surely this is the case with political studies. On that subject we are entirely justified, when dealing with a discipline that cannot effectively establish the bounds of truth and wisdom, in treating skeptically the organization's consensual teachings and in trying independently to pursue whatever nuggets of political insight are contained within the enormous amount of professional dross that political scholars have so far produced and will continue to amass.

Science and History

A commitment to dealing realistically with the juggernaut side of political science would be incomplete without considering what the substance of robinhooding might be. One practical way to begin is by compensating for the time-bound

50. *The Works of Thoreau* (Boston: Houghton Mifflin, 1937), p. 797.

quality of descriptive empiricism. Work done in this scholarly mode can supply us with basic information about many political entities and actors, from the Soviet Presidium to state legislatures, from the United Nations to American interest groups. Still, descriptive empiricism suffers from a scientific inclination to view politics as mainly a contemporary matter, to be analyzed chiefly in its immediate dimensions. Individual professors should therefore balance this tendency by placing more emphasis on history than does the discipline as a whole. Columns in the Temple of Science tend to stand separately, and this helps to explain why an American Political Science Association report could claim that the combination of historical and political scholarship, as it once existed in joint departments of even leading universities, "serves no useful academic purpose."[51] Nonetheless, any person's understanding of political reality can be greatly improved by reading history. After all, there can be no true appreciation of what is happening today unless we have some knowledge of how things came to be what they now are.

The troubles that plague Northern Ireland, for example, cannot be understood in isolation from their origins, nor can we thoroughly understand who the warring factions in that land are without some account of where and why they came into being. Similarly, the conduct of Congress today does not flow merely from the present structure of its committee system but also from a collective consciousness, however attenuated, of a historic struggle between the legislative and executive branches of government during the Watergate era. And the likelihood for lasting peace in the Middle East is a matter that can be computed, if at all, only on the basis of acquaintance with long-standing quarrels, indigenous to that region, that have yet to be resolved. Political science professors would do well, therefore, to use in their classrooms texts that illuminate the historical dimensions of political life, even if some of those texts must come from outside the discipline itself.

As a byproduct to bringing long-run factors into a curriculum overloaded with the short-run view, historical works can provoke students into developing reservations about how political analysis should be done in the first place. Mainstream practitioners sometimes forget that modern political analysis is really a latter-day version of writing history per se, and they therefore tend to suggest, explicitly or implicitly, that we can attain a much more precise grasp of things than any historian would expect to achieve. Historians know very well that the real world is complex, that its meaning is imperfectly understood even by contemporaries, and that whatever evidence we collect must be sifted by relying as

51. A Statement by the Committee of Standards of Instruction of the American Political Science Association, "Political Science as a Discipline," *American Political Science Review* (June 1962), p. 417.

much on discernment and intelligence as on what the available statistics seem, on the surface, to indicate. In this sense, to read history and to become aware of its ambiguities, is to be reminded constantly of the dangers of learning about politics from books and articles that overemphasize the worth of figures and models.

From first-hand acquaintance with their works, it becomes clear that historians have no scientific method at all, but just try to be "rational and resourceful, imaginative and conscientious."[52] These are exactly the qualities that students must learn to seek and appreciate in political science writings as they come to grips with political life, accepting only part of the collective standards that political science lays down for such learning. Their real problem, summed up succinctly by the historian E. H. Carr, will be what to do if asked to read a book by "that great scholar, Jones of St. Jude's." In that event, he answered, one should go "to a friend at St. Jude's to ask what sort of chap Jones is, and what bees he has in his bonnet. When you read a work of history, always listen for the buzzing."[53] It should be noted that Popper's central point was precisely the opposite, that true science proceeds by testing and falsifying, which together make cognitive buzzing inconsequential. Taking Carr as our guide, we must concede that students will not always be able to check very closely on every author they are assigned to read. But reading history can help them become aware of the problem of scholarly authority, and of how important it is to consider whenever possible, and to whatever extent, the real competence of whoever produced the writings they will encounter.

Morals and Good Books

The concomitant to overemphasizing the latest facts in political research is to neglect materials that deal with nontangible matters of principle and behavior. It is especially here that participation in society's great conversation flags. Teachers may therefore pass on to a second substantive act of robinhooding by requiring their students to read and discuss good books—from the past or present—in addition to professional writings. Once known as "great books," such works of quality formed the heart of college education as it developed over the centuries, and were long considered a sufficient basis for political instruction. They are still discussed by political theorists of the old school, but their importance to the discipline has declined along with that of traditional political theory and in proportion to the way in which its works have been overwhelmed in journals and libraries by articles and books in a more scientific style.

---

52. Jacques Barzun, *Clio and the Doctors: Psycho-History, Quanto-History and History* (Chicago: University of Chicago Press, 1974), p. 90.
53. *What Is History?* (New York: Macmillan, 1961), p. 23.

If political science is viewed more as an organization than a science, the case for paying increased attention to great books, and to their recent equivalents, becomes very strong indeed. The logic runs something like this. The discipline constantly issues a great many certified truths. But these should not be accepted as true merely because they are properly approved. In reality, only some of them are true, and therefore classroom studies should be based upon those contentions and not the others. But are these new political verities more true than those discovered by men in the past, or by nonpolitical scientists in the present? Not necessarily, unless we agree to the straight-line view of scientific progress, whereby knowledge achieved today appears to be superior to that of yesterday, or unless we accept the modern view of the Temple of Science, according to which political knowledge must come from only a single column rather than flow from a synthesis of knowledge drawn from the various columns that presently exist. At this point, once we challenge the notion that political science truths are inherently superior to those of the past or other disciplines today, we may ask if there is any reason why latter-day works by political scientists should continue to crowd out almost all other works in the discipline's curriculum. In fact, a considerable portion of the professional works assigned for reading in classrooms today are not patently impressive but are deemed important mainly because they help students "keep up with the literature" of professional political science. Woe to the potential practitioner, or so it is thought, who lags behind and is caught unprepared when someone asks if he has read Professor Smith's latest opus.

Here is where whatever potential gains may flow from continued reading of the modern syllabus should be measured against the certain losses that accrue to young people from the same exercise. Let us remember that keeping up with the literature means following a small conversation, based on specialized terms and expressed largely in jargon, which is itself shifting ground constantly as novelty wins out over wisdom and quantity of publication triumphs over quality. The profit from participating in that conversation for a number of years, through an entire program of studies, can only be meager, except for those few students who plan a career in academic political science and therefore must acquire an intellectual road map to the territory. For other students, the costs of reading in the prescribed style will surely outweigh its benefits.

Why not read only the best books from political science and add to them the best from other disciplines—such as sociology, economics, and English literature—when they have something worthwhile to tell us about public life? On the whole, good books are recognized as such because they deal with matters of importance to society rather than the needs of a single learned discipline. They therefore belong to the realm of substantive rather than functional rationality. Generally speaking, good books are also written in language that is comprehensible and speaks directly to issues of enduring concern.[54] They therefore help us to think clearly about what we must know in order to live decently together. And finally, good books are part of a long-lived moral and intellectual heritage summed up in society's great conversation. They therefore provide common reference points that people can acquire and then cite to one another in order to communicate accurately and share values effectively. Good books provide the social cement that great organizations do not.[55] They therefore deserve to be read and discussed in political science classrooms so as to insure that citizens educated there will emerge as men and women of culture rather than individuals possessing only technical skills.

Tragedy and Wisdom

So far as good, and great, books are concerned, we may turn to the concept of tragedy, as we have done several times before, to shed additional light on political science's predicament. In the theater, tragedy's goal is commonly defined as wisdom. The chorus of *Antigone*, for example, makes this clear: "If any man would be happy and not broken by Fate, Wisdom is the thing he should seek, for happiness lies there."[56] The same point is reiterated by numerous commentators.[57] It is interesting that this sort of reasoned insight into the nature of things is precisely what the great books bring into focus. If we take *The Federalist* as a case in politics, for instance, a recent essay by Gary Wills tells us that, "For Madison and Hamilton, the only thing that should recommend a man to his political fellows is the union of public virtue with wisdom."[58] And so the

54. Henry Steele Commager, *The Empire of Reason: How Europe Imagined and America Realized the Enlightenment* (Garden City, N.Y.: Doubleday, 1977), p. 130, speaks of Franklin, Washington, Jefferson, Hamilton, Sam and John Adams, Paine, Madison, Marshall, and other Founding Fathers, and remarks that "for all their learning, not one of them wrote in a language or style that his countrymen could not understand."

55. The disappearance from public life of books such as the Bible and *The Federalist*, along with the "spiritual common ground for society" which they used to provide, is deplored by Allan Bloom in "The Failure of the University," *Daedalus* (Fall 1974), pp. 59–60. The same dismay over a loss of cultural foundations was expressed by Lindsay Rogers, "Political Philosophy in the Twentieth Century: An Appraisal of its Contribution to the Study of Politics," in Roland Young, ed., *Approaches to the Study of Politics* (Evanston, Ill.: Northwestern University Press, 1958), pp. 200–01: "Crossword puzzles have too few addicts to permit the hope that there will be a general familiarity with ancient gods and goddesses. I have no doubt that one of our students, or a student of our students, will someday refer to the Sermon on the Mount and will find that he has no comprehending hearers."

56. *Antigone*, lines 1340–50.

57. For example, Herbert J. Muller, *The Spirit of Tragedy* (New York: Knopf, 1956), p. 36: and Robert W. Corrigan, "The Sun Also Rises: Ibsen's *Ghosts* as Tragedy?" in Corrigan, ed., *Tragedy: Vision and Form* (San Francisco: Chandler, 1965), p. 404.

58. *Explaining America: The Federalist* (Baltimore: Penguin, 1981), p. 186.

smaller world of tragic drama and the larger realm of great books may be said to share a concern for wisdom, and a conviction that we should seek it in every generation as our guiding light for social affairs.

The implications of this congruence are not to be underestimated. Political science's tragic condition indicates a need for practitioners to search out wisdom via renewed dedication to continuing a great conversation embodied in great books old and new. At the same time, this condition reflects the discipline's firm commitment to science, an exclusive value which, as we saw in previous chapters, is actually hostile to the notion of wisdom insofar as that entity may be discovered, grasped, and expounded by people who do not belong to scientific communities. This means that by taking into account important implications of the term "tragedy," we are once more brought to appreciate the intractability of political science's present pass. If the analogy holds at this point, it shows that we would be wrong to assume there is any chance of turning the discipline as a whole, rather than just a few of its members, in the direction of reform.

The Final Reckoning

Let us close by reconsidering a point raised in chapter 1. Political science resides in America's universities, where political scholars contribute to the training of men and women who go on to staff the nation's great organizations, including those of commerce, industry, government, communications, and the professions. Realistically speaking, we should not expect that such collective entities will fade away, although some counterculturists urge their dismantlement.[59] More likely, organizations will continue to dominate modern society, supplying essential goods and services, and employing large numbers of citizens from many occupations and professions. That being the case, life on a smaller scale, in a traditional frame of reference developed when society was less complex, grows increasingly difficult to maintain.

What are the grounds for holding out against at least part of this sort of progress? It really is a peculiar business. One might suppose that universities will provide the sort of information which human beings need not just for adjusting to their social environment, but for living well. If not, who will? Yet those same universities, and within them their departments of political science, are so thoroughly organized as often to lose sight of how stubbornly some aspects of the modern world must be resisted. Indeed, unless we take great care, political science will serve less as an instrument for solving problems than as a component part of the major problem itself, as it takes on more and more of the characteris-

59. E. F. Schumacher, *Small Is Beautiful: A Study of Economics as if People Mattered* (New York: Harper and Row, 1973).

tics of organizations more properly so-called. For example, bureaucracies stress qualities such as precision, stability, discipline, reliability, formal rationality, impersonality, and the like. Unfortunately, all of these also inform the standard view of how students should be taught to assess public life. In contrast, the larger concerns of people in society include justice, freedom, oppression, happiness, illness, death, victory, defeat, love, hate, salvation, and damnation.[60] Yet none of these is intrinsically important to political science.

But political science *cannot* deal with such affairs satisfactorily, a mainstream practitioner might say. They clearly belong to that category of problems, perhaps very important, which cannot be treated systematically and definitively according to standards of authoritative knowledge now prevailing in the world. Therefore to call for a revival of moral debate in political studies is as fruitless as trying to resurrect the polis in a world dominated by Rome. It is to reject whatever arguments have been made for more than a century, with considerable force and persuasiveness, about the impossibility of discovering the conclusive truth about such matters. Surely that is the sort of enterprise which a profession, by its very nature and proper role in modern society, must avoid undertaking.

The merit of such arguments should be acknowledged, based as they are upon distinctions that have long been drawn between facts and values, what is and what ought to be, tangible and intangible objects of inquiry. Yet they must also be set into perspective by a supplemental strategy for learning about political life. After all, whatever validity those distinctions enjoy, they at the same time suffer the grievous fault of directing political education away from the kind of speculation and analysis that must take place in order to foster citizenship appropriate to a good society.[61] And therefore, even though the same distinctions seem logically insurmountable, so also it is true that each of us, in his or her own life, every day, makes moral decisions and acts accordingly, with family, with friends, and with people whom we meet in public places. In *The Illusion of Technique*, William Barret takes up this theme, and notes that "Our moral vocabulary has been superseded by a psychoanalytic one," so that people are expected to speak less of good and evil than of "neuroses and complexes."[62] Yet in a world suffering from very powerful arguments as to why ethical decisions cannot be conclusively justified, most of us still live according to moral lights. And so, as Barret ob-

60. Ralph P. Hummel, *The Bureaucratic Experience* (New York: St. Martin's, 1977), pp. 56–57.

61. See Morris Janowitz, *The Last Half-Century: Societal Change and Politics in America* (Chicago: University of Chicago Press, 1978), p. 3: "Social control refers to the capacity of a social group, including a whole society, to regulate itself. Self-regulation must imply a set of 'higher moral principles' beyond those of self-interest."

62. *The Illusion of Technique: A Search for Meaning in a Technological Society* (Garden City, N.Y.: Doubleday, 1978), p. 232.

serves, there exists a "glaring discrepancy" between the terms of modern discourse and "actual life," for we still "distinguish the people we know by their virtues and vices, and deal with them accordingly." Indeed, "It clears the air sometimes to say of someone that he is a stinker, period, as if coming out of the psychological clouds we were at last touching solid ground."[63]

The point is that as individuals, rather than as professionals, we choose to suspend belief in the arguments of relativism and to live courageously in a realm of faith and good works. So let us concede that the discipline of political science will abide in the world of large organizations and will seek empirical certainty or high probability, since as a collective entity it cannot admit the utility of any other course. But let some political scholars, at least, extend a personal commitment to substantive rationality into their organizational habitat, regardless of how incongruous that effort may seem by the discipline's collective standards. While exploring the correlation of political facts to ethical principles, the goal should not be to impose any or all of the teacher's standards on students without restraint, but to insist on a sense of proportion now lacking in the discipline's work, between what is and what ought to be. Redressing this balance is, after all, the real challenge to society today. Modern man must refuse to let organizations sell the idea that what they do constitutes the sum total of what makes life worth living, and one must continually try to modify their product by paying attention to ideas and values that arise only outside of their bounds. As Henry S. Kariel says, we may be unable to change the world of organizational and administrative reality, but we must endeavor always to resist its ends in favor of our own, so as "to remain in touch with ourselves and others by bearing witness."[64]

What must be sought, in the end, is a personal rather than a collective understanding of politics, with due appreciation for the sense of mystery, glory, tragedy, leadership, courage, decency, and wickedness that goes under the name of wisdom. On the road that leads to political wisdom, there are no shortcuts, such as the scientific analysis of politics once promised. This is because just as politics is not chemistry, so also it is not engineering. Life is not a mechanical *puzzle*, where scattered parts of a confusing situation can patiently be ordered and assembled until, once a solution is found, the puzzle is solved for all time. What cry out for attention instead are social *problems* that will not yield to technical answers such as science pursues, but that may be ameliorated by patient and endless coping, such as the great conversation inspires.[65] This being the world we live in, political scientists would do well to step back from science and to admit to themselves that the truth about politics is not something which

63. Ibid., pp. 232–33.
64. "Perceiving Administrative Reality," *Journal of Politics* (August 1981), pp. 735–36.
65. On puzzles and problems, see Weldon, p. 193, n. 52 above.

can be squeezed neatly into a university curriculum, to be absorbed and digested there within the space of time allotted to ordinary studies. In fact, a program of political science that lasts each student for just a few years is only a way station on the road to political wisdom, and some students—and teachers—will never arrive at the final destination. Plato may have exaggerated the problem, but he did usefully warn us against hoping for shortcuts when he spoke of acquiring political wisdom in *The Statesman*:

> *Stranger:* Do you think that the multitude in the state can attain political science?
> *Young Socrates:* Impossible.
> *Stranger:* But perhaps in a city of fifty thousand men there could be a hundred or, say, fifty who could?
> *Young Socrates:* In that case, political science would be the easiest of all sciences; there could not be found in a city of that number as many really good players of checkers.[66]

66. "The Statesman," in *The Dialogues of Plato*, trans. B. Jowett (New York: Random House, 1937), vol. 2, p. 320.

Epilogue on Political Theory

The story of political science in this book is surely incomplete. It is a mathematical certainty, after all, that no one can acquaint himself with even a sizable fraction of the discipline's continuing output, and therefore any account of political studies over several generations must be selective. To some readers, such selectivity will be faulted for inevitably distorting the tale that I told. This is because political science research deals with a very wide range of social phenomena, in which case any partial reading of the discipline's findings is certain to slight works that some practitioners, at least, will regard as important milestones on the road we must travel in order to acquire useful and reliable political knowledge.[1]

Tragedy and Villains

Granted, the tale is incomplete. But this does not mean it cannot represent political science accurately. No automatic mechanism exists for deciding what to read and recount in such a study. Nevertheless, there can be well-founded reasons for considering this work or that, and the selectivity actually practiced may be warranted both in general and in specific terms.

In general, I intended to comment on a set of circumstances within which many talented political scholars find themselves working professionally. This condition I defined as tragic. Fortunately, it is a fact of literary tragedy that the play does not require evil acts. Thus when George Bernard Shaw wrote *Saint Joan*, he told of men faithfully defending Feudalism and the Church from Joan's Nationalism and Protestantism, and he observed that "There are no villains in

---

1. See Heinz Eulau, "Drift of a Discipline," *American Behavioral Scientist* (September/October 1977), pp. 6–7: "not even the 48 chapters of the recently published eight-volume *Handbook of Political Science* . . . fully reflect the kaleidoscopic quality of political science. . . . [Therefore] it is not only hazardous but false to make sweeping statements about political science 'as a whole.' "

the piece."[2] In tragedy, then, the price to be paid is levied against the good intentions of protagonists who have difficulty adjusting or moderating their pursuit of desirable ends so as to take into account the likelihood of undesirable results.

Accordingly, while telling the story of political science's tragic condition, I did not accuse any practitioners of taking deliberate steps against the public welfare, and I raised no ad hominem charges tantamount to dereliction of professional duties. A limited array of sources was indeed present, being mathematically unavoidable, but it held out no implication that those writers and works quoted were themselves responsible for the overall state of affairs. Other members of the community of political scholars might have been cited to the same effect, for the discipline's condition in general has endured for many years and is not the direct outcome of particular acts by identifiable practitioners. Thus I described a situation for which no one is exclusively culpable, and whose portrayal should give no one special offense.

The New Political Theory

That was the general picture, but what of specific selectivity, more narrowly focused? I left out of the story some people who were, at bottom, like the others whom I did include. But what of various scholars, missing from the tale, who may have been different? Perhaps they offered a solution to political science's condition, in which event we might overcome the tragic impasse by following their example of formulating and expounding the moral truths necessary to democratic life.

John Rawls is probably the most prominent scholar who, while not appearing in the story I told, may still be deemed a key character in the search for a way out of political science's dilemma. In *A Theory of Justice* (1971),[3] Rawls offered six hundred pages of maxims and considerations that combined elements of Kantian and Benthamite philosophy in order to argue for a largely egalitarian distribution of society's goods and services. This moral vision of a good life appealed to many scholars, and their reviews frequently praised Rawls's work.[4] Moreover, for or against, the sheer amount of critical attention paid to Rawls was remarkable. Over the years, hundreds of articles, anthologies, and books com-

---

2. *Saint Joan* (Baltimore: Penguin, 1951), p. 44.

3. (Cambridge, Mass.: Harvard University Press).

4. For example, H. L. A. Hart, "Rawls on Liberty and Its Priority," in Norman Daniels, ed., *Reading Rawls* (New York: Basic Books, 1975), p. 230: "No book of political philosophy since I read the great classics of the subject has stirred my thoughts as deeply as John Rawls's *A Theory of Justice.*" See also Douglas Rae, "Maximum Justice and an Alternative Principle of General Advantage," *American Political Science Review* (June 1975), p. 630: *A Theory of Justice* is "perhaps the bravest work of political theory written in this country since the times of Madison and Calhoun."

mented on his theory or on issues that became, in the light of his work, respectable subjects for professional debate.[5] Among these items, A *Theory of Justice* was followed shortly by Robert Nozick's *Anarchy, State, and Utopia* (1974),[6] which flatly rejected Rawls's egalitarianism in favor of an uncompromising laissez-faire theory as to who should receive society's products and which itself provoked considerable commentary in the discipline.[7] Contemporary political scholars have not dealt with any other living philosophers so extensively. So why not include Rawls, and perhaps Nozick, and the debate they inspired, as a sort of transition point toward future efforts at improving the state of our political knowledge?

There were two reasons for leaving Rawls, et al., out of this book, and with these I will draw my discussion of the discipline to a close. First of all, had I examined their works in detail, the very fact of highlighting exemplars in the field of what is today usually called political theory might have implied that that field has something uniquely important to tell us about political affairs. In my opinion, the implication would have been misleading. As a field, political theory does devote some time to the study of morals and therefore is worth some of our attention. But the goal should be wisdom based on an understanding of morals *and* political institutions, for only by staying in touch with the realities of public life can we expect to move them in the right direction. In this regard, much recent political theory is beside the point, for many recent works in that realm have ignored the findings of mainstream political scholars who strive to uncover the salient facts of political life, fleeting as those may be. This is the insularity that led George Kateb, in 1977, to note that "political theory . . . has, consciously or not, turned away from much political science," with the result that no compromise between the two is in sight.[8] Singling out works by practitioners of political theory might be taken to suggest, therefore, that I believe the field to

5. For bibliographies, see Gerald Tattershall, "A Rawls Bibliography," *Social Theory and Practice* (Spring 1973), pp. 123–27; Norman Daniels, "Selected Bibliography on John Rawls," in Daniels, *Reading Rawls*, pp. 348–50; and Robert K. Fullinwider, "A Chronological Bibliography of Works on John Rawls's *Theory of Justice*," *Political Theory* (November 1977), pp. 561–70. For major works, see Brian Barry, *The Liberal Theory of Justice: A Critical Examination of the Principal Doctrines in "A Theory of Justice" by John Rawls* (Oxford: Oxford University Press, 1973); Robert Paul Wolff, *Understanding Rawls: A Reconstruction and Critique of "A Theory of Justice"* (Princeton: Princeton University Press, 1977); and Michael J. Sandel, *Liberalism and The Limits of Justice* (Cambridge: Cambridge University Press, 1982).

6. (New York: Basic Books).

7. For example, see the symposium of six articles on Nozick in the *Western Political Quarterly* (June 1976), pp. 177–201, and the symposium of three articles on Nozick in *Political Theory* (May 1977), pp. 219–56.

8. "The Condition of Political Theory," *American Behavioral Scientist* (September/October 1977), p. 136.

constitute a special repository of the wisdom we need. But that is not my conviction. Good books, which are the wherewithal for wisdom, will turn up in many fields of political science and will be found outside the discipline as well.

Even if political theory per se is not the answer to our professional problem, some works of particular theorists might embody a special quality worth seeking out and pondering. True, some might. In the case of Rawls and Nozick, however, neither philosopher will take us very far in the direction we must go, and here was a second reason for leaving them out of the tale. Both men in fact offered schemes that exemplified the nonpolitical nature of much recent political theorizing. Rawls and Nozick differed with regard to policy recommendations. They agreed, though, that a citizen's goals in life are his or her private affair, which scholars have no right or competence to assess. And therefore they commented only on the means—the rules of justice—by which citizens should be permitted to realize their various ends.[9]

This sort of analysis leaves room for many fascinating speculations rooted in game theory, decision theory, theories of social choice, and so forth, concerning how people may most efficiently combine their desires. But it says little or nothing about the sticky and protracted issues of real political life, where strongly held goals clash and where some rank order or compromise must be made among them and among the interests they generate. Rawls, for example, did not address problems of language, race, religion, and national sentiment, although these can generate civil strife and even war,[10] and he neglected matters involving power, command, authority, and sanction, which are crucial, if sometimes unpleasant, attributes of governmental action.[11] Indeed, Rawls paid so little heed to political facts as to fashion no clear conception of the state, even though that agency would presumably have to maintain whatever standard of social justice he recommended.[12] Nozick, on the other hand, wrote passionately of the need for a minimal state, but his arguments were so far from being political, with so few references to concrete public problems, that the proposed state was more like a business firm for dispensing ad hoc services than an authoritative entity capable of dealing forcefully with matters of communitywide concern.[13]

Speculation of the Rawls-Nozick type may be elegant, powerful, and per-

---

9. Marc F. Plattner, "The New Political Theory," *The Public Interest* (Summer 1975), p. 127.

10. Vernon Van Dyke, "Justice as Fairness: For Groups?" *American Political Science Review* (June 1975), pp. 607–08.

11. Benjamin R. Barber, "Justifying Justice: Problems of Psychology, Measurement, and Politics in Rawls," ibid., p. 670.

12. Wolff, *Understanding Rawls*, p. 202.

13. Karen Johnson, "Government by Insurance Company: The Antipolitical Philosophy of Robert Nozick," *Western Political Quarterly* (June 1976), p. 177.

suasive. For our purposes, however, it advances along very narrow lines. In effect, it seeks to formulate a standard of pure justice, variously defined. By itself, that is a commendable aim. But taking a stand at the apex of political truth requires much wider perspectives. To return to our earlier formulation, at least some political scientists should serve as an educational force on the Temple of Science's roof. From there, they should help democratic citizens to think and behave so as to bring reasonable order to a world beset by contradictory conceptions of how civilized people can live together.[14] In light of that end, there was much common sense in Alan Bloom's complaint that Rawls tendered no advice on how to work out compromises and a middle path when we find, on occasion, that reason clashes with revelation, love opposes duty to one's country, life is at odds with dedication to the truth, and so on.[15] In fact, were we to search only for absolute justice, we would come right back to the tragedy of *Antigone*, where Creon and Antigone were both right but also unable to coexist in the same city without destroying each other.

14. For the broad view of what political scientists might contribute to citizenship training, see Donald W. Hanson, "The Education of Citizens: Reflections on the State of Political Science," *Polity* (Summer 1979), passim, but esp. pp. 476–77.

15. "Justice: John Rawls vs. the Tradition of Political Philosophy," *American Political Science Review* (June 1975), p. 659.

Index